_____ _____ presented his resignation
_____ of Coffee County which was accepted
_____ the Court —

On Motion of Goldman Green the Court
proceeded to _____ bind John Green which Indenture
is in the following words and figures —
I Adam Rayburn Chairman of the County
Court of Coffee County by the direction of the
Court and in their behalf do hereby bind
John Green an orphan of the age of Fourteen
Years to G. Green with him to live and work
as an apprentice untill he attains the age
of Twenty one Years during which time the
said John Green shall obey the lawful Com-
mands and faithfully Serve the said G
Green and be in all respects subject to
his authority and Control according to
Law and his duty as an apprentice —
And the said G Green on his part Covenants
that he will teach and instruct the said
John Green in the trade and occupation of
farming and to read and write and cypher
as far as the single Rule of three, or cause the
same to be done if he have sufficient Capacity — And he will Constantly find for the
said John Green sufficient diet lodging
washing and apparel and other necessaries
suited to an apprentice both in sickness and
in health, and also take Care of his moral
and treat him with humanity and at the
end of the time give him a horse saddle
and Bridle worth Eighty dollars and a
suit of good jeans clothes this 5th March
attest

MIDDLE TENNESSEE'S FORGOTTEN CHILDREN
Apprentices from 1784 to 1902

by

Alan N. Miller

CLEARFIELD

Printed for
Clearfield Company, Inc. by
Genealogical Publishing Co., Inc.
Baltimore, Maryland
2004

Reprinted for
Clearfield Company, Inc. by
Genealogical Publishing Co., Inc.
Baltimore, Maryland
2005

International Standard Book Number 0-8063-5246-9

Made in the United States of America

For Betty

A Texan with the
Tennessee Mountains
in her soul

Table of Contents

List of Abbreviations

Abt	about	mos	months
bnd	bound	orph	orphan
canc	cancelled	prev	previous(ly)
d	days	prob	probably
dau	daughter	req	request
dcd	deceased	resc	rescinded
FB	Freedmen's Bureau	ret	returned
GF	grandfather	sib(s)	sibling(s)
GM	grandmother	sur	surety
illeg	illegitimate	W/O	without
ind	indenture	yrs	years

Introduction

Apprenticeships have been known since ancient times, but the system which evolved in America had its roots in the England of the 16th century. The practice spread to the colonies along with other English customs but gradually became less of a method of training in the professions and crafts, evolving into a system whereby children who were or were likely to become indigent could be supported without cost to the local government.

When Tennessee became a state in 1796, she inherited the legal code of her mother state, North Carolina. Their laws of 1762 applicable to orphans specified the following:

1. Annually the names of all orphans who had no guardian or who were not previously bound were to be reported to the Orphan Court.
2. Where their estate was too small to support them, orphans or base-born children were to be bound as apprentices: the males until age 21, the females until age 18, and mulatto or mustee females until age 21.
3. The master was to provide "diet, clothes, lodging and accommodations, fit and necessary, and to teach or cause him or her to be taught to read and write."
4. At the expiration of the apprenticeship, the master was to pay the apprentice an amount specified by law [or in the indenture].
5. If the child were ill used or not taught as required, the court could cancel the indenture and rebind him or her.
6. The bond was to be by indenture, made between the presiding officer of the court (and his successor) and the master or mistress, recorded, and a copy kept in the clerk's office for the benefit of the apprentice.
7. Any ill-treated apprentice could prosecute in the name of the Justices of the Court and recover damages.

Originally, an orphan was considered to be any fatherless child. In 1825 Tennessee law was amended to include any child as bindable whose father had abandoned him or utterly failed and refused to support him, provided that the mother gave assent in open court. In the minutes these children also are sometimes referred to as orphans. In 1854 the courts were given the discretion to bind apprentices for shorter periods if desired. By 1858 the Code of Tennessee specified other changes, as follows:

1. No apprentice could be removed from the county without his consent and the consent of the court.
2. No householder could harbor or conceal any orphan child, or hire him, without first obtaining leave from some Justice of the Peace.
3. The apprentice was to be taught to read, write, and "cypher as far as the rule of three."
4. At the expiration of the indenture, in addition to the other stipulations, the master should pay to the apprentice $20 and furnish him with one good suit of clothes.
5. Illegitimate children could be bound out without their mother's consent if it were proved that she "disregarded their moral and mental culture and that she kept a house of ill repute, or lived in one."

Although these laws regarding the Master-Apprentice relationship remained in effect until the mid-20th century with few alterations, their application sometimes varied with court decisions and local practice. In different counties they seem to have been enforced with varying degrees of diligence. In no Middle Tennessee County was a record of an annual accounting found. Rather, they seemed to have been reported to the court at random by a JP or another interested individual, often the person to whom they were eventually bound. The mother's consent, when required and obtained, was not always recorded, leading at times to cancellation of the indenture.

Copies of the indenture were furnished to the Master, to the County Clerk and sometimes to the apprentice or his parent/guardian. Some indentures and bonds were recorded in full in the minutes, but most counties filed them in a Guardian Record Book or with Miscellaneous Bonds. Because copies of the indenture and accompanying bond seem to have vanished from most counties' archives, the Court Minutes are now the most complete record of these unfortunate children's fate. In some cases the complete indenture was recorded in the minutes along with the order binding the child; other clerks simply recorded that the child was bound, without further detail.

Of course not all bound children were indigent or orphans. A parent or guardian might bind a child in order to have a boy taught a useful trade or a girl the arts of homemaking. In a few cases financial arrangements were detailed in which the parent was to receive annual payments for the child's services. It was occasionally stipulated in a will that an heir was to be bound out and to whom. Also, not all indigent children were bound. Those not felt to have the physical or mental capacity to make a productive apprentice were relegated to care in the poor house or in a private home at county expense. Many ordered to be brought for consideration of binding could not be found by the sheriff so were not produced in court.

Orphanages began to appear before the Civil War -- in Davidson County by 1849. There the Protestant Orphan's Asylum reported 25 orphans in 1859, 29 in 1860, and 21 in 1868. Also in 1868, the St. Mary's Orphan Asylum was caring for 46 girls and 24 boys, somewhat more in later years. Annual reports were filed, usually with the names of the orphans, and semi-annual payments were made to the institutions for the orphan's care. Occasionally children to be apprenticed or adopted were taken directly from these institutions.

Following the Civil War, many functions of the state courts which might affect the rights of the freed slaves were suspended. Apprenticeships made by the local courts were allowed only with the approval of the local Freedmen's Bureau representative. During this period the Bureau's own court system handled most of the apprenticeships. On May 26, 1866 the State Assembly passed an act defining the legal rights of "Persons of Color," and the Freedmen's Bureau responded by abolishing their courts in Tennessee. Many of the apprentice indentures which had been approved by the Freedmen's courts were re-recorded in the County Court Minutes. Others included here are taken from the Bureau's own records and may be found in National Archives Record Group 105, micropublication M999, Roll 20.

The following pages contain records of apprenticeships in the counties of Middle Tennessee from the earliest surviving records until the practice became uncommon, usually in the late 1870's or 1880's. During the latter years of the Civil War few meetings of the County Courts were held, and it was not until after the war that apprenticeships again began to be recorded. The usual problems in handwriting interpretation were encountered, and names were spelled many ways, sometimes within the same document. Original spellings have been retained, but entries have been abbreviated and the names of the court officials and bondsmen omitted in most cases. In entries where the date of the original bond or indenture is not given, the information is from a later reference, such as the cancellation of the indenture.

When a name is found, it is suggested that the researcher consult the microfilmed minutes for several years before and after the event for further clues as to the parentage and circumstances of the child. Often an insolvent estate, provisions for pauper care or burial, a bastardy case, or orders to bring to court other family members may be found. Also, it is worth looking for the original bond, as the names of the sureties may be significant. A date following a fact in the notes points to the source of that fact. An asterisk after an entry or date directs the reader to a source for further data. It is hoped that these records will help researchers locate ancestors who, because they were penniless and often without living parents, might be recorded nowhere else.

Records were copied from microfilm obtained from the Tennessee State Archives, the Library of the Church of Jesus Christ of Latter Day Saints, and the Dallas Public Library. My thanks to Larry Butler of the Tennessee State Archives and to Lloyd Bockstruck and Sammie Lee Townsend of the Dallas Public Library for their assistance in making microfilm available for this project.

Bedford County

Name	Date	Age	Master	Notes
Shepperson, Elizabeth Margaret	2Jan1849	10 yrs	Phelps, Charles	Housewife. Daughter of D. B. Shepperson
Wise, Rhoda	1Oct1849	9 yrs	Stephens, Barnett	Orphan.
Wise, William R.	3Oct1849	13 yrs	Evans, William M.	Farming. Orphan
Hunt, Calvin	4Mar1850	17 yrs	Bomer, Joseph B.	Farming or husbandry. Orphan.
Nix, James R.	9Apr1851	13 yrs	Coats, Paton H.	Farming. Orphan
Stone, Minerva	5Apr1852		Stone, Solomon	Housewifery. Orphan
Newson, George W. H.	2May1852		Johnson, James M.	Farming. Request of mother, Susan Newsom. Rescinded 5June1854
Williams, Isaac	6Oct1852	15 yrs	Drumgoole, E. D.	Orphan
Chappel, Elijah	1Nov1852	14 yrs	King, C. R. P.	Orphan
Chappel, James	1Nov1852	7 yrs	King, C. R. P.	Orphan
Ward, William Henry	3Jan1853	10 yrs	Beck, William F.	Sadler. Orphan
Massey, Neoma	2May1853		Powell, John	Housewifery. Orphan
Cunningham, John Thomas	3Oct1853	7 yrs	Cunningham, George W.	Farming
Ward, William Henry	6Feb1854	12 yrs	Wilhoite, John	Orphan. Farming
Sharp, Granville L.	3Oct1854	5 yrs	Reese, James R.	Farming
Reed, John	6Nov1854	Abt 10 yrs	Hart, James	Farmer. Bound for 10 yrs. Wits: John Hart, Thomas Hart
Ellingsworth, Malissa	6Apr1858	16 mos	Givins, William	Deserted by her parents
Maddrn, John M.	1Aug1859	9 yrs	Landry, Thomas	Orphan. Farming
Maddrn, William A.	1Aug1859	13 yrs	Spencer, Philip	Orphan. Farming
Bearden, Lorenzo F.	5Apr1864		Bearden, J. A.	Orphan. Son of Benjamin Bearden 10Jan1867*
Lynch, Francis Marion	6Nov1865	Abt 5 yrs	Hopkins, W. W.	
Cannon, Elenor	7Nov1865	13 yrs	Cannon, Thomas B.	Of color. Consent of Freedmen's Bureau
Allen, George Washington	3Jan1866	8 yrs	Gosling, William	Of color. Consent of his mother (only living parent) and Freedmen's Bureau
Hays, William	8May1866		Swinney, L. J.	Orphan
Whitesell, John	4June1866	Abt 14 yrs	McAdams, Jesse B.	Cancelled 3May1869, as John Whitsell

Name	Date	Age	Master	Notes
Armstrong, Samuel	4Sept1866	Abt 8 yrs	Armstrong, James L.	Of color
Scott, Alexander Spencer	10Jan1867	Abt 6 yrs	Berron, Bxter	
Hall, Issabella	7Feb1867		Eakin, Lucretia	Consent of mother
Hall, Catherine	7Feb1867	Abt 8 yrs	Ward, Ishiel and Mary J.	Consent of mother
Dyer, John Fillmore	3June1867		Dyer, S. G.	Orphan, son of Robert Dyer, Dcd.
Dyer, James Robert	3June1867		Dyer, S. G.	Orphan, son of Robert Dyer, Dcd.
Davidson, Samuel	3June1867	Abt 11 yrs	Davidson, H. L.	Of color. Born a slave of Davidson. Cancelled 4Apr1871. Samuel a runaway, living with his grandmother
Davidson, Tempe	3June1867	Abt 9 yrs	Davidson, H. L.	Of color. Female. Cancelled 4Apr1871. Becoming unmanageable
Elizabeth	3Sept1867	8 yrs	Gill, W. W.	Of color. No father or mother
Amy	5Nov1867	8 yrs	Whitworth, Benjamin F.	Of color. No father or mother.
Malone, Ervin B. J.	3Mar1868	12 yrs	Cates, John S.	Consent of mother. Father dead
Dale, John Morgan	7Sept1868	6 yrs	Blackman, Bunell	Orphan
Rucker, Nancy Jane	10May1869	Abt 11 yrs	Taylor, Esq., William	Child of Jordan Rucker. 8Mar1870*
Cunningham, Margaret	7June1869	Abt 2 yrs	Shelton, Richard	Orphan. Both of color
Parker, Sam	3Aug1869	10 yrs	Parker, Esq., Daniel	Of color
Parker, Frank	3Aug1869	6 yrs	Parker, Esq., Daniel	Of color
Cowan, Eliza	7Oct1869	5 yrs	Cowan, Leah	Of color
Cowan, Sarah	7Oct1869	2 yrs	Cowan, Leah	Of color
Tarply, Millered Fellman	1Nov1869	Abt 13 yrs	Tarpley, London	Of color
Genir, Wade	17Nov1869	Abt 14 yrs	McRee, Wade H.	Of color. Orphan
Griffin, Julia Ann	17Nov1869	8 yrs	Griffin, Major	Both of color. Orphan
Griffin, Armstead	17Nov1869	12 yrs	Griffin, Major	Both of color. Orphan
Davidson, Samuel	7Apr1870	Abt 7 yrs	Davidson, Elizabeth	Of color. Neglected by father
Fields, Joseph B.	9Jan1871	17 yrs on 1Feb1871	Holt, Henry W.	Orphan
Houston, Green	24Feb1871	11 yrs	Payne, W. W.	Of color
Cooper, Duffy	3Oct1871	Abt 5 yrs	Frazier, Eliza	Of color. Orphan
Cooper, Adda	3Oct1871	Abt 7 yrs	Frazier, Eliza	Of color. Orphan

Name	Date	Age	Master	Notes
Brown, Mary Jane	3June1872	Abt 6 yrs	Green, Eliza	Of color
Connell, Henry Clay	2June1873	Abt 4 yrs	Burrow, William	
Taylor, William Vincent	18Aug1873	13 yrs	Taylor, James P.	Of color
Mackey, John Bill	1Dec1873	Abt 12 yrs	Phillips, S. B.	Orphan
Dale, Matilda	3Aug1874	5 yrs	Leathers, Catherine	Orphan
Odam, James William	17Oct1874	Abt 12 yrs	Patterson, Ready	Orphan. Consent of mother
Houston, William	7Dec1874	Abt 4 yrs	Ransom, B. F.	Of color. Consent of mother. Illegitimate
Mackey, Marian	3May1875	17 yrs	Hailey, S. R.	Male
Worthington, Eugene G.	3Dec1877	Abt 7 1/2 yrs	Sanders, Stephen	Consent of father, James M. Worthington
Airington, Jane	5Oct1880	Abt 6 yrs	Benford, J. W.	Orphan
Whitesides, Thomas	6Apr1881	Abt 8 or 9 yrs	Thurman, Calvin	Of color. Orphan
Johnson, Charles	7Nov1881	5 yrs on 28Jan1881	Glasscock, Charnel	Orphan
Allison, Lena	10Mar1882	Abt 6 yrs	Beachboard, Z. T.	Of color. Orphan
Short, Fannie	1Oct1883		Short, Sam	

Cannon County

Name	Date	Age	Master	Notes
Holland, George	3Oct1836	Abt 6 yrs	Williams, James W.	House carpenter. Illeg son of Omey Holland. Cancelled 3July1837
Farler, Thomas	2Jan1837		Rosebury, E. J.	Blacksmith. Name also spelled "Farly." Cancelled 7Jan1839
Pattrick, William	2Jan1837		Odam, Bengamin F.	Farming. Orphan of Levi Pattrick, Dcd
Smith, Jesse	3Jan1837	b. 29Sept1825	Nichols, Daniel	Orphan. Farming
Smith, William	3Jan1837	b. 17Jan1824	McEwin, Josiah	Orphan. Farming
Smith, Barnit G.	3Jan1837	b. 22Oct1827	McGee, Joseph C.	Orphan. Farming
Patrick, Jesse	6Feb1837	Abt 9 yrs	Higgins, William	Son of Levi Patrick, Dcd. On 7Aug1848 to care of mother, Katharine Patrick. Released 7Oct1851
Askue, John	7Feb1837	Abt 14 yrs	McClain, John	Orphan
Summars, Baldy H.	6Mar1837	Abt 13 yrs	Summars, Thomas D.	Orphan. Farming
Thomas, Hugh	6Mar1837	Abt 11 yrs	Jewel, Elihu B.	Orphan. Blacksmith. Cancelled 3June1839. Maltreatment charged by mother, Sarah Brogan
Summar, Matthew	6Mar1837	Abt 8 yrs	Summar, James B.	Orphan. Farming

Name	Date	Age	Master	Notes
Hatfield, John W.	6Mar1837	Abt 9 yrs	Hogwood, Dennison	Orphan. Taning
Farler, Burrel	7Mar1837	Abt 9 yrs	Elkins, Thomas	Orphan. Farming. Indenture altered 3Nov1845; schooling requirement dropped
Summar, Telitha	1May1837	Abt 9 yrs	Summar, Robert J.	Orphan. Cancelled 7Sept1840
Spears, George	1Jan1838	Abt 10 yrs	Coughanour, David	Orphan. Farming
Kincaid, Thomas	1Jan1838	Abt 12 yrs	Warren, Sr, Arthur	Orphan. Canc 2Aug1847. Thomas 21 yrs old
Joy, Robert K.	5Mar1838	Abt 9 yrs	Nichols, Joshua	Orphan
Escue, Charly	2Apr1838		Warren, David T.	Consent of Charly
Burket, Arthur H.	2July1838	Abt 9 yrs	Smith, Joseph H.	Orphan. Farming
Burket, George E.	2July1838	Abt 13 yrs	Brown, Joseph F.	Orphan. Farming
Hall, William J.	1Oct1838		Young, Thomas R.	Orphan. Taning & curying. Heir of John Hall, Dcd 6Jan1840. Canc 6Jan1840
Hall, John W.	1Oct1838		Young, Thomas R.	Orphan. Taning & curying. Heir of John Hall, Dcd 6Jan1840. Canc 6Jan1840
Sullivan, Eliza	2Oct1838	Abt 9 yrs	Fisher, John	Consent of mother, Onnah Sullivan
Stanley, William	5Nov1838		Ford, Henry	Bound by mother, Patsey Stanley. Cancelled 7June1841
Stanley, Angeline	5Nov1838		Ford, Henry	Bound by mother, Patsey Stanley. Cancelled 7June1841
Huggins, Benjamin F.	7Jan1839	Abt 13 yrs	Bryson, William	Orphan
Standley, Angaline	8Jan1839	Abt 8 yrs	Ford, Sr, Henry	Consent of mother & stepfather. Cancelled 7June1841
Standley, William Thomas	8Jan1839	Abt 6 yrs	Ford, Sr, Henry	Consent of mother & stepfather. Cancelled 7June1841
Holston, Richard	4Mar1839	Abt 15 yrs	Odam, Benjamin F.	Orphan. Farming
Hatfield, William C.	1Apr1839	Abt 14 yrs	Hogwood, Dennison	Orphan. Taning currying. Canc 7June1841
Farly, Thomas	1Apr1839	Abt 16 yrs	Kenedy, Washington	Orphan. Taning currying
Thomas, Hugh	3June1839		Brogan, Sarah	Orphan. Son of Sarah
Smith, Barnette G.	3Feb1840	Abt 13 yrs	Nichols, Daniel B.	Orphan
Summars, Telitha	7Sept1840		Duggan, James	Request of Telitha
Patrick, Polly Anne	7Sept1840		Hume, Gabriel	Orphan. Cancelled 6May1844
Couch, Sarah Jane	3May1841		Couch, Willis F.	Orphan. Richard C. Price apptd guardian to Sarah & to Willis F., William H., Barkley & Thomas B. Couch*. 5July1842*

Name	Date	To	Age	Notes
Hatfield, William C.	7June1841	Thompson, Hugh		Tanning
Stanly, Angalina	7June1841	Wood, Thomas G.		Orphan. Canc 3Apr1849, as Ann. To Patsy Gann, mother, & stepfather Willis Gann
Stanly, Thomas	7June1841	Wood, Thomas G.		Orphan
Rogers, James	5July1841	Jones, Levin	Abt 4 yrs	Orphan. Canc 5June1848. Jones getting old & James uncontrollable
Cantrill, David B.	4Oct1841	Evans, Charles C.	4 yrs	Orphan. Farming
Spears, Elizabeth Katharine	1Nov1841	Owen, Rebecca E.	4 yrs	Orphan. Housewifery
Hays, Mary Jane	7Feb1842	Hays, John	12 yrs	Orphan. Housewifery. Released 2June1851
Hays, Thomas	7Feb1842	Hays, John	12 yrs	Orphan. Farming. Released 2June1851
Hays, John Henry	5Apr1842	Hollis, Joseph	16 ys	Orphan. Farming. Cancelled 7Nov1842
Patrick, William F.	4July1842	Patton, Thomas J.	11 yrs	Orphan. Farming
Patrick, James A.	4July1842	Patton, Robert J.	7 yrs	Orphan. Farming. 5Oct1842*
Esque, George Grandson	1Aug1842	Lasiter, Luke	8 yrs	Orphan. Farming. Released 6Nov1854
Pollock, Joseph	1Aug1842	Knox, Joseph	10 yrs	Orphan. Farming. Cancelled 5Aug1844. To mother
Pollock, Daniel	1Aug1842	Knox, Joseph	7 yrs	Orphan. Farming. Cancelled 5Aug1844. To mother
Pollock, John	1Aug1842	Watson, Jones	4 yrs on 5Feb1843	Orphan. Farming. Cancelled 3July1843. To mother
Pollock, William	1Aug1842	Watson, Jones	6 yrs on 20th instant	Orphan. Farming. Cancelled 3July1843. To mother
Pogue, Samuel W.	5Sept1842	Sissom, James	13 yrs	Orphan. Farming. Canc 3Feb1845. To mother, who is to take them from the state.
Pogue, Absalom C.	5Sept1842	Sissom, James	8 yrs	Orphan. Farming. Canc 3Feb1845. To mother, who is to take them from the state.
Pogue, James M.	5Sept1842	English, Alexander	10 yrs	Orphan. Farming
Hays, John Henry	7Nov1842	Hays, David H.	16 yrs	Orphan. Farming
Hays, Nancy	5Dec1842	McBroom, Abel	8 yrs	Orphan. Housewifery
Hays, James	6Feb1843	Hays, John	11 yrs	Orphan. Farming. Released 5Sept1853
Coleman, Thomas F.	6Mar1843	McKnight, Samuel H.	7 yrs	Orphan. Farming
Brown, King Hiram	4Sept1843	Pelham, Isham	12 yrs	Orphan. Farming
Patrick, Polly Ann	6May1844	Patrick, Robert	15 yrs	Orphan. Housewifery
Young, Fielding M.	3June1844	Landsden, Hugh B.	8 yrs in Oct next	Orphan. Farming
McDougald, Margarett	2July1844	Weatherford, John Q.	11 yrs	Orphan. Housewifery. Cancelled 5Aug1844

Name	Date	Age	Master	Notes
McDougald, Margarett	5Aug1844	11 yrs	Herriman, John	Orphan. Housewifery
Pogue, Daniel M.	2Sept1844	9 yrs	Lasater, Jotham	Orphan. Farming. Canc 6Jan1846. To mother
Pogue, William C.	2Sept1844	8 yrs	Lasater, Hardy	Orphan. Farming. Canc 6Jan1846. To mother
Asberry, Albert	6Jan1845	5 yrs	Espy, George	Orphan. Cancelled 5July1847*
Brown, King Hiram	5May1845	15 yrs	Pelham, Isham	Orphan. Farming. Rebound at request of mother, Easter Brown
Sullivan, Franklin	3Mar1846	16 yrs	Miller, William C.	Orphan. Saddle making. Canc 6Apr1846
Sullivan, Franklin	6Apr1846	16 yrs	Thurston, George W.	Orphan. Planter. Cancelled 2Apr1849, Sullivan having left Thurston
Edwards, Samuel	6July1846	3 yrs	Leech, William C.	Orphan
Brown, Richard	1Feb1847	13 yrs	Wimberley, Jonathan	Orphan. 1July1850*
Asberry, Albert	5July1847		Saine, Noah W.	Cancelled 4Oct1847
Rogers, James	2Aug1847		Rogers, Elizabeth	Orphan
Rogers, John	2Aug1847		Rogers, Elizabeth	Orphan
Asberry, Albert	4Oct1847		Bynum, John	
Harris, James H. L.	3Apr1848	12 yrs	Finger, John L.	Orphan. Cancelled 5Mar1850
Harris, William P.	3Apr1848		Harris, Sarah	
Rogers, James	7Aug1848	11 yrs	Dotton, William	Orphan
Dalois, James P.	5Mar1850	5 yrs	Hollis, John	Orphan
Collins, Edmund	6Aug1850		Miller, William C.	Bound by mother, Harriet Collins. On 8Jan1856 bond cancelled, "Edward" returned to mother, Mrs McKnight
Buyer, Isaac	3Feb1851	10 yrs	Hawkins, Jacob B.	Orphan
Young, Fielding M.	6Oct1851	15 yrs	Smith, Zachariah	Orphan
Johnson, Eliza	2Feb1852		Prim, William	
Carter, Elizabeth	7Apr1852		Dabbs, Elijah	Bastard child
Young, Legrand	2May1853		Wilson, William N.	
Boren, Bezzel	4Oct1853	16 yrs on 1 1Sept1853	Young, William	Poor legibility. Spelling questionable
Hamilton, Harvey	4Apr1854	17 yrs	Turner, George	Orphan

Name	Date	Age	Owner	Notes
Blanton, John	6Nov1854		Jones, William B.	
Blanton, Mary	4Dec1854		Wood, James H.	Orphan. Son of Sarah. Cancelled 6Aug1860
Bankston, James	5Feb1855		Wilson, William	
Buyford, John	5May1856	Abt 12 yrs	Holt, Richard	
Peyton, Mary Jane	5May1856		Phillips, William	Until 16 years. Rescinded 8July1856
Peyton, Joshua	5May1856		Dodd David	
Bullard, James W.	1Feb1858		Hawkins, James	Orphan. Son of Elizabeth Bullard 5July1858*
Bullard, James W.	2Aug1858	11 yrs	Hawkins, James	Bastard child of Elizabeth Bullard
Wilson, Elizabeth Jane	5Sept1859	Abt 5 mo	Turner, Eli	Daughter of John Wilson
Davis, Thomas	7Nov1859	Abt 10 yrs	Wood, Thomas J.	Orphan
Davis, Robert	7Nov1859	8 yrs	Markum, Charles	Orphan. Canc 6Aug1860. Several runaways
Davis, William	7Nov1859	13 yrs	Wood, William	Orphan
Bank, James	2Jan1860		Blair, Isaac T.	
Quarles, William	4June1860	12 yrs	Milligan, John	Orphan. Child of Nancy Quarles. Sibs Judah & Sarah 2Apr1855
Blanton, Marey	6Aug1860		Wale, James H.	
Daughtry, James	Nov1860		Whitfield, M.	
Moon, Elvira	4Feb1861	11 yrs	Fowler, R.	Orphan. Canc 5May1862. Stolen away and locked up by Sallie Deloach
Jacobs, Alfred R.	6Oct1862	10 yrs	Curlee, P. B.	Orphan
Williams, Thomas	3Oct1865		Hollis, John	Orphan of Harry T. Williams, Dcd
Williams, John B.	4Dec1865	12 yrs	Williams, R. M.	Orphan of Henry T. Williams, Dcd. Canc 2Oct1871. Runaway. Child's name from 1871 entry
Cooper, Henderson Gerard	5Feb1866	8 yrs	Hollis, Joseph	Orphan
Green, James H.	5Mar1866		Ring, William	
Johnson, James	2Apr1866		Lawrence, H. J.	Orphan
McDaniel, Andrew	6Aug1866	4 yrs	Mitchell, H. A.	
McDaniel, James M.	6Aug1866	8 yrs	Covington, J. A.	Orphan
Northcutt, William A.	3Sept1866	14 yrs	Todd, J. A.	Orphan. Canc 7Sept1868. Runaway
Northcutt, Adrian F.	3Sept1866	12 yrs 9 mo	Tenpenny, Tobias	Orphan. Cancelled 5Aug1867. Runaway
McDaniel, Losson	3Sept1866	5 yrs	Preston, H. L.	Orphan

Name	Date	Age	Master	Notes
Bush, Bery Zachariah	3Dec1866	b. 3Oct1859	Oliver, J. R.	Son of F. R. Bush & Barberry E. Bush
Blackwell, Joseph	5Aug1867	15 yrs	McFerrin, B. L.	Orphan
Orran, Ann	6Aug1867	8 mo	Jones, Aaron F.	Orphan. Cancelled 3Sept1867
Orran, Samuel	6Aug1867	2 yrs	Jones, Aaron F.	Orphan. Cancelled 3Sept1867
Parton, William P.	7Oct1867		King, Sampson G.	Orphan of J. L. Parton, Dcd*
Holt, James	3Feb1868	8 yrs on 15Oct1867	Holt, B. A.	Orphan. Assent of mother. Canc 6Feb1871, as James Ashly. Mother remarried
Wood, Franklin	7Apr1868	11 yrs 1/3 mo	Wood, Washington	Orphan. Both of color. Canc 1Feb1869
Wood, Ellen	2June1868	16 yrs	St John, M. E.	Orphan. Of color
Wood, Franklin	1Feb1869	12 yrs	St John, M. E.	Of color
Covington, Jane	7June1869	15 yrs 5 mo	Fugitt, Jr, Benjamin	Orphan. Of color. Father & mother dead
Bush, Harvey	6Dec1869	7 yrs 8 mo	Gray, Samuel W.	Request of mother, Barberry Ellen Bush
Covington, James	3Jan1871	12 yrs	Mason, J. E.	Orphan. Of color
Marcham, S. T.	8Oct1872		Carson, William	Bound by mother, Margaret Marchant
Roe, Allen	3Feb1873	11 yrs	Elkins, J. D.	Orphan. Farming
Crawford, Jack	3Mar1873	12 yrs	Walling, J. K.	Orphan. Farming
Brothers, W. T.	3Mar1873	14 yrs last Sept	Thomas, J. W.	Orphan. Farming
Martin, Mart	8Apr1873	11 yrs	Walkup, J. D.	Orphan. Farming
Whorly, Pleasant A.	5May1873	3 yrs	Arnold, J. B.	Orphan. Farming
Martin, William	1Sept1873	7 yrs	Hawkins, J. B.	Orphan. Farming
Petty, Newton	6Oct1873	11 yrs	Laseter, Sr, Luke	Orphan. Farming
Bethel, Price	7Oct1873	Abt 10 yrs	Gordon, John H.	Orphan. Farming. Marginal note dated 3June1884 is receipt from Bethell for bond's demands. Bethell now over 21 yrs
Bryant, Albert	4May1874	11 yrs	Odom, C. B.	Orphan. Farming. Siblings John & 2 others 6Apr1874
Brooks, John R.	7Sept1874	11 yrs	Lasiter, Luke	Orphan. Farming
Brooks, Benjamin F.	7Dec1874	14 yrs	Reed, H. B.	Orphan. Farming
Goin, Thomas P.	1Feb1875	3 yrs	Goin, J. C.	Orphan. Farming

Name	Date	Age	Master	Notes
Bryant, Samanthy	2Aug1875	7 yrs	Ring, B. S.	Indenture dated 4May1874. Orphan. Siblings John, Albert & one other 6Apr1874
Bryant, Reps	2Aug1875	9 yrs	Ring, B. S.	Indenture dated 4May1874. Orphan. Siblings John, Albert & one other 6Apr1874
Mooningham, John E.	2Aug1875	14 yrs	Shacklett, John L.	Orphan. Farming
Bogle, Robert	5Sept1875	17 yrs	Milligan, Joel	Orphan. Farming
Worrick, Westly	4Oct1875	9 yrs	McMahan, Westly	Orphan. Farming
Lockard, Samuel F.	6Dec1875	7 yrs	Ring, William	Orphan. Farming
Blancit, Thomas	1May1876	11 yrs	Hoover, T. N.	Orphan. Farming
Rackly, Andrew J.	6Nov1876	14 yrs	Gooding, Joseph A.	Orphan. Farming
Byford, William M. A.	6Nov1876	11 yrs	Williams, J. R.	Orphan. Farming. Cancelled 4Apr1881
Cooper, William White	3Dec1877	16 yrs	McMahan, William	Orphan. Farming
Parton, Marnetta	5Aug1878	13 yrs	Fugitt, M. S.	Orphan. Household work
Parton, Isaac	5Aug1878	10 yrs	Fugitt, M. S.	Orphan. Farming
Howlin, William H.	7Oct1878	10 yrs	Todd, J. P.	Orphan. Farming
Bowers, Nancy J.	8Mar1879	14 yrs	Holt, Millie	Orphan
Brown, Billey	6Oct1879	12 yrs	Goodloe, J. E.	Orphan. Cancelled 5Apr1880
Higden, Edney	6Oct1879	9 yrs	Robertson, R. S.	Orphan
Higden, James	6Jan1880	8 yrs	St John, H. J.	Illegitimate son of Eliza Higden, who cannot support him
Duke, John	4Oct1880	14 yrs	Dobbs, John H.	Orphan
Ratler, Polly	6Feb1882	11 yrs	Sissom, Thomas	Orphan

Cheatham County

Name	Date	Age	Master	Notes
Durard, Joseph	14Sept1857	16 yrs	Felts, William E.	Orphan. Blacksmith. Prob son of Timothy & Ruth Durard 14Sept1857* 3Oct1859*
Proctor, W. W.	4Jan1858	2 yrs	Demumbra, William	Orphan. Farmer
Binkley, Sarah Ann	6June1859	7 yrs	Felts, William E.	Orphan. Domestic duties. Dau of William Binkley, Dcd
Solomon	1Jan1866	Abt 13 yrs	Allen, J. R.	Of color. Farming. Former slave of Allen
Nathan	1Jan1866	Abt 13 yrs	Allen, J. R.	Of color. Farming. Former slave of Allen

Name	Date	Age	Master	Notes
Proctor, Wilson	1Oct1866	Abt 12 yrs	Demumbra, Wilson	Farming
Six, Maria Jane	4Jan1869	Abt 6 yrs	Turner, J. E.	Of color. Orphan
Six, Billy	4Jan1869	Abt 6 yrs	Turner, J. E.	Of color. Orphan
Gray, Sevetus Cross	4Sept1871	Abt 11 yrs	Nichol, Lydia T.	
Gray, James J.	5Feb1872		Perdue, T. B.	Farming
Speight, John	5May1873	13 yrs	Williams, Lewis	Farming. Williams of color. James Speight, surety
Lankford, Robert	4May1874		Easterly, B. H.	Of color. Farming
Swar, Robert	4Oct1875	8 yrs	McCormack, Joseph	Illegitimate. Farming. Mother unable to provide
Swar, Samuel	4Oct1875	5 yrs	McCormack, Joseph	Illegitimate. Farming. Mother unable to provide
Blanchard, F. U. H.	7Feb1876	5 yrs	Pardue, Martha A. (Mrs)	Orphan. Farming. Consent of Blanchard

Clay County

Name	Date	Age	Master	Notes
Alread, Sarah Alice	2June1873	6 yrs	Burris, Timothy C.	Daughter of John and Sarah Ann Alread. Abandoned by father 5May1873* Cancelled 3Aug1874
Alread, Tennessee	2June1873	Abt 4 yrs	Cullam, D. W.	Daughter of John and Sarah Ann Alread. Abandoned by father 5May1873*
Maris, Marthy	6Jan1874		Massee, James	Daughter of Lucy Maris
Henry, Samuel T.	2Feb1874		Clements, Andrew J.	Cancelled 4May1874. Runaway
Armor, James	2Feb1874		Clements, Andrew J.	Other sibs Adeline, 11 yrs & Lucretia, 3 yrs. Cancelled 4May1874. Runaway
Armor, Sarah Francis	2Feb1874		Clements, Andrew J.	Surname may be Henry 4May1874. Cancelled 4May1874. Runaway
Armor, Louisa	2Feb1874		Clements, Andrew J.	Other sibs Adeline, 11 yrs & Lucretia, 3 yrs. Cancelled 4May1874. Runaway
Alread, Sarah Allice	3Aug1874		Johnson, R. M.	
Shields, James	5June1876		Plumlee, B. S.	Consent of Fannie Shields, mother. Of color. Cancelled 3July1877. To mother
Moss, William	188-		Hibit, Laura B. (Mrs)	Original order not found. Cancelled 5Nov1883. Master now Laura B. Fowler

Coffee County

Name	Date	Age	Guardian	Notes
Carroll, Willis	4July1836	16 yrs next August	Charles, John	Waggon making
McEwin, George W.	4July1836		Lusk, William	
Ellis, John	3Oct1836		Brantley, James A.	Saddler
Ragsdale, Thomas	7Aug1837	Abt 13 yrs	Webster, Jonathan (Col)	On petition of his mother, Jane Ragsdale, widow of Pleasant Ragsdale, Dcd
Campbell, Fyander S.	7Aug1837		Lusk, William	Orphan
Williams, James	4Dec1837	16 yrs on 28Feb next	Maxwell & Shanklin	Orphan. Tanner
Green, John	5Mar1838	14 yrs	Green, G.	Orphan. Farming
Littleton, Samuel H.	7May1838	13 yrs	Keele, James W.	Orphan
Caloway, Patton	6Aug1838	10 yrs	Clay, Sidney	Orphan. House carpenter
Farmer, George W.	6Aug1838	14 yrs	Keeling, James	Orphan. Canc 3May1841
Davis, Robert G.	3Sept1838	16 yrs on 7Apr next	Lackey, Robert (Esq)	Farming. Cancelled 4July1842
Carroll, Thomas L.	3Sept1838	5 yrs on 7March1838	Pea, David W.	Orphan. Hatter
Ellis, John	7Oct1838		Smith, Daniel W.	Saddler. Securities released from bond 6July1840
Davis, John	3Dec1838	16 yrs on 15Nov1838	Smith, Daniel W.	Orphan. Consent of his mother. Saddler
Harris, John	4Mar1839	18 yrs	Wilkins, Peter P.	Orphan. Blacksmith
Brown, Anderson	4Mar1839	Abt 10 yrs	Blackburn, Robert	Farmer
Call, Thomas J.	5Aug1839	11 yrs	Burrows, Thomas	Orphan. Faming
Spanglin, William L.	4Nov1839	4 yrs on 16th inst	Brandon, John	Farming
Jefferson	2Dec1839	9 yrs next March	Huffman, John	Orphan. Farming. Of color
Misser, Robert	4May1840	16 yrs	Jenkins, Benjamin F.	Orphan. Farming
Farmer, George W.	3May1841	16 yrs on 25Dec1841	Mitchell, Thomas	Taner
Adams, Joseph B.	6Sept1841	7 yrs	Clay, Green	Orphan. Carpenter
Adams, Menty	6Sept1841	11 yrs	Hill, Thomas	Orphan
Call, Jefferson	4Oct1841	13 yrs	Taylor, Robert	Orphan. Taning

Name	Date	Age	Master	Notes
Redden, Susan Jane	1Nov1841	8 yrs	Roberts, Philop	Orphan. Until 21 yrs
Redden, Wiley	1Nov1841	4 yrs	Roberts, Philop	Orphan
Brown, Joshua	4July1842	14 yrs	Hickerson, William A.	
Brown, Anderson	4July1842	15 yrs	Hickerson, William A.	
Thompson, Robert	5Sept1842	16 yrs	Cunningham, John	Orphan
Gilliam, William R. B.	4Sept1843	9 yrs	Ewell, David	Orphan. Farming
Collins, John	5Aug1844	11 yrs	Collins, William	Orphan. Farming
Smith, John	5Aug1844	14 yrs	Sutton, William	Orphan. Farming
Foster, A. Edward	7Dec1846	12 yrs	Williams, William B.	Orphan. Saddler
Mary Ann	6Sept1847	4 yrs	Cunningham, Nancy	Mulatto
Jack	3Jan1848	17 yrs 9 mo	Isom, James M.	Blacksmith. Of color
Foster, Edward	4Dec1848	14 yrs	Buckner, William L.	Taylor
Collins, James W.	2Apr1849	12 ys	Haggard, Robert M.	Child of Lewis Collins, Dcd. Farming. Security changed 7May1849
Collins, Robert M.	2Apr1849	8 yrs	Haggard, Robert M.	Child of Lewis Collins, Dcd. Farming. Security changed 7May1849
Hill, Mary Jane	2Dec1850	4 yrs	Kuykendoll, Abraham	Dau of Benjamin Hill
Mary Ann	4Aug1851	8 yrs	Cunningham, Jr, John	Mulatto
Freeman, James	6Feb1854	10 or 11 yrs	Blackburn, Robert	Orphan
Freeman, Bird B.	6Feb1854	14 or 15 yrs	Hickman, Lille D.	Orphan
Wiggs, William	1May1854	7 yrs	Brown, Robert	Farming. Mulatto. On motion of William E. Lynn, "Riggs" taken from Brown 8Jan1861
McEwen, Thomas W.	5June1854	10 yrs	Webster, Jonothan S.	
McEwen, Thomas W.	7Aug1854	10 yrs 6 mo	Webster, Jonothan S.	Son of Mary E. McEwen. Farming. Rebound with different surety
Tosh, Andrew J.	7May1855	3 yrs on 1May1855	Muckleroy, Isaac	Orphan. Farming
Thomas, Mary Ann Elizabeth	7Mar1859	8 yrs on 18Apr1858	Sumers, A. J.	House keeping. Canc 7Aug1860. Summers leaving the state

Name	Date	Age	Guardian	Remarks
Thomas, John	7Mar1859	7 yrs on 9Mar1859	Sumers, A. J.	Farming. Canc 7Aug1860. Summers leaving the state
Tosh, Frances Jane	5Dec1859	10 yrs on 18Jan1860	Redwine, Elbert	Orphan. Housekeeping
Weathers, Ephraim	4June1860	7 yrs on 1Jan1860	Carden, James A.	Orphan. Farming. Along with Rebecca Jane Withers, ordered to court on 5Jan1859
Freeze, M. F.	4June1860	10 yrs on 16July1860	Holden, James	
Freeze, Malinda E.	4June1860	8 yrs on 9June1860	Holden, James	
Freeze, Mary Jane	4June1860	4 yrs in Sept1860	Myrick, M. V.	Orphan
Thomas, John	7Aug1860	8 yrs on 9Mar1860	Summers, John H.	Farming
Thomas, Mary Ann Elizabeth	7Aug1860	10 yrs on 18Apr1860	Garrett, Robert E.	
Wiggs, William	4Feb1861	13 yrs	Lynn, William E.	Orphan. Farming. Of color
Parker, Harvey	1July1861	5 yrs on 1Dec1861	Scott, Thomas N.	Orphan. Bricklaying
Toliver, James T. A.	3Sept1861	10 yrs on 10Mar1862	Wiser, J. B.	Orphan. Farming
Bird, James	3Oct1865	13 yrs on 1Dec1865	Norton, N. P.	Orphan. Farming
Austin, John Morgan	3Oct1865	3 yrs on 1Dec1865	Hall, Samuel W.	Orphan. Farming
Winsett, James Elijah	6Nov1865	12 yrs	Winsett, N. A.	Orphan. Farming
Winsett, Ruana Jane	6Nov1865	8 yrs	Winsett, N. A.	Orphan
Gray, William	2Apr1866	7 yrs in January1866	Jernigan, Cary	Orphan. Farming
Short, Jack	7May1866	9 yrs in Dec1866	Short, J. B.	Farming. Mulatto
Crawly, Martha Narissa	4June1866	11 yrs on 15Dec1865	Ford, William P.	Orphan. Farming
Crawley, Thomas Jasper	4June1866	6 yrs on 15Apr1866	Ford, William P.	Orphan. Farming
Finch, Charlotte	4Dec1866	7 yrs on 1Oct1866	Martin, Matt	Housekeeping. Consent of mother. Of color
Cothern, Thomas B. Springs	8Jan1867	10 yrs on 1Oct1866	Ferrell, Robert R.	Farming. Consent of mother. Cancelled 3Sept1867
Cothren, John	8Jan1867	12 yrs on 21Jan1867	Rodes, Iverson T.	Farming. Consent of mother
Mosely, Henry	4Feb1867	15 yrs on 4July1867	Britt, John C.	Farming. Of color

Name	Date	Age	Master	Notes
Maupin, Hannah	2Apr1867	15 yrs	Maupin, Abner	Orphan. House keeping. Of color
Walden, John	1July1867	3 yrs on 1Apr1867	Roberts, Zepheniah	Orphan. Farming
Cavit, Eliza	5Aug1867	8 yrs on 5Aug1867	Messick, Chrisley	Orphan. House keeping. Canc 3Feb1868. At mother's wish, child now living with her sister, who has lately married N. B. Daniel
Cavit, Thomas	6Aug1867	13 yrs on 6Aug1867	Carlisle, R. B.	Orphan. Farming
Cunningham, Bill	8Oct1867	15 yrs on 15Nov1867	Cunningham, Thomas	Farming. Of color
Hays, Henry	7Jan1868	7 yrs on 1Nov1868	Harrison, James B.	Orphan. Farming
Taylor, James H.	5Jan1869	9 yrs on 16Nov1868	Carden, Robert C.	Orphan. Consent of father, James R. Taylor. Farming. Canc 5July1869. To father. Will of James Taylor filed 7Nov1870. On 6Dec1870 Emaline J. Taylor, widow, dissented
Brown, Anthony	1Feb1869	15 yrs	Campbell, G. R.	Orphan. Farming
Ashley, Mary	7June1869	11 yrs on 13Nov1868	Emerson, Hiram S.	Orphan. House keeping. Of color. Consent of mother, blind & in poor house
Ashley, Jennie	7June1869	9 yrs in March last	Emerson, Francis W.	Orphan. House keeping. Of color. Consent of mother, blind & in poor house
Holt, Matilda	5Oct1869	13 yrs	Holt, A. M.	Orphan. Housekeeping. Of color
Holt, Monroe	5Oct1869	10 yrs	Holt, A. M.	Orphan. Farming. Of color
Holt, Wheeler	5Oct1869	6 yrs	Holt, A. M.	Orphan. Farming. Of color
Swope, George	7Dec1869	11 yrs	Swope, W. C.	Orphan. Farming. Of color
Dial, Mary Jane	7Feb1871	5 yrs in April 1871	Carroll, James K. P.	Illegitimate. House keeper
Ashley, Betty	5May1871	Abt 6 yrs	Waggoner, J. W.	House keeping. Of color
Osborne, Joe	3Oct1871	8 yrs	Davidson, L. W.	Orphan. Farming. Of color
Holder, Thomas Joseph	?		McDonald, J. A.	Orphan previously bound. Canc 8 June1875. McDonald leaving county
Ashley, James	1July1875	8 yrs	King, William N.	Orphan. Farming. Of color
Madison, William	2Aug1875	10 yrs	Montgomery, Sandy	Orphan. Farming
Ellison, Letha	5Jun1876	8 yrs	Scott, T. N.	Orphan. General house keeping
Alison, Laura	4July1876	6 yrs	Carlisle, James S.	Orphan. House keeping

Name	Date	Age	Surety	Remarks
Collins, Seth	4Dec1876	Abt 10 yrs	Hickerson, Wiley	Mother dead, father in poor house. Farming. Poor house census 5Jan1878 lists a Thomas Collins, 67or 68 yrs, blind
Brown, Isaac H.	2Oct1877	14 yrs last August	Miles, W. T.	Orphan. Farmer
Thrower, James T.	3Dec1877	4 yrs 4 mo	Logan, J. M.	Orphan. Farming
Eastman, John W.	8Jan1878	6 yrs on 28Nov1877	Emory, George & Catherine	Farming. Son of Sarah Jane (Emory) Eastman. Grandson of Emorys. Abandoned by father*
Roughton, Henry	4Feb1878	8 yrs	Carlisle, James S.	Orphan. Blacksmith & farming. Of color
Dye, Jimmie	3Feb1879	Abt 5 yrs	Scott, T. N.	Son of Malinda Dye. Farming
Speace, John	1Dec1879	13 yrs in May1879	Christian, S. J.	Farming. Of color. Cancelled 6Feb1883, boy having left Christian on abt 20Oct1882
Spiece, Charles	1Dec1879	15 yrs in Dec1879	Christian, S. J.	Farming. Of color. Cancelled 6Feb1883, boy having left Christian on abt 20Oct1882
McBride, Wesley	8Jan1880	Abt 9 yrs	Witherspoon, A. B.	Farming
McGill, David	2Aug1880	Abt 5 yrs	Jacobs, Samuel	Farming
Proscer, Raymond Nathan	7Feb1881	14 mo	Foster, Hugh A.	Farming
Drake, John William	6June1881	11 yrs	Keeling, E. L.	Orphan. Farming
Drake, Eliza Jane	6June1881	6 yrs	Keeling, E. L.	Orphan. Housekeeping
Crosslen, William Harvey	1Aug1881	10 yrs on 29Apr1881	Waganer, J. W.	Orphan. Farming
Hill, Thomas Hickman	6Sept1881	10 yrs in Sept1881	Casey, W. B.	Orphan. Farming
Bradford, Martin	2May1882		Fletcher, Green	Orphan. Farming
Shipp, George	5June1882		Powers, Thomas H.	Orphan. Farming
Johnson, Mollie	5Sept1882	Abt 2 yrs	Roberts, W. R.	House mistress. White
Bradford, Martin	3Oct1882		Winton, John	Farming. Rescinded 3Oct1882
Crosslen, Harvey	6Nov1882	11 yrs	Carlisle, R. B.	Orphan. Farming. Cancelled 7Apr1884 at request of Polly Ann Crosslen, mother*
Womack, Mollie	2July1883	12 yrs on 15Jan1883	Whitworth, E. M.	Orphan. Housekeeping
Womack, Mattie	2July1883	6 yrs on 1May1883	Willis, Jr, John K.	Orphan. Housekeeping. On 25Jan1886 F. M. Womack released as bondsman. Willis ordered to secure new surety

Name	Date	Age	Master	Notes
Starnes, William	6Aug1883	9 yrs	Carden, Lewis	Orphan. Farming
Williams, James Edmund	5Nov1883	14 yrs	Duncan, Ellender	Orphan. Farming. Cancelled 5July1886 at request of Williams
Womack, David P.	5Oct1884	6 yrs on 22July1884	Byrom, H. L.	Orphan. Farming
Brown, Hiram P.	4Oct1886	9 yrs	Duncan, Ellender	Orphan. Farming
Nevills, Marius A.	7Feb1887		Pulley, Paul	Son of George & Angeline Nevills, Dcd. Of color. Resc 4Apr1887, as Anthony Nevil

Davidson County

Name	Date	Age	Master	Notes
Pierce, John	Jan1784	13 yrs	Gallaspy, William	Orphan. House carpenter
Lefevre,	Jan1785		Armstrong, Francis	Orphan of Isaac Lefever July1785* Bound by Cathrine Levevre
Lefevre	Jan1785		Armstrong, Francis	Orphan of Isaac Lefever July1785* Bound by Cathrine Levevre
Barrnett, Peter	Apr1785			Mulatto. Indenture given by Barrnett on himself cancelled
Phelps, John	5July1785	9yrs 1mo	Martin, Joseph	Orphan of Solomon Phelps, Dcd
Phelps, Mary	5July1785	9yrs 1mo	Martin, Joseph	Orphan of Solomon Phelps, Dcd
Phelps, Elisha	5July1785	10yrs 9mo	Barton, Samuel	Orphan
Phelps, Micajah	5July1785	7yrs 5mo	Armstrong, Francis	Orphan
Lefever, Mary	4Oct1785	6 yrs	Armstrong, Francis	Orphan. Ill treatment alleged 15Jan1793 & 8Apr1793
Lefever, Marget	4Oct1785	4 yrs	Armstrong, Francis	Orphan. Ill treatment alleged 15Jan1793 & 8Apr1793
Dunbar, Thomas	10Apr1788	14yrs 7mo	Glaver, Michael	Orphan. Weaving
Vernor, Samuel	5Oct1789	11yrs 2mo	Stuart, William	Orphan. Farmer. Canc 11Apr1791, returned to mother
Wallace, William	5Oct1789	6yrs 6mo	Mitchel, William	Orphan. Weaving
Vernor, James	5Oct1789	14 yrs	Shaw, William	Orphan. Saddler
Ozburn, Samuel	8Oct1789	19 yrs	Singletery, John Stern	Orphan. House carpenter
Ozburn, Budd	8Oct1789	16yrs 8mo	Lancaster, William	Orphan. Blacksmith
McFaddin, Elias	5Jan1790	17yrs last July	Motheral, John	Orphan. Wheel wright. Bound for 3yrs 2mo from 1Jan1790
Bushnel, Ezra	13Jan1792	14 yrs	Murry, Thomas	Orphan. Carpenter & joiner. Father, Eusebius Bushnell, living
Morgan, Thomas	12Apr1792	11 yrs	Rice, Elisha	Orphan

Name	Date	Age	Bound to	Notes
Phelps, Micajah	11Apr1793	15yrs 2mo	Young, Daniel	Orphan. Hatter. On 16Jan1794 Young subpoened to answer charges of mistreatment
Phelps, Elisha	11Apr1793	18yrs 6mo	Young, Daniel	Orphan. Hatter. On 16Jan1794 Young subpoened to answer charges of mistreatment
Lockett, Nancy	14Oct1794		Gamble Edmond	Orphan. Until 14 y/o or until claimed by relations. Has sister Lucy Lockett? 15Oct1795
Lockett, Royal	14Oct1794		Hill, Dan	Orphan. Until 16 y/o or until claimed by relations. Has sister Lucy Lockett? 15Oct1795
Kuykendall, Jessee	15Jan1795	14 yrs	Murry, Thomas	Orphan. Joiner and carpenter. Annulled 13July1796. To mother
Lincoln, John	13July1795	15 yrs	Murry, William	Orphan. Carpenter & joiner
Lockett, Joel	13Oct1795		Hart, Susannah	Until 16 y/o. Orphan of Pleasant Lockett, Dcd.
Hogan, James	14Apr1796	14 yrs	Murry, Thomas	Orphan. House carpenter and joiner
McGaugh, Robert	15Apr1796	18yrs 11mo	Smith, Thomas	Orphan. Hat maker
Shoat, Ruth	12July1796	7 yrs last May	Byrns, James	Orphan. Knit, sew & spin. Resc 14Apr1800
Fry, Patsey	12July1796	Nearly 14 yrs	Joiner, Jemima	Orphan
Lockett, Joel	10Apr1797	Abt 6 yrs	Dougherty, James	Orphan
Moss, Betsey	13July1797	7 yrs last Feb	Rozzel, Nehemiah	Orphan
Oliver, Enoch	13July1797	12yrs 2mo	Beaty, David	Orphan. Until 20 y/o
Loughlin,	12Oct1797		Love, Joseph	Dau of Peter Loughlin. Indenture binding her to Edward G. Rasford on 12Jan1796 canc.
Phelps, Charles	10Apr1798	Abt 12 yrs	Oliphant, James	Orphan. Wheel right
Lockett, Nancy	11July1798		Gamble, Edmond	Orphan. Until 18 y/o
Gentry, Nicholas	13Oct1798	16 yrs on 15Sept last	Boyd, James	Orphan of Nicholas Gentry, Dcd. Wheel wright
Watkins, Samuel	8July1799	5 yrs on 18Mar last	Turnbull, William	Orphan. Annulled 29Jan1805. Mistreatment
Nolin, Micajah	10July1799	Abt 14 yrs	Stuart, John	Until 18 yrs. Orphan. Flax and cotton wheel wright
Castillo, Abraham	13July1799	9 yrs on 24Dec1799	Montgomery, William	Orphan
Kelly, Hugh	16Oct1799	18 yrs on 1Jan1800	Childress, Henry	Orphan
Kelly, Alexander	16Oct1799	Abt 16yrs 6mo	Childress, Henry	Orphan

Name	Date	Age	Master	Notes
Kelly, James	16Oct1799	Abt 14 yrs	Childress, Henry	Orphan
Haythorn, William	16Oct1799	Abt 7 yrs next Mar	Donnelly, James	Orphan. Cancelled 18July1810
Haythorn, John	16Oct1799	Abt 5 yrs next Feb	Donnelly, James	Orphan. Cancelled 18July1810
Williams, Joseph	13Jan1801	4 yrs last 25Dec	Shaw, Hugh	Orphan. Taylor
Thompson, Thomas	13Jan1801	17yrs on 4Feb next	Thompson, James	Black smith
Carson, William	13Jan1801	17 1/2 yrs	Eagleman, Joseph	Butcher
Lucas, Fany (Fawny)	14Jan1801	8 yrs	Sappington, Roger B.	Orphan. Alias Fany Sappington. Sheriff to find & put her into master's possession
Moore, David	15Jan1801	14 yrs	Lintz, William	Orphan. Shoemaker
McCutchen, John	15Apr1801	15 yrs on 15Nov last	McBride, Joseph	Orphan. Cabinetmaker & house joiner
Kindsiah, Sterling	17Apr1801	9 to 10 yrs	DiMills, Benjamin	Orphan. May be canc after 4 yrs by Co Ct
Ransom, Ferebee	11Oct1801	b. 22Mar1792	Lewis, Joel	Orphan. Of color.
Ransom, Martin	11Oct1801	b. 5Jan1796	Lewis, Joel	Orphan. Of color. Cancelled 28Apr1815, as son of Holdy? Ransom
Ransom, Polly Rawlings	11Oct1801	b. 22Sept1798	Lewis, Joel	Orphan. Of color. Cancelled 31Jan1812
Ransom, Dempsy	11Oct1801	b. 10May1800	Lewis, Joel	Orphan. Of color. Canc 24Oct1815
Unnamed	16Jan1802		Guthrie, Henry	Bound by James Care. Child not named
Smith, James	16Jan1802	13 y/o last Sept	Deadridge, Thomas	Cabinett workman
Stuart, Thomas	14Apr1802	Abt 19 yrs	Newsom, William	Orphan. Millwright
Williams, Josiah	14Oct1802	Abt 6y/o next 25Dec	Lassiter, Frederick	Orphan
Hopkins, Jason	11Jan1803	16 yrs on 26th inst	McBride, Joseph	Cabinet maker
Adams, James	14Jan1803	18 yrs on 15Sept last	Smith, Alexander	Orphan. Hatting. Joel Lewis, Esq, was guardian. 12Oct1802
Adams, Daniel	14Jan1803	12 yrs on 30th inst	Smith, Alexander	Orphan. Hatting. Joel Lewis, Esq, was guardian. 12Oct1802
Brown, William	9Apr1803	9 yrs	Moore, Amos	Orphan
Kindrick, Sterling	13Apr1803	12 yrs next August	Brown, Sterling	Orphan. Brown to be paid $8 yearly for 2 yrs
Slaughter, Mary Hodge	15July1803	10 yrs on 2June last	Hodge, Francis	
Slaughter, Francis Hodge Asbury	15July1803	8 yrs on 29Aug next	Hodge, Francis	

Name	Date	Age/Term	Master	Notes
Slaughter, William	15July1803	5 yrs on 19Jan last	Hodge, Francis	Orphan. Mother dead, deserted by father. 16July1802*
Connelly, George	14July1803	Abt 5 yrs	Cashboh, Robert	
Harding, Thomas	17Jan1804	17 yrs on 1Jan1804	Lintz, William	Shoe & boot maker
Whitsett, William	21Apr1804	16yrs on 15Sept1804	Raymond, Nicholas	Orphan. House carpenter
Griffin, James	17July1804	17 yrs on 1June last	Jones, Jarvis	
Stanley, Benjamin	19July1804	16 yrs	Smith, William	Orphan. Blacksmith
Liner, Nancy	15Oct1804	14 yrs on 1Feb	Hoffman, Michael	Orphan.
Awl, Samuel	23Oct1804	9 yrs	McCreary, Nathanial	Orphan. Taylor
Awl, Sophia	23Oct1804	7 yrs	McCreary, Nathanial	Orphan
Watkins, Samuel	29Jan1805	Abt 12 yrs	Watkins, Isaac	Orphan. House carpenter
Walker, James	21July1805	Abt 14 yrs	Becham [Bakem] & Russell	Orphan. Windsor chair making & painting. Rescinded 7Jan1806, ill treatment at hands of William Bakem
Hudson, Jessee	22July1805	15yrs 5mo	Moore, Samuel	Orphan. Blacksmith
Drumgold, James	21Oct1805	Abt 11 yrs next June	Young, Daniel	Orphan. Hat maker
Hickman, John _oyer	31Jan1806	17yrs on 9Sept1805	Deadrick, George M. & Summerville, John	Orphan of Edwin Hickman, Dcd. Bookkeeping & merchandising
Vincent, John	23Apr1806	4 yrs last August	McConnell, John P.	Orphan. Hatting. Cancelled 20July1812
Walker, James	30Apr1806		Eastin, Thomas	Orphan. Bound for 5 yrs. Printing
Berry, William Lawson	30Apr1806		Eastin, Thomas	Orphan. Bound for 3 yrs. Printing
Berry, John G.	30Apr1806		Eastin, Thomas	Orphan. Bound for 3 yrs 6 mo. Printing
Martin, Campbell	25July1806	15 yrs	Young, Daniel	Hatting
Harding, James	31July1806	17yrs on 15May1806	Green, Thomas	Black smith
Green, Eldridge	7Jan1807	15yrs on 20Sept last	Goodloe, John M.	Orphan. House carpenter. Canc 26Oct1810*
Bishop, Sally	30Apr1807	12 yrs	Matheson, James	Orphan
Bishop, Betsey	30Apr1807	6 yrs	Matheson, Charles	Orphan. Cancelled 23July1816, as Charles Mulheren
Wiggans, John	27July1807	9 yrs	Crossway, Nicholas	
Wiggans, David	27July1807	4 yrs	Cole, Edward	
Burnett, Ally	30July1807	5 yrs	Hays, Charles	Orphan
Burnett, Peter	30July1807	10 yrs	Hays, Charles	Orphan

Name	Date	Age	Master	Notes
Burnett, Venis	30July1807	8 yrs 6 mo	Hays, Charles	Orphan. Until 21 yrs
Burnett, Rachael	30July1807	7 yrs	Hays, Charles	Orphan. Until 21 yrs
Brown, William	29Oct1807	13yrs on 2Aug last	Allan, Lewis	Of color. Orphan. House carpenter
Murrell, Benjamin	29Oct1807	11yrs on 29April next	Elleston, Joseph T.	Silversmith & jeweller. Canc 21July1810
Murrel, Peter	29Oct1807	9yrs on 5Dec next	Elleston, Joseph T.	Silversmith & jeweller
Woodroff, Dolly	28Jan1808	11 yrs	Hinton, Jeremiah	Orphan
Bishop, Epson	19Apr1808	12yrs on 31Oct next	Sayers, Foster	Orphan. Blacksmith
Vinson, Rebeccah	22Apr1808	8 yrs	Vinson, Richard	Orphan
Wathinson, Alexander	25Apr1808	12 yrs	Bean, David M.	Orphan. Cabinet maker
Mills, Edward	25Apr1808	12yrs on 11July next	Cole, William	Orphan. Cancelled 27Oct1809
Ingram, Sterling	29Apr1808	7 yrs 6 mo	Cabiness, Charles	Orphan
Ingram, John Collier	29Apr1808	9 yrs	Cabiness, Charles	Orphan
Berry, Charles M.	30Apr1808	13 yrs	Read, Henry	Orphan. Shoe maker
Read, James	30Apr1808	15 yrs	Eastin, Thomas	Orphan. Printer
King, John	25July1808	16 yrs	Condon, James	Orphan. Taylor
Cantchloe, James	26July1808	16yrs on 3Sept next	Deathrige, John & Thomas	Orphan. Cabinet work
Jones, Lomas	17Apr1809	17yrs on 28Nov next	Williamson, John S.	Orphan. Saddler
Douglass, Wyatt	21Apr1809	13yrs on 25Jan last	Stump, Christopher	Orphan. Roap making. Canc 27Oct1814
Vaughan, John	21Apr1809	14 yrs	Stump, Christopher	Orphan. Roap making
Vaughan, Edward	21Apr1809	12 yrs	Stump, Christopher	Orphan. Roap making
Stump, Jacob	21Apr1809	14 yrs	Stump, Christopher	Orphan. Roap making
Harris, Edward G.	21Apr1809	14 yrs next October	Bradford, Thomas G.	Orphan. Printer & bookbinder
Harris, Benjamin Franklin	21Apr1809	16 yrs next Sept	Eastin, Thomas	Orphan. Printer
Williams, Isham A.	28July1809	17 yrs last 1June	Bass, Peter	Orphan. Tanner & currier
Smith, William	28July1809	16yrs on 15April last	Powell, John	Orphan. House carpenter

Name	Date	Age/Term	Bound to	Notes
Suras, John	16Oct1809	16yrs on 15June last	Winstead, Samuel	Orphan. Shop joiner or cabinet workman
McClendon, Bright	16Oct1809	10 yrs	Gray, Newell	Orphan. Shop joiner or cabinet workman
McClendon, Bright	17Oct1809		Allan, Lewis	Orphan. Bound two years. House carpenter
Pace, Harnet	18Oct1809	12yrs on 25Dec next	Williamson, John S.	Orphan. Saddler. Cancelled 29Jan1814, as Barnet Pace
Deshan, Leach	25Oct1809		McConnell, John P.	Orphan. Of color. Bound 9 yrs. Hatter
Harding, George	26Oct1809	12 yrs 7 mo	Harding, John	Orphan. Cabinet workman
Burnet, Fanney	26Jan1810	6 yrs	McFadden, Candor	Of color. Plain weaving
Harriet	26Jan1810	2 yrs 6 mo	McFadden, Candor	Of color. Spinning & plain weaving
Merrel, Bekah	26Jan1810	11 yrs 6 mo	Compton, William	
Haynes, James	17Apr1810	15 yrs	Goodloe, John M.	Orphan. House carpenter
Short, Theophilus	19Apr1810	19 yrs	Last, Alexander	Orphan. Bricklayer & stone mason
Alston, William	20Apr1810	14yrs on 14Oct next	Williamson, John S.	Saddler
Lee, Sally	22Apr1810	10 yrs last March	West, George & wife	Orphan
Brownston, Daniel	16July1810	2yrs on 11Jan last	Conaway, Timothy	Orphan
Brownston, Isaac	16July1810	4yrs on 28April last	Conway, Timothy	Orphan
Haythorn, John	18July1810	15 yrs last February	Craig, Alexander	Orphn. Weaver
Haythorn, William	18July1810	17 yrs last March	Harding, John	Orphan
Murrell, Benjamin	21July1810	14yrs on 29Apr last	Lintz, William	Shoe & boot maker
Murrel, Susanna	27July1810	14 yrs next April	Carney, Elijah	Orphan. On 31July1813 Carney ordered to show cause why indenture should not be revoked for ill treatment
Bennett, James	17Oct1810	12yrs on 7th this mo	White, Thomas	Orphan. House carpenter
Ford, John	23Oct1810	17yrs on 4Nov next	Eakin, Moses	Orphan. Hatter
Wallace, Moses	21Jan1811	19yrs on 17Nov last	Wallace, William	Orphan. Boot & shoe making
Chavis, Jacob	21Jan1811	8 yrs next May	Horton, Josiah	Of color. Orphan. Farming
Chavis, Polly	21Jan1811	10 yrs next Nov	Horton, Josiah	Of color. Orphan. Housekeeping
Chavis, Nancy	21Jan1811	5 yrs next June	Horton, Josiah	Of color. Orphan. Housekeeping

Name	Date	Age	Master	Notes
Stobuck, William	31Jan1811	13 yrs	Stobuck, Adam	Orphan. Black smith. Cancelled 27Apr1813, request of Rebeca Stabuck
Molton, Amos	2Feb1811	7 yrs	Lintz, William	Orphan. Shoe & boot maker
Lucy	15Apr1811	9 yrs	Crook, Bignal	Of color. Orphan
Adams, Williamson	19Apr1811	Abt 18 yrs	Shackleford, Thomas	Orphan. Brickmaking. Bound until 4Mar1814
Howell, Sterling	15July1811	16yrs on 15July1811	McBride, James	Orphan. Cabinett business
Page, George	15July1811	8yrs on 14Feb next	Carney, Elijah	Orphan. Cancelled 27Oct1814
Stump, John	24July1811	15 yrs	Williamson, Thomas	Orphan. Sadler
Echols, Silas	24July1811	15yrs on 28Sept next	Moore, John	
Scruggs, John	24July1811	Abt 14 yrs	Shackleford, Thomas	Orphan. Brickmaking & laying
Cain, John	25July1811	16yrs on 25June last	Lentz, William	Orphan. Shoe & boot making
Wilson, Isaac	21Oct1811	12 yrs	Shackelford, Thomas	Brickmaker & layer
Hall, George	22Oct1811		Hall, Elihee S.	Servant. George binds himself for 3 yrs
Oliver, Roderick	29Oct1811	11yrs on 15Feb last	Williamson, Thomas	Orphan. Saddler. A prior indenture to Candaur McFadden cancelled
White, Samuel	30Oct1811	16yrs on 7Oct1811	Tyre, Richardson	Orphan. Taylor
Pitman, David	25Jan1812	4yrs on 31May next	Benning, James	Orphan. Of color. Brick making & laying
Pitman, Edmond	25Jan1812	2yrs on 2May next	Benning, James	Orphan. Of color. Brick laying & making
Carter, William	29Jan1812	17 yrs	Johnson, George	Orphan. Of color. Farming
Linear, Garrison	31Jan1812	12yrs on 1Sept next	Criddle, John	Orphan. Saddling
Linear, Robert	31Jan1812	16yrs on 2 Sept next	Criddle, John	Orphan. Sadling
Ransom, Polly Rawlings	31Jan1812	14yrs on 22Sept1812	Herbert, Richard	Of color
Clay, Mark	21Apr1812	17 yrs on 19Dec last	Davis, Absalom	Orphan. Cabinet making

Name	Date	Age	Master	Notes
Thweatt, Isom R.	30Apr1812	17 yrs on 8Sept next	Lientz, William	Orphan. Shoe & boot making
Elliston, Andrew	1May1812	11 yrs next July	Probart, William Y.	Orphan. Tayloring. Cancelled 31July1812
Vincent, John	20July1812	11 yrs next August	Payzer, George	Orphan. Spinning in cotton factory
Douglass, Sally	21July1812	5 yrs last mo	McAdams, William R.	Orphan
Bennett, John	21July1812	14 yrs on 7Oct next	Woodcock, John	Orphan.Saddling & harness making. Cancelled 27July1814 for ill treatment
Elliston, Andrew	31July1812	10 yrs on 18May last	Probart, William Y.	Orphan. Tayloring
Liddon, William Abraham	31July1812	17 yrs 6 mo	Raworth, Edward	Orphan. Jeweler & silver smith
Corbett, Samuel Wright	1Aug1812		Goode, Samuel	Orphan. Black smith
Brandon, Frederick	?		Hartley, Charles	Of color. Data from cancellation entry 20Oct1812
Patton, James	24Oct1812	Abt 14 yrs	Williamson, John S.	Orphan. Saddling & harness making
Campbell, Samuel	28Oct1812	18 yrs	Stump, John	Orphan, Black smith
Kenedy, William	31Oct1812	17 yrs	Maddox, Ellis	Orphan. Black smith
Ransom, Aggy	31Oct1812		Lewis, Joel	Child of Holdy Ransom. Of color
Ransom, James King	31Oct1812		Lewis, Joel	Child of Holdy Ransom. Of color
Ransom, Sarah King	31Oct1812		Lewis, Joel	Child of Holdy Ransom. Of color
Ransom, Miriam	31Oct1812		Lewis, Joel	Child of Holdy Ransom. Of color
Ransom, John Lewis	31Oct1812		Lewis, Joel	Child of Holdy Ransom. Of color
Roach, John Griffin	25Jan1813	16 yrs on 15Nov last	Bass, Peter	Orphan. Tanner & currier
Parish, James	30Jan1813	16 yrs on 15Apr next	Garrett, Thomas	Orphan. House carpenter & joiner
Washpeen, James	20Apr1813	16 yrs	Jackson, William	Wheel wright
Waddle, Allan	29Apr1813		Maddox, Ellis	Orphan
Kennedy, Betsy	30Apr1813	13 yrs on 30Aug next	Hutton, Charles	Orphan. Spin, sew & knit
Casebier, William Lytle	30Apr1813	6 yrs on 10Dec next	Hutton, Charles	Orphan. Farming

Name	Date	Age	Master	Notes
Harlow, Maria	20July1813	13 yrs on 13July1813	Cramer, Henry	Orphan. Spin, sew & knit
Patton, John	20July1813	17yrs on 20Sept next	Ward, Joseph	Orphan. Cabinet workman
Harlow, William	20July1813	Abt 15 yrs	Garrett, Richard	Orphan. Waggon making
Hutson, John B.	26July1813	15 yrs last June	Stainback, Robert	Orphan. Tayloring
Hudson, Jefferson B.	26July1813	14 yrs on 1June last	Luntz, William	Orphan. Shoe & bootmaking
Philips, Mark	27July1813	16 yrs on 23 this mo	Hewlett, Edmund & George	Orphan. Saddler
Harlow, Patsy	27July1813	5 yrs on 1Aug next	Allen, David	Orphan. Sew, knit, spin & housekeeping
Harlow, Anne	27July1813	3 yrs on 1May last	Allen, David	Orphan. Sew, knit, spin & housekeeping
Kain, Andrew	29July1813	16 yrs	Stainback, Robert	Orphan. Tayloring. Canc 29Jan1814, as Cain
Ransom, John Lewis	30July1813		Lewis, Joel	Orohan. Farming. Of color
Ransom, Miriam	30July1813		Lewis, Joel	Orphan. Sew, knit, spin & housework. Of color
Ransom, Aggy	30July1813		Lewis, Joel	Orphan. Sew, knit, spin & housework. Of color
Ransom, Sarah King	30July1813		Lewis, Joel	Orphan. Sew, knit, spin & housework. Of color
Ransom, James King	30July1813		Lewis, Joel	Orohan. Farming. Of color
Short, John	31July1813		Lientz, William	Orphan. Shoe & bootmaking. A prior indenture with William Wallace cancelled
Short, Zachariah	31July1813		Lientz, William	Orphan. Shoe & bootmaking. A prior indenture with William Wallace cancelled
Caffrey, William	31July1813	16 yrs on 16Apr next	Whitson, George	Orphan. Black smith. One of 6 or 8 orphans of Peter Caffrey, Dcd. 29July1813. Cancelled 26Jan1814
Caffrey, James S.	31July1813	12 yrs on 5Sept1813	Smith, Richard	Orphan. Cabinet maker. One of 6 or 8 orphans of Peter Caffrey, Dcd. 29July1813.
Caffrey, George Washington	31July1813	9 yrs on 5Sept next	Smith, Richard	Orphan. Cabinet maker. One of 6 or 8 orphans of Peter Caffrey, Dcd. 29July1813.
Caffrey, Thomas	31July1813		Elliston, Joseph L.	Orphan. Silver & gold smith. One of 6 or 8 orphans of Peter Caffrey, Dcd. 29July1813.

Name	Date	Age/Term	Master	Notes
Cain, James	18Oct1813		Marshall, Elihu	Orphan.
Harlow, Samuel	19Oct1813	8 yrs	Fowler, Mason	Orphan. Cooper
Shaw, William	17Jan1814	15 yrs next August	Blair, John	Orphan living with John Cairy. Farming. Cancelled 20July1816
Maxwell, Richard	18Jan1814	18yrs on 28June next	Shackleford, Thomas	Orphan. Brick laying
Fletcher, Robert A.	18Jan1814	17 yrs on 8July1813	Garner, John	Orphan. Silver smith, clock & watch repairing. Garner apptd administrator of estate of James H. Fletcher, Dcd. Jane Fletcher, relict, relinquishes her right
Smith, Alexander	24Jan1814	Abt 5 yrs	Benning, James	Orphan. Making, burning & laying brick
Caffrey, William	26Jan1814	16 yrs on 16Apr next	Lientz, William	Orphan. Boot & shoe making
Kain, Andrew	29Jan1814	16 yrs on 29July1813	Benning, James	Orphan. Brick making & laying
Pace, Barnet	29Jan1814	16 yrs on 25Dec1813	McKernan, Bernard & Stout, Samuel V. D.	Orphan. Cariage, harness & triming making
Pope, Kendred (Kennedy?)	18Apr1814	15 yrs on 28Nov last	Hanks, Richard	Orphan. House joiner & carpenter
Cartmell, Martin	18Apr1814	17 yrs on 1Nov next	Williamson, Thomas	Orphan. Saddling & harness making
Pace, Lucinda	26Apr1814	12 yrs	Hughes, Robert	Orphan. Spin, knit` weave & house work. Cancelled 19Oct1814
Pace, Richard	26Apr1814	11 yrs	Ballentine, Charles	Orphan. Shoe & boot making. Cancelled 19Oct1814
Patton, James	27Apr1814	15 yrs on 29Dec next	Ward, Joseph	Until 20 yrs 8 mo. Orphan. Cabbinett maker. Ward also chosen as guardian
Berry, John	18July1814	13 yrs on 9Oct last	Beaty, William	Orphan. Wheel right
Lewallen, Elizabeth	22July1814	Abt 14 yrs	Thompson, Ephraim	Orphan. Thompson also chosen as guardian
Moran, Charles	23July1814	18 yrs in Jan last	Hicks, James G.	Orphan. Cabinett business
Bennett, John	27July1814	16 yrs on 7Oct next	Standly, Benjamin	Orphan. Blacksmith. Cancelled 21Oct1815
Cain, James	29July1814	14 yrs on 5June	Marshall, Elihu	Orphan. Shoe & bootmaker
Spears, Polly	25Oct1814	7 yrs on 13Sept1814	Lenear, Buchanan	Orphan. Spin, knit & sew

Name	Date	Age	Master	Notes
Woodfin, Rayland	25Oct1814		Gamble, Edmund (Esq)	Until 14 yrs. Orphan. Not a formal indenture. Gamble also apptd guardian
Woodfin, Silas	27Oct1814	Abt 12 yrs	Bradford, Thomas G.	For 5 yrs. Orphan
Wilks, William Albert	25Jan1815	14 yrs on 6Apr next	Gray, James	Until 20 yrs. Plastering. Orphan
Morris, Daniel	27Jan1815	14 yrs on 22Dec last	Elliston, Joseph T.	Silver smith & jeweller
Morris, Thomas	17Apr1815	8 yrs in Sept next	Knight, William	Brick maker & layer
Harris, Charles	19Apr1815	16 yrs	Shackleford, Thomas	Brick maker & layer
Seaborn, James	24Apr1815	17 yrs in May next	Mosley, Septha	Orphan. Brick maker & layer
Cato, Roland	25Apr1815	14yrs on 25Sept1815	Ross, Daniel	Orphan. Blacksmith
Woodfin, Silas M.	18July1815	12 yrs last January	Bradford, Thomas G.	Printing
Dyer, David	18July1815	9 yrs on 19Oct next	Bradford, Thomas G.	Printing
Dyer, William	18July1815	11yrs on 11Sept next	Bradford, Thomas G.	Printing
Caffrey, Polly	18July1815	14 yrs	Hart, Robert W.	Orphan. Knit, sew, & spin. On 20Jan1815 orphans of Peter Caffrey, Dcd and Nancy Caffrey ordered brought to court
Alexander, Joseph	18July1815	9 yrs on 21June1815	Williams & Cheatham	Orphan. Cabinet maker
Alexander, John Millige	18July1815	10 yrs on 25Dec1814	Williams & Cheatham	Orphan. Cabinet maker
Alexander, James	24July1815	14 yrs	Lynch, William	Orphan. Turning business
Pirkins, Edmund Barker	25July1815	14 yrs on 8Mar1815	Shackleford, Thomas	Orphan. Brick maker & layer. Cancelled 28July1820
Caffery, Simon Peter	27July1815	8 yrs	Condon, James	Taylor. On 20Jan1815 orphans of Peter Caffrey, Dcd and Nancy Caffrey ordered brought to court. Cancelled 15Jan1816
Waddle, Allen	28July1815	12 yrs	McKernan & Stout	Orphan. Coach harness making & triming
Caffrey, Nancy	16Oct1815	Abt 6 yrs	McFaddin, Robert	Orphan. Housewifery. On 20Jan1815 orphans of Peter Caffrey, Dcd and Nancy Caffrey ordered brought to court

Name	Date	Master	Description
McPherson, Abner	17Oct1815	12 yrs 11 mo on 3Nov1815	Phelps, Josiah	Orphan. Wheel right & turner
McPherson, James	17Oct1815	14 yrs on 3Nov1815	Phelps, Josiah	Orphan. Wheel right & turner
Morris, Isaac	24Oct1815	17 yrs on 1Dec next	Woodcock, John	Orphan. Saddling & harness making
Murrel, John	24Oct1815	13 yrs	Murrel, William	Orphan. Brick making & laying
Ransom, Dempsy	24Oct1815	14 yrs on 10May1815	Rutherford, William	Carpenter & house joiner. Of color
McGraw, Jason	25Oct1815	10 yrs on 23Jan next	Shackleford, Thomas	Orphan. Brick making & laying. Cancelled 28July1820
McGraw, Elijah	25Oct1815	13yrs on 10June next	Shackleford, Thomas	Orphan. Brick making & laying. Cancelled 28July1820
McGraw, George	25Oct1815	15yrs on 20June next	Shackleford, Thomas	Orphan. Brick making & laying. Cancelled 28July1820
Mosier, Daniel	25Oct1815		Shackleford, Thomas	Orphan. Brick making & laying. Son of Christian Mosier, Dcd 18Oct1815* Cancelled 28July1820
Mosier, David	25Oct1815		Shackleford, Thomas	Orphan. Brick making & laying. Son of Christian Mosier, Dcd 18Oct1815*
Edney, William Britan	25Oct1815	17 yrs	Manning, William	Orphan. House carpenter & joiner
Caffrey, Simon Peter	15Jan1816	8 yrs in July last	Beaty, William	Orphan. Wheel wright & turner
Wiggins, Harry	16Jan1816	7 yrs	Donelson, William & Cantrell, Jr, Stephen	Orphan. Farming. Of color
Wiggins, Sarah	16Jan1816	11 yrs	Donelson, William & Cantrell, Jr, Stephen	Orphan. Spin, weave & housework. Of color
Wiggins, Nancy	16Jan1816	15 yrs on 4Oct1816	Donelson, William & Cantrell, Jr, Stephen	Orphan. Spin, weave & housework. Of color
Hardin, Peter Perkins	17Jan1816	10 yrs	Harville, Frederick	Brick making & laying
Dyar, James	24Jan1816	14yrs on 29Sept1816	Folwell, John	Orphan. Tayloring
Dyar, Wiley	24Jan1816	15yrs on 26June1816	Folwell, John	Orphan. Tayloring

Name	Date	Age	Master	Notes
Murrell, Mary	24Jan1816	10 yrs on 10Oct1815	Folwell, John	Orphan. Knit, sew & housework
McPherson, George	15Apr1816	11yrs on 10June next	West, Henry	Orphan. Shoemaker. Cancelled 24Apr1821
Bailey, Montgomery	15Apr1816	17 yrs on 17May1816	Beaty, William	Orphan. Turner & wheel wright
Moore, William	16Apr1816	16 yrs in Aug next	Snow, David C.	Orphan. Tin plate working
Moore, James D.	16Apr1816	11 yrs	Snow, David C.	Orphan. Tin plate working
Davis, Robert	23Apr1816	17 yrs on 28Nov last	Hewlett, Edmond & George	Orphan. Saddling
Koen, Milton	25Apr1816	16 yrs on 26Oct next	Houston, James B.	Orphan. Cabinet making
Williams, Benjamin Franklin	25Apr1816	15 yrs	Houston, James B.	Orphan. Cabinet making
Smithsom, Sylvanus	26Apr1816	18 yrs on 12Dec1815	Shackleford, Thomas	Orphan. Brick laying
George	15July1816	4 yrs on 1Sept next	Boothe, Robert	Orphan. Farming. Of color
Thomas, George	17July1816	11 yrs	Fuqua, Joshua	Cabinett business. Cancelled 21Oct1817
Thomas, James	17July1816	13 yrs	Fuqua, Joshua	Cabinett business. Cancelled 21Oct1817
Darden, James	20July1816	17 yrs on 4May last	Luntz, William	Shoe & boot making
Darden, Jesse	20July1816	16 yrs on 4May last	Luntz, William	Shoe & boot making
Shaw, William	20July1816	17 yrs in Aug next	East, Edward H.	Orphan. Black smith
Casebien, William Lytle	20July1816	9 yrs in Dec next	Benning, James	Brick making & laying
Roach, John	22Oct1816	8 yrs on 3Mar next	Roads, James	Orphan. Brick making & laying
Thompson, Riley	24Oct1816	17 yrs on 20Jan next	Crabb, Henry	Of color
Gladden, Joseph	29Oct1816	12 yrs	Stobaugh, John	Orphan. Blacksmith
McCane, Elisha	29Oct1816	12 yrs in June last	Folwell, John	Orphan. Tayloring
Smith, Henry	29Oct1816	9 yrs	McClelan, George	Orphan. Carpenter
McFerrin, William	29Oct1816	18 yrs on 5June last	Arthur, William	Orphan. Stone cutting

Name	Date	Term	Bonded to	Remarks
Smith, Jesse	29Oct1816	16 yrs on 20Feb next	Setler, Isaac & James W.	Orphan. Tin plating
Coldwell, John	30Oct1816	12 yrs	Luntz, William	Orphan. Shoe & boot making
Moore, Alford	1Nov1816	14 yrs last May	Hewlett, Edmond & George	Orphan. Sadling
Oliver, Roderick	1Nov1816	16 yrs on 15Feb last	Martin, Peter	Orphan. Sadler
Drake, James C	2Nov1816	14 yrs on 16Jan next	Hewlett, Edmond & George	Orphan. Sadler
Scruggs, Willie	20Jan1817	15 yrs	Condon, James	Orphan. Taylouring
Seabourn, Howell	20Jan1817	17 yrs	Brooks, Moris (Moses?)	Orphan. Black smith. Cancelled 15Jan1821
Ben	23Jan1817	4 yrs	Balch, Alfred	Orphan. Compleat body servant. Of color. Cancelled 17Apr1826
Price, William	24Jan1817	15 yrs next June	Hicks, John C.	Orphan. Cabinet maker
Boggs, William C.	24Jan1817	16 yrs on 3Feb1817	Smiley, Robert	Orphan. Tayloring
Boggs, Charles W.	24Jan1817	15yrs on 17Sept1817	Smiley, Robert	Orphan. Tayloring
Murrell, Polly	24Jan1817	13 yrs next June	Marshall, Elihu	Orphan. House keeping
Armstead	28Jan1817	18 yrs	Pryor, Nicholas B.	Orphan. Carpenter & house joiner. Of color
Bill	28Jan1817	17 yrs 6 mo	Pryor, Nicholas B.	Orphan. Carpenter & house joiner. Of color
Moser, Joseph	28Jan1817	17 yrs on 8?Oct next	Dunlap, Alexander	Orphan. Carpenter & house joiner
Nancy	28Jan1817	8 yrs	Berryhill, William M.	Orphan. Read, sew, knit & housework. Of color
Franky	30Jan1817	18 yrs	Walker, Robert T., Gordon, James, & Bell, Robert	Of color
Andy	30Jan1817	12 yrs.	Gordon, James	Orphan. Of color
Alfred	30Jan1817	14 yrs	Bell, Robert	Orphan. Of color
Lorenzo	30Jan1817	10 yrs	Walker, Robert T.	Orphan. Of color

Name	Date	Age	Master	Notes
Nelly	30Jan1817	8 yrs	Walker, Robert T., Gordon, James, & Bell, Robert	Orphan. Of color
Othello	30Jan1817	4 yrs	Walker, Robert T., Gordon, James, & Bell, Robert	Orphan. Of color
Ursey	30Jan1817	6 yrs	Walker, Robert T., Gordon, James, & Bell, Robert	Orphan. Of color
Hudson, Baxter	30Jan1817	14 yrs	Buck, James	Orphan. Shoe & boot making
Price, Acquella	31Jan1817	16 yrs last June	Pick, Nathaniel	Orphan. Carpenter & house joiner
Anderson, Timothy	1Feb1817	15 yrs	Ward, Allen	Orphan. Tayloring
Kirkpatrick, John	1Feb1817	14 yrs next March	Lynch, William	Orphan. Tanning
Wheelin, George Tatnel?	22Apr1817	14 yrs	Scott, Charles	Orphan. Until 20 yrs. Blacksmith
Tyre, Parilee	29Apr1817	8 yrs on 13Aug next	Patton, William	Orphan. Seamstress
Price, John	29Apr1817	9 yrs on 3Oct next	Patton, William	Orphan. Tayloring
Parker, Paradise	30Apr1817	17 yrs 6 mo	Buie, Daniel	Orphan. Gun smith
McCutchen, Jason H.	23July1817	10 yrs on 22Oct1817	Cayce, Thomas	Orphan. Waggon making. Canc 21Oct1823
Linton, Jacob	24July1817	17 yrs 2 mo	Miller, Dennis	Orphan. Tobaconist
Miller, John	24July1817	14 yrs	Elliston, John	Orphan. Silver smith & jueler
Waddle, James	26July1817	16 yrs	Clark, Solomon	Orphan. Brick laying & making
Oliver, George	29July1817	15 yrs on 15July1817	Martin, Peter H.	Orphan. Sadler
Kennedy, Alfred	2Aug1817	14 yrs on 17June last	Pryor, Nicholas B.	Orphan. Carpenter & house joiner
Ransom, Aggy	2Aug1817	14 yrs	Allen, John L.	Of color. Cancelled 21Jan1822
Ransom, Sally	2Aug1817	8 yrs	Allen, John L.	Of color. Cancelled 21Jan1822

Name	Date	Term/Age	To whom	Notes
Ransom, John	2Aug1817	6 yrs	Allen, John L.	Of color. Cancelled 29Apr1823. Son of Holdy or Holda Ransom (fe) 29Oct1822*
Ransom, Nancy	2Aug1817	7 yrs	Allen, John L.	Of color. Cancelled 29Apr1823. Dau of Holdy or Holda Ransom (fe) 29Oct1822*
Williams, John.	2Aug1817	15 yrs on 27Dec next	Shackleford, Thomas	Until 19 yrs 4 mo. Orphan. Brick making & laying. Cancelled 28Jan1820
Thomas, James	21Oct1817	14 yrs 3 mo	Chandler, William	Orphan. Cotton spinning
Thomas, George	21Oct1817	12 yrs 3 mo	Chandler, William	Orphan. Cotton spinning
Hicks, Thomas	22Oct1817	17 yrs on 4Dec last	Alfred Osbourn & Co	Cabinet making
Hicks, Elijah	22Oct1817	15 yrs on 3July last	Alfred Osbourn & Co	Orphan. Cabinet making
Farmer, George	22Oct1817	15 yrs 9 mo	Stump, John	Orphan. Cabinet making
Isaac	29Oct1817	12 yrs	Pryor, Nicholas B.	Orphan. House joiner & carpenter. Of color
Henry	29Oct1817	7 yrs on 25Dec1817	Washington, Jr, Thomas	Orphan. Complete body servant including shaving. Of color
Smith, Edwin	30Oct1817	16 yrs 10 mo	Houston, James B.	Orphan. Cabinet business
Brown, James	31Oct1817	14 yrs	Folwell, John	Orphan. Tayloring
Knight, John	1Nov1817	4 yrs next April	Allen, John L.	Orphan. Cotton manufacturing
Cain, Joseph	19Jan1818	19 yrs 31Mar next	McIntosh, Daniel	Orphan. Tayloring
Watson, James	19Jan1818	17 yrs 5 mo	Adams, Richard K.	Orphan. Carpenter & house joiner
Eldridge, Samuel	19Jan1818	11 yrs on 4Oct last	McIntosh, Daniel	Orphan. Tayloring
Seabourn, Benjamin	19Jan1818	14 yrs on 24Mar	Brooks, Moses T.	Orphan. Blacksmith
Anderson, James	29Jan1818	11 yrs on 18June last	Lomax, Alfred	Orphan. Carpenter & house joiner. Cancelled 23Jan1821
Alfred	30Jan1818		Pryor, Nicholas	Orphan. Carpenter & house joiner. Of color
Boyd, Lawrence	20Apr1818	5 yrs on 15Jan next	Coffman, Isaac	Orphan. Farmer
Moore, John	21Apr1818	16yrs on 10June next	Martin, Peter H.	Orphan. Saddler
Judy Eliza	23Apr1818	3 yrs on 2Sept next	Stratton, Thomas	Until 18 yrs. Orphan. Of color
William David	23Apr1818	1 yr on 20 April	Stratton, Thomas	Orphan. Of color

Name	Date	Age	Master	Notes
Pleasants, Naddison	23Apr1818	5 yrs on 25June1818	Stratton, Thomas	Orphan. Of color
Cooke, Washington	1May1818	10 yrs 6 mo	Osborn, Alfred M.	Orphan. Talouring
Murrell, John	1May1818	16 yrs	Elliston, John	Orphan. Silver smith
Lucy	1May1818	16 yrs	McLean, Sarah	Orphan. Of color
Lewis, Henry H.	1May1818	14 yrs on 4th this mo	League, Josiah	Orphan. Farmer
Wilks, Albert	31July1818	17 yrs on 5Apr1819	Goodwin, William	Until 20 yrs. Plastering
Collins, William	31July1818	12yrs on 13May next	Wilson, Robert	Orphan. Cabinet maker. Canc 19July1819
Collins, James	31July1818	7 yrs next May	Coldwell, Jr, William	Orphan. Tanning & currying. Cancelled 19July1819
Collins, Ebsworth	31July1818	8 yrs next February	Coldwell, Jr, William	Orphan. Tanning & currying. Cancelled 19July1819
Harris, Robert	31July1818	Abt 15 yrs	Wood, Alexander H. & William R.	Orphan. Chair making
Cox, John	1Aug1818	12 yrs on	Hewlett, George & Harper, William	Orphan. Saddling
Wright, Francis	1Aug1818	17 yrs	Houston, James B.	Orphan. Cabinet making
Brown, John E.	19Oct1818	7 yrs on 5May last	Miller, James D.	Orphan. Blacksmith. Cancelled 15Apr1822
Brown, Benjamin H.	19Oct1818	4 yrs on 4Mar last	Miller, James D.	Orphan. Blacksmith
Brown, Alfred S.	19Oct1818	10 yrs on 4Jan next	Miller, James D.	Orphan. Blacksmith. Cancelled 15Apr1822
Webb, John W[esley]	19Oct1818	10 yrs on 17June last	Porter, Emmer J.	Orphan. House carpenter. Canc 28July1820. To mother, Polly Rainey.17July1820*
Webb, Daniel A[nderson]	19Oct1818	8 yrs on 11July last	Porter, Emmer J.	Orphan. House carpenter. Canc 28July1820 as David. To mother, Polly Rainey. 17July1820*
Webb, Northlett E.	19Oct1818	5 yrs on 8Nov next	Porter, Emmer J.	Orphan. House carpenter. Canc 28July1820. To mother, Polly Rainey.17July1820*
Ransom, Mary Ann	20Oct1818	4 yrs last mo	Moore, John	Of color
Miller, Hannah	22Oct1818	12 yrs on 14Apr1818	Garret, Richard	Orphan. Millinary

Name	Date	Age	Master	Notes
Ragan, Joseph	25Jan1819	12 yrs on 15July last	Terrass, Henry	Orphan. Confectioner. Cancelled 28Jan1823
Ragan, Daniel	29Jan1819	10 yrs	Lomax, Alfred	Orphan. Carpenter & house joiner
Coffee, Joseph	29Jan1819	17 yrs next Nov	Jones, Oakley	Orphan. Carpenter & house joiner
Spear, Aaron	29Jan1819	9 yrs this day	Earthman, Lewis	Orphan. Farmer
Murrell, James	29Jan1819	10 yrs next June	Gordon, Robert	Orphan. Silversmith
Ragan, Daniel	29Jan1819	10 yrs	Lomax, Alfred	Orphan. Carpenter & house joiner. Alias Daniel Cowan. Cancelled 23Jan1821 as Daniel Corn
Fambrough, William	19Apr1819	14 yrs on 1Oct1819	Terhune, Peter	Orphqn. Waggon making
Ubanks, George	19Apr1819	18 yrs on 20July1819	Houston, James B.	Orphan. Cabinet making
Ubanks, Stephen	19Apr1819	16 yrs on 26Dec1818	Houston, James B.	Orphan. Cabinet making
Hays, Lorenzo Dore?	29Apr1819		Hewlett, William	Orphan. Saddling. Cancelled 1May1819. To be delivered to George Chandler
Cook, Thomas	29Apr1819	7 yrs	Adams, Williamson	Orphan. Brickmaking & laying
Kannady, William	29Apr1819	13 yrs	Hicks, John C.	Orphan. Cabinet making. Canc 29Jan1820
Crenshaw, Richard	29Apr1819	16 yrs	Hicks, John C.	Orphan. Cabinet making. Canc 29Jan1820
Woodfin, Roland	29Apr1819	13 yrs	Hicks, John C.	Orphan. Cabinet making. Canc 29Jan1820
Whitfield, Bryant	29Apr1819	16 yrs on 2July next	Folwell, John	Orphan. Tayloring
Wallace, William P.	29Apr1819	13 yrs	Hicks, John C.	Orphan. Cabinet making
Thomas, Wilson	29Apr1819	18 yrs on 5th this mo	Hewlett, William	Orphan. Saddling
Hailey, Eliza	19July1819	13 yrs	Forehand, George	Orphan
Trice, Washington	19July1819	15 yrs	Hewlett, William	Orphan. Saddling
Nail, Willis	19July1819	17 yrs on 3Feb last	Hewlett, William	Orphan. Saddling
Frances, Joseph Clark	20July1819	9 yrs	Dickson, John M.	Orphan. Painting & chairmaking
Cox, John	20July1819	12 yrs on 9Dec last	Harper, William	Orphan. Sadlering. A prior indenture to George Howlett cancelled
Cain, James	30July1819	18 yrs on 5June last	Glenn, Simon	Orphan. Shoe & bootmaking

Name	Date	Age	Master	Notes
Henry	30July1819	8 yrs 6 mo	Lettler, James W.	Copper smith. Of color. A prior indenture to Thomas Washington cancelled at request of Washington. Cancelled 16July1821
Cook, John	18Oct1819	7 yrs	Vaughn, Archibald	Orphan. Blacksmith
Campbell, Caroline	18Oct1819	3 yrs on 16Dec next	McAslin, John	Orphan
Pitman, Edmond	26Oct1819	9 yrs on 1May1810 [sic]	Clark, Solomon	Orphan. Brick making & laying & stone laying. Of color
Pitman, David	26Oct1819	11 yrs on 1June1819	Clark, Solomon	Orphan. Brick making & laying & stone laying. Of color
Martin, Jeremiah	17Jan1820	16 yrs	Glenn, Simon	Orphan. Shoe & boot making
Price, William	17Jan1820	18 yrs next ?	McCombs, James	Orphan. Cabinet maker
Powers, William	28Jan1820	16 yrs on 1January	Jewell, Joseph	Orphan. Black smith
Wallace, Hartwell	28Jan1820	17 yrs	Stout, Samuel V. D.	Orphan. Coach making
Wallace, William P.	28Jan1820	13 yrs on 3Feb next	McMannis, Samuel	Orphan. Tinplate working. Canc 27July1824
Green, Tyre Dates	28Jan1820	16 yrs 6 mo	Clark, Solomon	Orphan. Brick making & laying
Woodfin, Richard?	29Jan1820	14 yrs on 30Apr next	McCombs, James	Orphan. Cabinet making
Kannady, William	29Jan1820	14 yrs on 30Apr next	Barker, Willis	Orphan. Shoe & bootmaking
Krenchaw, Richard	29Jan1820	15 yrs on 30Apr last	Webb, Kendall	Orphan. Cord warner?
Price, John	28Apr1820	12 yrs 6 mo	Barker, Willis	Orphan. Shoe & boot making
Cartwright, Nelson	28Apr1820	16 yrs on 6May next	Houston, James B.	Orphan. Cabinet making
Mulharrin, Jr, James	28Apr1820	15 yrs on 9Sept next	Welch, Thomas	Son of Charles Mulharrin. Bound at request of James Mulharrin, Esq. House carpenter & joiner
Frances, Menerva	28Apr1820	6 yrs	Moore, Joseph	Orphan. Sew, knit, spin & weave. Cancelled 23Apr1822
Smithin, Joshua	17July1820	15 yrs	Crutcher, John H.	Orphan. Shoe & boot making
Carlisle, Robert	28July1820	16 yrs	Welch, Thomas	Orphan. House carpenter & joiner. Cancelled 29Oct1822
Wiggins, Sarah	28July1820	14 yrs	Donelson, Severn	Orphan. Of color
Wiggins, Harry	28July1820	10 yrs	Donelson, Severn	Orphan. Of color

Name	Date	Age	Master	Notes
Peggy	28July1820	8 yrs on 4th this mo	Perkins, Sophia	Orphan. Of color
Stephen	28July1820	6 yrs in May last	Perkins, Sophia	Orphan. Of color
Jefferson	28July1820	4 yrs in Oct next	Perkins, Sophia	Orphan. Of color
Williams, John	29July1820	18 yrs on 27Dec next	Sigler, John	Until 19 yrs 4 mo. Orphan. Brick maker & layer
McGraw, Jason	29July1820	15 yrs on 23Jan next	Sigler, John	Orphan. Brick making & layer
McGraw, Elijah	29July1820	18 yrs on 10June last	Sigler, John	Orphan. Brick making & layer
Mosier, Daniel	29July1820		Sigler, John	Orphan. Brick making & layer
Perkins, Edmund B.	29July1820	19 yrs on 8Mar last	Sigler, John	Orphan. Brick making & layer
Chavis, James	29July1820	2 yrs on 4th this mo	Horton, Josiah (Esq)	Orphan. Farming
Samuel	27Oct1820	11 yrs	Nichols, John	Orphan. Indian
Archibald	27Oct1820	9 yrs	Nichols, John	Orphan. Indian
Hannah	27Oct1820	7 yrs	Nichols, John	Orphan. Indian
Matilda	27Oct1820	4 yrs	Nichols, John	Orphan. Indian
Jacob	27Oct1820	2 1/2 yrs	Nichols, John	Orphan. Indian
Cato	27Oct1820	6 mo	Nichols, John	Orphan. Indian
Smith, John R.	27Oct1820	15 yrs	Burton, Moses	Orphan. Carpenter & house joiner
Roland, Delilah	27Oct1820	12 yrs	Jewell, Joseph	Orphan. Seamstress. Dau of Jordan Roland, Dcd. Widow also brought to court*
Roland, Rebecca	27Oct1820	10 yrs	Balch, Alfred	Orphan. Seamstress. Dau of Jordan Roland, Dcd. Widow also brought to court. * Cancelled 24Apr1820
Roland, John	27Oct1820	9 yrs	Wells, David	Orphan. Coopering business. See above
Gulledge, George	15Jan1821	17 yrs on 1Jan1821	Cox, William B.	Orphan. Blacksmith
Gordon, Jonathan	15Jan1821	13yrs on 26Sept next	Stout, Samuel V. D. & Co	Orphan. Coach & harness making & trimming
Gordon, John	15Jan1821	15 yrs on 7Sept next	Barker, Willis	Orphan. Shoe & bootmaking
Anderson, James	23Jan1821	14 yrs	Pryor, Nicholas G.	Orphan. Carpenter & house joiner

Name	Date	Age	Master	Notes
Corn, Daniel	23Jan1821	12 yrs	Pryor, Nicholas G.	Orphan. Alias Ragan. Carpenter & house joiner
Vest, Berry	24Jan1821	10 yrs next March	George, William	Orphan. Carpenter & house joiner
Grimes, John	16Apr1821	10 yrs	Allen, John L.	Orphan. Cotton spinning & carding
Grimes, James	16Apr1821	8 yrs	Allen, John L.	Orphan. Cotton spinning & carding
Oliver, Sally	16Apr1821	12 yrs	Allen, Sr, William	Orphan. Sew & spin. Of color
Oliver, Polly	16Apr1821	8 yrs	Allen, Sr, William	Orphan. Sew & spin. Of color
Henry	16July1821		Houston, Samuel	Orphan. Body servant. Of color
Washington, George	16July1821	4 yrs	Matlock, John	Orphan. Farming
Ledgirth, William	15Oct1821	16yrs on 22May next	Evrett, Jesse J.	Orphan. Farming. On 23Oct1821 Nancy Ledgirth & her 3 youngest children allowed support
Curtis, Greenberry	15Oct1821	9 yrs	Williamson, Thomas	Orphan. Farming
Huddleston, William W.	15Oct1821	12 yrs	Brooks, Isaac W.	Orphan. Blacksmith. Cancelled 21July1823
Martin, Henry	15Oct1821	11 yrs	Edmondson, Samuel	Orphan. Sadling
Ledgirth, John B.	23Oct1821	13 yrs	Jordon, Benjamin	Orphan. Farming. Same date Nancy Ledgirth & her 3 youngest children allowed support
Hardy, William	23Oct1821	12 yrs on 1Jan next	Kent, William	Orphan. Waggon making. Canc 16July1827
O'Briant, John	23Oct1821	16 yrs	Brooks, Moses T.	Orphan. Blacksmith
Ledgirth, Daniel R.	23Oct1821	8 yrs	Everett, Simon	Orphan. Shoe & boot making. Same date Nancy Ledgirth & her 3 youngest children allowed support
Gower, Ephraim	21Jan1822	17yrs on 27Jan1822	Miller, James D.	Orphan. Blacksmith. Cancelled 15Apr1822
Lockhart, Joseph	24Jan1822	Abt 21 yrs this date	Wilkinson, Benjamin	Certificate of Freedom granted. Mulatto. Born free & bound in Powhatan Co, VA. Moved to Davidson Co with Williamson about 5 yrs ago. Carpenter*
William	29Jan1822	8 yrs	Martin, Thomas	Mulatto. Property of Donelson Caffrey. Bound by him by attorney
James	29Jan1822	6 yrs	Martin, Thomas	Mulatto. Property of Donelson Caffrey. Bound by him by attorney
Lucy	29Jan1822	4 yrs	Martin, Thomas	Until 18 yrs. Mulatto. Property of Donelson Caffrey. Bound by him by attorney

Name	Date	Term	Master	Remarks
Hail, Thomas J.	30Jan1822	17 yrs on 8Sept next	Webb, Kendal	Orphan. Shoe & boot making
O'Brian, James	15Apr1822	13 yrs in August last	Brooks, Moses T.	Orphan. Blacksmith. Cancelled 21Apr1823
Gower, Ephraim	15Apr1822	17 yrs on 27Jan last	Miller, David T., Vanleer, Bernard & Hynes, Andrew	Orphan. Blacksmith
Brown, Alfred S.	15Apr1822	14 yrs on 4Jan last	Miller, David T., Vanleer, Bernard & Hynes, Andrew	Orphan. Blacksmith. Cancelled 21July1823
Brown, John E.	15Apr1822	9 yrs on 5May next	Miller, David T., Vanleer, Bernard & Hynes, Andrew	Orphan. Blacksmith. Cancelled 21July1823
Campbell, George W.	22Apr1822	16 yrs on 19Oct last	Lanier, Robert	Orphan. Sadler. Cancelled 29Oct1822
Saludes, Aron B.	23Apr1822	16 yrs on 11Apr1822	Smiley, Robert	Orphan. Tayloring
Gower, Ziba?	23Apr1822	16yrs on 25Sept next	Knight, John	Male orphan. Blacksmith
McCutchen, James	23Apr1822	11 yrs on 1Jan last	Crenshaw, William T.	Orphan. Carpenter & house joiner
Hopper, John	23Apr1822	15yrs on 20May next	Thomas, John	Orphan. Farming
Graham, John	23July1822	16 yrs 5 mo	Welch, Thomas	Orphan. Carpenter & house joiner
Colthorp, John	21Oct1822	10 yrs	Colthorp, Norvell	Orphan. Farming
Colthorp, William	21Oct1822	7 yrs	Colthorp, Norvell	Orphan. Farming
Powell, Bennett W.	22Oct1822	10 yrs	Houston, James B.	Orphan. Cabinet making
Dyer, David	25Oct1822	16 yrs	Darby, Patrick H. & Van Pelt, Henry	Orphan. Printing
Dyer, Simpson	25Oct1822	12 yrs next March	Darby, Patrick H. & Van Pelt, Henry	Orphan. Printing
Goode, William	25Oct1822	17 yrs	Darby, Patrick H. & Van Pelt, Henry	Orphan. Printing
Rowland, John	29Oct1822	12 yrs	Faulkner, William	Orphan. Farming. Son of Patsey Rowland 21Oct1822
Oliver, Polly	29Oct1822	9 yrs on 16April last	Everett, Jesse J.	Orphan. Housework & sewing. Of color

Name	Date	Age	Master	Notes
Rowland, Deliah	29Oct1822	14 yrs	Newland, John	Until 21 yrs. Orphan. Spinning, weaving, etc. Daughter of Patsey Rowland 21Oct1822
Carlisle, Robert	29Oct1822	18 yrs	Gingery, Joseph	Orphan. House carpenter & joiner
Campbell, George W.	29Oct1822	17 yrs the 19th inst	Robertson, Norvell H.	Orphan. Sadler
Murrell, James	2Nov1822	14 yrs on 17July last	Elliston, John	Orphan. Silver smith & jeweller & watch & clock repairer
Binyard, Rosetta A.	20Jan1823	7 yrs on 9Nov last	Winfrey, Valentine	Orphan
Roland, Jordon	20Jan1823	10 yrs 6 mo	Faulkner, James	Orphan. Farmer
Wells, Moses	20Jan1823	9 yrs	Wells, Hiram	Orphan. Shoe & boot making
Wells, David	20Jan1823	13 yrs next March	Wells, Hiram	Orphan. Shoe & boot making
Grimes, James	28Jan1823	7 yrs	Towns, Herbert	Orphan. Shoe & boot making
O'Briant, James	21Apr1823	15 yrs 8 mo	Miller & Merrell	Orphan. Silver smith & watch repairing
Brown, James M.	21Apr1823	11 yrs	Short & Clifford	Orphan. Shoe & boot making
Ledgirth, Daniel R.	29Apr1823	10 yrs next Nov	Thompson, William	Orphan. Brick making & laying. On 28Oct1823 Nancy Ledgirth & her 3 children allowed county support
Oliver, Sarah	29Apr1823		Allen, Sarah	Orphan. Sew, knit, spin, weave & other housework. Of color
Jenkins, Harman R.	29Apr1823	17 yrs	Cartmell, Henry R.	Orphan. Sadling & harness making
Ransom, John	29Apr1823	14 yrs 6 mo	Fly, Micajah	Orphan. Carpenter & house joiner. Of color
Henry	1May1823	12 yrs 3 mo	Currey, Isaiah	Orphan. Barber & hair dresser. Of color
Brown, John E.	21July1823	10 yrs on 5May next	McDaniel, Alexander	Orphan. House carpenter & joiner. Cancelled 19Oct1829
Brown, Alfred S.	21July1823	15 yrs on 4Jan last	McDaniel, Alexander	Orphan. House carpenter & joiner
Wilson, James	22July1823	18 yrs on 20June last	Watson, Liven	Orphan. Shoe & boot making
Price, Nimrod	29July1823	13 yrs	Thornton, Nelson	Orphan. Hatter
Knighten, James	29July1823	13 yrs	McCombs, James W.	Orphan. Cabinet making
Coltharp, John	20Oct1823	11 yrs	Murdock, William	Orphan. Blacksmith. On 30Oct1823 ordered brought to court by Norvelle Colthorp, guardian. Indentures cancelled 19Jan1824

Name	Date	Master	Term	Notes
Coltharp, William	2Oct1823	Murdock, William	9 yrs on 7Dec next	Orphan. Blacksmith. On 30Oct1823 ordered brought to court by Norvelle Colthorp, guardian. Indentures cancelled 19Jan1824
England, Joseph	2Oct1823	Young, Mark	16 yrs on 4Jan next	Orphan. Blacksmith
Wair, George L.	2Oct1823	Robertson, Norvell H.	15 yrs on 4April last	Orphan. Sadlery business
Nesbitt, Moses	31Oct1823	Houston, James B.	18 yrs on 5Dec next	Orphan. Cabinet business
Ransom, John	31Oct1823	Clark, Solomon	10 yrs	Orphan. Brick making & laying. Of color
Hampton, Collins	19Jan1824	Cartwright, David	16 yrs	Orphan. Farming
Farrow?, Thomas	19Jan1824	Davis, Loyd	17 yrs	Orphan, Shoe & boot making
Lifteller?, Henry	27Jan1824	McCann, William	11 yrs	Orphan. Cooper
Martin, William	27Jan1824	Sutton, Stephen	10 yrs	Orphan. Blacksmith. Cancelled 18July1825
Page, Warren	28Jan1824	Houston, James B.	17 yrs on 1May next	Orphan. Cabinet making. On same date, Patsey Page, widow of Absalom Page, Dcd, applies for dower
Osborne, William	19Apr1824	Neal, John	18yrs on 17June next	Orphan. Waggon making
Box, Robert F.	19Apr1824	Hoover, Philip	16 yrs in Sept next	Orphan. Saddlery business
Sluder, Aron	19July1824	McIntosh, Daniel	18 yrs on 11April last	Orphan. Tayloring
Cantwell, Barney	20July1824	Snow, Johnson & Moore	17 yrs	Orphan. Tin plate working
Miller, James	27July1824	Welch, Thomas	15 yrs 6 mo	Orphan. House carpenter & joiner
Bell, Richard	29July1824	Osborne, Alfred M.	12 yrs	Orphan. Tailoring
Walker, Westley Franklin	30July1824	Woodcock, John	7 yrs	Orphan. Sadling & whip making
Walker, Benjamin	30July1824	Woodcock, John	9 yrs	Orphan. Sadling & whip making
Colthorp, John	31July1824	McManus, Samuel		Orphan. Tin plate working. 27Apr1824*
Price, Jemima	18Oct1824	Cobb, Robert S.	9 yrs	Orphan. House business
Webb, Daniel A.	2Oct1824	Welborn, Enoch	14 yrs on 11July last	Orphan, Jeweller & silversmith
Webb, John W.	2Oct1824	Garner, William	15yrs on 17June1824	Orphan. Cabinet making
Webb, Norflet E.	2Oct1824	Garner, William	10 yrs on 8Nov1824	Orphan. Cabinet making
Williams, Elmon W.	26Oct1824	Gooch, David R.	14 yrs	Orphan. Farming. Cancelled 18July1825

Name	Date	Age	Master	Notes
Williams, Benjamin	26Oct1824	15 yrs	Kimbrough, Joseph	Orphan. Farming, Cancelled 18July1825. Kimbro living in Rutherford Co
Foster, David	26Oct1824	18 yrs	Mays, Joseph	Orphan. Coopering business
Walker, Benjamin	25Jan1825	8 yrs	Dougal, Joseph	Orphan. Farming
Roland, Joel	25Jan1825	8 yrs	Hinton, William N. (or M)	Orphan. Farming
Francis, Mason	25Jan1825	8 yrs	Taft & Collins	Orphan. Cotton spinning
Jones, George	25Jan1825	13 yrs	Patterson, Robert	Orphan. Farming. Had been living with Susan Jones 18Jan1825
Turner, Creacy	18Apr1825	11 yrs in May next	Thomas, Margaret	Orphan. Sew, knit, cook & other housework. Cancelled 24Jan1826
Jones, George	18Apr1825	13 yrs 3 mo	Patterson, Matthew	Orphan. Wheelwright
Trigg, James	19Apr1825	10 yrs in July next	Wright, James	Orphan, Farming
Harding, Peter	26Apr1825	18 yrs	Clark, Solomon	Orphan. Brickmaking & laying
Martin, William	18July1825		Hewlett, William	Orphan. Sadler
Wiggins, James T.	20July1825	16 yrs	Cartmell, Henry R.	Orphan. Sadler
Spears, Rebecca	17Oct1825	10 yrs	Cameron, Daniel	Orphan. House business
Ubanks, Thomas	25Oct1825	18 yrs on 18June last	McIntosh, Daniel	Orphan. Tayloring
Sawyer, Matthew	25Oct1825	17 yrs on 19Aug last	McIntosh, Daniel	Orphan. Tayloring
Tindal, Henry	25Oct1825	16 yrs on 1Jan next	Garner, William	Orphan. Cabinet maker
Pate, Lucinda	25Oct1825	8 yrs	Dorris, Elizabeth	Until 21 yrs. Orphan
Nighten, George W.	16Jan1826	13yrs on 17June next	Greenhalgh, Jacob	Orphan. Tayloring. Canc 25Apr1816, as Knighten
Harrison, William J.	16Jan1826	17 yrs in Dec last	Gingry, Joseph	Orphan. Carpenter & house joiner
Rodgers, Joseph	23Jan1826	16 yrs	Clark, James	Orphan. Waggon maker
Champ, William	23Jan1826	18yrs on 26June next	Burnett, John P.	Orphan. Waggon maker
Johnston, Isaac	24Jan1826	16 yrs	Brim, Daniel	Orphan. Rope making
Johnston, Edwin	24Jan1826	9 yrs	Brim, Daniel	Orphan. Rope making
Turner, Creacy	24Jan1826	12 yrs in May next	Patteson, Thomas	Orphan. Knit, cook & house business

Name	Date	Term	To whom bound	Notes
Cook, Thomas	26Jan1826	14 yrs	Stout, Jacob V. D.	Orphan. Tayloring
Cook, Washington	26Jan1826	18 yrs in Nov last	Stout, Jacob V. D.	Orphan. Tayloring
Green, Samuel	25Apr1826	13 yrs on 8June next	Dotson, Jeremiah	Until 20 yrs. Orphan. Tayloring
Beazley, Charles C.	25Apr1826	14yrs on 23June1826	Debrell, Edwin	Orphan. Carpenter & house joiner
Washington, George	17July1826	7 yrs	Cartwright, Thomas N.	Orphan. Farming
Gallagher, John	24July1826	8 yrs on 18Jan next	Greenhalgh, Jacob	Orphan. Tayloring
Mary	25July1826		Jourdan, Benjamin	Orphan. Weave, sew, & other house business. Of color
Galagher, Charles	25July1826	10 yrs on 8Nov next	McKinney & Sumner	Orphan. Saddling
Taylor, Caroline	25July1826	7 yrs 3 mo	Fryer, Alfred	Orphan
Taylor, Julia Ann	25July1826	4 yrs in June last	Fryer, Stokeley	Orphan
Roland, Elizabeth	25July1826	13 yrs	Newland, John	Orphan
Wright, Polly	16Oct1826	7 yrs	Burnett, Parnell	Orphan. House wife
McElway, John	24Oct1826	15 yrs next Xmas	Stout, Jacob V. D.	Orphan. Tayloring
Page, Jesse	24Oct1826	16 yrs on 10Nov next	Mount, Joseph	Orphan. Silver smith
Page, Jefferson	24Oct1826	16 yrs	Hewlett & Peterson	Orphan. Sadling
Sluder, Ezekial	23Jan1827	14 yrs on 21July last	Thomas, James	Orphan. Saddlering
Pate, Lucinda	23Jan1827	9 yrs on 5Oct last	Murrell, William	Orphan. Milliner
Crosswey, Elias	16Apr1827	15 yrs	Peacock & Williams	Orphan. Tayloring
Melvin, Edmond	26July1827		Vanderville, John	Orphan. Blacksmith
Thompson, Alfred	15Oct1827	12 yrs	Johnson & Moore	Orphan. Tin plate working. Canc 23Oct1827
Way, James	15Oct1827	14 yrs on 30Aug last	Johnson & Moore	Orphan. Tin plate working
Bell, Mary	23Oct1827		Cunningham, Alexander	Orphan. Until 21 yrs. House business. Cancelled 28July1828
Jackson, Andrew	23Oct1827	7 yrs	Hood, John	Orphan. Waggon making
Parrish, George W.	21Jan1828	15 yrs in Nov last	Johnson & Moore	Orphan. Tin plate working
Feribee, Thomas H.	21Jan1828	17 yrs on 3Mar next	McCombs, Baptist	Orphan. House carpenter & joiner. McCombs also his guardian
Cork, John	29Jan1828	10 yrs	Adams, Thomas A.	Orphan. Farming
Bradburn, William P.	29Jan1828	14 yrs	Simpson, John S.	Orphan. Printing

Name	Date	Age	Master	Notes
Johnson, Thomas J.	21Apr1828	14 yrs	Smith, Jesse L.	Orphan. Tin plate working. Canc 4May1832
Simons, Jane	30Apr1828	11 yrs	Lawrence, John	Orphan. House keeping. Resc 26Oct1829
Hodges, Wilson	2May1828	18 yrs in Feb last	Stout, Samuel V. D.	Orphan. Coach making
Bell, Mary	28July1828	14 yrs	Barrett, James	Orphan. House business. Of color
Crooks, Robert	28July1828	17 yrs on 1Mar next	McCombs, Baptist	Orphan. Carpenter & house joiner
James, George W.	28July1828	17yrs on 26May next	McIntosh, Daniel	Orphan. Tayloring
Hanley, James	1Aug1828	10 yrs	Patterson, John	Orphan. Farming. Cancelled 16July1833
Hanley, Peter	1Aug1828	13 yrs	Patterson, John	Orphan. Farming. Cancelled 16July1833
Binkley, Charles	27Oct1828	14 yrs on 19July last	Hunter, Isaac	Orphan. Tanning. Cancelled 20Apr1829
Gholston, John	27Oct1828	16 yrs	McIntosh, Daniel	Orphan. Tayloring
Herndon, George	27Oct1828	18 yrs on 13July1828	Webb, Kendal	Orphan. Boot & shoe making
Bateman, Charles	28Oct1828	15 yrs on 3June last	Robertson, James C.	Orphan. Cabinet making
Forbes, James	19Jan1829	6 yrs	Yarborough, James	Orphan. Shoe & boot making
Carlisle, Samuel	19Jan1829	12 yrs	Davis, Loyd	Orphan. Shoe & boot making
Koin, Daniel	?		Sayers, Nicholas B.	Indenture cancelled 20Apr1828
Jones, Anderson	27Apr1829	14 yrs in March last	Sawyer, Amos	Orphan. Carpenter & house joiner
Hooper, Samuel	27Apr1829	10 yrs	Shule, James C.	Orphan. Gun smithing
Cockrill, Mark R.	1May1829	14 yrs	McCombs & Robinson	Orphan. Cabinet making
Williams, John S.	1May1829	13 yrs	McCombs & Robinson	Orphan. Cabinet making
Beech, George W.	1May1829	14 yrs 9 mo	Lawrence, John	Orphan. Carpenter & house joiner
Jackson, Betsey	20July1829	6 yrs	Winfrey, Valentine	Orphan. Knit, cook & house business. Of color
Tarver, Bird	22July1829	16 yrs	March, Jesse D.	Orphan. Sadler
Campbell, Thomas	27July1829	15 yrs	Hewlett, William	Orphan. Sadler
Burt, Tenham	28July1829	19 yrs on 1April next	McCombs, Baptist	Orphan. Carpenter & house joiner
Wallace, John M.	28July1829	15 yrs on 27Dec next	McCombs, Baptist	Orphan. Carpenter & house joiner

Name	Date	Age	Master	Notes
Green, James	19Oct1829	13 yrs on 18Sept last	Ament, William B.	Orphan. Brickmaking & laying
Green, William	19Oct1829	11 yrs in Nov next	Ament, William B.	Orphan. Brickmaking & laying
Fry, Richard	19Oct1829	13 yrs on 1May last	Ament, Thomas W.	Orphan. Brickmaking & laying
Cooper, George	22Oct1829	12 yrs on 20Dec next	Musgrove, Edward	Orphan. Tayloring
Brown, John E.	24Oct1829	16 yrs on 5May last	Brown, Alfred S.	Orphan. House carpenter & joiner
Brown, James M.	26Oct1829	17 yrs	Lawrence, John	Orphan. Carpenter & house joiner
Cockrill, Robert	26Oct1829	13 yrs	Austin, George	Orphan. Brickmaking & laying
Connelly, George	26Oct1829	12 yrs	Austin, George	Orphan. Brickmaking & laying
Henry, Lemuel B.	27Oct1829	16 yrs on 3April last	Anderson, William	Orphan. Tayloring
Simons, Jane	27Oct1829	12 yrs on 30April last	Read, James	Orphan. Milliner
Wood, James C.	29Oct1829	18 yrs in Feb next	Moore, William & J.	Orphan. Tin plate working
Watkins, Younger P.	30Oct1829	17 yrs	Hall, Allen A.	Orphan. Printing
Cragg, James T.	30Oct1829	15 yrs on 11Jan next	Hall, Allen A.	Orphan. Printing
Adams, John M.	21Jan1830	16 yrs	Anderson, William	Orphan. Tayloring
Sneed, Burwell E.	2Feb1830	19 yrs in Dec last	Gilman, Timothy W.	Orphan. Carpenter & house joiner
Joseph	19Apr1830	10 yrs in Nov last	Boothe, Robert	Orphan. Farming. Of color
John	19Apr1830	7 yrs	Boothe, Robert	Orphan. Farming. Of color
Hill, Thomas J.	19Apr1830	16 yrs on 4Oct next	Woodcock, John	Orphan. Saddle harness and whip making
Price, Levi	30Apr1830	15 yrs on 7Mar last	Speice, Thomas L	Orphan. Brickmaking & laying
Pitman, George	5May1830	16 yrs on 11Mar last	Stout, Samuel V. D.	Orphan. Coach making
Thompson, John	31July1830	17 yrs in March last	Hazel, Samuel K.	Orphan. Cabinet maker
Hodges, Jesse	18Oct1830	16 yrs on 15Mar1830	Cartmell, Henry R.	Orphan. Saddler
Bigley, Thomas	25Oct1830	18 yrs on 5Nov 1830	Goss, John D.	Orphan. Cabinet maker

Name	Date	Age	Master	Notes
Cannon, John	29Oct1830	12 yrs on 15Aug1830	March, Jesse D.	Orphan. Saddleing
Carmon, Josiah	2Nov1830	15 yrs	Dotson, Jeremiah	Orphan. Tayloring
Anderson, Robert	4Nov1830	16 yrs in March last	Webb, Kendal	Orphan. Shoe & boot making
Micah, William	6Nov1830	9 yrs	Tilford, Samuel	Orphan. House & body servant. Of color
Thompson, Alfred F.	24Jan1831	14 yrs on 28May1830	Dougal, Joseph	Orphan. Tailoring
Manscoe, Archibald E.	24Jan1831	7 yrs on 14June last	Stone, Levi B.	Orphan. House carpenter & joiner
Finney, Thomas J.	18Apr1831	16 yrs in Sept last	Tannehill, Wilkins	Orphan. Printing
Baker, John	25Apr1831	17 yrs on 17Mar last	Thomas, James	Orphan. Saddler
Fitzgerald, Leroy	25Apr1831	7 yrs	Ralston, David	Orphan. Farmer. Cancelled 17Oct1831
Virgin, Samuel J.	17Oct1831	13 yrs	Dotson, Jeremiah	Orphan. Tayloring
Fitzgerald, Leroy	17Oct1831	7 yrs	Ralston, William	Orphan. Farming
Lee, Ralph Smythe	18Oct1831	16 yrs on 17Dec last	Hunt Tardiff & Co	Orphan. Printing
Holder, William	25Oct1831	Abt 15 yrs	Cobler, Davis	Orphan. Shoemaking. Of color 17Oct1831
Harrison, Nicholas	4Nov1831	15 yrs in Sept last	Hall, Allen A.	Orphan. Printing
Martha	16Jan1832	Abt 4 yrs	Collins, Thomas	Orphan. Housekeeping. Of color
Martin, Blackman	23Jan1832	Abt 16 yrs	Yarborough, James	Orphan. Saddler
Scott, Warner L.	24Jan1832	17 yrs in Dec last	Dotson, Jeremiah	Orphan. Tailoring
White, Robert	26Apr1832	16 yrs	Spicee?, Thomas L.	Orphan. Brickmaking & laying
Cooper, George	28Apr1832	15 yrs	Anderson, William	Orphan. Tailoring
Brown, Benjamin H.	1May1832	18 yrs on 4Mar1832	Watkins, George W.	Orphan. House carpenter & joiner
Johnson, Thomas J.	4May1832	18 yrs on 4Dec1831	Moore, William & James D.	Orphan. Tin plate working
Quisenbury, John	16July1832	13 yrs	Page, Jesse W.	Orphan. Saddlery & harness making
Davis, Zachariah	23Jan1832	6 yrs 6 mo	Lowry, George	Orphan. Making cotton carding & spinning machines. Canc 7Nov1834, as David Lowry
Johns, Benjamin F.	30July1832	5 yrs	Parke, Joseph	Orphan. Carpenter & house joiner
Johns, Melinda	30July1832	8 yrs	Parke, Joseph	Orphan. Good housewife

Thompson, Alfred F.	2Aug1832	16 yrs on 28May last	Link, Joseph	Orphan. Saddlery & harness making. Cancelled 28July1834
Barton, John	15Oct1832	16 yrs	Pegram, William	Orphan. Farming
Hobbs, Edwin	16Oct1832	13 yrs on 13Nov1832	Goss, John D.	Orphan. Cabinet making
Graves, Henry	3Nov1832		Moore, William H. & James D.	Orphan. Tin plate working
Graves, Sutton	3Nov1832		Moore, William H. & James D.	Orphan. Tin plate working
Graves, Samuel	3Nov1832		Moore, William H. & James D.	Orphan. Tin plate working
Gilliam, Lemuel	21Jan1833	10 yrs	Watkins, George W.	Orphan. Carpenter
Gilliam, Martha	21Jan1833	9 yrs on 13Nov last	Watkins, George W.	Orphan. Spinster
Owens, James	21Jan1833	11 yrs on 1Feb1833	Thomas, James	Orphan. Saddle making
Gilliam, John	21Jan1833	11 yrs 6 mo	Yarborough, James	Orphan. Sadle & harness making
Gilliam, Edward	21Jan1833	16 yrs	Curfman, William & Atkinson, William	Orphan. Waggon making
Ney, William C.	9Feb1833		Hall, Allen A.	Orphan. Printing
Hobbs, William H.	9Feb1833		Hall, Allen A.	Orphan. Printing
Harrison, Romulus	9Feb1833		Hall, Allen A.	Orphan. Printing
Gilliam, Edna Ann	9Feb1833		Neely, Samuel	Orphan. Seamstress
Bow, Samuel	23Apr1833		Vaughn, John	Orphan. Rope making. Of color
Phulfar, Joseph	23Apr1833	13 yrs	Hurt, Floyd	Orphan. Plastering
Goodwin, George W.	27Apr1833	17 yrs on 19Dec next	March, Jesse D.	Orphan. Saddle making
Hall, Bayless	3May1833	13 yrs on 1Oct last	Garner, William	Orphan. Cabinet making
Brown, Albert	15July1833	6 yrs	Richmond, Braddock	Orphan. Waggon making. Of color
Hanley, Peter	16July1833	16 yrs in August next	Hunter, Isaac	Orphan. Tanning
Crighton, Joseph	17July1833	12 yrs	Linck, Joseph	Orphan. Sadler

Name	Date	Age	Master	Notes
Cantrell, James	22July1833		Call, Joseph	Orphan. Barber. Of color
Rainey, Samuel	22July1833		Ferguson, Anderson	Orphan. Farming & planting
Buck, Thomas M.	22July1833		Moore, William H. & James D.	Orphan. Tin plate working
Phulfar, Lucinda	25July1833	8 yrs	Corbit, William A.	Orphan. Sew, knit & other house business. Cancelled 31Oct1833
Thompson, James H.	27July1833	13 yrs on 23Oct next	Harris, William	Orphan. House & sign painting
?	25Oct1833		Weakley, Robert L.	Indenture signed by William Hill, Nancy Williams, F. A. Henry & William Hill, Jr. Name of apprentice not specified
Weakley, Thomas	26Oct1833	13 yrs	Cartmell, Henry R.	Orphan. Sadler & harness making
Phulphar, Lucinda	31Oct1833	8 yrs	Baker, Obyah	Orphan. House business
Bow, William Samuel	2Nov1833	8 yrs on 23April last	Wilburn, Enoch	Orphan. Silversmith. Of color
Turner, Thomas	8Nov1833	16 yrs	Vaughan, Archibald	Orphan. Blacksmith
Hogan, Franklin	9Nov1833	12 yrs	Peterson, Morton	Orphan. Sadler & harness making
Wright, Martha	11Nov1833		Irwin, John	Orphan. Of color
Wright, James	11Nov1833		Irwin, John	Orphan. Of color
Woodruff, George W.	7Feb1834	13 yrs	Johnson, Thomas B.	Orphan. Farming
Pryor, Cornelius D.	7Feb1834	13 yrs on 29Apr next	Hunt, William Hassell	Orphan. Printing. Cancelled 27Apr1835
Hobbs, Collin S.	7Feb1834	14 yrs on 20Nov1833	Hunt, William Hassell	Orphan. Printing
Moore, Mark H.	7Feb1834	15yrs on 24Sept1833	Hunt, William Hassell	Orphan. Printing
Humphreys, Oliver H.	21Apr1834	16 yrs	Saffanans, David	Orphan. Tinning
Roland, James	21Apr1834	1 yr	Roland, William	Orphan. Farming
Hall, Shelby	22Apr1834	3 yrs	Murrell, James	Orphan. Brickmaking & laying
Hall, George	22Apr1834	16 yrs	Shelby, John	Orphan. Miller. Cancelled 1May1835
Hall, John	22Apr1834	10 yrs	Shelby, John	Orphan. Miller. Cancelled 1May1835
Nelson, Thomas H.	23Apr1834	4 yrs	Winfrey, Valentine	Orphan. Farming

Name	Date	Age	Master	Notes
Edy	24Apr1834		Tally, Nelson	Until 18 yrs. Orphan. Spin, knit & cook. Of color
Stevens, James	24Apr1834	8 yrs	Winfrey, George W.	Orphan. Blacksmith
Pryor, William L.	26Apr1834	15 yrs	Hall, Allen A.	Orphan. Printing
White, Ephraim	5May1834	14 yrs	Call, Joseph	Orphan. Barber. Of color
Malory, Thomas Eaton	6May1834	15 yrs	Burton, George H.	Orphan. Carpenter
Chatham, John	21July1834	10 yrs	Stout, Samuel V. D.	Orphan. Coach painting & harness making
White, Hiram	21July1834	17 yrs	Thomas, James	Orphan. Saddling
Martha	25July1834	12 yrs	Sluder, Aaron B.	Until 18 yrs. Orphan. Sew, knit & house business. Of color. Cancelled 26Apr1836
Thompson, Alfred F.	28July1834	18 yrs	Page, Jesse W.	Orphan. Saddling & harness making
Shepperd, John R.	28July1834	16 yrs on 9Oct next	Goss, John D.	Orphan. Cabinet maker
Ray, John F.	4Aug1834	15 yrs on 19Oct next	Savage, Richard	Orphan. Saddle & harness making
Ray, William J.	4Aug1834	13 yrs on 1April last	Savage, Richard	Orphan. Saddle & harness making
Fawbush, James	27Oct1834	8 yrs	Ralston, David	Orphan. Farming
Hodges, Robert	4Nov1834	14 yrs	Dotson, Jeremiah	Orphan. Tayloring
Thompkins, Washington	4Nov1834	14 yrs	Washington, Gilbert G.	Orphan. Tanning. Cancelled 22Apr1835
Davis, Zachariah	7Nov1834	8 yrs 9 mos 14 days	Bashaw, Joseph E.	Orphan. Cotton carding & spinning machine making
Berry, David W.	7Nov1834	10yrs on 11May next	Bashaw, Joseph E.	Orphan. Cotton carding & spinning machine making
Whitehead, Lanier	8Nov1834	15 yrs last October	Lanier, Robert	Orphan. Saddler
Casselman, James	19Jan1835	17 yrs last August	Thomas, James	Orphan. Saddlery
Baker, James M.	19Jan1835	15yrs on 15June next	Adkinson, William J.	Orphan. Waggon making
Rhodes, Joseph	19Jan1835	12 yrs last Xmas	Peterson, Morton	Orphan. Saddlery business
Owens, Andrew	26Jan1835	12 yrs	Turner, William W.	Orphan. Farming. Cancelled 1Apr1839
Owens, Amanda	26Jan1835	12 yrs	Turner, William W.	Orphan. Common house business. Cancelled 1Apr1839
Thompson, James	26Jan1835	15 yrs	Hill, Robert S.	Orphan. Blacksmith
Leigh, Gilbert	26Jan1835	16yrs on 25May next	Goss, John D.	Orphan. Cabinet making

Name	Date	Age	Master	Notes
Johnson, Willis	3Feb1835	16 yrs last Sept	Anderson, Andrew & Nehemiah S.	Orphan. Brass & iron foundry
Haynes, Margaret	4Feb1835	15 yrs	Read, Jane	Orphan. Milliner
Thompkins, Washington	22Apr1835		McNeill, John	Orphan. Farming
Worley, Martha	23Apr1835	13 yrs	Burton, Thomas	Orphan. Seamstress. Cancelled 5Sept1837
Owen, William	24Apr1835	14 yrs on 16Aug next	Saffarans, David	Orphan. Tinning
Wright, Emily H.	27Apr1835	13 yrs next October	Frazer, Ketturah	Orphan. Milliner. 20Apr1835*
Wright, Arristine	27Apr1835	15 yrs on 13Nov next	Frazer, Ketturah	Orphan. Milliner. 20Apr1835*
Gossett, Martin	27Apr1835	15 yrs last November	Dotson, Jeremiah	Orphan. Tayloring
Swinney, Thomas	27Apr1835	15 yrs on 8Aug next	Thomas, James	Orphan. Saddlery
Graham, Mary B.	28Apr1835	7 yrs	Graham, Reuben P.	Orphan. Seamstress
Hobbs, William H.	5May1835	18 yrs on 6Feb last	Nye, Shadrack	Orphan. Printing
Harrison, Romulus	5May1835	16 yrs on 5June next	Nye, Shadrack	Orphan. Printing
Harrison, Nicholas	5May1835	19yrs on 25Sept next	Nye, Shadrack	Orphan. Printing
Caton, Catherine	6May1835	12 yrs	Brown, Berryman	Orphan. Seamstress
Barker, Ellen	1Aug1835	5 yrs	Washington, William L.	Orphan. Housekeeping
Barker, Barbara	1Aug1835	3 yrs	Washington, William L.	Orphan. Housekeeping
Barker, James	1Aug1835	9 yrs	Stout, Samuel V. D.	Orphan. Coach making
Gleaver, John E.	2Aug1835	12 yrs last March	Ewing, Orville	Orphan. Apothecary
Fox, Charles James	8Aug1835	14 yrs on 2Nov1835	Ewing, Orville	Until 19 yrs 9 mos. Orphan. Apothecary
Hogg, John B.	20Oct1835	18 yrs 3 mo	Hall, James	Orphan. Druggist. See Samuel Hogg
Hartwell, Eliza Jane	26Oct1835	6 yrs	Chichering, John	Until 18 yrs. House waiting. Of color
Guy, James	26Oct1835		Yarborough, James	Orphan. Saddlery
Hughes, Robert	26Oct1835	2 yrs	Hughes, John L.	Orphan. House waiting

Name	Date	Age	To whom	Notes
Owens, Carroll	26Oct1835	12 yrs	Allen, William H.	Orphan. Blacksmith
Gleaves, James	5Nov1835	17 yrs last June	Smith, James	Orphan. Printing
Virgil, Samuel	7Nov1835	18 yrs	March, Jesse D.	Saddlery & harness making
Alexander, Stephen	18Jan1836	10 yrs	Reeves, William	Orphan. Farming. Of color
Alexander, William	18Jan1836	16 yrs	Kellum, Henry	Orphan. Farming. Of color
Loftin, Robert	18Jan1836	5 yrs	Allison, William	Orphan. Turning business
Beavers, Thomas J.	18Jan1836	19yrs on 20June next	Sears, Charles	Orphan. Boot & shoe making. On 25Jan1836 Beavers petitioned by next friend John C. Beavers to cancel indenture. Denied 29Jan
Billings, William	25Jan1836	15 yrs	Peabody, John	Orphan. Jeweller
Bradford, Joseph S.	30Jan1836	17 yrs last October	Moore, William H. & G. B.	Orphan. Tin making
Clark, Theoderick	30Jan1836	11 yrs last March	Moore, William H. & G. B.	Orphan. Tin making
Stephen	2Feb1836	2 yrs	Esselman, John N.	House waiting. Of color
Margaret	2Feb1836	8 yrs	Esselman, John N.	Until 18 yrs. House waiting. Of color
Becky	2Feb1836	3 yrs	Esselman, John N.	Until 18 yrs. House waiting. Of color
Martha	26Apr1836	14 yrs in July next	Williams, William	Until 18 yrs. Sewing, knitting & housekeeping. Of color. Canc 6Feb1837
Rogers, Edward H.	3May1836	16 yrs on 22Feb last	Nye, Shadrack	Orphan. Printer
Betsey	3May1836	13 yrs in July next	Thomas, John	Until 18 yrs. Housekeeping. Of color
Johnson, George K.	6June1836	12 yrs on 8Oct next	Anderson, Andrew & Nehemiah S.	Orphan. Foundry
David, Felix R	7June1836	19yrs on 16Sept next	March, Jesse D.	Until 12Aug1838. Orphan. Saddler
Johnson, Richard	7June1836	18 yrs on 30Jan last	March, Jesse D.	Until 1Nov1838. Orphan. Saddler
Smith, James	1Aug1836	13 yrs	Anderson, Benjamin C.	Blacksmith
Ramar, Daniel	3Aug1836	15 yrs	Peterson, Morton	Orphan. Sadler
William	5Sept1836	7 yrs	McCabe, William	Orphan. Tayloring. Of color
Henry	5Sept1836	10 yrs	Brown, Berryman	Orphan. Carpenter. Of color
Ramer, William	5Sept1836	Between 12 & 13 yrs	Lowry, Overton	Orphan. Farming
Ramer, Jane	5Sept1836	12 yrs	Lowry, Overton	Orphan. Farming

Name	Date	Age	Master	Notes
Lucas, Caleb	3Oct1836	12 yrs on 24June last	Burton, George H.	Orphan. Carpenter
Lucas, Starlin Brown	3Oct1836	13 yrs on 5May last	Gunter, G. B.	Orphan. Waggon making. Voided 3Apr1837
Lacy, Ann	3Oct1836	11 yrs	McCabe, William	Orphan. Serving & housekeeping. Of color
Alexander, Stephen	3Oct1836	11 yrs on 7 this mo	Hutton, William D.	Orphan. Tanning
Westley	5Dec1836	8 or 9 yrs	Richmond, Barton	Orphan
Mitchell, Willie	5Dec1836	16 yrs	Mitchell, Martha	Orphan. Hack driving & keeping horses
Bradley, Sarah Ann	6Dec1836	13 yrs in Feb next	Ferguson, James B.	Until 18 yrs. House keeping. Mulatto
Bushrod	7Dec1836	12 yrs	Hill, Richard J.	Orphan. Farming. Of color
Martha	6Feb1837	15 yrs next July	Kieruliff, Jacob	Sewing, knitting & house waiting. Of color. Cancelled 5Feb1838
Cagle, William J.	6Feb1837	14 yrs	Cagle, George	Orphan. Cooper. Cancelled 7Feb1837
Thompson, Thomas R.	7Feb1837	14 yrs on 28Jan1837	Nye, Shadrack	Orphan. Printing
Leake, James	8Feb1837	14 yrs on 14Apr next	Nye, Shadrack	Orphan. Printing
Loftin, Albert	6Mar1837	Abt 3 yrs	Walker, John S.	Farming. Of color
Newland, William P.	4Apr1837	16 yrs last Sept	Newland, William	Orphan. Farming
Pittser, William J.	5Apr1837	15 yrs on 25Dec last	Goss, John D.	Orphan. Cabinet maker
Green, Joseph S.	1May1837	8 yrs on 12Apr last	Chandler, William	Orphan. Farming. On 3June1839 Chandler called to answer petition by _____ Green to cancel indenture. Dismissed 2July1839
Luallen, James M. M. C.	3July1837	Abt 14 yrs	Parkerson, James B.	Orphan. Blacksmithing
Ball, David S.	6Nov1837	17 yrs on 23Mar last	Carpenter, John C. & Lyon, Matthew	Orphan. Printing. Cancelled 7Aug1838
Stewart, Florian	4Dec1837	5 yrs on 20Aug last	Walder, Priscilla	Orphan. Sewing & housekeeping. Cancelled 4Mar1839 as Flora Ann. Returned to father
Fagg, Martha Jane	4Dec1837	6 yrs	Frederick, William W.	Orphan. Housewifery
Green, Jonathan J.	1Jan1838	13 yrs on 19Dec last	Tally, Banister	Orphan. Farming
Jackson, Richard	1Jan1838	17 yrs in Oct1838	Wyatt, Spencer R.	Waggon making. Cancelled 7Sept1840

Lacy, William	2Jan1838	Abt 8 yrs	Cole, Robert A.	Saddling. Of color
Martha	5Feb1838	16 yrs next July	Couch, John A.	Orphan. Sewing, knitting & house waiting. Of color
Williams, Benjamin F.	6Mar1838	10 yrs the 1st inst	McCann, William	Orphan. Cooper
Kyle, James	4Apr1838	15 yrs on 4July next	Morrison, Andrew	Orphan. Tailoring
Clemmons, Andrew E.	4Apr1838	18 yrs on 1Mar1838	Wright, Moses & Aaron	Orphan. Tailoring
Owen, William	5Apr1838		Maxy, Powhatan & Hagen, John W.	Orphan. Tin plate business
Hobbs, John	5Apr1838	16 yrs on 17July next	Maxy, Powhatan & Hagen, John W.	Orphan. Tinning business
Iredell, Alfred	5Apr1838	14yrs on 14May next	Maxy, Powhatan & Hagen, John W.	Orphan. Tin plate business
Garner, William	5Apr1838	17 yrs on 30Aug next	Graham, Reuben P.	Orphan. Barber. Of color, "yellow"
Reppete, William	7May1838	10 yrs next October	White, John	Orphan. Plastering
Runnels, Martha	8May1838	13 yrs on 27Mar last	Call, Joseph	Until 18 yrs. Housekeeping. Of color
Runnels, Jane	8May1838	10 yrs on 17July next	Call, Joseph	Until 18 yrs. Housekeeping. Of color
Runnels, Betsey	8May1838	4 yrs on 12Sept last	Call, Joseph	Until 18 yrs. Housekeeping. Of color
Wilson, Eliza	5June1838	Abt 9 yrs	Read, Jane	Orphan. Milliner
Goodwin, Jeremiah V.	7July1838		Morrow, John	For 5 yrs from 3rd this mo. Orphan. Saddling
Cagle, Jonathan	6Aug1838	8 yrs on 7Feb last	Cagle, George J.	Orphan. Farming. Cancelled 5Oct1840
Bell [Ball], David G.	7Aug1838		Dunn, William H.	Orphan. Printing. Ordered returned to court 6Feb1839. Cancelled 3Apr1839. To mother, Evelina Ball
Waggoner, William	4Sept1838	Abt 15 yrs	Puckett, Etheldred B.	Orphan. Saddler
Hogg, Samuel	3Oct1838	14 yrs on 9Mar1838	Hall, James H. M.	Until 19 yrs. Druggist & apothecary. One of 6 children of John B. Hogg (d. 24May1833) & grandson of Capt. Samuel Hogg, a Rev. War veteran. James P. Grundy, apptd guardian 5June1838*. 7Nov1838*
Blakemore, Jesse T.	3Dec1838	17 yrs in Apr1839	Morrow, John	Orphan. Saddlery

51

Name	Date	Age	Master	Notes
Simpson, Robert H.	7Jan1839	14 yrs in Aug1839	Sledge, John P.	Orphan. Turning
Biggs, John	8Jan1839	16 yrs on 6Feb next	Booker, Anderson	Orphan. Carpenter
Owens, Andrew	1Apr1839		Briley, John G.	Farming
Coslett, Joseph	2Apr1839	Abt 16 yrs	Combs, James W. M. & Carson, N. D.	For 5 yrs. Cabinet maker
Nichol, Felix R.	8Oct1839	14yrs on 11May next	Anderson, William	Orphan. Tailoring
Lott	4Nov1839	2 yrs	Pegram, Roger	Foundling. Farming. Of color
Patrick, Timothy	4Nov1839	Abt 12 yrs	Orton, Ray S.	Orphan. Tanner
Duff, Joseph	5Nov1839	12 yrs last July	Anderson, William	Orphan. Tailoring
Smith, Daniel	5Nov1839	10 yrs	Moody, Robert	Orphan. Blacksmith
Gavin, Andrew	6Jan1840	Abt 15 yrs	Greer, Henry	Orphan. Farming
Bowen (?Brown), James C.	2June1840	Abt 16 yrs	Nye, Shadrick	Printing
Jackson, Richard W.	7Sept1840		Allen, Samuel M.	Wagon making
Sweeney, Josiah	7Sept1840	17 yrs in Feb1840	Baynes, Marcus H.	Blacksmithing
Rodgers, John H.	7Dec1840		Allen, S. M.	
Barbee	4Jan1841	10 yrs in Aug next	March, Jesse D.	House business & sewing
Frances	7Jan1841		Madden, William	Of color
Mathes, Levy J.	7Jan1841		Anderson, Henry M.	Orphan
Colley, Richard R.	7Jan1841		Bosworth, William	Orphan
Reynolds, John B.	6Apr1841		Nye, S.	Orphan. Printing
Owen, Hannibal	3May1841		Stewart, William	Blacksmith
Blannan, Jane Ann	4May1841		Warren, William	Housekeeping. Alias ?Brewer
Leake, Greenwood	7June1841		Maxey, P. W.	Orphan. Tin plate business
Leake, John M.	6July1841		Tooly, Joseph H.	Orphan. Machine making
Lamb, Augustus L.	2Aug1841		Harris, William	Orphan. House & sign painting
Yorke?, James M.	3Aug1841		Saffrans, Weller O.	Orphan. Tinning
Rich, William	1Nov1841		Winfrey, Thomas A.	Orphan. House servant
Morton, Wright H.	8Dec1841		McCombs, James W.	Cabinet making

Name	Date	Master	Occupation
Mechem, William	8Dec1841	McCombs, James W.	Cabinet making
Swinney, James	8Feb1842	McCann, William	Orphan. Coopering. Cancelled 5Aug1846
Swinney, Silas N.	8Feb1842	McCann, William	Orphan. Coopering
Gentry, John R	8Mar1842	Porter, Solomon	Orphan. Barber
Tienon, Charles	3May1842	Maxey & McClure	Orphan. Tin & sheet iron business
Lewallen, Bennet	8July1842	Scott, William	Orphan. Farming
Lewallen, Jesse	8July1842	Pegram, John P.	Orphan. Farming
Lewallen, John S.	8July1842	Usery, William	Orphan. Farming
Jim	5Sept1842	Johnson, Charles	Orphan. Farming. Of color
John	5Sept1842	Johnson, Charles	Orphan. Farming. Of color
Melinda	5Sept1842	Johnson, Charles	Until 18 yrs. Orphan. Housekeeping. Of color
Caroline	5Sept1842	Gray, John	Orphan. Housekeeping. Of color
Martin, Thomas	5Sept1842	Maxwell, Jene	Orphan. Farming
Johnson, Michael	6Sept1842	Jones, Lewis	Orphan. Farming
Harrison, Joseph M.	4Oct1842	Turley, Charles A.	Orphan. Hat manufacturing
Brown, Lewis	5Nov1842	McClure, William	Orphan. Farming. Of color
Brown, Sarah A.	5Nov1842	McClure, William	Until 18 yrs. House servant. Of color
Westley	6Feb1843	Stewart, Peter	Shoe making. Of color
Duren, Emeline	7Feb1843	Plasants, Lucy	Orphan. Washing
Stewart, Elizabeth	7Feb1843	Dreyfus, Lucy	Until 21 yrs. Orphan. Sewing & housewifery
Glasgow, Enoch	3Apr1843	Scott, St Clair	Orphan. Farming
Burnett, Kinchen	4Apr1843	Hays, Charles	Farming. Of color
White, Samuel	6June1843	Singleton, Robert W.	Orphan. Farming
Bagwell, George	6July1843	Cowerden, Collin M.	Orphan. House carpentry & joining
Richard	3Sept1843	Woods, David	House capentering. Both of color
Haly, Susan	4Sept1843	Couch, Peter J.	Orphan. Housekeeping
Saunders, Luiza Frances	2Oct1843	Ramer, Henry	Orphan. Housekeeping
Allford, James	7Nov1843	Austin, George M.	Orphan. Farming
Allford, John	7Nov1843	Briley, John G.	Orphan. Farming
Allvord, Thomas	7Nov1843	Gilman, Alva	Orphan. Farming
Buchanan, Laban	6Feb1844	Allen, M. S.	Orphan. Black smith

Name	Date	Age	Master	Notes
Camp, Benjamin T.	6May1844		Moore, William H.	Orphan. Tin plate working. Canc 1Dec1845
Camp,	6May1844		McKenna, B. R.	Orphan. Printing
Carroll, Louiza	6Aug1844		Hill, John G.	Orphan. Housekeeping. Of color. Cancelled 9Oct1944. Restored to Humphrey Clinker
Loftin, Robert	2Sept1844		Pegram, John P.	Orphan. Farming
Steele, George	8Oct1844		Turner, Thomas	Orphan. Black smith. Of color
Scott, George	9Oct1844		Henderson, Adam	Orphan. Shoe making. Of color
Carroll, Louisa	4Nov1844		Clinker, Humphrey	Until 18 yrs. Orphan. House keeping. Of color
Fletcher, Francis	3Dec1844		Manon, John	Orphan. Saddling. Of color
Johnson, William	3Dec1844		Maxey, P. W. & McClure, N.	Orphan. Tin manufacturing
Buchanan, James B.	3Mar1845		Allen, Samuel M.	Orphan. Waggon making
Laughlin, William M.	7Apr1845		Elliston, William	Orphan. Turning
Henry, Rebecca	9Apr1845		Fudge, John	Orphan. House keeping
Childress, Desey	9Apr1845		Curtis, Francis	Orphan. House keeping. Of color
Childress, Eliza	9Apr1845		Curtis, Francis	Orphan. House keeping. Of color
Poates, Lewis L.	3June1845		McKennie, B. R.	Orphan. Printing
Gentry, John R	1Sept1845		Rawlings, William	Orphan. Barber & hair dressing. Of color
Washington, Ann	2Sept1845	13 yrs	Fogg, Francis B.	Orphan. Mantan (Mantua?) making
Johnson, George M.	7Oct1845		Yenie?, Samuel J.	Orphan. Segar making
Hunter, William A.	7Oct1845		Jewel, H. G.	Orphan. Drugg business
Matthis, William H.	7Oct1845		Curry, Richard A.	Orphan. Drugg business
Matthis, Mary J.	7Oct1845		Curry, Richard A.	Orphan. House keeping
Winters, Seaborn	1Dec1845		Berry, A. D.	Orphan. Tailoring
Camp, Benjamin L.	1Dec1845		Payne, G. W. G.	Orphan. Tin plate business
Johnson, Charles	2Mar1846	17 yrs on 22Apr1846	Huff, John	Orphan. Brick laying
Garner, William	2Mar1846	15 yrs on 1May1846	Huff, John	Orphan. Brick laying
Hall, Susan	7July1846		Drake, Susan	Orphan. Seamstress

Name	Date	Master	Notes
Yates, William F.	3Aug1846	Cartmell, H. R.	Orphan. Saddling
Swinney, James	5Aug1846	Whiteman, William S.	Paper making
Sommers, Carnie F.	7Sept1846	Denning, William	Orphan. Boot & shoe making. Cancelled 8Nov1848
Taylor, James	7Dec1846	Crouch, Thomas J.	Orphan. Farming
Jaco?, John J.	1Feb1847	Hyronomus, F.	Orphan. Tailoring
Williams, George W.	1Feb1847	Foster, Henry W.	Orphan. Farming
Fagg, Martha J.	1Feb1847	Warren, W. B.	Orphan. Housekeeping
Morton, Solomon	7June1847	Moore, William T.	Orphan. Farming
Morton, John B.	2Aug1847	Whitemore, F.	Orphan. Farming
Sellkirk, William	3Aug1847	Williams, William D.	Orphan. Farming
Haley, Henry C.	6Sept1847	Jones, William	Orphan. Carpentering
Childress, Susan M.	6Sept1847	McCain, William	Orphan. Housekeeping. On 4Dec1854 McCain & wife allowed to remove Susan Margaret from Tennessee*
Collier, John A.	7Sept1847	Shivers, A. C.	Orphan. Saddlering
Williams, William	1Nov1847	Barnes, John F.	Orphan. Farming
Gess, Richard	7Feb1848	Shivers, Asa	Orphan. Butchering
Childress, Minerva	15Mar1848	Jackson, William	Orphan. Housekeeping
Bennett, Henry	4Apr1848	Hamilton, George F.	Farming. Of color
Bennett, Thomas	4Apr1848	Hamilton, George F.	Farming. Of color
Beazley, Harriett	1May1848	Ramer, Henry	Until 21 yrs. Orphan. Cancelled 6Feb1850
Female, Unnamed	7Aug1848	Ellison, William	Orphan. Of color
Barham, Robert A.	3Oct1848	Stout, S. V. D.	Orphan. Coach making
Chamberlain, Mathew	6Nov1848	Drake, Wesley	Orphan
Glasgow, W. W.	5Mar1849	Smith, W. B.	Orphan. Farming
Kem?, John	3Apr1849	Alexander, J. N.	Orphan.
Mann, Eudora M.	4Apr1849	Hitchcock, Ann	Orphan. Hitchcock was President of the Orphan's Assylum
Mann, Sarah V.	4Apr1849	Hitchcock, Ann	Orphan. Hitchcock was President of the Orphan's Assylum
Mann, George	4Apr1849	Hitchcock, Ann	Orphan. Hitchcock was President of the Orphan's Assylum
Mann, Josiah	4Apr1849	Hitchcock, Ann	Orphan. Hitchcock was President of the Orphan's Assylum
Reddick, Thomas	7Aug1849	Burke, E. K.	Orphan. A. C. Norvell appointed guardian to Thomas & and an unnamed sibling

Name	Date	Age	Master	Notes
Strachauer, Emil	6Nov1849		Lyon, James M.	Orphan
Roberts, M. T	3Dec1849		McKinnie, B. R.	Orphan
Clark, Frank	8Jan1850		Days, L.	
Powell, Mary A.	5Feb1850		Powell, Charles	Until 21. Orphan
Williams, George	4Mar1850		Leonard, Peyton	Orphan
Celia	2Apr1850		Taylor, Rachel	Until 18 yrs. Orphan. Housekeeping. Of color
Chisenhall, Caroline	2Apr1850		Lane, William T.	Orphan. Taken from mother, Rhoda A. Chisenhall, for immoral conduct 6Mar1850*
Chisenhall, William	2Apr1850		Lane, William T.	Orphan. Taken from mother, Rhoda A. Chisenhall, for immoral conduct 6Mar1850*
Nicholson, Jeremiah N.	10Aug1850		Weller, Benjamin S.	Orphan. Tinning
Smith, Francis (fe)	10Oct1850		Lindsley, Mary Ann	Until 18 yrs. Orphan. House keeping. Of color
Summer, John	4Nov1850	10 yrs	Stalcup, Alexander	Orphan. Gun smithing
Carter, George W.	2Dec1850	14 yrs	Bowen, Jeremiah	Orphan. Tanning
Carter, Archibald P.	2Dec1850	11 yrs	Bowen, Jeremiah	Orphan. Tanning
Hunter, Francis Elizabeth	5Mar1851		Moss, James S.	Until 18 yrs. Orphan. House keeping. Of color
Tatem John	8Apr1851	12 yrs	Barett, Charles	Hack driver. Of color. On 11July1856 as John Tate ordered discharged form apprenticeship on 12Mar1859, when 21 yrs
Sullivan, Chesterfield W.	8Apr1851		Deaderick, Fielding	Canc 5July1854. To mother, Lucy Lucky (Lacky). Order stayed next day. Made final 11Aug1854
Capley, Amanda	4June1851	12 yrs	Taylor, Ellenor	Orphan. Milliner
Julia Caroline	4Aug1851	5 yrs	Tyree, Henry P.	Until 18 yrs. Of color
John Henry	4Aug1851		Stevenson, Volney S.	Of color
Jones, Charles	1Sept1851		Temple, L. M.	Of color
Stewart, William B.	2Sept1851		Stewart, William	Orphan. Black smith. Cancelled 12Feb1855
Smith, John	7Oct1851		Teag, James	Orphan. Farming
Pollard,_____ (fe)	7Oct1851		McCullough,____	Orphan. Milliner
McBride, Thomas	7Jan1852	17 yrs	Shaffer, R. W.	Orphan. Brick laying
Rose, Moses M. R. R.	2Mar1852	Abt 7 yrs	Sherman, Charles S.	Orphan. Harness making

Name	Date	Master/Employer	Age	Notes
Gray, Hardy B.	5Mar1852	Chilcutt, B. F.	13 yrs	Orphan. Farming
Tucker, George M.	3May1852	Page, Thomas B	7 yrs	Orphan. Farming
Tucker, Samuel G.	3May1852	Page, Thomas B	5 yrs	Orphan. Farming
Foster, John	6Dec1852	Carper, A.	10 yrs	Orphan. Farming. Of color 9Apr1853. On 2May1853 Green Carper ordered to return John to Alexander Carper
Johnson, Sophia	9Dec1852	Fergason, Sarah A. (Mrs)	13 yrs	Housekeeping. Mulatto
Lewis, Henry	9Dec1852	Daderick, F.	Abt 13 yrs	Of color
Baker, Susannah E.	9Dec1852	West, Charles B.	8 yrs	House keeping
Patton, Francis M.	6June1853	Mansmill?, John	Abt 14 yrs	Orphan. Butcher
Mann, George W. M.	6June1853	Noakes, E. B.	8 yrs	Orphan. Saddler
Walker, Tennessee (fe)	6June1853	Stratton, Mary	Abt 6 yrs	Orphan
Green, Thomas	6Sept1853	Golden, Thomas	8 yrs	Orphan. Gas fitting
Johnson, John Thomas	8Sept1853	Hawkins, Richard M.	13 yrs	Orphan. Saddler
Jenkins, Joseph	6Oct1853	Jenkins, Obediah	8 yrs	Orphan.
Jenkins, John	6Oct1853	Jenkins, Obediah	4 yrs	Orphan
Jenkins, Mary	6Oct1853	Jenkins, Obediah	9? Yrs	Orphan
Jenkins, Elizabeth	6Oct1853	Jenkins, Obediah	6 yrs	Orphan
Barnes, Benjamin D.	7Nov1853	Roller, John	8 yrs	Orphan. An adjacent incomplete entry suggests that another Barnes child was also bound
Hall (Hale?), Guman S.	5June1854	Pugh, John R.	10 yrs	Orphan. Farming. Cancelled 10Aug1854. To care of Aaron Wright
Powell, Ann	4July1854	Haslum, Samuel	9 yrs	Orphan. House keeping
Dawes, Lafayette	7July1854	Chilton, Thomas W.		Father, James Dawes, failed to provide
Dawes, Sarah Francis	7July1854	Chilton, Thomas W.		Father, James Dawes, failed to provide
Dawes, Mary V.	7July1854	Chilton, Thomas W.		Father, James Dawes, failed to provide
Dawes, Susannah	7July1854	Chilton, James M.		Father, James Dawes, failed to provide
Dawes, Robert	7July1854	Chilton, James M.		Father, James Dawes, failed to provide
Dawes, Isaac	7July1854	Chilton, James M.		Father, James Dawes, failed to provide
Burnett, Thomas	7Aug1854	Powers, R. F.	8 yrs	Orphan. Farming
Patton, Soleman	7Aug1854	Ruckles, Robert	8 yrs	Orphan. Lock smithing & bell hanging
Johnson, Melissa	7Aug1854	Maddux, William D.	12 yrs	Orphan. House keeping

Name	Date	Age	Master	Notes
Rose, Rachel Ann	7Aug1854	13 yrs	Shankling, David	Until 18 yrs. Housekeeping. Both of color
Johnson, Monroe	8Aug1854	7 yrs	Stewart, Michael S.	Until 15 yrs
Lakey, Chesterfield	11Aug1854		Wright, Aaron	Of color. See Chesterfield W Sullivan
Barnett, Isaac	15Aug1854	10 yrs	Paul, Isaac	Orphan. Brick or stone mason. Paul to pay $20 yearly to court for use of the mother. Same date Harriett Barnett declared of unsound mind
Barnett, Wiley	15Aug1854	Abt 7 ys	Paul, Isaac	Orphan. Brick or stone mason. Paul to pay $20 yearly to court for use of the mother. Same date Harriett Barnett declared of unsound mind
Foster, Sylvester B.	4Sept1854		Meacham, William F.	Orphan.
Cross, Thomas	11Sept1854	8 yrs	Hill, Henry	Orphan. Carpenter
Bush, Louisa	8Nov1854		Boyd, William L.	Orphan. Housekeeping. Of color
Roberts, M. T	9Dec1854		Stuit?, Ira A.	Orphan. Coach making
Huskey, Emma	5Jan1855		Byrne, William T.	On 10July1857 Byrne ordered to answer petition to cancel apprenticeship
Huskey, Henry	5Jan1855		Byrne, William T.	On 10July1857 Byrne ordered to answer petition to cancel apprenticeship
Huskey, Willis	5Jan1855		Byrne, William T.	On 10July1857 Byrne ordered to answer petition to cancel apprenticeship
Bush, Jane	6Mar1855		Conley, R. D.	Orphan. Washing, ironing etc. Of color
Parks, George	7Mar1855		Felts, J. W	Orphan
Martin, Nancy	8Mar1855		Harlam, James	Orphan
Chanis?, Leonard	7May1855		Livery, Peter	Orphan. Farming. Both of color
Chanis?, Alfred	7May1855		Livery, Peter	Orphan. Farming. Both of color
Stereman, Rebecca	11Aug1855		Wilken, D. T.	House keeping. Of color
Call, Virginia	5Sept1855		Stratton, Mary	Orphan. Of color. On 3Oct1855 Ann McKinney ordered to deliver Virginia to L. M. Temple, her guardian
Day, Madison	8Nov1855		Day, Jane	Until 17 yrs. Of color
Day, Jacob	8Nov1855		Day, Jane	Until 17 yrs. Of color
Day, Abraham	8Nov1855		Day, Jane	Until 17 yrs. Of color

Name	Date	Age	Master/Guardian	Notes
Day, Margaret Ann	8Nov1855		Day, Jane	Until 18 yrs. Of color
Day, Thomas	8Nov1855		Day, Jane	Until 17 yrs. Of color
Day, John	8Nov1855		Day, Jane	Until 17 yrs. Of color
Paull?, Wiley B.	7Dec1855		Simms, Wiley	Orphan
Mosely, Jasper N.	15Jan1856		Felts, James W.	Tin working
McDaniel, James	4May1857	8 or 9 yrs	Williams, William T.	Orphan. Farming
Young, Boyd	11Mar1858	15 yrs	P. W. Maxey & Co.	Orphan. Tin & sheet iron work. Cancelled 6July1863
Sitton, Henry	11Mar1858	7 yrs	Hickman, Willis	Of color
Mayo, Amanda Jane	7Apr1858	5 yrs	Ezell, James	
Jefferson, James	8Apr1858	15 yrs	Parrish, Frank	Hair dressing & barbering. Of color
Husky, Emma	10Apr1858	15 yrs	Freeman, Zachias	House keeping. Of color.
Foster, John Houston	21June1858	14 yrs	McGavock, R. W.	Orphan. Barber. Of color
West, Claiborne	24July1858	15 yrs	Young, Edward E.	Orphan. Tinner etc
Ann Eliza	14Aug1858	12 yrs	Zimerman, J. M.	Orphan. House keeping & needlework
Husky, Henry	21Dec1858	12 yrs	Maxey, P. W.	Orphan. Tin plate & sheet iron worker. Of color. 1Nov1858*
Husky, Willis	21Dec1858	10 yrs	Cornelius, W. R.	Orphan. Tin plate & sheet iron worker. Of color. 1Nov1858*
Coffee, Humphrey	24Dec1858	7 yrs	Barr, Hugh	Orphan. Cooper
Laurent, Alexander J.	8Feb1859	16 yrs	Jacker, M.	Orphan. Machinist
Laurent, Edgar	8Feb1859	12 yrs	Bohme, Oscar	Orphan. Pasementier
Laurent, Eugene L.	11Feb1859	19 yrs	Wells, Thomas	Orphan. Apothecary & druggist
Brock, Cornelia	11Feb1859	Abt 8 yrs	Allen, William C.	Until 21 yrs. Orphan. Housekeeping
Celia	6Apr1859	10 yrs	Taylor, Jesse & Maria	Until 18 yrs. Orphan. Housekeeping. Of color
Cockrill, George	5June1860	6 yrs	Cook, A. B.	Orphan. Farming. Of color
Walker, Tennessee	16Aug1860	14 yrs	Creighton, Joseph	Abandoned by her parents. Housekeeping
Inglishly, Emily	7Nov1860	15 yrs	Whiteman, H. W.	Orphan. Housekeeping. Edmund O'Connor & wife removed as guardians
Craighead, Alexander	1Dec1860	10 yrs	Turner, Abner	Until 16 yrs. Hosteler. Of color
Craighead, James	1Dec1860	8 yrs	Turner, Abner	Until 16 yrs. Hosteler. Of color
Voorvaart, Henry	5Dec1860	15 yrs	Thomas, Charles S.	Orphan. Butcher
Brok, Emily	21Sept1861	4 yrs 6 mo	Hefty, Mathew	Housekeeping
Hynes, Thomas	12Apr1862	10 yrs	O'Donnell, Connell	Until 18 yrs. Orphan. Stonemason or farming

Name	Date	Age	Master	Notes
Knight, Frances	5May1862	14 yrs	Bruce, M. C.	Orphan. Nurse & house keeping
Hamilton, Lewis	20May1865		Lapsley, Daniel L.	Orphan. Barbering. Both of color
Johnson, Flora	27May1865		Johnson, Anthony W.	Orphan. House keeping. Of color
Smallwood, Richard	24June1865	13 yrs	Harris & Pearl	Orphan. Barbering. Of color
Lewis, Mary Francis	29July1865	12 yrs	Lewis, William B.	Orphan. Farming. Of color
Lewis, Henry	29July1865	10 yrs	Lewis, William B.	Orphan. Farming. Of color
Rehberger, Ann	11Nov1865	6 yrs	Lauther, Adam	Orphan. House keeping
Noel, Calvin	16June1866	13 yrs	Noel, S. A. G.	Orphan. Farming & dining room servant. Of color
Noel, Henry	16June1866	7 yrs	Noel, S. A. G.	Orphan. Farming & dining room servant. Of color
Thompson, Ann	30June1866	10 yrs	Shafter, William R.	Orphan. House keeping. With Ann's permission, Shafter allowed to remove her from state. Of color
Barber, Milly	21July1866	9 yrs	Noland, R. C.	Orphan. House keeping & farming. Milly agrees to move to Rutherford Co. Of color
Foster, Mathias	13Oct1866	9 yrs	Forehand, G. B	Orphan. Wheelwright
Etherly, Margaret	11Dec1866	12 yrs	King, E. Douglas	Orphan. House keeping. Of color
Wigdon, John	15Dec1866	10 yrs	Paul, James A.	Orphan. Farming
Forrester, Wilburn	5Jan1867	16 yrs	Reguin, C. F.	Orphan. House & sign painter. Annulled 13Mar1869
Wilson, Robert	9Jan1867	10 yrs	Cox, A. D.	Orphan. Farming. Of color
Cox, Mary Jane	9Jan1867	8 yrs	Cox, A. D.	Orphan. House keeping. Of color
Johnson, Scott	19Jan1867	17 yrs	Fanning, A. J.	Consent of father. Farming. Of color
Johnson, Nathan	19Jan1867	9 yrs	Fanning, A. J.	Consent of father. Farming. Of color
Minor, Pauline	2Mar1867	9 yrs	Lishey, Louis C.	Orphan. Consent of mother. House keeping. Of color. Cancelled 30July1870 with consent of all parties
Edmund	18May1867	Abt 8 yrs	Davis, S. J. (Mrs)	Orphan. Of color
Simpkins, Mary	27July1867	Abt 8 yrs	Nance, Ann D. (Mrs)	AKA Mary Drake. Orphan. House keeping. Of color
Jordan, Ned	17Aug1867	8 yrs	Whitsett, William A.	Orphan. Farming. Of color
Mowry, John	17Aug1867	10 yrs	Burnsides, Nancy	Orphan. Farming
Kelly, Isaac	31Aug1867	12 yrs	Whitsett, William A.	Orphan. Farming
Hutchinson, Alice	9Oct1867	8 yrs	Barnes, R. A.	Orphan. House keeping. Of color

Name	Date	Age	Bondsman	Notes
Johnson, Frank	19Oct1867	11 yrs	Hill, H. B.	Orphan. Farming. Of color
Green, Martha Elizabeth	12Nov1867	7 yrs	James, John D.	Orphan. House keeping
Hood, James	23Nov1867	Abt 14 yrs	Haggard, William D.	Orphan. Farming
Hood, William	23Nov1867	Abt 12 yrs	Haggard, William D.	Orphan. Farming
Taylor, Bettie	12Sept1868	Abt 8 yrs	Mahoney, Timothy T.	Testimony that mother, Nancy Taylor, was cruel and unfit. Father dead.
Harrison, Charles	4Jan1869	12 yrs	Rankin, W. R.	Orphan
Madison, Murphy	9Jan1869	5 yrs	East, Benjamin J.	Orphan. Brick-laying
Alexander, William	1Feb1869	12 yrs	Herrin, Thomas	Orphan. Farming
Joslin, Sallie	22Feb1869	8 yrs	Davidson, Sam B.	House keeping. Of color. Cancelled 1Dec1871, Sallie having left Davidson
Harper, Mintha	27Feb1869	6 yrs	Lewis, Granville	Orphan. Both of color. House keeping
Lindsley, Jennie	13Mar1869	8 yrs	Sledge, Ella	Orphan. Sempstress. Estate of Dr N. Lawrence Lindsley partitioned same date
Moore, George	24Apr1869	8 yrs	Harris, Laetitia J.	Orphan. Housekeeping & farming. Of color
Warren, Sarah	13Nov1869	13 yrs	Johnson, A. W.	Orphan. Housekeeping
Link, Samuel	3Feb1870	6 yrs	Link, Joseph	Orphan. Farming. Of color
Scott, Mary	12Feb1870	11 yrs	Eason, E. J. (Mrs)	Orphan. House keeping. Of color
Jones, Robert	9Apr1870	11 yrs	Barrett, A. R.	Orphan. House servant. Of color. On 16Apr1870 Mrs Barrett allowed to take Robert to New York State
Potter, Susan	16Apr1870	14 yrs	Parkes, Thomas	Orphan. House servant. Of color. Cancelled 3Nov1871, Susan having left Parkes
Rucker, Archie	16Apr1870	8 yrs	Grinstead, A.P.	Orphan. Farming. Of color
Thompson, Robert	30Apr1870	12 yrs	Foster, William Henry	Orphan. Farming. Of color
Graham, Mahala	5July1870	9 yrs	Sanford, A. G.	Orphan. House servant. Of color. Sanford allowed to take Mahala from county. Permission revoked 27Aug1870. Apprenticeship cancelled 5Sept1870
Morgan, Ida	30July1870	10 yrs	Compton, Emily G	Consent of father. House servant
Morgan, Cabal	30July1870	12 yrs	Compton, Emily G	Consent of father. Farming
Carter, Mahala	16Sept1870	10 yrs	McCall, Aileen O. (Miss)	Orphan. House servant. Of color
Campbell, Samson	22Sept1870	14 yrs	McIver, Frank	Orphan. Both of color

Name	Date	Age	Master	Notes
Woods, Susan	19Oct1870	16 yrs	Abrahams, H.	Until 21yrs. Orphan. House servant. Of color
Noel, Henry T.	31Oct1870	12 yrs	Noel, Tennessee E. (Mrs)	Orphan. House servant. Of color
Hesselbein, Charles D.	19Nov1870	13 yrs	Heuser, John J.	Until 18 yrs. Orphan. Merchandising. Cancelled 14June1872, with Charles' mother & sister present in court & consenting
Manley, Pinkney Fillmore	21Jan1871	14 yrs	Maxey, P. W. (Esq)	Orphan. Farming
Davenport, Harriet Ann	6Feb1871	8 yrs	Kinnaird, R. M.	Until 21yrs. Orphan. House servant. Of color. Cancelled 1Feb1872
Hudson, Peyton	10Mar1871	10 yrs	Bittick, Josephus	Orphan. Farming. Of color
Dickey, Sims	8Apr1871	9 yrs	Dickey, Ebenezar	Orphan. Farming. Both of color
Bass, Calvin	25Apr1871	Abt 13 yrs	Wilkerson, B. F.	Orphan. Farming. Of color
Harris, Lizzie	29May1871	11 yrs	Lewis, Granville	Orphan. House servant. Both of color
Watson, Jane	29May1871	11 yrs	Watson, Samuel	Orphan. House servant. Both of color
White, William	22July1871	14 yrs	March, Lewis	Orphan. Farming. Both of color
Goodall, Martha Jane	22July1871	1 yr	March, Lewis	Orphan. House servant. Both of color
Goodall, John Nelson	22July1871	4 yrs	March, Lewis	Orphan. Farming. Both of color
McCullough, John	29July1871	12 yrs	Smith, Pleasant A.	Orphan. Farming. Of color
McClure, Caroline	18Sept1871	Abt 9 yrs	Howell, Robert M.	Orphan. House servant. Of color. Cancelled 17July1875
Harris, Edward	30Sept1871	9 yrs	Lipscomb, George	Orphan. Farming. Both of color
Hughes, Henry	28Oct1871	6 yrs	Whitsitt, William A.	Orphan. Farming. Mother consents. Of color
Hughes, Mary	28Oct1871	3 yrs	Whitsitt, William A.	Orphan. House servant. Mother consents. Of color
Burnett, Cora Aldridge	1Nov1871	5 yrs	Hooper, George J.	Orphan. House servant
Perrin, Jerry	1Jan1872	14 yrs	Alexander, James	Orphan. Farming. Of color
Holland, Fannie	26Mar1872	8 yrs	Graham, Lizzie	Request of mother. Dress making. Both of color
Murrell, John Morgan	24May1872	10 yrs	Noel, O. F.	Mother consents. Farm hand
Achey, Jeffy	18June1872	Abt 9 yrs	Achey, P. H. (Esq)	Orphan. House servant. Of color
Curran, Catherine	24June1872	10 yrs	St Marys Orphan Asylum	Daughter of Mary Connally, a dissipated & incompetent woman
Connally, Margaret	24June1872	5 or 6 yrs	St Marys Orphan Asylum	Daughter of Mary Connally, a dissipated & incompetent woman

Name	Apprenticed to	Date	Age	Remarks
Curran, Bridget	Griffith, J. O.	24June1872	Abt 13 yrs	House servant. Daughter of Mary Connally, a dissipated & improper woman. Father dead
Robertson, Charles	Bell, Stanley H.	27June1872	Abt 9 yrs	Farmer. Betsy P. Robertson, his mother & guardian, consents. Of color. Bell allowed to remove Charles to his home in Alabama
Mathias, Treas	Blair, John Z.	28June1872	Abt 15 yrs	Orphan. House servant. Of color
Woods, Pricilla	Abrahams, H.	26July1872	16 yrs	Orphan. House servant. Of color
O'Connell, Maggie	Brew, Michael R.	20Aug1872	13 yrs	Orphan. House servant
Foster, John	Wharton, Joseph	3Sept1872	Abt 13 yrs	Orphan. Blacksmith. Both of color
Gray, Simon	Sexton, A. (Esq)	26Sept1872	15 yrs	No father or mother. Farmer. Of color
Brown, Josephine	Warner, John	4Nov1872	6 yrs	Mother & father dead. House servant. Both of color
Brown, Ophelia	Greenlee, Harvey	6Nov1872	5 yrs	Mother & father dead. House servant. Both of color
Edwards, Josephine	Butler, Jemima	7Dec1872	6 yrs	Orphan. House servant. Both of color
Bibee, Johnnie	Chandler, W. J.	18Jan1873	Abt 3 1/2 yrs	Orphan. Farming. Mother dead. Father unknown to court
Williams, Sarah D.	Rains, W. B.	17Feb1873	8 yrs	Orphan. House keeper
Smith, Arthur	Seat, Maria	25Apr1873	5 mo	Orphan.
Shaw, James	Shaw, Christopher	25Apr1873	5 yrs	Father & mother dead. Farmer. Of color
Epsley, George Thomas	Nance, C. W.	12July1873	9 yrs	Orphan. Farming
McClinchy, Johnnie	Power, Chris	22July1873	13 yrs	Orphan. Butchering
Hanifin, John J.	Power, Chris	22July1873	13 yrs	Father & mother dead. Butchering
Hadley, Jane	Fowles, Abram	12Aug1873	10 yrs	Given to Fowles to rear by father 5 yrs ago. Sewing & keeping house. Both of color. Canc 22Aug1873. To father, Monroe Hadley
Martin, Robert	Trabue, Henry	27Aug1873	9 1/2 yrs	Orphan. Farming. Both of color
Pheiffer, Fanny	Maney, W. B.	1Sept1873	13 yrs	Orphan. Housekeeper
Hunt, Johnnie	Parrish, Henry	22Sept1873	7 yrs	Father dead. Farming. Both of color. Cancelled 10Dec1875. Returned to mother
Dickerson, Francis	South, George M.	29Sept1873	Abt 14 yrs	Father & mother dead. Farming
Dickerson, James	South, George M.	29Sept1873		Father & mother dead. Farming
Dickerson, Jefferson	South, George M.	29Sept1873		Father & mother dead. Farming
Dickerson, George	South, George M.	29Sept1873	Abt 4 yrs (youngest)	Father & mother dead. Farming

Name	Date	Age	Master	Notes
Nichol, Peyton	4Oct1873	14 yrs	Smith, Abram	Father & mother dead. Both of color
Epsley, Jesse F.	24Oct1873	8 yrs	Jones, Amzi	Father & mother dead. Farming. Jones allowed to remove Jesse to Rutherford Co, his present home, or to any other location.
McGarock, Albert	22Nov1873	16 yrs	Connell, William	Consent of father. Farming. Of color. Canc 18Apr1874, Albert having left Connell
McGarock, Anderson	22Nov1873	14 yrs	Phillips, William	Consent of father. Farming. Of color. Canc 19June1874, Anderson having left Phillips
Hughes, Samuel	31Dec1873	14 yrs	Hyde, Peter	Orphan. Farming. Of color
Cartwright, Sarah E.	8Jan1874	12 yrs	Cartwright, P. A.	Orphan. House keeper. Of color. On same date M. T. Cartwright granted administration of estate of Elvira E. Cartwright, Dcd. Race?
Sadler, Benjimin B.	24Jan1874	12 yrs	Cato, Jr, John	Orphan. Consent of mother. Farming
Johnson, Lizzie	24Jan1874	8 yrs	Miller, Ellen D. (Mrs)	Parents dead. House keeper
Mullen, Fidellous	6Feb1874	14 yrs	Jordan, J. H.	Orphan. Farming
Baudle, Sophia	13Feb1874	13 yrs	Seifried, Sigman	Child of Andrew Baudle, who consents. House keeper
Baudle, Carrie	13Feb1874	9 yrs	Seifried, Sigman	Child of Andrew Baudle, who consents. House keeper
Cato, Isaac	15Feb1874	10 yrs	Cato, Edmund	Orphan. Farming. Of color
Nettie	12 Mar1874	2 yrs	Smith, Benjamin	Orphan. House keeper. Both of color
Copley, Charlie	21Mar1874	5 yrs	Crockett, W. W. T.	Orphan. Farming
Booker, Catherine	24Mar1874	8 yrs	Booker, Polk	Orphan. House keeper. Both of color
Milam, Duffield (Duffie)	30Mar1874	10 yrs	Payne, J. A.	Orphan. House keeper. Of color
Cook, John	23Apr1874	16 yrs	Satterwhite, S. T.	Parents dead. Farming. Of color. Cancelled 4Aug1875. Cook fled to Kansas
Carter, William	27Apr1874	9 yrs	Johnson, Steve	Orphan. Hostler. Of color
Wright, Orpha	7May1874	9 yrs	Bondurant, J. J.	Orphan. House keeper
Floyd, Jack	16May1874	Abt 16 yrs	Johnson, Thomas B.	Orphan. Farming. Of color
Copley, Amanda	6June1874	9 yrs	Weakley, Olin of D. C.	Orphan. House keeper
Copley, Bettie	6June1874	12 yrs	Butman, John H.	Orphan. House keeper

Name	Date	Age	To whom bound	Notes
Bowling, Lee	30June1874	5 yrs	Turner, Thomas A.	Orphan. Farming. Turner allowed to remove apprentice to Cheatham Co
Selle, Fred	30June1874	13 yrs	Turner, Thomas A.	Orphan. Farming. Turner allowed to remove apprentice to Cheatham Co
Beasley, Charles Felix	26Aug1874	Abt 14 yrs	Johnson, George S.	Mother dead. Abandoned by father. Farming
Craddick, Elizabeth	12Sept1874	Abt 8 yrs	Winters, J. J.	Illegitimate child. Mother of base morals & lewd habits etc. House keeping
Cash, Byron	22Sept1874	11 yrs	Roberts, John G.	Orphan. Farmer. Of color
Browder, Joseph	28Sept1874		McNulty & Co	Carpenter. For 3 yrs, until 25Aug1877. Bound by his mother, Mary Browder, who is to be paid monthly for his services and to furnish his tools.
Weimer, Alexander	30Sept1874	Abt 13 yrs	Washington, F. W.	Orphan. Farmer
Baker, Lena	20Oct1874	6 yrs	Chrisman, George	Orphan. House keeping
Thomas, Jim	7Nov1874	12 yrs	Ford, A. B.	Orphan. Farmer. Of color
Collins, Wade	29Dec1874	12 yrs	Cheatham, N. B.	Orphan. Hostler. Of color
White, Ellen	1Feb1875	11 yrs	Bass, Irvin	Orphan. House keeping. Both of color
White, Eddy	1Feb1875	4 yrs	Bass, Irvin	Orphan. Farmer. Both of color
Waggoner, Henry	26Apr1875	Abt 9 yrs	Saunders, W. H.	Orphan. Farmer. Of color
Winbourn, Willie	3May1875	Abt 3 yrs	Winbourn, Letty Ann	Abandoned by parents, who are unknown. Called Willie Winbourn by Letty Ann with court's permission. Both of color.
Williford, Thomas	25May1875	Abt 9 yrs	Cato, Martha	Orphan. Living with Cato past 2 yrs. Farmer
Rogers, John W.	29June1875	3 yrs	Toney, Thomas	Orphan. Farmer
Lassater, Abraham C.	24Aug1875	13 yrs	Hamblen, John A.	Orphan. Farmer. Of color
Schild, Annie	30Aug1875	15 yrs	Wilkin, D. F.	House keeping
Green, George W.	14Sept1875	12 yrs	Baldwin, James	Farmer. Both of color
Vaughan, Richard	27Sept1875	8 yrs	Cato, Joseph	Orphan. Farmer. Of color
Cato, Eugene	27Sept1875	3 yrs	Cato, Joseph	Orphan. Farmer. Of color
Vowel, Thomas	31Dec1875	10 yrs	Nance, C. P.	Orphan. Farmer
Lattimer, J. A.	4Jan1875	10 yrs	Griggs, T. K.	Farmer
Grant, Tom	27Jan1876	8 yrs	Harding, John	Orphan. Farmer. Of color

Name	Date	Age	Master	Notes
Jackson, Calhoun M.	5Feb1876		Bratton, W. S.	Orphan. Farmer. Of color
Wilson, Matthew	13June1876	10 yrs	Flintoff, Henry C.	Orphan. Farmer
Wilson, William	13June1876	9 yrs	Flintoff, Henry C.	Orphan. Farmer
Sellie, Christopher	9Aug1876	12 yrs	Stuart, W. H.	Farmer
Ridley, John	16Nov1876	9 yrs	Carter, W. J.	Orphan. Farmer. Of color
Stambers, John (or Slambers)	12Jan1877	8 yrs	Underwood, Noah	Orphan. Farmer. Of color
Clemmons, Jonas	30Jan1877	11 yrs	White, R. C.	Until 17 yrs. Orphan. Farming. Of color
Bransford, Louis	20Feb1877	9 yrs	Bransford, John S.	Orphan. Gardner. Of color
Clements, William W.	6Apr1877	8 yrs	Hagar, James W.	Orphan. Farmer
Hicks, John	18June1877	14 yrs	Traylor, H. F.	Orphan. Farmer
Young, Henry	23June1877	12 yrs	Young, Mose	Orphan. Farmer. Both of color
Thompson, Henry	24July1877		Toney, Thomas	Bound by mother, Alice Thompson. Father, Emanuel Thompson, in State Penitentiary. Farmer. Of color
Taylor, Jack	6Aug1877	Abt 9 yrs	Taylor, John	Orphan. Farmer
Fisher, Charles G.	27Aug1877	9 yrs	Cuppet, G. W.	Until 18 yrs. Consent of father, Charles G. Fisher. Farmer
Bently, Sam	26Jan1878	12 yrs	Hill, Willis	Mother, Mary Bently, consents. Farmer. Both of color
Dowling, Leny	6Apr1878	Abt 5 yrs	Dowling, Jordan	Farmer. Of color
Ragan, John W. E.	11Oct1880	12 yrs	Caldwell, J. F.	Race horse riding
Simms, Charles	6Jan1881	14 yrs	Holt III, Henry	Until 18 yrs. Farming
Ferguson, Andrew	15Jan1881	12 yrs	Knight, W. A.	Farming. Of color

DeKalb County

Name	Date	Age	Master	Notes
Finley, Caroline Matilda	2May1842	11 yrs	Finley, Gemima	Orphan
Prentice, Robert	3July1843		Parsly, Nicholas	
Rigsby, Layfayette	3July1843	10 yrs	McDowell, Luke	
Rigsby, Frances Malvina	3July1843		McDowell, Luke	
Rigsby, William T.	3July1843		McDowell, Luke	
Rankhorn, George W.	1Jan1844		Rankhorn, Craford	
Chapman,	1Jan1844		Chapman, Thomas	

Name	Date	Age	Master	Notes
Rogers, James Edward	1July1844	16 mo	West, Thomas W.	Orphan
Ray, Joseph	6July1846	5 yrs	Ray, Thomas	Orphan
Brashears, William	6July1846		Rice, Eleanor	Orphan. Eleanor late the wife of William Rice, Sr, Dcd. William Rice, Jr, Surety
Stites, John	2Nov1846	11 yrs	Griffith, Amos	Orphan
Rose, Joseph	7June1847	12 yrs	Seller, George W.	Orphan. Henry, James and John Rose also ordered brought to be bound. Released 6Sept1847. Father, John Rose, Sr. returned
Rose, Samuel	7June1847	14 yrs	Adcock, Isaac	Orphan* Released 6Sept1847. Father, John Rose, Sr., having returned to county
Rose, John M.	7June1847	6 yrs	Tyree, Samuel S.	Orphan* Released 6Sept1847. Father, John Rose, Sr., having returned to county
Cantrell, Abram C.	7June1847	5 yrs	Durham, Thomas	Orphan
Rose, Henry	7June1847	9 or 10 yrs	Perkins, James W.	Orphan. Annulled 5July1847, returned to mother
Murphey, Tolbert	5July1847	16 yrs on 6Oct next	Cameron, Henry	Orphan
Hutchins, Albert G.	6Sept1847	12 yrs	Johnson, Wesley	Orphan
Strong, Green	?		Robinson, Edward	On 6Sept1847 Robinson released from requirement for schooling Strong
Hutchins, Charles D.	1Nov1847	15 yrs on 11Apr1848	Bunton, Henry	Orphan
Hannon, Barton	3Apr1848	Abt 3 yrs	Bond, J. L.	Consent of mother. On 3Sept1849 Bond ordered to bring Hannon to court to answer charges of mistreatment
Taylor, James	3July1848	10 yrs	Taylor, Line	Orphan. Approval of mother
Green, Thomas J.	4Sept1848	13 yrs 2 mo	Whaley, Seth M.	Orphan. Request of mother
Redmond, James	2Oct1848	16 yrs	Camron, Henry	Orphan
Pack, Monroe	4Dec1848	15 mo	Pack, Bartemus	Orphan
Pack, Nancy	4Dec1848	Abt 3 yrs	Pack, Bartemus	Orphan
Snider, David	1Jan1849	9 yrs	Taylor, Jacob	Orphan. 4Dec1848, 6Nov1848*
Baily, Asa	2July1849	Abt 12 yrs	Measles, William	Orphan
Fish, Claiborn	5Jan1857	12 yrs on 25Mar1857	McClellan, William A.	Illegit son of Tempy Fish, who consents

Name	Date	Age	Master	Notes
Cantrell, Lawson	3May1858	15 yrs on 23May1858	Cope, H. B.	
Pack, Matilda	7Feb1860	Abt 12 yrs	Mandlebeum, Henry	On petition of John Pack
Pack, Mary	7Feb1860	Abt 6 yrs	Martin, M. T.	On petition of John Pack
Kerley, John	6Nov1865	10 yrs on 12Oct1865	Davis, Solomon	Orphan
Anderson, Thomas	5Mar1866		Parker, John	Cancelled 2May1870*
Williams, Litan	1June1868	Abt 13 yrs	McLellan, S. W.	Of color
Patterson, J. L.	7Mar1870		Hutchison, Charles	Orphan of Lee Patterson, Dcd. 7Dec1869*

Dickson County

Name	Date	Age	Master	Notes
Holligan, Jeremiah	Dec1805	8 yrs in April next	Wright, James	Orphan
McCammon, Thomas	17Mar1806	3 yrs 10 mo	Gilmore, Matthew	Illegitimate child. Blacksmith
Humphry, William Pearce	6Apr1812	6 yrs next June	Peacock, William	Son of Nancy Pearce Humphry & Hardy Pearce Humphry
Humphry, Elizabeth Pearce	6Apr1812		Molton, Michael	Daughter of Nancy Pearce Humphry & Hardy Pearce Humphry
Hedge, William	6Jan1817		Hedge, William	Voided 7Jan1817
Grivit, Henry	?		Wingate, Joseph	On 8Jan1817 ordered returned to court, Wingate now deceased
Grivit, William	?		Wingate, Joseph	On 8Jan1817 ordered returned to court, Wingate now deceased
Grevit, Henry	7Apr1817		Kirk, Jesse L.	
Grevit, William	7Apr1817		Kirk, Jesse L.	Gravit maltreated & removed from co by Kierk. Ordered returned 4Oct1824
Gainer, Jesse	8July1817		Williams, Buckner	
Beavers, William	7Apr1817		Hedge, William	Resc 9Oct1817. To mother, Kesiah Bevers
Dodd, David	8Jan1818		Maybon, John	
Booker, James Madison	4Oct1824	6 yrs	Holliway, John	Orphan
Gravit, William	3Jan1825		Bishop, William	Orphan

Name	Date	Age	Bound To	Notes
Jernigan, Lewis	6Apr1825	17 yrs	Bishop, William	Making saddles
Austin, Eliza	2Jan1826	9 yrs	Austin, David	
Booker, Joseph	2Jan1826	3 yrs	Grayham, Soloman	
Brown, Benjamin	3July1826	Abt 12 yrs	Cunningham, Willis	Orphan
Blount, George W.	2Oct1826	7 yrs	Richardson, Thomas	Orphan
McQuarter, Reubin	2Oct1826	Abt 11 yrs	Hunt, Spencer T.	Orphan
Right, Nelly	1Jan1827	16 yrs	Deloach, Simon	
Worley, Elisha	1Jan1827	10 yrs	Handlin, Joseph	Farming
Harris, Arum	5Oct1827	12 yrs	Welden, John R.	Orphan. 7Apr1828* 7July1828*
Harris, Mark	5Oct1827	16 yrs	Bibb, Minor	Orphan. Farming. This date Bibb appt Adm of estate of Daniel Harris, Dcd. 7Apr1828* 7July1828*
Harris, Everitt	5Oct1827	13 yrs		Orphan. Millwright. 7Apr1828* 7July1828*
Harris, John	5Oct1827	7 yrs	Pullin, Archibald	Orphan. 7Apr1828* 7July1828*
Austin, John	5Oct1827	14 yrs	Reeder, Levi H.	Orphan. Farmer
Malugin, William	5Oct1827	15 yrs	Gallion, George	Orphan. Potter
Smith, William	7Apr1828	6 yrs	Gilmore, Matthew	Farmer
Baker, Jr., William	3Jan1831		Duke, Robert	Farmer. Bound by father, William Baker, Sr.
Harris, Aaron	5Apr1831		Tilly, George	Farmer
Malugian, Jonathan	6Apr1831		Adamson, G.	Blacksmith
Lyle, John	4July1831	14 yrs	Daniel, Woodson	Orphan. Farming
Hall, Isaac	2July1832		Tatom, George W.	Son of Joseph Hall, Dcd. 2Jan1832* Resc 2Dec1839, Hall having left
Durell, John	8Jan1833	15 yrs	Matthews, William	Orphan. Farmer
Read, James	8Jan1833	15 yrs	Brown, Andrew A.	Orphan. Mill right
Hamilton, David	4Jan1836	15 yrs	Piner, Thomas	Farming
Murphey, Thomas	1Aug1836	15 yrs	Phillips, William	Orphan. Bound at Murphy's request
Nolin, Robert	5Sept1836		Perry, Ruffin	Orphan. Farmer. Canc 6Feb1843. Runaway
Nesbitt, Andrew	Oct1836		Tycer, Ellis	Orphan. Not in Oct1836 minutes. See 6Dec1842. New bond on 2Jan1843 with Allen Nesbitt, Surety
Green, John	6Dec1836		Philips, William	Orphan. Refining of iron
Dunagan, Andrew	2Jan1837		Dunagan, William	Orphan

Name	Date	Age	Master	Notes
Dunagan, Andrew	6Mar1837		Dunagan, William	Orphan. Bonded on 7Aug1837
Baker, R. N. W.	4June1837		Hunt, S. T.	Orphan of Dicy Baker 1May1837
Sears, Moses	4June1837		Gaston, Richard	Orphan
Chumbley, Wilson	3July1837		Humphreys, E. W.	Orphan
Patengell, Samuel	5Nov1837	Abt 6 yrs	Williams, Joseph	Orphan
Reaves, Pleasant	1Jan1838		Cunningham, Willis	Orphan
Green, William	2Apr1838		Brown, Andrew A.	Orphan
Dyer, Caroline	1Oct1838		Daniel, James	Orphan. Dau of Martha Hach?, free woman of color 2July1838*
Dunnegin, James	5Nov1838		Dunnegin, Andrew	Orphan of John Dunagan, Dcd. 7May1838*
Dunnegin, Benton	5Nov1838		Dunnegin, John	Orphan of John Dunagan, Dcd. 7May1838*
Dunnegan, Norman	7Jan1839		Hannah, William	Orphan of John Dunagan, Dcd. 7May1838* 5Dec1842*
Brazel, Richard	7Jan1839		King, Samuel	Orphan. ?Has sister Caroline 10Oct1838. 5Dec1842*
Nesbitt, Rebecka	4Feb1839		Massee, Absolum	Until 21 yrs. Canc 5Dec1842, sureties dead
Baker, Mitchell	1June1840	8 yrs	Dunagan, Mateson	Orphan
Brassell, John W.	6July1840	Abt 12 mo	Willey, William	Orphan
Nesbitt, Rebecca	2Jan1843		Nesbitt, Nancy	Orphan
Tidwell, Henry C.	6May1844		Tidwell, Richard	Orphan
Tidwell, Nancy A.	6May1844		Tidwell, Richard	Orphan
Johnston, Asa	1July1844		Hicks, George W.	Orphan
Ballard, Richard	2June1845		Parrish, Huel	Req of mother, Arena Ballard
Sherron, Harriet	2Mar1847	11 yrs	Eubank, John	Orphan
Chumbley, Ann R.	7June1847		Murrell, Thomas	Orphan. Canc 2Apr1849
Chumbley, Elizabeth	7June1847		Hickerson, Ezekiel	Orphan. Canc 6Nov1848, Hickerson's wife having died
Vineyard, Orren	6Sept1847		Vineyard, John	Orphan
Carroll, Epps	6Sept1847		Wells, John	Orphan
Chumbley, Elizabeth	6Nov1848		Willy, Sr, William	Orphan
Washborn, Lucy H.	6Nov1848	7 yrs	Lewis, George	Orphan
Tramell, James	1Jan1849		Holland, Greer	

Name	Date	Age	Bound to	Notes
Jones, Thomas	5Mar1849		Stokes, John	Orphan
Chumly, Ann R.	2Apr1849		Cathy, Joshua	Orphan
Sherman, Harriet	3Sept1849	Abt 13 yrs	Bowen, B. B.	Orphan
Sherman, James	1Oct1849		Fussell, J. W.	A prior binding to William Dodson canc at Sherman's request
Baker, W. T.	5Nov1849		Grymes, Cornelius	Orphan
Pottergale, John	4Mar1850		Proctor, Henderson	Orphan
Jones, Sally A.	4Mar1850		Bateman, William D.	
McGiven, Robert W.	7July1851		Mattock, D. L.	Orphan. Alias Davis
Nolin, William L.	5Jan1852	6 yrs	Binkley, F. M.	Orphan
Nolen, Nancy	6Jan1852	4 yrs	Chickester, Cyrus	Orphan
Jarnigan, Andrew J.	Abt Nov1858	Abt 14 yrs	Parrish, Huel	4Nov1861* Jarnigan, now 17 y/o, in CSA Army. Indenture cancelled
Hampton, Thomas Martin	2Nov1857	5 yrs	Winfrey, W. E.	Data from June1862 binding. Cancelled 2June1862, Winfrey dead
Hampton, Thomas Martin	2June1862	9 yrs 7 mo	Winfrey, Ann M. (Miss)	
Dyer, John W.	Sept 1858		Norris, W. W.	Free child of color. Father took child in March 1865. On 2Oct1865* Sheriff ordered to return him to Norris. Same on 6Sept1869*
Dyer, Filmont	Sept 1858		Norris, W. W.	Free child of color. Father took child in March 1865. On 2Oct1865* Sheriff ordered to return him to Norris. Same on 6Sept1869*
Mayberry, John Daniel	1Jan1866	5 yrs	Baker, Blount	Orphan
Jackson, Isaac	2Jan1866	16 yrs	Leech, Jacob	Orphan
Kirk, Robert	2Jan1866	6 yrs	Hendrick, Thornton W.	Orphan
Collin, Riley	6Feb1866	14 yrs on 4Mar last	Malone, Meredith Erskine	FB. Orphan. Household & farming.
Jackson, Rosetta	5Feb1866	16 yrs on 27Oct next	Jackson, Willis	FB. Orphan. Until 16Oct1868 [sic]. Household & farming.
Jackson, Vilet	5Feb1866	14 yrs on 1Mar next	Jackson, Willis	FB. Orphan. Household & farming.
Bell, Wiley	6Feb1866	16 yrs on 6July last	Bell, Elisha	FB. Orphan. Farming.
Bell, Isaac	6Feb1866	13 yrs on 4June last	Bell, Elisha	FB. Orphan. Farming
Jackson, James H.	6Feb1866	16 yrs on 4Sept last	Nicks, A. D.	FB. Farming

Name	Date	Age	Master	Notes
Bowen, William H.	6Feb1866	15 yrs on 13Aug last	Bowen, B. B.	FB. Orphan. Farming
Leech, George W.	26Feb1866	11 yrs	Leech, P. F.	FB. Orphan. Farming
Cooksey, Jacob	27Feb1866	9 yrs on 20Dec last	Nichols, T. W.	FB. Orphan. Farming
Cooksey, Isaac	27Feb1866	11 yrs on 8Jan last	Parchmen, M. J.	FB. Orphan. Farming
Hall, James Edward	5Mar1866	11 yrs on 25Nov last	Hall, N. M.	FB. Orphan. Farming
Hall, Solomen	5Mar1866	13 yrs on 11Apr last	Hall, N. M.	FB. Orphan. Farming
Binkley, Charles	5Mar1866	9 yrs on 1Jan last	Bell, B. W.	FB. Orphan. Farming
Binkley, Elenora	5Mar1866	5 yrs on 25Jan last	Bell, B. W.	FB. Orphan. Housework & farming
Binkley, Henry	5Mar1866	7 yrs on 1Mar last	Bell, B. W.	FB. Orphan. Farming
Binkley, Samuel	5Mar1866	8 yrs on 1Jan last	Williams, J. J.	FB. Orphan. Farming
White, Kittie	5Mar1866	4 yrs on 1Jan last	Williams, J. J.	FB. Orphan. Housework & farming
Binkley, Jerry	5Mar1866	7 yrs on 8Jan last	Williams, J. J.	FB. Orphan. Farming
Steel, William	10Mar1866	9 yrs on 5Jan last	Steele, Margaret	FB. Orphan. Farming
Weakley, Nancy	31Mar1866	3 yrs on 15Feb1866	Kiggins, Michael L.	FB. Orphan. Housework & farming
Weakley, Rachel	31Mar1866	13 yrs 1Mar1866	Kiggins, Michael L.	FB. Orphan. Housework & farming
Weakley, Emma	31Mar1866	13 yrs on 20Jan1866	Kiggins, Michael L.	FB. Orphan. Housework & farming
Weakley, George	31Mar1866	5 yrs on 1Jan1866	Kiggins, Michael L.	FB. Orphan. Farming
Weakley, Bellfield	31Mar1866	6 yrs on 9Feb1866	Kiggins, Michael L.	FB. Orphan. Farming
Holt, Alexander	2Apr1866	12 yrs on 1Jan1866	Holt, James M.	FB. Orphan. Farming
Holt, Mary	2Apr1866	7 yrs on 12Jan1866	Holt, James M.	FB. Orphan. House & farming
Holt, Lewis	2Apr1866	9 yrs on 20Feb1866	Holt, James M.	FB. Orphan. Farming
Roberts, Dilla	14Apr1866	10 yrs on 1Jan1866	Caps, William J.	FB. Orphan. Housework & farming
Roberts, Hellen	14Apr1866	6 yrs 20Jan1866	Marsh, A.	FB. Orphan. Housework & farming
Roberts, Robert	14Apr1866	8 yrs on 1Feb1866	Marsh, A.	FB. Orphan. Farming
Langston, James	1Apr1867		Pardue, G. M.	FB. Orphan
Holland, Isaac L.	1July1867	10 yrs on 30Apr last	Baker, Absolum	Orphan
Thompson, Robert L	1July1867	16 yrs on 15Oct next	Larkins, J. C.	Orphan. On 3Aug1868* child ordered returned to father, Lewis Thompson

Name	Date	Age	Master	Notes
Thompson, Samuel	1July1867	Abt 6 yrs	Larkins, J. C.	Orphan. On 3Aug1868* child ordered returned to father, Lewis Thompson
Steeley, Jesse	2Sept1867		Shelton, George C.	Orphan
Winnick, John W.	7Oct1867	8 yrs	Dickson, Marena M.	Orphan. Alias J. W. Hill 3Sept1877. Canc 3Sept1877, Waynick uncontrollable
Girl, Unnamed	4Nov1867		Wiley, E. H.	Of color. Orphan. Until age 21
Binkley, Ellen	4Nov1867		Binkley, F. M.	Of color. Orphan. Until age 21
Boy, Unnamed	2Dec1867		Wiley, E. H.	Of color. Orphan
Woods, John	2Dec1867	Abt 12 yrs	Vanhook, William	Orphan
Seals, Richard T.	1June1868		Hughes, L. T.	Orphan
Seals, Elizabeth	1June1868		Hughes, L. T.	Orphan
Baker, Thomas R.	1Feb1869		Harris, William	Orphan
Baker, John E.	1Feb1869		Harris, William	Orphan
Cunningham, Phillis	1Mar1869	6 yrs	Cunningham, E. W.	Of color. Orphan
Cunningham, Marina	1Mar1869	11 yrs	Cunningham, E. W.	Of color. Orphan
Cunningham, Sallie	1Mar1869	4 yrs	Cunningham, E. W.	Of color. Orphan
Cunningham, Phillip	1Mar1869	8 yrs	Cunningham, E. W.	Of color. Orphan
Hamilton, John	1Nov1869		Clifton, J.K.	Orphan
Bramlet, Aaron M.	6Dec1869	Abt 13 yrs	Stokes, W. D.	Orphan
Jackson, John	2May1870		Jackson, John V.	Of color. Neither father nor mother
Holland, Isaac S.	4July1870	14 yrs	Baker, Absolum	Bond renewed
Hunter, Joanah	7Nov1870	10 yrs	McMahan, G. W.	Of color. Orphan. Until age 21
Weakley, George	3Jan1871		McNichol, Thomas	Of color. Orphan. Renewed 2Feb1874
Weakley, Nancy	3Jan1871		McNichol, Thomas	Of color. Orphan. Renewed 2Feb1874
Neper, James Jorden	6Mar1871		Rye, H. C.	Cancelled 4Nov1872, as James J. Nipper
Nepper, Joann	6Mar1871		Lilly, P. A.	Orphan
Neper, George Cooley	6Mar1871		Lilly, P. A.	Orphan
Jackson, Pasly	5June1871		Jackson, Jasper	Of color. Orphan
Jackson, Jake	5June1871		Jackson, Jasper	Of color. Orphan
Lock, Joseph	7Aug1871		Carsaw, S. H.	Orphan
Seals, Allen	6Nov1871		Milum, Benjamin	Consent of mother, Eliza Seals

Name	Date	Age	Master	Notes
Baker, John	5Feb1872		Carrot, E. M.	Son of Parilee Baker. 2Jan1872*
Vanlier, Daniel	5Feb1872		Proctor, H.	Of color. Orphan
Vanlier, Tennessee	5Feb1872		Proctor, H.	Of color. Orphan
Pickett, Alford	1Apr1872	11 yrs	Pickett, J. J.	Of color. Orphan
Boy, Unnamed	1July1872	7 yrs	Richardson, Squire	Of color. Orphan
Bomer, Robert	5Aug1872	14 yrs in Oct next	Schnistton, W. S. V. (fe)	Orphan
Nipper, James J.	4Nov1872		Alsbrooks, G. W.	Orphan. See James Jordon Neper
Boy, Unnamed	7July1873	14 yrs	Hammond, William	Orphan
Higdon, James J.	1Sept1873		Cunningham, John F.	Consent of Mrs. Higdon
Appleton, Charles	5Jan1874		Winn, E. A. (fe)	Orphan
Kelsaw, Bell	2Feb1874	11 yrs	Leech, D. R.	Of color. Orphan. 3Nov1873*
Kelsaw, Martha	2Feb1874	9 yrs	Kendrick, J. H.	Of color. Orphan. 3Nov1873* Canc 4May1874, req of Mrs T. W. Hendrick
Kelsaw, Mary	2Mar1874	6 yrs	Reynolds, C. S.	Of color. Orphan. 3Nov1873*
Fox, Joseph	6Apr1874		Petty, G. H.	Request of Fox
Kelsow, Martha	4May1874	9 yrs	Bowers, J. M.	Of color. Orphan
Hayes, Emily A.	1June1874	5 yrs	Daniel, John R.	Orphan
Ellison, John	3Aug1874		Hutton, Ann	Of color. Orphan. Previously bound to S. H. Carsaw
Mixon, Nuton	2Nov1874		Stokes, W. D.	Of color. Consent of mother, Mrs. Mixon
Price, Jarome	3May1875		Price, J. J.	1Mar1875* Canc 7July1879. Jerome gone
Price, Harret E.	3May1875		Price, D. W.	1Mar1875*
Price, H. E.	3Jan1876		Chadowins, Jessee	Cancelled 6Aug1877 as H. M. Price. Chadowin's wife deceased
Price, H. M.	6Aug1877		Price, D. W.	
Lethers, John	3Sept1877		McMahand, A. W.	Orphan. Mother, Miss Lethers 6Aug1877*
Morgan, Salley	1Oct1877		Overton, Thomas & E.	Orphan. ? Dau of Miss Lethers 6Aug1877*
Moor, James	?		Petty, James D.	Canc 1Oct1877, Moor having left
Rollins, Virgil Homer	4Feb1878	Abt 4 yrs	Rollins, A. M.	Mother, Mary Ann Rollins, consents by letter
Eavins, W. H.	4Feb1878		Timmins, Solemn	Request of Timmins, stepfather of Evins

Name	Date	Age	Master	Notes
Mariah	1Apr1878		Clingan, J. M.	Orphan. Of color
Leech, Emil T	5Aug1878	4 yrs in Spring 1878	Leech, Isham	Consent of mother, Georgi Ann Leech
Porter, Andrew	2Sept1878		Tidwell, Robert	Of color. Orphan. Cancelled 4Feb1884
Alsbrooks, G. D.	2Aug1880		Colman, W. D.	Orphan. Grandson of Coleman
McCartey, J. A.	5Mar1883	9 yrs last Oct	Sugg, J. D.	Orphan
Eleazer?, Mike			Petzer, George	Bond renewed 1Oct1883
Porter, Andrew	4Feb1884		Steele, Robert	Of color
Easley, Cora	4Feb1884		Grigsly, T. K.	Of color. Abandoned by mother, father dead 7Jan1884*
Easley, Ida	4Feb1884		Grigsly, W. L.	Of color. Abandoned by mother, father dead 7Jan1884* Cancelled 7Apr1884, returned to mother
Unnamed male	7Apr1884		Stone, R. B.	Of color. Taken from jail by order of Circuit Judge
King, Granvill S.	4Aug1884		Hickerson, Henry M.	Orphan. Canc 3Aug1885
Jacks, W. J.	6Oct1884		Jackson, Freeman	Consent of mother
Carrot, E. W.	3Nov1884		Weekly, W. T.	Orphan
Carrot, A. B.	3Nov1884		Weekly, W. T.	Orphan
Deloach, W. T.	2Mar1885	6 yrs	Nicks, B. W. S	Request of father, Gid Deloach
Deloach, Ann	2Mar1885	4 yrs	Nicks, B. W. S.	Request of father, Gid Deloach
King, Granvill S.	3Aug1885		Roberts, William	Orphan
Young, James M.	3Aug1885		Gaston, Maury	Orphan

Franklin County

Name	Date	Age	Master	Notes
Reynolds, Haywood	3Sept1832	12 yrs last January	Hammons, Elijah	Orphan. Indenture canc 28May1832
Wilder, William	5Sept1832	14 yrs last 20April	Stewart, William	Hatter
Ransom, James			Allen, Hudson & Adams, Abner	Coach maker
McEwen, William	26Nov1832	7 yrs on 19Dec next	Rutherford, John A.	Saddle tree maker
McEwen, Mary Ann	26Nov1832	4 yrs on 26Dec next	Rutherford, John A.	
McEwen, Nancy	26Nov1832	11 yrs next 29Dec	Lush, James	Until age 21 yrs
Wilder, William	3Dec1832	12 yrs last January	Thompson, Bryant B.	Prob son of Nathaniel Wilder (d. Feb 1832) & Margaret Wilder*

Name	Date	Age	Master	Notes
Brooks, William	25Feb1833		Bradford, Joseph	For 3 yrs from 1Jan1833. Saddling
Bradley, Jonathan	?		Bradford, Joseph	Orphan. Indenture canc 4March1833
Gage, Maryann	27May1833	18 mo	Huddleston, Jr, Joseph	
Jared, Sarah	2Aug1833	Abt 12 yrs	Barrier, Henry	
McCoy, William	?		Logan, Thomas S.	Coach making. Indenture canc 2Dec1833
Hampton, James	3Mar1834	12 yrs	Rowland, George	
Stamps, Nathan	3Mar1834	15 yrs	Rowland, George	
Hunter, John	3Mar1834	14 yrs next 17Nov	Olium?, Robert H.	Orphan. Until age 19 yrs
Kenedy, Jackson	1Sept1834	15 yrs	Harris, Richmond P.	Cotton spinning. Canc 3June1839, Harris having died
McLaughlin, Richard H.	1Dec1834	16 yrs last 1Oct	Bradford, Joseph	Saddle making. ?Orphan son of Thomas McLaughlin 23Feb1835.* Left for Seminole Campaign on 1Nov1837. 5Mar1838
McLaughlin, William	1Dec1834	10 yrs last 7June	Logan, Thomas S.	Carriage making. ?Orphan son of Thomas McLaughlin 23Feb1835*
Lynch, Geter	24Feb1835	16 yrs next April	Allen, Hudson & Curle, Portland J.	Harness triming
Gatny, Westly	?		Moore, Richard B.	Indenture cancelled 25May1835
Parish, Richard	26May1835	12 ys	Parish, David	
Sherwood, Joseph	2Jan1837		Williamson, Robert	
Hopkins, Edith	6Feb1837		Coleman, Thomas A.	
Hopkins, S. D.	6Feb1837		Coleman, Thomas A.	
Haws, Hampton H.	4May1837	13 yrs last Oct	King, Amazan	Orphan. Until 20 years. Brick laying
Thomasan, Martha	5June1837	10 yrs	Roberts, Phillip	
Thomasan, John	5June1837	5 ys	Roberts, Phillip	
Cawan, James C.	6Nov1837	10 yrs	Cawan, Harvey C.	Orphan of James B. Cawan, Dcd. 3Oct1837
Cawan, Mary A.	6Nov1837	8 yrs	Cawan, Harvey C.	Orphan of James B. Cawan, Dcd. 3Oct1837
Cawan, Margaret A.	6Nov1837	6 yrs	Cawan, Harvey C.	Orphan of James B. Cawan, Dcd. 3Oct1837
Dorsan, Leurinda M.	4Dec1837	4 yrs	Hill, Reuben	
Williams, James	1Jan1838	6 yrs	Woods, Sr, Charles	Orphan

Name	Date	Age/Term	Bound to	Notes
Brown, Micajah	6Mar1838	14 yrs	Williams, James	Orphan. Saddle making
Faris, Cannon B.	2July1838	14 yrs	Lyons, William	Orphan
Faris, Porter	2July1838	16 yrs	Haily, Thomas	Orphan
Faris, Antum	2July1838	13 yrs	Haily, Thomas	Orphan
Goin, Alphonzo J.	?	Abt 16 yrs in 1838	Lewis, David C.	Mulatto. Indenture cancelled 1Oct1838* 2Oct1838*
Thomas, John F.	5Feb1839		Gore, Joshua	
Forgeson, Henry	3June1839	10 yrs	Summers, Sr, Samuel	
Forgeson, Nancy	3June1839	9 yrs	Summers, Sr, Samuel	
Forgeson, John	3June1839	7 yrs	Summers, Sr, Samuel	
Forgeson, Sally	3June1839	5 yrs	Summers, Sr, Samuel	
Forgeson, Samuel	3June1839		Summers, Jr, Samuel	
Tucker, Kenton	4June1839		Bradford, Joseph	Orphan. Saddle making. Term of 4 yrs from 18Apr1839
Brawn, Elijah	1July1839	12 yrs	Custer, Michael	
Partin, Peter	5Nov1839	16 yrs	Starne, William	Orphan. Farming. Rescinded 6Jan1840
Swinn, Sally M.	6Apr1840	2 yrs	Adkins, Joseph	Orphan
Shropshire, William	5Apr1841		Gunn, Thomas L.	Son of Joseph Shropshire, Dcd. Tanning. Bound by mother
Car, Martha Ann	7June1841	2 yrs	Miller, Joseph	Spinning. Bound until 21 yrs.
Shropshire, James W.	8June1841	17yrs on 19Aug1841	Hooker & Williamson	Son of Joseph Shropshire, Dcd. Coach making. Bound by mother. Canc 7Feb1843
Miles, General Jackson	1Sept1841	11 yrs in July1842	Roseborough, Samuel M.	Farming. Bound by mother, Malissa Miles
Shropshire, Benjamin	1Sept1841	16 yrs on 22Oct1841	Owen, M. P.	Son of Joseph Shropshire, Dcd. Cabinet making. Bound by mother. Canc 7Mar1842
Thomas, William	1Nov1841	16yrs 21May1842	Custer, Michael	Taning. Bound at request of Thomas
Coleman, William Henry	2Nov1841	8yrs on 2Jan1842	Porter, Madison	By authority of Samuel Roseborough
Hoozier, Mahalie	1Feb1842	13 yrs	Smith, Robert	Until age 18 yrs or gets married
Hunt, Samuel	4Apr1842	12 yrs	Robertson, David W.	
McLaughlin, Elijah	5Apr1842	14 yrs on 22Aug1842	Hooker & Williamson	Triming & harness making. Canc 3Mar1845
Shropshir, Benjamin F.	2May1842	17yrs on 22Oct1842	Robinson, M. W.	Cabinet making. Mother consents. Canc 7Feb1843
Gillaspie, Arguile C.	5Sept1842	13yrs on 6Dec1842	Turner, Roberson J.	Taning. Consent of Mrs. Gillespie
McLaughlin, George T.	5Dec1842	16yrs on 1Aug1843	Reeves, William	Carpenter

Name	Date	Age	Master	Notes
Adcock, William	7Feb1843	Abt 15 yrs	Foster, James B.	Farming
Starne, Benjamin C.	5June1843	15 yrs	Orear, William	Heir of William Starne, Dcd.
McCoy, John	6May1844	9 or 10 yrs	Custer, Michael	Taning. ?Son of Sally McCoy 2Apr1844*
Hill, Mary Elizabeth	3June1844	5yrs on 16Feb1845	Hill, Benjamin	Housekeeping. Until 21 yrs or marries
Gaither, Philip D.	4Feb1845	6 yrs	Darrell, Augustus	Carriage making. Darrell GF of Gaither
Gillaspie, Tipton L.	3Mar1845	12rys on 1Feb1845	Turner, John B.	Blacksmithing
McLaughlin, Elijah	3Mar1845		Brooks, William G.	Harness making
Baggett, Martin V.	4Mar1850	12 yrs	Smith, David D.	Farming
Baggett, Mary Jane	4Mar1850	6 yrs	Burt, Fredrick	Housewifery
Johnson, Amelia	5Aug1850	4 yrs	Johnson, Sally	Until 21 yrs. Housewifery
Johnson, Amelia	2Sept1850	4 yrs	Embry, Simpson J.	Of color. Seamstress & housewife. No mention of prior indenture
Wortham, Henry	8Oct1850	13 yrs	Brazelton, W. W.	
Lewis, Francis M.	4Nov1850	10 yrs on 1Dec next	Smith, Loranzo A.	Son of Gabriel Lewis, Dcd.
Lewis, William	2Dec1850	Abt 13 yrs	Connel, Robert	Son of Gabriel Lewis, Dcd.
Lewis, James K. P.	4Aug1851	7 yrs	Tunes, Demarous M.	Farming
Hutton, Alexander	1Dec1851	15 yrs	Franklin, Joseph	Farming. Canc 3Sept1855, request of father, William H. Hutton
Owen, Logan			Pearson, Meredith	Canc 1Dec1851. Data from 1851 indenture
Owen, Logan	1Dec1851	18 yrs	Franklin, Benjamin	Farming
Loggins, James	3May1852	15 yrs 6 mo	Faris, Cornelius	Of color. Farming
Miller, John M.	2Aug1852	12 yrs	Armstrong, John	Farming
Nichols, Sarah Ann	4June1853	9 yrs	Hall, Henry	Housewifery
Ford, Nelson	5Dec1853	9 or 10 yrs	Ford, William	Farming. Cancelled 6Feb1854
Damron, Joseph	2Oct1854	9 yrs	Cheatham, Robinson V.	Child of Ona Damron, Dcd. Canc 2Apr1855
Nevills, Benjamin F.	4Nov1854	Abt 11 yrs	Riddle, Linton	Child of Elizabeth Nevills, formerly Elizabeth Brown
Damron, Joseph	2Apr1855	10 yrs	Edward, James A.	Orphan of Oney Damron, Dcd. Farming. Canc 3Apr1854
Damron, Joseph	3Apr1855	10 yrs	Prince, William	Heir of Oney Damron, Dcd. Farming
David	7May1855	13 yrs	Oliver, George W.	Child of Mindy, Dcd., free woman of color

Name	Date	Age	Notes
Hines	7May1855	9 yrs	Child of Mindy, Dcd., free woman of color
Mary	7May1855	11 yrs	Child of Mindy, Dcd., free woman of color
Charlotte	7May1855	4 yrs	Child of Mindy, Dcd., free woman of color
William	7May1855	1 yr	Child of Mindy, Dcd., free woman of color
Mitchell, John	6Oct1856	7 yrs 7 mo	
Corm, Meredith	6Apr1857	8 yrs 8 mo	
Lokey, Claibourne	6Oct1857	13 yrs 3 mo	Son of James Lokey, Dcd. & Lucy Lokey. 3Jan1859, 7Feb1859* Canc 1July1861*
Lokey, John W.	6Oct1857	7 yrs 5 1/2 mo	Son of James Lokey, Dcd. & Lucy Lokey. 3Jan1859, 7Feb1859* Canc 3Nov1862*
Teasdale, James	2Feb1858		Child of Martha Teasdale. 2Apr1866*
Teasdale, Allice	2Feb1858		Child of Martha Teasdale. 2Apr1866*
Teasdale, Robertson	2Feb1858		Child of Martha Teasdale. 2Apr1866*
Teasdale, Emily	2Feb1858		Child of Martha Teasdale
Gross, Billy	4Jan1859		Illeg mulatto child. Mother, white, gone. Taken from care of Isaac Gross
Riddle, Enoch	4Jan1859		Orphan of Enoch Riddle, Dcd. Canc 1Feb1862. Enoch ill used. To his uncle, Sinton Riddle
Gist, John Tollison	4Jan1859		Orphan of Hyram Gist, Dcd.
Buzby, Cyntha Margarett	1Aug1859	14 yrs 11 mo	Housekeeping. Dau of Thomas Buzby, who has absconded. Consent of mother
Barnes, Susanah Susan	7Nov1859	9 yrs 14 days	Housework. Orphan of Jemema Barnes
Hill, William	4Feb1861		Child of Nancy Hill. Nancy taken to Lunatic Asylum 1July1861*
Hill, John	5Feb1861		Child of Nancy Hill. Nancy taken to Lunatic Asylum 1July1861*
Scott	2Jan1866	7 yrs	Mother, Jane, died 1862. Of color
Lewis	2Jan1866	5 yrs	Mother, Jane, died 1862. Of color
Peter	2Jan1866	4 yrs	Of color. Mother, Jane, died 1862
Henry	2Jan1866	8 yrs	Of color.
John	4Jan1866	9 yrs	Of color

Oliver, George W.		
Oliver, John		
Oliver, John		
Oliver, John		
Smith, Tobias D.		
Bean, C. H.		
Byrom, Thomas		
Byrom, Thomas		
Fanning, William C.		
Fanning, William C.		
Fanning, J. W.		
Fanning, J. W.		
Faris, Sanders		
McKelvey, Samuel		
Delzell, William		
Farris, Hezekiah		
Adair, James		
Taft, William M.		
Sharp, James		
Simmons, George		
Simmons, George		
Simmons, George		
Gray, Isaac		
Keith, William P.		

Name	Date	Age	Master	Notes
Frank	5Jan1866	8 yrs	Wilhoit, Pearce	Of color. Orphan
Jim	7Feb1866	6 yrs	Lymbough, Wilburn	Abandoned by mother, father unknown. Of color
Frank	7Feb1866	3 yrs	Lymbough, Wilburn	Abandoned by mother, father unknown. Of color
Flora	7Feb1866	3 yrs	Lymbough, Wilburn	Abandoned by mother, father unknown. Of color
Carter, Adeline	4Sept1866		Carter, M. K. (Mrs)	Of color. Orphan. Dau of Harriet
Temple, Matilda J.	1Oct1866	14 yrs	Byrom, H. L.	Also called Matilda J. Byrom. Of color. Dau of Eastes Temple.
Ness	3Dec1866	13 yrs	Turney, H. L. (Mrs)	Of color. Bound until 25Dec1867. Renewed for 1 yr 2Dec1867, 7Dec1868
Ellen	5Feb1867	Abt 13 yrs	Wood, Ira G.	Mulatto. House servant
Kenerly, Albert	5Aug1867	Abt 14 yrs	Kenerly, J. T.	Farming. Of color
Scott	5Mar1868	5 yrs	Simmons, George	Of color. Bond revoked same day
Leuis	5Mar1868	7 yrs	Simmons, George	Of color. Bond revoked same day
Moses	5Mar1868	9 yrs	Simmons, George	Of color. Bond revoked same day
Hudleston, Jason	1June1868	Abt 5 yrs	Elkins, Allen	Of color
Hudleston, Georgia Ann	1June1868	Abt 6 yrs	Harris, John	Of color
Moore, Della	8Oct1869	Abt 8 yrs	Word, Thomas A.	Of color
Lewis, Elizabeth	17Nov1869	Abt 12 yrs	Brooks, William G.	House servant. Mulatto. Alias Elizabeth Moor. Orphan
Miller, Wallace E.	5Sept1870	Abt 13 yrs	Miller, Sr, John	Of color. Farming. Consent of Jackson Steel, next friend & uncle
Woods, Doughlas	7Sept1870	10 yrs	Lipscomb, John	Orphan. Farmer
Smith, Mariah J.	11Nov1870	9 yrs	Barney, A. M.	Orphan. Of color
Moore, Della	2Apr1872		Word, Sarah J.	Orphan. Of color
Mallard, Cyrus	9Apr1873	Abt 13 yrs	Cowan, R. H.	Orphan. Farming. Mother dead
Mallard, Mary	9Apr1873	Abt 11 yrs	Cowan, William M.	Orphan. Housework. Mother dead
Farris, John	1Feb1875	2 yrs	Kennerly, John P.	Abandoned by mother. Of color

Giles County

Name	Date	Age	Master	Notes
Scott, George W.	11Mar1814		Pickins, James H.	Orphan. Probable sibs Samuel, Edney

Scott, Edney	7June1814	Tinnen, James	Sibs George W., Samuel 11Mar1814*
Stegall, Elizabeth	8Dec1814	Lester, German	Conditionally bound
Stegall, Lucinda	8Dec1814	Thompson, William F.	Conditionally bound
Estep, Isabella	9Dec1814	Pearson, Samuel	aka Eba Estep
Scott, Samuel	6June1815	Kerley, William M.	Orphan
Foster, Rachel	5Sept1816	Loyd, Henry	Orphan
Weir, John Washington	17Nov1823	Nichols, John A.	Orphan
Hicks, Charlotte	24Nov1823	Tacker, John	
Russell, Bartlett	17May1824	Huckeby, John	
Strickland, Rhoda	17May1824	Lane, Willis	Orphan. Previously bound to Alexander Barron, who has left the county 16Feb1824. Resc 28Feb1825, petition of Thomas Hicks
Barber, Bearzley	24May1824	Story, Archibald	
Russell, Gray	16Aug1824	Williamson, Edmund	
Russell, Nancy	16Aug1824	Holcomb, Hardy H.	
Samuel, Achillis	15Nov1824	Samuel, Stephen	Canc 28Nov1825. Achillis to Henry Phenix
Samuel, Ulysses	15Nov1824	Samuel, Ethelbert	
Beazley, William	28Feb1825	Mabrey, Francis H.	Orphan. Resc 20Feb1827
McCabe, Hugh	?	Cooper, Henry J.	Indenture rescinded 28Feb1825
Strickland, Rhoda	28Feb1825	Hicks, Thomas	Orphan 16May1825
Campbell, William	16May1825	Reynolds, Enoch	Orphan
Kirby, David M.	15Aug1825	Farmer, Nathan	Orphan
Riddle, Robert	?	Patterson, Nelson	Indenture voided 22Aug1825
Harwell, Ransom	?	Harwell, Sterling	Indenture voided 22Aug1825
Wilson, Sarah Ann	24Nov1825	Shields, Samuel	
Hemenway, Martha Ann	21Nov1825	Beal, Benjamin	
Carpenter, Dangerfield	28Nov1825	Crowder, Isaac	Rescinded 26Feb1827
sham,	22Feb1826	Amiss, John	Part of page with child's name missing
Duty, Henry	27Feb1826	Rivers, John H.	
Duty, Malinda	27Feb1826	Pullen, Jesse	
Cody, Sally	27Feb1826	Cody, Pierce	

Name	Age	Date	Master	Notes
Glover, Benjamin		15May1826	Dodson, Jordan	
Alexander, Jefferson		22May1826	McIntyre, Peter	
White, John M.		22May1826	Sellers, George	
Defoe, Polly		21Aug1826	Stone, John	
Moore, William		20Nov1826	Mayfield, William C.	A prior indent to Enoch Reynolds rescinded
Carlisle, John		20Nov1826	Burkett, Burgess	
Carpenter, Claibourne		?	Samuel, Anthony	Indenture rescinded 27Nov1826
Kennedy, Francis		19Feb1827	Nance, Joseph	
Carpenter, Dangerfield		26Feb1827	Gilham, Samuel	
Cobbs, Paulina		21May1827	White, John	A prior indenture to James Kimbrough rescinded
Eli, Jacob		21May1827	Browning, Martin	
Harmond, Nancy		20Aug1827	Derr, Daniel	
Bailey, John		20Aug1827	Draper, Jefferson	
Wilson, John		20Aug1827	Thomson, Alexander	
Childress, William P.		20Aug1827	Cooper, Henry J.	
Davidson, William S.		?	Patteson, Moses	Indenture voided 26Nov1827
Davidson, Nicholas		?	Thompson, Hugh W.	Indenture voided 26Nov1827
Jones, Isaac W.		26Nov1827	Kerr, Samuel	Orphan
Hicks, Alfred		18Feb1828	Cheatham, John	Orphan
Burch, Bernard		28Feb1828	Anderson, Samuel Y.	A prior indenture to James Lynch cancelled
Davenport, Cary A. H.		28Feb1828	Childress, Robert B.	Orphan
Cheatham, Henry		19May1828	McKenzie, Ulysses	Orphan
Martin, James		19May1828	Pearson, Simon	Orphan
Childress, Robert		19May1828	Hatchell, Bannister	Orphan. Cancelled 18May1829
Martin, John		23Aug1828	Shelton, James N.	Orphan
Martin, Susanna		25Aug1828	Brown, William A.	Orphan
Baker, Mary Ann		24Nov1828	Baker, Nancy	
Coleman, Mary Ann		25Nov1828	Field, William H.	Orphan
Jeffries, Franklin	13 yrs	16Feb1829	Gardiner, Samuel G.	Orphan

Name	Date		Name 2	Note
Joplin, William	23Feb1829		Lynch, William	
Walker, Charles H.	23Feb1829		Usery, William	Orphan
Walker, William C.	23Feb1829		Montgomery, John J.	Orphan
Hunt, Andrew	18May1829		Boyce, Meshech	Orphan
Childress, Robert	18May1829		Woods, William W.	
Clements, Alfred Hayes	18May1829		Bodenhamer, David	Orphan. Rescinded 18Nov1833
Smith, William	19May1829		Shell, James N.	Orphan
Smith, James	19May1829		Storey, Archibald	Orphan
Beard, Edward	Nov 1829		McKnight, Thomas	Rescinded 24Feb1834 (only record)
Aidy, John	18Feb1833		Muncrief, William S.	
Parrett, Thomas J.	18Feb1833		Muncrief, William S.	
Walker, Charles	25Feb1833		Wooldridge, John R.	Rescinded 20May1833
Spaulding, Koziah	25Feb1833		Harwell, Josiah	
Walker, Charles	20May1833		White, John	Orphan. Rescinded 18Nov1834
Foster, Betsy	27May1833	Abt 12 yrs	McNeese, James	Orphan
Gatewood, William	27May1833		Carithers, Samuel	Orphan
McDonald, Mary	1June1833		Harwell, Coleman	Child of James McDonald
McDonald, Martha	1June1833		Harwell, Coleman	Child of James McDonald
McDonald, Catharine	1June1833		Harwell, Coleman	Child of James McDonald
McDonald, Nancy	1June1833		McDonald, Robert W.	Child of James McDonald
McDonald, Malvina	1June1833		McDonald, Robert W.	Child of James McDonald
McDonald, Jonas	1June1833		McDonald, Robert W.	Child of James McDonald
Tucker, Jackson	18Nov1833		Tucker, John	
Ervin, Ann	25Nov1833		Pullen, Jesse	A prior indent to Lucy Ballard rescinded
Condry, John W.	27May1834		Burch, Bernard M.	
Condry, Alpheus A.	27May1834		Burch, Bernard M.	
Condry, Edward	27May1834		Talbot, Lewis	
York, William H.	?		Dowers, David	Rescinded 18Aug1834
York, William H.	25Aug1834		Alderson, Josiah	
Patterson, John	25Aug1834		Davidson, Robert	Of color
Patterson, Mary	25Aug1834		Davidson, Robert	Of color

Name	Date	Age	Master	Notes
Horn, William A.	17Nov1834		Laird, Martin	
Horn, Edward G.	17Nov1834		Bugg, Robert M.	
Deavenport, Nathan	24Nov1834		Stevenson, William	
Unnamed	6Mar1837		Paisley, James	Name of apprentice not given
Unnamed	6Mar1837		Whitfield, Copeland	Name of apprentice not given
Unnamed	6Mar1837		Devenport, Thomas	Name of apprentice not given
Litle, James	6Mar1837		Tacker, Seaborn M.	
Litle, George	6Mar1837		Angus, Gustavus	
Gilbert, Eliza	3Apr1837	Abt 7 yrs	Busick, L. J. M.	Orphan
Craften, George W.	4Sept1837		Parks, John L.	Orphan
Craften, John B.	4Sept1837		Parks, John L.	Orphan
Wilson, Reuben	7May1838	Abt 16 yrs	Field, William H.	Orphan
Unnamed	2July1838		Lester, Fountain	Bound by Amy Walton
Prior, Isaac	14July1838		Jones, Homer R. & Dennis, Briant	Bound by mother, Amy Walton
Shadden, William	3Sept1838		Howard, William	
Wall, Jesse	5Nov1838		Wall, George	Orphan of Jesse Wall, Dcd.
Guthrie, Nancy Amanda Caroline	1Apr1839		Shields, John N.	Child of Robert Guthrie
Guthrie, Courtney Jane	1Apr1839		Beal, Thomas S.	
Guthrie, Lydia Marie	6May1839		Webb, Washington	Daughter of Robert Guthrie, Jr
Guthrie, Grandison G.	6May1839		Beal, Charles F.	Son of Robert Guthrie, Jr
Guthrie, Thomas S.	6May1839		Guthrie, Sr, Robert	Son of Robert Guthrie, Jr
Coker, John M.	3June1839		Barrett, Thomas	A prior indent to Washington Armon canc
Walton, Anderson	6Sept1847		Smith, Buckner	Child of Amy Walton. Of color
Walton, Mary	6Sept1847		Smith, Buckner	Child of Amy Walton. Of color
Bob, Caroline	6Sept1847		Ford, Jonathan	Child of Peggy Bob, free negro. Of color
Bob, Neuton Francis	1Nov1847	10yrs on 1Mar1848	Tacker, Edward C.	Child of Peggy Bob, free negro. Of color
Bob, Abagail	1Nov1847	2 yrs this date	Tacker, Edward C.	Child of Peggy Bob, free negro. Of color

Name	Date	Guardian	Age/Birth	Notes
Foster, John	6Dec1847	Taylor, John	7 yrs this date	
Hannah, George W.	5Feb1849	Collins, Joseph A.		
Gant, William M.	3Sept1849	Taylor, Phineas	Abt 9 yrs	Orphan. Cancelled 3Dec1849
Crosswhite, Elijah	1Oct1849	Mitchell, Calvin W.	19 yrs next 17Nov	
Dickey, Benjamin	1Oct1849	Massey, John	Abt 12 yrs	Rescinded 3June1850
Ezell, John James	3Dec1849	Childers, Joseph B.		Father deceased
Estes, Julia Ann	7Jan1850	Estes, Thomas P.	b. 8Aug1842	Child of William Estes. Thomas her GF
Estes, Thomas Jasper	7Jan1850	Estes, Thomas P.	b. 17July1844	Child of William Estes. Thomas his GF
Estes, Sarah William	7Jan1850	Estes, Thomas P.	b. 3Jan1847	Child of William Estes. Thomas her GF
King, Napoleon	4Mar1850	Cox, William	13 yrs on next 7Apr	
Dickey, William Henry	1Apr1850	Davis, John		
Hubbard, John W.	1Apr1850	Johnson, Cosby B.	2 yrs 8 mo	Orphan
Dickey, William Henry	1Apr1850	Davis, John	9 yrs	Orphan
Hubbard, Mary B.	1Apr1850	Johnson, William R.	11 yrs 8 mo	Orphan
Hubbard, Sarah Elizabeth	6May1850	Abernathy, John	4 yrs 9 mo	Orphan
Hubbard, Paralee	6May1850	Pullen, Jesse	7 yrs on 6Feb1850	Orphan
Peak, Gilliam A.	3June1850	Handry, James L.	10 yrs on 25Aug1850	
Wilson, Andrew	7Oct1850	Riddle, Thomas S.	17 yrs	Orphan
Mills, Martha	4Nov1850	Hays, Howell C.	b. 1Apr1840	Child of Emily F. Mills, free woman of color
Mills, William	4Nov1850	Hays, Howell C.	b. 5July1844	Child of Emily F. Mills, free woman of color
Mills, Francis	4Nov1850	Hays, Howell C.	b. 20July1845	Child of Emily F. Mills, free woman of color
Mills, John	4Nov1850	Hays, Howell C.	b. 27June1847	Child of Emily F. Mills, free woman of color
Mills, Barbara	4Nov1850	Hays, Howell C.	b. 9Nov1849	Child of Emily F. Mills, free woman of color
Peregin, William	4Nov1850	Parsons, Samuel A.	8 yrs on 20Feb1850	
Peregin, Mathew	4Nov1850	Abernathy, Wyatt H.	3 yrs on 2Dec1849	
Gilbert, James	2Dec1850	Worsham, John H.		
Cox, Mackey	17Jan1869	Burch, Irvin		Both of color. Mother consents
Boaz, Marvin Jefferson	1Feb1869	Higdon, D. K.		Orphan
Rackley, Jesse	12Apr1869	Chapman, James M.	Abt 13 yrs	Orphan. Of color. Cancelled 1Sept1873

Name	Date	Age	Master	Notes
Dean, Alick	6Sept1869		Webb, Henry	Webb of color. Dean's race not given. Canc 5Oct1870, petition of mother, Julia Dean
Yokely, Amanda Ann	6Sept1869		Yokely, Samuel	Of color
Yokely, Lindsay B.	6Sept1869		Yokely, Samuel	Of color
Smith, Sallie	4Oct1869		Hart, Mary Ann (Mrs)	Of color
Hill, Tennessee Alice	12Nov1869		Harwell, Claburn	Of color
Hopkins, Alfred	7Mar1870		Hopkins, G. A.	Of color. Child of Claburn Hopkins, who petitioned unsuccessfully for his return. 4Apr1870, 4Oct1870*, 14Oct1870* Canc 12Apr1875, child having left 2 yrs ago
Hopkins, Noragr? (or Noray)	7Mar1870		Hopkins, G. A.	Of color. Child of Claburn Hopkins, who petitioned unsuccessfully for his return. 4Apr1870, 4Oct1870*, 14Oct1870* Canc 12Apr1875, child having left 2 yrs ago
Hopkins, Warner (or Waren)	7Mar1870		Hopkins, G. A.	Of color. Child of Claburn Hopkins, who petitioned unsuccessfully for his return. 4Apr1870, 4Oct1870*, 14Oct1870* Canc 12Apr1875, child having left 2 yrs ago
Gorden, Joseph	4Apr1870		Anderson, W. G. S.	Of color. Canc 24July1876
Stanley, John	4Apr1870		Wade, T. B.	Of color. Orphan. 10Oct1870*
Stayer, Edward Leroy	7Nov1870		Coats, William	Consent of mother, Sarah Frances Stayer
Burke, Henry Alonzo	5Dec1870	6 yrs	Harmond, James T.	Consent of mother, Matilda Ann Burke, widow. Harmond also his Guardian
Pointer, Jr, Major	6Dec1870	14 yrs	Pointer, Major, the elder	Orphan. Both of color. Brickmason
Burke, Melissa Ann	9Dec1870	9 yrs	Moore, John T.	Consent of mother, Matilda Ann Burke, widow. Moore also her guardian. Rescinded 9June1871
Beverly, Thomas B.	May 1867		Hart, William	Orphan. Rescinded 3Jan1871, request of Mary Anne Hart, widow of William Hart
Beverly, Thomas B.	3Jan1871		Williamson, Nathan R.	Orphan
Burke, Malissa Ann	9June1871	Abt 9 yrs	Oliver, Lem	Orphan. Housekeeper. Consent of mother
Atkins, Ben	11Aug1871	Abt 8 yrs	Young, Richard	Orphan. Farmer. Cons of mother. All of color
Atkins, Sam	11Aug1871	Abt 4 yrs	Young, Richard	Orphan. Farmer. Cons of mother. All of color

Name	?	Age	Name	Notes
Waldrup, Julia			Parson, David N.	Canc 15Sept1871, child now 12 yrs, mother remarried, now Frankie Barlen
Hancock, Cannon	4Oct1871	Abt 8 yrs	Paisley, John M.	Farmer. Both parents dead. Of color
Holt, George W.	5Feb1872		Collins, Samuel F.	Orphan. Consent of mother
Caldwell, John F.	4Apr1872		Vinson, E. L.	
Caldwell, Mary J.	4Apr1872		Vinson, E. L.	
Abernathy, Millard (or Wilson)	19Aug1872	Abt 5 yrs	Wilkins, F. W. & Angelina	Orphan. Of color. Consent of mother, Angeretta (or Henrietta) Abernathy. Canc 12May1873. Child ill, needs mother's care
Maxwell, Cannis (fe)	23Dec1872	Abt 10 yrs	West, D. K.	Of color. Consent of father, Samuel Maxwell
Cox, Lizzie	17Feb1873		Simmons, James M.	Orphan
Davis, Laura	17Feb1873		Aymett, H. H.	Of color. Orphan
Parton, Forest	3Mar1873	Abt 6 yrs	Alexander, T. B.	Orphan
Hays, Monroe	5May1873	Abt 8 yrs	Coates, William A.	Orphan. Consent of mother, Sallie Hays
Higdon, Thomas	2June1873		Boyd, James P.	Orphan. Of color. Son of Coley Higdon, Dcd
Walker, Flora	2Feb1874		Johnson, John C.	Of color
Miller, Mary	27July1874		Anderson, James P.	Orphan. Of color. Anderson also appt guard
Miller, George	27July1874		Anderson, James P.	Orphan. Of color. Anderson also appt guard
Brunson, Edmund	10Aug1874		Brunson, James	Orphan. Both of color
McKam, Jeff	2Nov1874	Abt 12 yrs	Tarpley, William F.	Of color
Nichols, William C.	2Nov1874	Abt 6 yrs	Case, Isaac Y. (or V.)	Request of mother. Canc 13Sept1875, returned to mother at her request
Harwell, David	9Nov1874		Harwell, Thomas B.	Orphan. Of color
Harwell, John	9Nov1874		Harwell, Thomas B.	Orphan. Of color
Reed, Ada Bell	7Dec1874		Smith, W. W.	Orphan. Of color
Walker, Bitha	1Feb1875		Walker, Robert J.	Orphan. Of color
Walker, Morgan	1Feb1875		Walker, Robert J.	Orphan. Of color
Barnett, William	8Feb1875		Morris, Margaret J. (Mrs)	Infant son of George Barnett, who petitions for the indenture
Williamson, India	26Apr1875		Williamson, Thomas S.	Orphan. Of color
Williamson, Mariah	26Apr1875		Williamson, Thomas S.	Orphan. Of color
Scott, Robert	6Mar1876		Walls, Z. T.	Orphan

Name	Date	Age	Master	Notes
Gordon, Joseph	24July1876	13 yrs	Gordon, David	Both of color

Grundy County

Name	Date	Age	Master	Notes
Henderson, Campbell	2Feb1846		Smith, Andrew C.	
Smith, Alexander	2Feb1846		Smith, Andrew C.	
Thomas, Ruful	2Feb1846		Smith, Andrew C.	
Cagle, Artemesa Emeline	3July1848		Wilson, Ballard G.	Until 21 yrs. One of two daughters of Telitha Cagle, who consents 5Jun1848*.
Fults, Marshall	1Jan1849		Fults, John	
Pearson, William J.	1Jan1849	Abt 2 yrs	Bryant, John	
Loryan	1April1850	6 yrs	Walker, John J.	Of color
Jackson, William	7Oct1850	13yrs on 15Jan next	Conn, Joel N. W.	Consent of mother, Rebecca Jackson
Summers, Minton	3Mar1851		Roberts, William	
Ingrum, Joseph	7June1852	11 yrs	Humble, Wiat M.	Orphan
Cagle, Georgia Ann	3Oct1853		Knight, George	Bastard child of Tabitha Cagle. "Given" to Knight, the reputed father, and name changed to Georgia Ann Knight. Indenture or adoption?
Cagle, Darkey A. E.	3Oct1853	Abt 6 yrs	Hughes, John C.	Child of Tabitha Cagle 5Sept1853*
Cagle, Elizabeth	3Oct1853	Abt 8 yrs	Bost, D. L.	Child of Tabitha Cagle 5Sept1853*
John	3Oct1853	Abt 7 yrs	Walker Jr, John J.	Child of Malvina, free woman of color
Georgia	3Oct1853	Abt 5 yrs	Walker Jr, John J.	Child of Malvina, free woman of color
Myres, George Perry	3Oct1853	Abt 16 yrs	Northcut, Archibald	Orphan of Casper & Tabitha Myers, Dcd 4July1853* Later changed to guardianship
Myres, Casper	3Oct1853	Abt 14 yrs	Nunly, John	Orphan of Casper & Tabitha Myers, Dcd 4July1853* Later changed to guardianship. Canc 5June1854
Gaines, Andrew	1Aug1854		Northcut, William E.	Orphan strolling from place to place 3July1854
Fily Ann	1Jan1855	Abt 11 yrs	Walker, Elizabeth (Miss)	Of color. Bond filed 5Feb1855. Cancelled 7June1858. To mother, Malvina Chaney

Name	Date	Age	Bound to	Notes
Campbell, Cleirsey L. Jane	7July1856	7 yrs	Nunly, John	Orphan. Consent of mother. Sibs Mary Adeline & Juleta Virginia Campbell bid out*
Whitman, William	6Oct1856	1 yr	Bost, Noah	Orphan of Seally Whitman 4Jan1858* Canc 5Apr1858*
Nunly, Wesley	2Nov1857	7 yrs	Smith, Martha	Orphan of John Nunly, Dcd. Until 14 yrs. Bound on application of Jesse Nunly. On 4Jan1858 Moses Patrick apptd guardian
Myres, Abby	8Dec1857	8 yrs 10 mo	Bagget, John S.	Orphan of Casper Myers, Dcd 2Feb1857* Canc 7Jan1861. Bagget out of county. To brother, Holen Mires
Morton, Hamman	1Feb1858	10 yrs 4 mo	Countiss, P. H.	Orphan
Whitman, William Henry	5Apr1858	3 yrs 7 mo	Jones, Abraham	Orphan
Chaney, F. E. (fe)	7Feb1859	15 yrs in April next	Gilliam, Harris	Of color. For 5 yrs
Stylls, John	7Mar1859	Abt 13 yrs	Fults, Elsberry	Canc 2Apr1860. Fults out of county. To Mrs. Harris' possession
Joseph	7Nov1859	5 yrs 8 mo	Moony, Loucinda	Of color
Kenedy, Richard	2Sept1861	4 yrs 6 mo	Smith, William C.	
Sanders, Russell	3Nov1862	9 yrs on 1Mar1862	Sartian, L. D.	Orphan. Canc 7July1874. Sanders gone
Burrows, Russel	7Jan1867	9 yrs	Sartin, Susanah	Orphan
Burrows, Victory	7Jan1867	10 yrs	Meeks, Benjamin	Orphan. Female
Smartt, George	1June1868	12 yrs	Nunly, Commodore	Orphan. Canc 6Mar1871. Nunly dead
Burrows, Russel	3May1869	11 yrs	Sartin, James	Orphan
Meeks, George	6Mar1871		Countiss, P. H.	Orphan
Myres, Martha Elizabeth	6May1872	6 yrs 6 mo	Stoner, William H.	Minor heir of Holland Myres, Dcd. Stoner of Warren Co
Myres, Mary C.	7July1873		Masengale, M. C.	Orphan. Masengale of Warren Co
Crow, Lucinda	7Apr1874		Goodman, S. P.	Until age 21. Orphan
Thomas, Albert	6July1874	Abt 7 yrs	Gillam, Samuel	Orphan
Ward, Child of Catharine (male)	3July1876		Brazele, Elias	Taken from Stephen Kilgore. No bond recorded
Wildman, Taylor Campbell	2Apr1877		Sims, E. M.	Child of Bell Wildman
Dugan, Bethel	3Nov1879	6 or 7 yrs	Morton, William	Child of Ford & Eliza Dugan
Dugan, John	3Nov1879	12 or 13 yrs	Morton, John J.	Child of Ford & Eliza Dugan

Name	Date	Age	Master	Notes
Qualls, Unnamed	5Sept1881		Sanders, Jordan	Bastard child of Sarah Qualls 4July1881. Ret to mother 3Oct1881*
Qualls, Unnamed	5Sept1881		Tate, Goodman	Bastard child of Sarah Qualls 4July1881. 3Oct1881* Bond 4Oct1881
Qualls, Thomas	5Sept1881		McCarver, Elias	Bastard child of Sarah Qualls 4July1881. On 3Oct1881 returned to mother. Unsound mind
Qualls, Unnamed	5Sept1881		McCarver, Elias	Bastard child of Sarah Qualls 4July1881. 3Oct1881* Bond 4Oct1881
Qualls, Martha	5Sept1881		Green, William R.	Bastard child of Sarah Qualls 4July1881. 3Oct1881* Bond 4Oct188 Returned to mother 6Feb1882

Hickman County

Name	Date	Age	Master	Notes
Savage, Savannah C.	3Dec1866	11 yrs	Savage, Asa	Orphan. Of color
McAlister, William A.	6May1867	8 yrs	Brown, W. W.	Orphan
McAlister, Sarah F.	6May1867	6 yrs	Brown, W. W.	Orphan
McAlister, George	6May1867	3 yrs	Brown, W. W.	Orphan
Crow, Nelly	6May1867	10 yrs	Puckett, Jr., J. N.	Orphan. Abandoned
Huston, General	3June1867	12 yrs	Giles, Care J.	Orphan
Beddin, Margaret P.	3June1867	12 yrs	Carothers, J. H.	Orphan
Howell, W. H.	5Aug1867	8 yrs	Darden, Alfred	Orphan
Gibbs, Sarah F.	1Mar1869	14 yrs	Smith, Rich A.	
Gibbs, James F.	1Mar1869	8 yrs	Smith, Rich A.	
Gibbs, John	1Mar1869	10 yrs	Grimes, Thomas L.	Orphan. Cancelled 2Apr1877
Gibbs, Mary	1Mar1869	14 yrs	Grigsby, W. H.	
Hawkins, Ann	4Oct1869	8 yrs	Cathy, Jethro B.	Orphan. Of color
Nunnellee, Lucretia	8Feb1870	11 yrs	Nunnellee, George	Orphan
Nance, Louisa	3May1870	5 yrs in Sept1870	Perry, Macinas G.	Orphan. Mother unable to provide
Hassell, John	5July1870	Abt 5 yrs	Hornbeak, John W.	Of color
Lovett, Michael	3Oct1870	8 yrs in April1870	Miller, David C	Orphan. Farmer. Consent of mother

Name	Date	Age	Master	Notes
Fielder, John Thomas	3Oct1870		Jones, Orin A.	Orphan. Farmer. Consent of mother
Bowen. Sherman	7Nov1870	3 yrs on 3Oct1870	Wells, Eli	Orphan. Farmer. Consent of mother
Satterfield, Beauragard	2Jan1872	9 yrs	Easly, W. T.	No father or mother. Farmer
Watts, Colombus	3June1872	11 yrs on 1May1872	Darden, B. G.	Abandoned by father. Consent of mother, who is unable to provide. Farmer
Watts, Robert E. Lee	3June1872	8 yrs	Darden, B. G.	Abandoned by father. Consent of mother, who is unable to provide. Farmer
Askins, David	3June1872	11 yrs in Nov1872	Carothers, H. R.	No father or mother. Farmer
Capps, Mary E. P.	3June1874	13 yrs on 6May last	Hassell, John	
Dockrey, Minnie A.	1Nov1875		Defoe, John W.	
Nat, Samuel	5Jan1876	12 yrs	Eason, J.R.	Farming. Father & mother dead
Nat, Willie	5Jan1876	8 yrs	Eason, J.R.	Farming. Father & mother dead
Barbaror, Mary E.	6Mar1876		Cornelias, Mary E.	
Powers, John	5June1876	14 yrs next January	Berryman, H. T.	Farming. Without means of support
Powers, Arch	5June1876	12 yrs on 2June1876	Berryman, H. T.	Farming. Without means of support
Mays, Amanda	4June1877	4 yrs in March1877	Easley, J. B.	Of color
Pinkerton, James H.	6Aug1877	10 yrs in Dec1877	Woods, James	Orphan
Flowers, Caroline	6Aug1877	8 or 9 yrs	Clagett, H.	Orphan. Of color
Linch, Daniel	5Feb1878	3 yrs on 1March1878	Smith, R. A.	Orphan. Abandoned by reputed father, who denies being parent*. Mother dead. Farmer
Swift, William	5Aug1878	12 yrs on 12Aug1878	Tidwell, L. J.	Farming. Father dead. Mother unable to maintain him, consents
Flowers, Walter R.	4Aug1879	7 yrs in June last	Garner, Renfro	Orphan. Of color
Lawson, Samuel	8Oct1880	16 yrs in Sept1880	Weatherspoon, C.	Orphan

Houston County

Name	Date	Age	Master	Notes
Monroe, Ed	8Apr1873	5 yrs	Pollard, J. J.	Farming.Of color. Abandoned by parents
Monroe, Marshall	8Apr1873	3 yrs	Pollard, J. J.	Farming.Of color. Abandoned by parents

Name	Date	Age	Master	Notes
Patterson, Andrew	3Aug1874	17 yrs	Potter, Perry	Orphan. Farming. Both parents dead. Potter also gave bond as guardian. 2Apr1877*
Jenkins, Thomas H.	6Dec1875	9 yrs	Allen, S. T.	Farming. No parents
Hankins, Richard	2Oct1876	9 yrs	Dickson, J. C.	Farming. Consent of mother. Abandoned by father
Jones, Willie	7Aug1882	17 yrs on 10Aug1882	Sensing, J. D.	Orphan. Abandoned by father
Kelly, Nathan	3Jan1883		Wilcox, George P.	Of color. Order to be investigated 2Apr1883
McCants?, William	1Oct1883		Adams, S. B.	Infant son of Mrs. S. J. Jordan, who requests her son to be bound

Humphreys County

Name	Date	Age	Master	Notes
Slaughter, George B.	7Mar1842	14 yrs	Guthrie, William H.	Orphan
Christopher, Susan E.	8Nov1843		Massey, John	Of color. Baseborn
Duncan, Coleman H.	6Oct1845		McCastland, Andrew	Orphan child of Sarah Duncan, Dcd
Hall, Zodac	2Feb1846		Massey, M. M.	Orphan
Henson, Cathom W.	1Feb1847	Over 14 yrs	Cooley, E. J.	Request of Henson
Seets, Thomas	5Apr1847		Simpson, D. M.	Orphan
Parker, Pityl M.	7Feb1848		Parker, James M.	Orphan of John Parker, Dcd
Parker, Katherine E.	7Feb1848		Dunlap, Robert R.	Orphan of John Parker, Dcd
Duncan, Levi	3Sept1849	Abt 13 yrs	Hendrix, Laban	Orphan
Warren, William	7Aug1883	15 yrs on 1May1883	Sinks, G. B.	Orphan. Agriculture
Young, John P.	5May1884	10 yrs on 1Jan1884	Wasson, J. F.	Orphan. Farmer. Cancelled 7Mar1887, Young having left Wasson abt 15Nov1886
Hall, Artha	5May1884	10 yrs on 6Feb1884	Wasson, J. F.	Orphan. Farmer
Hall, Osco	5May1884	6 yrs on 14Mar1884	Wasson, J. F.	Orphan. Farmer
Dotson, Harvey	?		Gunn, G. W.	Canc 5July1886, Dotson having left Gunn
Pickard, Mary Elizabeth	5July1886	7 yrs in August1886	Pickard, Spencer	Orphan. General housekeeping & housework

Name	Date	Age	Master	Notes
Morrisett, Zachariah	?	Over 21yrs 2Aug1886	Warren, Zachariah	Apprenticeship completed 2Aug1886
Hadley, Minnie B.	4Oct1886		Kimmons, W. J.	Abandoned by father, J. J. Hadley. Mother dead
Hadley, Stella B.	4Oct1886		Kimmons, W. J.	Abandoned by father, J. J. Hadley. Mother dead
Hadley, Katy	4Oct1886		Kimmons, W. J.	Abandoned by father, J. J. Hadley. Mother dead
Hadley, Lossie	4Oct1886		Kimmons, W. J.	Abandoned by father, J. J. Hadley. Mother dead
Marchbanks, Walter	2July1888	Abt 4 yrs	Reece, H. R.	Mother dead. Father not known
Randolph, Ernest	7May1889	9 yrs	Brown, F. G.	Father dead. Mother not capable of caring for him. Of color

Jackson County

Name	Date	Age	Master	Notes
West, Jr, William	?		Fowler, Franklin	On 7Oct1872 indenture cancelled with 4 yrs to serve. West married & has left Fowler
Darwin, Nelson	4Nov1872	15 yrs	Darwin, G. C.	Of color
Darwin, Adenille [Adeline]	4Nov1872	4 yrs	Darwin, G. C.	Of color. Cancelled 6Nov1876, as Adeline. G. C. Darwin now dead. Returned to mother
Cherry, Beauregard	4Nov1872	12 yrs	Sweezy, Matthias	Orphan. Cancelled 3Nov1873. Sweezy leaving county & Cherry refusing to go. Minor heir of William Cherry 6Oct1876
Smith, Fielding	186_		Smith, Elijah	Orphan. On 7Apr1873 Smith ordered to replace burned records. Fielding returned to court 1June1874
Myers, James	8Apr1873	13 yrs	Murray, John P.	Of color
Allen, George	5May1873		Craighead, W. H.	
Bright, Lizzie L.	1871		Hare, Achilles	Orphan of Cassie Bright. Hare ordered to replace burned records
Glisson, John	1Sept1873		Harris, America	Orphan. In care of Harris nearly 2 yrs
Smith, Bird C.	11Sept1873	4 yrs next November	Cox, Peter G.	Of color. ? son of Nancy Smith 7Aug1873*
Smith, Alford J.	1Dec1873	6 yrs in July1873	Cox, W. G.	Of color. ? son of Nancy Smith 7Aug1873*
May, Lee	12Jan1874	4 yrs next July	Gipson, John M.	Of color
Pryor, Sydney S.	2Feb1874	14 yrs on 1Sept last	Johnson, Samuel	

Name	Date	Age	Master	Notes
Hudson, James M.	?		Hawes, Daniel W.	Cancelled 1Mar1875. Hudson to receive $50 on 1Oct next, when 21 yrs old
Roberts, James M. F.	2Mar1874	12 yrs last January	Hawes, Daniel W.	Cancelled 18Apr1874. Roberts a runaway
Roberts, Squire L. E.	2Mar1874	5 yrs next May	Whitiker, William	Cancelled 1June1874, as Lewis E. Roberts, orphan of Julia Roberts
Pryor, Charley	2Mar1874	8 yrs next Sept	Loftis, James M.	
Pryor, John	4May1874	13 yrs on 1May1874	Myers, Henry	
Hunter, Francis	1June1874		Hare, Samuel E.	Female orphan of Jessee and Milly Hunter
Hudson, Albert	?		Read, Nimrod	Bond renewed 6July1874
Hudson, William	?		Read, Nimrod	On 6June1874, mother, Elizabeth Hudson, charges cruelty. Read's right to control of William confirmed 17July1874
Hudson, William	7Sept1874	Abt 14 yrs	Read, Nimrod	Orphan. Rebound. Prior bond records destroyed in courthouse fire 14Aug1872
Smith, James	7Sept1874	13 yrs	Young, N. B.	Orphan of Nora Smith. Cancelled 7Feb1876. Smith left Young on 6Feb1876, now running at large. Now termed illegitimate son of Leanna Smith
Richardson, Rachel	5Oct1874		Jourdan, G. C.	
Richardson, Thena	5Oct1874		Kirkpatrick, Albert	Female
Johnson, William Henry	2Nov1874	10 yrs on 15Jan1875	Loftice, Labin	Cancelled 4Aug1879, Johnson having left
Richmon, Elisabeth	3May1875		Darwin, G. C.	Child of Malinda Richmon. Of color
Richmon, Silas	3May1875		Darwin, G. C.	Child of Malinda Richmon. Of color. Cancelled 7Aug1876, as Silas Darwin, son of Malinda Darwin, G. C. Darwin having died. 6Apr1875*
Goolsby, Milton	7June1875	15 yrs in Dec1875	Mosley, Milton B.	Consent of Mary Goolsby, mother. Cancelled 6Sept1875
Scisco, William	6Sept1875	16 yrs on 10Aug last	Scisco, Hubbard	Abandoned by mother. Canc 3July1876. Mother, Sarah M. Scisco, able to support
Harris, Jessie	4Oct1875	8 yrs	Richmond, Frankliin	Mary Harris, mother, consents 5July1875
Price, John	6Dec1875		Richmond, William	Child of Nancy Price
Price, George	6Dec1875		Richmond, William	Child of Nancy Price

Name	Date	Age	Placed With	Notes
Jones, David	6Dec1875	15 yrs	Richmond, Frank	Son of Ann Jones. Cancelled 6Jan1880. David ungovernable & a 3 time runaway
Hightower, William P.	1867 or 68		Burris, John M.	Original records burned. Re-recorded 6Mar1876. William now 21 yrs 10Jan1876*
Loftis, John	1May1876	12 or 13 yrs	Myres, S. S.	Orphan. Farming
Hawkins, William	4Dec1876	13 yrs	McCarver, Pinkey	Of color
Sutton, James	5Mar1877	11 yrs on 16May1877	Morgan, J. W.	Consent of mother
Sutton, A. D.	5Mar1877	7 yrs on 26Mar1877	Dowel, J. M.	Consent of mother
Jones, David	6Aug1877	Abt 15 yrs Dec1875	Richmond, Frank	Rebound. Mother's (Ann Jones) suit for custody denied. Appealed to Circuit Court
McGee, Elizabeth	4Nov1878	11 yrs	Hawes, Daniel W.	On 6Jan1879 payment made for hauling Catharin McGhee & 2 children to poor house
McGee, Emily Jane	2Dec1878	9 yrs	Hoover, William M.	Orphan. Re-recorded as McGhee same date
McGee, Mary Francis	7Oct1879	4 yrs	Crowder, M. N.	Daughter of Nancy McGee, pauper
Fann, John	1Aug1881	8 yrs on 1June1881	Ragland, James	
Hawkins, John	7Nov1881	3 yrs	Herod, Margaret A.	Consent of mother
Fann, Wiley Howell	5Dec1881	11 yrs in Apr1882	Bybee, L. S.	
Dennis, Will Henry	5Feb1882	Abt 3 yrs	Brotherton, Annie	
Dennis, Susan Ann	5Feb1882	Abt 13 mo	Brotherton, Annie	
Loftis, William	3Mar1884	7 yrs	Burris, John M.	Farmer or miller. Orphan son of Clarinda Loftis, who consents
Hamlet, Annie	26Mar1900	Abt 8 yrs	Van Hooser, P. F.	Illegitimate. Abandoned by mother
Burton, Edith	3Mar1902	Abt 14 yrs	Burton, John P.	Father, Jack Burton, unable to support
Burton, Mattie	7Apr1902	Abt 10 yrs	Burton, D. L.	Father, Jack Burton, unable to support
Pickens, Louise	2June1902	Abt 12 yrs	Johnson, D. B.	Father & mother dead

Lawrence County

Name	Date	Age	Master	Notes
Davis, John	1Feb1819		McIntire, John	
Farmer, Joseph	2Feb1819		Edmondson, James	Had been living with Jacob Adair 2Nov1818
McGee, James	3Oct1820		McDonald, John	Orphan of Polly McGee. Tan, curry & dress leather. Cancelled 2Apr1821, McDonald having left county
Nichols, Coleman	3July1821		Blythe, Lemual	Orphan
McGee, James	7July1821		Howard, Thomas	Shoe & boot maker. On 6April1822 Mary McGee allowed to keep her two daughters
Jones, Willmi? Carni Lucy	1Oct1821		Cranister, Adam	Orphan
Burk, Arter?	1Oct1821		Cook, Charles	Orphan. Cancelled 1Apr1822
Lendry, Caswell	1Oct1821		Stockton, Douglas H.	Orphan. Cancelled 7Jan1822
Alias?, Betsy	1Apr1822		Mathews, Daniel	Orphan. For 8 yrs
Burk, Arter?	1Apr1822		Burk, Ruthy	
Holland, Esquire	6Apr1822	17 yrs	Potter, William	Orphan. Hatting
McGee, Female	6Apr1822		McGee, Mary	Daughter of Mary
McGee, Female	6Apr1822		McGee, Mary	Daughter of Mary
McGee, James	1July1822		Killbourn, Amas	Orphan
Sutton, Jesse	5July1822		Blythe, Jacob	Cancelled 2Apr1832, Jesse having eloped
McGee, Sally	?		McConnell, James M.	Orphan. Indenture cancelled 6Jan1823
Smith, Myram	6Jan1823	Abt 2 yrs	Smith, James	Female orphan
Smith, Lovesy	6Jan1823	Abt 2 yrs	Smith, James	Female orphan
Hettan, William	5Apr1824		Crisp, Mansil	Orphan. Bond & security given 10Apr1824
Horn, Pinkney H.	4July1825		Horn, Thomas	Orphan
Glover, Joseph	3July1826	Abt 10 yrs	Stribling, John B.	Orphan
Webby, Matilda	3July1826	Abt 14 yrs	Murphy, Archibald	Orphan
Grimes, Henry	2Oct1826		Grimes, Luke	Orphan
Basham, Johnston	2Apr1827		Basham, James	Blacksmith. Heir of William Basham, Dcd
Basham, Susan	2Apr1827		Basham, James	Heir of William Basham, Dcd

Name	Date	Age	Name	Notes
Basham, William	2Apr1827		Basham, James	Blacksmith. Heir of William Basham, Dcd
Basham, Ezekiel	2Apr1827		Basham, Nathan	Carpenter. Heir of William Basham, Dcd
Basham, Malinda	2Apr1827		Basham, Nathan	Heir of William Basham, Dcd
Paine, Robert	2July1827	10 yrs	Paine, Hardin	Guardianship also. Heir of James Paine, Dcd. Guardianship cancelled 6Oct1828
Paine, Winsted	2July1827	9 yrs	Paine, Hardin	Guardianship also. Heir of James Paine, Dcd. Guardianship cancelled 6Oct1828
Paine, Maryan	2July1827	4 yrs	Paine, Hardin	Guardianship also. Heir of James Paine, Dcd. Guardianship cancelled 6Oct1828
Paine, Martha Jane	2July1827	4 yrs	Paine, Hardin	Guardianship also. Heir of James Paine, Dcd. Guardianship cancelled 6Oct1828
Richards, Willson	6Oct1828		Richards, George W.	Black smith
Driscal, Nicholas B.	5Oct1829		Bell, John J.	Orphan. Cancelled 7Apr1831
Driscal, Ruthy A. G.	5Oct1829		Sullivan, Jordan	Until 21 yrs. Orphan
Campbell, Jacob	5Oct1829		Sullivan, Jordan	Orphan
Arp, William	4Oct1830		Thompson, Ebenezer	Orphan
Arp, Martin	4Oct1830		Thompson, Ebenezer	Orphan
Arp, Robert Bolin	4Oct1830		Morrow, Benjamin	Orphan
Kendrick, R. C.	?		Kendrick, Judith	Orphan. Cancelled 7Apr1831
Wise, Polly An	3Oct1831		Glover, Jesse B.	
Pearce, Anna	3Oct1831		Woolsey, Samuel	Orphan
Jack, Polly Berry	2Jan1832		Tally, John W.	Orphan
Jack, Love Amanda	2Jan1832		Tally, John W.	Orphan
Jack, Elizabeth Ann	2Jan1832		Tally, John W.	Orphan
Castelon, Edward	2Apr1832		Wisdom, John	
Bolden, Elliott	1Oct1832		Davis, David H.	Orphan
Beardin, John	1Oct1832		Sessums, Blount A.	Orphan
Horn, Davis	7Jan1833		Springers, Aaron	Orphan
Basham, Jonston	1Apr1833		Basham, James	Orphan
Basham, William	1Apr1833		Basham, James	Orphan
Brashers, Alexander	1Apr1833		Brashers, Alexander	Orphan

Name	Date	Age	Master	Notes
Brashers, William C.	1Apr1833		Brashers, Alexander	Orphan
Walker, Benjamin	2July1833	Abt 6 yrs	Parks, Wilie S.	Orphan. Cancelled 7Mar1842
Walker, Wesley	2July1833	Abt 3 yrs	Denton, Lemuel B.	Orphan
Basham, Ezekiel	7Oct1833		Johnston, John	
Crosley, Josiah	7Oct1833		Blythe, Jacob	
Daniel, James	6Jan1834		Springer, Jonas	Orphan. Alias James Green
[McManus], Hiram	7Apr1834		Fondren, John	Orphan. Of color. Terms of indenture completed 2Jan1854.* Given free papers
Roberson, Lucinda	7Apr1834		Blythe, Jacob	Orphan
Jackson, Matilda	8Apr1834		Woodard, Fielder	Orphan
Campbell, Jacob	6Jan1835		Evans, William W.	Orphan
Davidson, Alexander	4Jan1836		Tarkington, James W.	Orphan
Greenwood, William	6Mar1837		Boren, Doss	Cancelled 5Mar1838, Greenwood having married and left Boren
Pearce, Samuel	4June1838	Abt 14 yrs	Gabel, Barnabas	Heir of Spencer Pearce, Dcd. Gabel also apptd guardian of heirs of Spencer Pearce
Stewart, William	3Sept1838	Abt 6 yrs	Counce, Peter	Orphan. Cancelled 5Feb1849
Kimbell, Basel	1Oct1838		Moulders, Abel	Blacksmith
Kimbell, King G.	1Oct1838		Moulders, Abel	Blacksmith
Watters, George	5Nov1838	19 yrs	Smith, Francis	Orphan
Watters, John A.	5Nov1838		Weaver, Zebidey	Orphan
Male, unnamed	5Nov1838	10 yrs	Herrin, Charles J.	Orphan
Male, unnamed	5Nov1838	Abt 13 yrs	Hicks, Charles	Orphan
Randell, Michel Uriah	5Oct1840		Harris, Henry H.	Orphan of Thomas Randell, Dcd
Smith, Nancy	5Oct1840		Campbell, Alexander	Orphan of Thomas Randell, Dcd
Nevel?, Marg	4Jan1841		Litteral, Rodman	Orphan
Pitts, Elizabeth F.	2Aug1841		Brown, Catharine C.	Orphan
Kelly, William Edward	3Jan1842		Carter, Jarrett	Orphan
Walker, Benjamin	7Mar1842		Edmiston, William A.	Orphan

Name	Date	Age	Guardian/Master	Notes
Montgomery, Cynthia Ann	5Dec1842		Hefly, William	
Green, Frances Rebecca	2Oct1843		Green, Asa	
Thorn, Alexander	6Nov1843		Goff, John	
Thorn, [Jasper Newton]	6Nov1843		Goff, Ira C.	On 2Mar1852 Effa Thorn petitioned to have indenture canc, alleging cruelty and intent to remove from county. Dismissed 5Apr1852
Gardner, Hughey	4Dec1843	6 yrs 9 mo 26 d	Parker, William	
Pitts, Elizabeth	2Jan1844		Roundtree, Thomas P.	Cancelled 10Apr1848
Coker, Mary	4Nov1844		Baucum, Cader	Orphan. Cancelled 1Nov1845
Coker, Mary	1Nov1845		Coker, Job	
Jackson, William Noah	1Dec1845		Parker, Noah	Canc 3Sept1856 at request of grandfather
Stewart, Martin D.	2Feb1846	Abt 8 yrs	Ratliff, Joseph	Bound at request of Lucretia Stewart, mother. Cancelled 6Sept1847
Stewart, Andrew J.	2Feb1846	Abt 6 yrs	Ratliff, Joseph	Bound at request of Lucretia Stewart, mother. Cancelled 6Sept1847
Grinaway, Robert	5Oct1846		Anthony, John M.	Cancelled 7Jan1850, as Greenway
Grinaway, Thomas	4Jan1847	15 yrs	Pennington, Isaac D.	Orphan. Cancelled 3Apr1848, as Greenway
Stewart, Daniel Martin	6Sept1847		Pennington, Philip M.	At request of Lucretia Stewart, mother
Stewart, Andrew Jackson	6Sept1847		Pennington, Jacob W.	At request of Lucretia Stewart, mother. Cancelled 7Jan1850. To mother, Lucretia Ham, formerly Stewart
Prince, John	7Feb1848	14 yrs	Colier, Brown L.	Orphan. Cancelled 10Apr1848
Greenway, Thomas	3Apr1848	16 yrs	Pennington, James J.	Orphan
Pitts, Elizabeth	10Apr1848		Boswell, Martha G.	
Ratliff, Alfred	6Nov1848		Parke, George	
Stewart, William	5Feb1849		Estes, Calvin	Blacksmith
Smith, Silas	6Aug1849	Abt 4 yrs	Smith, Thomas M.	Orphan. Cancelled 4Oct1852
Ezell, Allen	5Nov1849		Ezell, Charles G.	Orphan
Ezell, Cynthia	5Nov1849		Ezell, Charles G.	Orphan
Greenway, Robert	7Jan1850		Burch, Stephen	
Greenway, Robert	8Jan1850		Goff, Ira C.	Canc 8Jan1850, Burch refusing to give bond
Vancleve, James B.	1July1850		Burch, Stephen C.	

Name	Date	Age	Master	Notes
Blanchet, Eliza C.	5Aug1850		Arnold, Winston	Cancelled 3Feb1851
Clark, William M.	?		Norman, Wilson B.	Cancelled 7Oct1850
Miles, Reuben	2Dec1850		Haynes, Joseph	Canc 6Jan1851. Miles declared a pauper
Miles, Mary Jane	2Dec1850		Haynes, Elizabeth	Cancelled 1Sept1856 by Joseph Haynes
Miles, James K. P.	2Dec1850		Haynes, Elizabeth	Cancelled 1Sept1856 by Joseph Haynes
Johnson, Samuel	3Feb1851		Austin, Philip G.	Bound upon petition of George W. Shelton
Richardson, James K. P.	8Apr1851		Chaffin, John	Orphan of William Richardson, Dcd. Canc 1Dec1856, James having left Chaffin
Richardson, John Willis	8Apr1851		Chaffin, John	Orphan of William Richardson, Dcd. Canc 1Dec1856, John having left Chaffin
Foster, Sarah	4Aug1851		Richardson, Amos	Cancelled 6Feb1854
Bishop, John W.	1Dec1851		Estes, John	
Blair, Lewallen Sanford	1Dec1851		Chaffin, Elihu M.	Cancelled 2Aug1852
Bishop, Lindsey B.	1Dec1851		Estes, James D.	Cancelled 8July1856
Bishop, William James	1Mar1852		Bishop, Alfred	Canc 5July1852 at request of Wiley Bishop
Seaton, John	1Mar1852		Petty, David	
Bishop, Gabriel A.	1Mar1852		Sandusky, John	
Jones, James	5Apr1852		White, Daniel J.	Orphan
Bishop, W. J.	5July1852		Bishop, Wiley	Canc 7Apr1853
Smith, Silas	4Oct1852	7 yrs	Bently, Leonidas M.	Illegitimate child. Of color
Seaton, Martha	6Dec1852	3 yrs	Martin, John B.	Cancelled 4Apr1853
Whitley, Thomas H.	6Dec1852	3 mo	Williams, Thomas	Grandchild of Williams
Fisher, Elizabeth	4Apr1853	6 yrs	McKey, Charles.	Orphan
Fisher, William	4Apr1853		McKey, Charles.	
Anne, Miss	4Apr1853		Bumpass, Mary	Orphan. Cancelled 7Apr1856
Bishop, William James	7Apr1853		Estes, H. N.	Orphan. Cancelled 3Sept1853
Griggs, Doctor M. M.	2May1853		Duncan, John W.	Consent of mother & stepfather, Nicholas Spears & Sarah Spears
Seaton, James	2May1853		Sellers, William C.	

Name	Date	Age	Bound to	Notes
Seaton, Martha	4July1853	4 yrs	Joyce, William	
Bishop, William J.	3Sept1853		Miles, Willis F.	Cancelled 6Nov1854
Foster, Sarah	6Feb1854		Parks, William	Cancelled 3May1858
Smith, Green B.	6Feb1854	Abt 10 yrs	Cunningham, George A.	New bond given 4Aug1856
Smith, James L.	6Feb1854	Abt 4 yrs	Cunningham, George A.	New bond given 4Aug1856
Smith, Jasper J.	6Feb1854	Abt 4 yrs	Cunningham, George A.	New bond given 4Aug1856
Durham, Napoleon B.	7Aug1854	17 yrs	Durham, John	
Bishop, Eliza J.	6Oct1854	4 yrs	Estes, Sarah	Until 15 yrs. Orphan. New bond 1Sept1856
Lovel, Loranza D.	7Oct1854	10 yrs	Stewart, John W.	Orphan
Bishop, William J.	6Nov1854	Over 14 yrs	Buler, Mary F.	Buler selected by William
Smith, Sarah Ann M.	1Jan1855	3 yrs	Myres, George	Orphan
Bishop, William J.	1Jan1855		Buler, Mary F.	Orphan. Buler gave bond
Wilson, Mary D.	6Jan1855	9 yrs	Brown, Catharine C.	Orphan
Ezzell, Allen	2Apr1855	Abt 14 yrs	Council, John R.	Orphan. Cancelled 6Oct1857
Hamilton, Margarett	2Apr1855	9 yrs	Campbell, Jacob	Orphan
Howard, John W.	2Apr1855	11 yrs	Ratiff, Owen	Orphan. Cancelled 3Aug1857
Ezzell, Elizabeth	6Aug1855		Ezzell, William	
Hughes, Jesse B.	3Sept1855	10 yrs	Davis, John S.	Orphan
Monk, William J.	3Sept1855	3 yrs	Jones, James W.	Orphan. Appealed under Pauper Act to Circuit Court by Elizabeth Monk, mother, and William J. Monk
Hughes, Samuel D.	1Oct1855	13 yrs	Powell, A. J.	Orphan. Cancelled 6June1859, David S. Hughes having left Powell
Shields, John	1Oct1855	10 yrs	Evans, William A.	Orphan
Hamilton, Margarett L.	1Oct1855	9 yrs	Tomlin, James S.	Orphan. Canc 7Apr1856. To grandmother
Anne	7Apr1856	Abt 13 yrs	Martin, John B.	Until 18 yrs. Orphan. Cancelled 11Apr1857, Anne having left Martin
Bishop, Lindsey B.	8July1856	11 1/2 yrs	Tripp, G. W.	Orphan
Haney, William	8July1856	15 yrs	Smith, John L.	Orphan
Bennett, William	4Aug1856	14 yrs	Pennington, Jacob M.	Cancelled 1Nov1859. To father
Miles, J. K. P.	1Sept1856		Ross, M. G.	Orphan
Miles, Mary Jane	1Sept1856		Ross, M. G.	Orphan

Name	Date	Age	Master	Notes
Wafford, John	1Dec1856		White, D. J.	
Howard, John W.	3Aug1857	13 yrs	White, Baker	Until 19 yrs. Cancelled 3Dec1860, Howard wishing to apprentice himelf to Isaac B. White of Maury Co
Howard, John W.	3Dec1860		White, Isaac B.	Cancelled 2Feb1863
Bishop, [L. B.]	6Oct1857		Dotson, S. H.	Orphan. Cancelled 4Apr1859. To Wilie Bishop, grandfather
Foster, Sarah	3May1858		Simonton, William	
Hail, John	7June1858	10 yrs	Blake, H. J.	Orphan. Canc 6Feb1858. To grandfather
Hubbar[d], John W.	Sept1859	12 yrs	Chaffin, William	Cancelled 3Dec1860, Hubbard having left
Williams, Cornelia Jane	5Mar1860		Hix, Thomas	
Bailey, Bill	5Aug1861	2 yrs	White, John	Of color. Consent of reputed mother, Emiley Bailey
Smith, Orange	?		Smith, William	Cancelled 8Oct1867. A runaway. Of color
Scott, Absolam	Nov1866		Chaffin, William	Data from 8Aug1870, when indenture cancelled because of Chaffin's death
Franks, Lydia Ann	?		Pennington, Jacob M.	Cancelled 2Sept1867. To mother, Adeline Franks. Of color
Franks, Indiana	?		Pennington, Jacob M.	Cancelled 2Sept1867. To mother, Adeline Franks. Of color
Jordan, George L.	5Dec1867	Abt 11 yrs	Davis, G. B.	Orphan
McLean, Clark	6Nov1868	Abt 9 yrs	McLean, Charles	Of color
McLean, Jerry Lewis	6Nov1868	Abt 7 yrs	McLean, Charles	Of color
McGee, Martha	?		Linun, W. P. H.	Canc 9Jan1869. To mother, Patsy McGee
Hopkins, Matthew	13Sept1869		Herrin, C. J.	Orphan
Hopkins, Elizabeth	13Sept1869		Herrin, C. J.	Orphan
Willis, William	8Nov1869		Welch, John L.	Orphan
Brittin, John	7Feb1870	8 yrs	Harwell, M. B.	Cancelled & John adopted by W. B. Chaffin 10June1870. Name changed to William B. Chaffin II
Hopkins, Matthew	14Mar1870		Hardin, M. J.	Orphan
Simpson, George A.	10June1870	8 yrs	Flippo, A. A.	
Williams, Edward B.	7July1870		Pennington, James J.	
Bird, John	1Aug1870		Simms, P. L.	Orphan

Scott, Absalom	Wright, W. N.	8Aug1870		Appealed to Circuit Court by William Chaffin's executors. Of color. Cancelled 12Oct1871
Melton, J[ohn]. T.	Bently, D. A.	5Dec1870	13 yrs	Consent of father. Cancelled 7Nov1872, John having left Bently
Eaton, George W.	Wright, Robert	6Mar1871		Orphan
Finney, Anna M.	Howser, F. A.	3July1871		Until 21 yrs
Scott, Absolan	Chaffin, M. A. [Miss]	11Oct1871		Of color
Herbert, James	Herbert, S. B.	7Nov1871	9 yrs	Of color
Simpson, Henry	Bentley, W. R.	15Dec1871		Orphan. Farming
Scott, Frederick	Paine, Susan J.	15Dec1871		Orphan. Farming
Clayton, Thomas	Bryan, Mary	5Feb1872		Orphan
Pope, W. F.	Curry, J. N.	4Mar1872	Abt 9 yrs	Orphan
Pope, James	Blue, A. W.	4Mar1872	Abt 14 yrs	Orphan. Farming
Pope, John	Curry, D. W.	4Mar1872	Abt 11 yrs	Orphan. Farming
Bridges, H. E. D.	Slagal, John	1Apr1872		Orphan. Farming
Bridges, John E.	Grimes, R. J.	1Apr1872		Orphan. Farming
Bridges, Mary	Bently, William R.	25May1872	Abt 8 yrs	Orphan. Until 21 yrs
Crawford, Abraham L.	Neal, W. W.	1July1872		Father unknown. Mother unable to educate and maintain
Williams, William	Williams, A. J.	22Nov1872	Abt 8 yrs	Orphan. Farming
Coutts, Ned	Springer, Jonas	2Dec1872	5 yrs	Farming. Of color
Spears, James C.	Flippo, Thomas	3Mar1873	Abt 2 yrs	Orphan. Farming
Smith, John H.	Powell, James M.	2May1873		Orphan
Thompson, Samuel	Strickland, S. D.	6May1873	Abt 10 yrs	Orphan. Farming
Blair, Jane	Pickard, John	26Mar1874	Abt 13 yrs	Until 21 yrs. Orphan. Of color
Currey, Elizabeth	Malone, H. R.	23July1874		Until 21 yrs. Orphan
Brailey, Causis	Green, Golman	22Feb1875		Until 21 yrs. Female
Williams, Malisse	Pickard, John	14Oct1875	5 yrs	Until 21 yrs. Orphan. House keeping
Bird, John	Simms, E. C.	29Aug1877	Abt 13 yrs	Orphan
McLaren, Elizabeth	Balz, John P.	6Jan1879	18 yrs in 1885-188_	No father or mother. Of color
Snow, Dora	Bitter, Bernard	13Jan1879	Abt 5 yrs	Orphan. Housekeeping

Name	Date	Age	Master	Notes
Johnson, Amanda E.	5May1879	9 yrs	Hughes, D. J.	Consent of father, Alexander Johnson
Blackwell, Mary	1June1880	Abt 11 yrs	Neal, W. W.	Orphan
Crews, Lilly	25July1881	Abt 8 yrs	Buchanan, W. J. (Mrs)	Orphan. Housekeeping
Tucker, Marion	25July1881	7 yrs	Welch, Sallie	Orphan. Farming
Tucker, George W.	25July1881	9 yrs	Welch, Sallie	Orphan. Farming
Webster, Willie Francis	26Mar1883	Abt 5 yrs	Orth, Peter	Orphan
Mason, Calvin Marion	9Apr1883		Herbert, S. B.	
Varen, Friet?	11June1883	Abt 13 yrs	Benedict, Joseph	Orphan
Haskin, John	2Oct1883		Hall, G. C.	
Haskin, Joseph	2Oct1883		Wall, Allen	
Woods, Will	4Jan1884		Paulk, James L.	Of color

Lewis County

Name	Date	Age	Master	Notes
Sharp, Samuel	6Aug1866	9 yrs	Sharp, William P.	Consent of Mary Sharp, mother. Of color. Farmer
Sharp, Judah A.	6Aug1866	6 yrs	Sharp, William P.	Consent of Mary Sharp, mother. Of color. Farmer. Mistreatment alleged 4Mar1872
Losson, Jerry	6Nov1866	12 yrs	Napier, William C.	Farmer. Of color
Losson, Eliza	6Nov1866	14 yrs	Napier, William C.	Farmer. Of color
Ray, Henry	4Mar1872	11 yrs	Bell, Marion	Orphan. Farmer. Of color
Ray, Richard	4Mar1872	12 yrs	Bell, Marion	Orphan. Farmer. Of color
Campbell, Miles	1April1872	8 yrs	Jordan, Henry	Orphan. Farmer. Of color
Sharp, Judah	1April1872	13 yrs	Sharp, William P.	Orphan, dau of Mary Sharp. Housewifery. Of color
Saxton, John H.	1Dec1873	9 yrs	Fain, Charles	Orphan
Moris, George W.	5Aug1878	12 yrs	Johnston, R. S.	Orphan. Farmer. Consent of Moris

Lincoln County

Name	Date	Age	Master	Notes
Middleton, Benjamin F.	28May1810	9 yrs on 4Sept1809	Clark, Thomas	Blacksmith. Orphan
Middleton, Deily E.	29May1810		Duvall, Alexander	Spinning & weaving. Orphan

Name	Date	Age	To whom bound	Notes
Browning, Brinkley	29May1810		Sebastian, Isaac	Millwright. Orphan
Tramble, Hollingsworth	26Aug1811	4 yrs	McKinley, David	Orphan
Westbrook, John	26Aug1811	13 yrs this October	Brinker, Henry	Orphan
Middleton, Dicea Emiline	25Feb1812	8 yrs in June 1812	Murphey, John	Orphan
Philips, Rebecah	1Aug1814	11 yrs	Enochs, Gabriel	Orphan. James Cohron & Israel Philips appt adm of estate of Elizabeth Philips same day
Phillips, John	1Aug1814	13 yrs	Enochs, John	Orphan. James Cohron & Israel Philips appt adm of estate of Elizabeth Philips same day
Lot, Matilda	7Nov1814	9 yrs last May	Nolan, Easter	Orphan. Weaving, spinning, sewing & nitting
Philips, Britain	6Feb1815	15 yrs	Archer, George	Orphan. Shoemaking business. James Cohron & Israel Philips apptd adm of estate of Elizabeth Philips 1Aug1814
Dark, Thomas	7Feb1815	15 yrs last November	Beavers, Stephen	Orphan. Cabinet business
Shelton, Thomas	6May1815		Sweazy, Charles	Orphan. Blacksmith. Cancelled 6Nov1815
Hammons, Charles	6May1815		Dusenberry, John	Until March 1820
Shelton, Alfred M.	7Aug1815	8 or 9 yrs	Beavers, Jr, William	Orphan
Coats, Thomas	6Nov1815	15 yrs	Simmons, John	Blacksmith
Hurt, Ranson	5Aug1816		Callaghan, Patrick O.	Orphan of John Hurt, Dcd. Bricklaying
Hurt, William P.	5Aug1816		Callaghan, Patrick O.	Orphan of John Hurt, Dcd. Bricklaying
Ross, Peter	?		Sprinkle, Charles	Previously bound. On 24Jan1820 suit alleging maltreatment dismissed. Appealed
Warren, William G.	23Oct1820		Dusenberry, John	Tanner
Baggett, Lemuel	26Oct1822		Dickson, Robert	
Warren, Jinsey	2Jan1826		Smoot, John H.	Orphan
Warren, Selma	2Jan1826		Hunter, Ruben	Orphan
Warren, Beda	3Apr1826		Ginnings, William	
Waren, Salina	3Apr1826		Pilant, Pinkney	
Hollandsworth, Abner	3Apr1826		Rosebrough, William	Blacksmith
Sawyers, Payton	7Apr1826		Sawyers, Abner G.	Until 20 yrs. Blacksmith
Reed, Amos	3July1826	14 or 15 yrs	McElroy, Jr, Micajah	Orphan. Farming

Name	Date	Age	Master	Notes
Dodd, Mary	2Oct1826	7 yrs	Byers, James	Orphan
Warren, James	2Oct1826		Holding, Samuel S.	Orphan. Cabinet maker
Jeffrey	7Oct1826		Thompson, David	Shoemaking. Of color
Cummins, Andrew	9Oct1826		Pugh, Spencer A.	Orphan of Thomas Cummins, Dcd. Sadling
Parrish, Mary Ann	9Oct1826	Abt 13 yrs	Buchanan, Moses	Orphan
Bean, Isaac	15Jan1827		Cheatham, John	Boot & shoemaking
Holman, William	15Jan1827		Alford, James D.	Cabinet maker
Warren, John	16July1827	Abt 8 ys	Holden, Samuel S.	Consent of Henry Warren, Guardian. Cabinet business
Coventry, Amelia	?		Walker, Zedock	Cancelled 23July1827. To care of guardian, Robert Beard
Lisk, Polly	15Oct1827	Abt 10 yrs	Shorter, James	Orphan of Josiah Sisk, Dcd
Hunt, John	28Jan1828	Abt 8 yrs	Shipp, Lewis	Farming. "Yellow boy"
Sisk, Solomon	28Jan1828	Abt 6 yrs	Cole, Eli	Farming
Young, Ezekiel	28Jan1828	Abt 12 yrs	Wallace, Joseph H.	Cord winding business. Canc 19July1831
Dennis, Samuel	28Jan1828		Wallace, Joseph H.	Shoe & boot making. Cancelled 19Jan1831
Baggot, Benjamin	28July1830		Dickson, Robert	Sadling business
Findley, Joel	28July1830	Abt 4 yrs 6 mo	Dickson, Robert	Tanner & currier. Entry crossed out
Zively, John	18Oct1830		Morgan & Jones	Son of John H. Zively, Dcd. 27July1830. Cancelled 2July1838
Holloway, James	18Oct1830		Hulme & Wiagart	Son of Betsey Holloway 27July1830
Mayfield, John	18Oct1830		Hague, James	Son of Archibald Mayfield, Dcd. Has brother, Robert 27 & 28July1830
Young, Ezekiel	19July1831		Young, James	
Findley, Joel	23July1831	7 yrs on 12 June last	Crawford, James A.	
Gibson, Lewis	19Oct1831		Vernon, William	Of color
Hicks, John	23Jan1832		Cranfield, Isom	Cabinet maker
Swinford, Amanda Jane	23July1832		Beach, Benjamin	
Swinford, Susan Catherine	23July1832		Beach, Benjamin	
Troop, James M.	21Jan1833		Moore, William	

Name	Date	Age	Master	Notes
Throup, Sally	21Jan1833		Campbell, Parker	
Throup, Francis	21Jan1833		Beaty, William	
Furgerson, Nelson	15Apr1833		Polson, William G.	On 29Jan1833 John Furgerson, orphan, ordered brought to court
Hinkle, Samuel	21Oct1833	Abt 16 yrs	Call, Daniel H.	
Frame, Lucinda Adaline	20Jan1834		Turney, Jacob B.	Until 21 yrs
Martin, Mary C.	21Apr1834		George, David W.	
Martin, William	21Apr1834		Reeves, Malachi	
Moyers, Hampton	21Apr1834		Phillips, John H.	Until older child [which?] is 21 yrs. Cancelled 27Jan1835. To father
Moyers, Benjamin F.	21Apr1834		Phillips, John H.	Until older child [which?] is 21 yrs. Cancelled 27Jan1835. To father
Jackson, William	?		Norton, John C.	Of color. On 21April1834 released from giving further (>4 mo) schooling
George	28Apr1834		Fincher, Francis M.	Son of Peggy Akin, of color. 21Apr1834*
Nancy Jane	28Apr1834		Brewer, William	Dau of Peggy Akin, of color. 21Apr1834*
Sarah	28Apr1834		George, William	Dau of Peggy Akin, of color. 21Apr1834*
Gravall, Jack	?		Jordan, Hezekiah	Of color. On 21July1834 released from giving further schooling
Stricklin, Jane	28July1834	Abt 9 yrs	Beard, Jr., Absalon	
Spears, Samuel	21Oct1834		Vernon, William	
Abels, Alexander	21July1835		Pybas, Benjamin	Heir of Jeremiah Abels, Dcd
Abels, Mahala	21July1835		Pybas, Benjamin	Heir of Jeremiah Abels, Dcd
Teurey, Thomas Jefferson	21Oct1835		Morgan, John T.	Sadler. Name is probably Towrey
Roach, John	18Apr1836		Parks, William	Farming
Roach, James	18Apr1836		Ellis, James	
Roach, William D.	2May1836	Abt 11 yrs	Short, Merrit H.	Orphan
Vines, Milly	6June1836	Abt 8 yrs	Morgan, John S.	Orphan
Towrey, James	6June1836	Abt 17 yrs	Stonebraker, Jacob	Orphan. Cancelled 1Oct1838
Vines, Benjamin	6June1836	Abt 3 yrs	Wilshire, Thomas L.	Orphan

Name	Date	Age	Master	Notes
Vines, Betsey	4July1836		Goodrich, John	On 4Nov1836 Elizabeth Vines ordered taken to poor house, then brought to court at next term
Lee, Jasper	Aug1836		Weigert, John	Orphan
Moyers, Joel S.	Aug1836		Berry, William L.	Orphan of Henry or Peter Moyers 4July1836
Roach, Martha	3Oct1836		Bryant, William R.	
Russell, Emily	5Dec1836		Pitts, William A.	
Myers, Sterling A.	6Feb1837	Abt 8 yrs	Myers, James	Orphan
Towrey, Josiah	5June1837		Hague, James & William L.	
Moyers, Peter	5June1837		Gullett, Solomon	Son of Henry Moyers, Dcd 6Mar1837
Russell, Mary Ann	Aug1837		Bright, Jr, William	
Nott, Mary	4Sept1837		Shaw, Sr, William	Orphan
Moyers, William	5Feb1838		Bell, Samuel	Orphan of Henry Moyers, Dcd 6Mar1837
Ziverly, John H.	2July1838		Stone, Joel L.	Orphan
Houston, Robert	2July1838		Moore, A. S. & Stonebraker, George	Orphan. Tanning & currying
Martha	6Aug1838		Kidd, George	Mulatto. Child of a free negro late of this county named Stephen
Mackanaw	6Aug1838		Kidd, George	Mulatto. Child of a free negro late of this county named Stephen
Calvin	3Sept1838		Nowlin, Bluford	Mulatto. Son of Stephen Husk, late of this county
Kingsley, [Mary] Adeline	1Oct1838		Roland, Richard W.	Orphan 3Sept1838
Kingsley, Elizabeth	1Oct1838		Gibson, Albert G.	Orphan 3Sept1838
Philips, Cynthia Ellen	5Nov1838	Abt 8 yrs	Cole, John	Orphan. On 7Oct1839 James Locker apptd adm of estate of James Philips
Philips, Francis	5Nov1838	Abt 8 yrs	Cole, Elizabeth	Orphan. On 7Oct1839 James Locker apptd adm of estate of James Philips
Philips, Fanny	5Nov1838	Abt 8 yrs	Butler, William	Orphan. On 7Oct1839 James Locker apptd adm of estate of James Philips

Name	Date	Age	Other	Notes
Brown, James E.	7Jan1839		Conger, M.	
Thomas, Alfred	4Feb1839	Abt 12 yrs	Leatherwood, Basil	Same date William B. Robinson apptd adm of estate of William Thomas
Thomas, Calvin	4Feb1839	4 or 5 yrs	Benston, Mathias	Same date William B. Robinson apptd adm of estate of William Thomas. 4Aug1845*
Thomas, James	4Feb1839	Abt 3 yrs	Benston, Mathias	Same date William B. Robinson apptd adm of estate of William Thomas. 4Aug1845*
Roach, Susan S.	3June1839		Sims, Hampton	
Waggoner, Catherine	5Aug1839		Laws, David	Orphan
Hand, Harris C.	7Oct1839		English, Joseph S.	
Hedgpeth, Louisa	3Aug1840		Hedgepeth, Jeremiah	Cancelled 5July1847
Hedgpeth, Charlotte	3Aug1840		Hedgepeth, Jeremiah	Cancelled 5July1847
Hedgepeth, Cornelius	3Aug1840		Hedgepeth, Jeremiah	Cancelled 5May1850. Jeremiah's will probated July1851
Eddington, Mary Jane	7Sept1840		Beard, Robert	Orphan. Eli Hindman apptd guard 4Apr1842
Eddington, Elizabeth Eleanor	7Sept1840		Beard, Robert	Orphan. Eli Hindman apptd guard 4Apr1842
Eddington, Rebecca Frances	7Sept1840		Beard, Robert	Orphan. Eli Hindman apptd guard 4Apr1842
Eddington, Edward J.	7Sept1840		Beard, John P.	Orphan
Eddington, Miles Newton	7Sept1840		McBride, John	Orphan. Eli Hindman apptd guard 4Apr1842
McCoy, John	7Sept1840		Phillips, John H.	
McCoy, James	7Sept1840		Phillips, John H.	
Hulme, William	5Apr1841		Harris, Joel M.	Tanning
Vines, Benjamin	3May1841		Mayfield, John	Tanning. On 5Aug1844 Mayfield allowed to remove Vines to Alabama
Pruitt, Catharine	2Aug1841	Abt 13 yrs	Caughran, Andrew	Orphan. Has a sister 5April1841*. On 4Oct1841 Larry Epps apptd guardian of Ann Pruitt, orphan, abt 6 yrs old
Moyers, William	1Nov1841		Smith, Austin G.	Orphan
Towery, William	6Dec1841		Morgan, John T.	Orphan
Norris, Thomas J.	6Dec1841		Cobb, James H.	Cancelled 2May1842
Hill, Houston C.	2May1842		Collins, William	Orphan. Farming
Hill, Jesse	2May1842		Oliver, George	Orphan. Farming
Steed, William F.	5Sept1842		Philips, Lewis	Orphan. Farming

Name	Age	Date	Master	Notes
Hill, Houston C.		5Sept1842	McAfee, William	Orphan. Farming
Husk, Richard C.		5Sept1842	Caughran, Andrew	Orphan. Farming. Mulatto
Philips, Frances		3Oct1842	Cole, John	Pauper
Bias, James Abner		5Dec1842	Woodall, James	Orphan
Hill, Samuel		3Apr1843	Timmins, Ambrose	Orphan
Senton, Gillespie		3Apr1843	Riley, Samuel G.	Orphan. Cancelled 4Mar1850
Senton, Perry Lee		3Apr1843	Riley, Samuel G.	Orphan
Eddington, John E.		3July1843	Beard, Robert	Farming. Eli Hindman apptd guard 4Apr1842
Watson, David		7Aug1843	Pitts, William	Farming
Williams, William A.		4Mar1844	Williams, William	Farming
Ward, George		3June1844	Moore & McClain	Tanner. Orphan, one of three children of Elizabeth Ward 1Apr1844
Stator, Cornelius N.		1July1844	Aaikin, T. D.	Saddler. Cancelled 6Apr1846
Gunter, Jasper		6Jan1845	Wallace, Samuel	Farming. Cancelled 5Sept1853
Rutledge, Henry		3Mar1845	Brown, Samuel D.	Farming. On 5Feb1845 Joseph, son of Joseph Rutledge, Dcd, ordered to court
Rutledge, Margret		3Mar1845	Brown, Samuel D.	House business. See above
Gunter, Claiborn		3Mar1845	Wyatt, William	Farming
Burnet, Thomas B.		5May1845	Beardin, Francis M.	Black Smith
Medcalf, John T.		4Aug1845	Edde, Moses P.	
Medcalf, William L.		4Aug1845	Walker, Andrew W.	
Sharp, Mary		1Sept1845	Lowe, Mathew	
Lopea, Amilda		5Jan1846	Wallis, William	Rescinded 2Feb1846
Edwards, William W.		2Mar1846	Timmons, William	Farming
Staten, Cornelius T.		6Apr1846	Morgan, John T.	
Metcalf, Charles A.		1June1846	Edde, Moses P.	
Tucker, Samuel L.		7Sept1846	Trip, Jonathan	Shoemaker
Briant, Thomas		5Apr1847	Brant, Wright	
Briant, Louisa A.		5Apr1847	Brant, Wright	

Name	Date	Age	Master	Notes
Hedgepeth, Louisa J.	5July1847		McAfee, William	Until 21 yrs
Hedgepeth, Charlotte	5July1847		McAfee, William	Until 21 yrs
Swan, John A.	5Oct1847		Gill, Alanson G.	Farming
Rainy, Thomas W.	1Nov1847		Colier, John E.	Orphan. Farming
Medciff, Charles A.	1Nov1847		McBride, James	Saddling. Cancelled 4Mar1851
Thomas, James	6Dec1847		Stephens, John	Blacksmith. Cancelled 3May1852
Thomas, Calvin	6Dec1847		Brum?, Joshua D.	
Gibbs, William	3Jan1848	10 yrs 6 mo	Douthit, Campbell	Orphan. Cancelled 3July1848 for abuse
Smith, Adison Lewis	6Mar1848		Aikin, L. D.	Saddler
Gibbs, William	3July1848		Hamilton, William	
Durham, Nancy	7Aug1848		Scroggins, Abner	
Metcalf, John R.	4Sept1848		Freeman, Thomas H.	Saddling
Wise, Mary Ann	3Sept1849		Stafford, A. L.	Housekeeping
Wise, Thomas	3Sept1849		Cooper, B. W.	Farming
Hall, William	3Dec1849		Tool, James	Has a brother, Anderson 5Nov1849
Sinton, Gillaspie	4Mar1850	Abt 17 yrs	Jinkins, John F.	Orphan. Farming
Metcalf, Charles A.	4Mar1850		Hamilton, John	Orphan. Farming
Owen, Joseph	4Mar1850		Fincher, Aarin	Orphan. Farming
Section, Elijah	4Mar1850		Jinkins, John F.	Orphan. Farming. Prob should be Sinton
Sinton, Eliza	?		Riley, Samuel J.	Orphan. Cancelled 4Mar1850
Hedgepeth, Cornelious	6May1850	Abt 13 yrs	McAfee, William	Orphan. Farming
Hall, Palmyra E.	3June1850	Abt 12 yrs	Howel, Charles S.	Orphan. Housekeeping
Maloney, Nathaniel	1July1850		Hobbs, William P.	
Butts, Alexander	5Aug1850		Amey, L. F.	Blacksmithing
Hall, William	5Aug1850		Cole, F. M.	Until 20 yrs. Farming. James Tool, previous master, dead
Timms, Rosanna	1Sept1851		Dennis, Lemuel P. M.	
Bryant, Louisa	1Sept1851		Carter, William E.	
Doss, Marion	6Oct1851		Brown, R. L.	Farming
Harrison, Thomas	5Jan1852		McAfee, William	
Timms, James	5Apr1852	Abt 13 yrs	Smith, John N.	Orphan. Farming
Thomas, James	3May1852	Abt 16 yrs	Downing, Alexander G.	Orphan. Tanning, currying, & finishing

Name	Date	Age	Master	Notes
Hank, Isaac	7Feb1853	Abt 16 yrs	Steed, Augustus	Orphan
Witt, Polly Ann	5Sept1853		Jobe, Jane	Orphan
Moffett, James S.	5Sept1853		Cathron, Lucy	
Gunter, Jasper	5Sept1853		Landess, Felix G.	Tanning
Marshall, Balis L.	2Oct1854		Stewart, James	Until 20 yrs. Farming
Rainy, John C.	2Oct1854	Abt 15 or 16 yrs	Prossen, John D.	Orphan. Farming
Reynolds, Mark	5Feb1855		Callier, Mark	Farming
Bray, Willis	5Feb1855		Bray, Hanan	Farming
McAfee, Lawsen L. W.	3Sept1855		Steelman, Silas	Farming
Renegar, Cordelia	3Sept1855		Hoots, Jacob	Until 21 yrs
Pool, William	3Mar1856	Abt 4 yrs 6 mo	Scoggins, Abner	
Halland, Jimry	5May1856		McBride, John	Female
Sharp, William	1Dec1856		Proper, J. A.	
Beavers, Eli H.	2Feb1857		Moyers, George W.	
Cook, John	2June1857		Cole, William F.	
Cook, John	5Aug1857		Cole, William F.	Duplicate entry
Taylor, William H.	3May1858	Abt 15 mo	Taylor, William H.	Foundling. Farming. Probably a corrected entry
Taylor, William T.	7June1858	14 & 15 mo	Taylor, William H.	
Uptain, Amanda M. A.	7June1858	12 yrs on 4Dec last	Roberts, James A.	Orphan. Seamstress & housekeeping
Johnson, Angus A.	4Oct1858	Abt 13 yrs	Marshall, Benjamin	Orphan
Martin, Martha A. A.	6June1859	10 yrs	Pylant, Pinkney	Orphan. Domestic housewifery
Martin, Sarah Ann Josephfine	6June1859		Sorrells, Isham	Orphan. Domestic housewifery
Bryant, Sterling	4July1859		Prosser, W. P.	Orphan. Farming
Bryant, John P.	4July1859		Prosser, Perry G.	Orphan. Farming
Porter, Elizabeth	1Aug1859		Roberts, James A.	Orphan. Housewifery & sewing or tailoring
Jackson, William	3Oct1859		Philpot, Franklin	Orphan. Farming
Echols, Martha Ann	5Dec1859	Abt 11 yrs	Anderson, John	Orphan. Housewifery

Name	Date	Age	Master	Notes
Perry, William W.	5Dec1859	Abt 7 yrs	Anderson, John	Orphan. Farming. Canc 7June1869, Perry having left Anderson in May 1868
Echols, Augustus T.	5Dec1859	Abt 9 ys	Anderson, John	Orphan. Farming. On 1Apr1872 terms of indenture certified by Echols as completed
Anderson, William J.	5Dec1859	Abt 13 yrs	Anderson, John	Orphan. Farming. On 2Sept1867 apprentice's surname corrected to "Echols"
Perry, Robert R.	5Dec1859	Abt 5 yrs	Millikin, John H.	Orphan. Farming. Rescinded 2Dec1872. Millikin dead
Norvell, William	7Feb1860	Abt 15 yrs	Prosser, A. M.	Orphan. Farming
Hobbs, Littleberry	5Mar1860	Abt 17 yrs	Sugg, William C.	Orphan. Farming
Hall, James V.	3July1860	Abt 7 yrs	Roach, James P.	Orphan. Farming
Porter, Elizabeth	3Oct1860	Abt 10 yrs	English, James E.	Orphan. Housewifery
Porter, Robert	5Nov1860		Taylor, Catharine	Orphan
Williamson, William	1Apr1861	13 yrs 10 mo	Hagen, John R.	Orphan. Architecture & house building
Jones, James	2Dec1861	Abt 13 yrs	Moore, W. E.	Orphan. Farming
Couch, Susan	2Oct1865		Smith, Richard	Orphan
Yarboro, Sarah. J. E. M.	5Feb1866	18 yrs on 6Jan1869	Fairbank, William	Request of mother, Nancy A. E. Yarboro (Mrs)
McCrary, Joseph D.	5Mar1866	6 yrs on 6May1866	White, Thomas	Orphan. Agreement with mother, Madeline McCrary
Patterson, Tom	2July1866	10 yrs	Patterson, Elizabeth R.	Farming. Of color
Sherrell, Albert	2July1866	10 yrs	Sherrell, Joseph L. (Dr)	Of color. Farming
Kimbrough, Woos	2July1866	14 yrs on 2June1866	Kimbrough, Bradley	Farming. Of color
Whitaker, Joe	2July1866	13 yrs on 1Oct1866	Whitaker, N. H.	Farming. Of color
Whitaker, Benton	2July1866	11 yrs on 1July1866	Whitaker, N. H.	Farming. Of color
Colter, Alexander	3Sept1866	13 yrs on 4Apr1866	Colter, H. H.	Farming. Of color
Grisard, Delpha	5Nov1866	11 yrs on 24Dec1866	Grisard, Margaret A.	House servant. Orphan. Of color
Stewart, Tom	3Dec1866	15 yrs on 10Dec1866	Stewart, George	Farming. Orphan. Of color
Douthit, Violet	3Dec1866	10 yrs on 1Apr1867	Douthit, Calvin Y.	Housekeeping. Of color

Name	Date	Age	Master	Notes
Jones, Martha	8Jan1867	10 yrs on 1May1867	Jones, Sarah F.	Housekeeping. Orphan. Of color. On 8Apr1867 sheriff ordered to deliver Martha to Jones from Peter G. McMullen. 13May1867*
Parks, Jim	8Jan1867	4 yrs on 1Jan1867	Kimbrough, Bradley	Consent of mother, Nancy Parks. Farming. Of color
Pitts, James	8Jan1867	7 yrs on 12Feb1867	Pitts, E. B.	Request of mother, Louisa Pitts. Farming. Of color
Pitts, Clarke	8Jan1867	9 yrs on 11Feb1867	Pitts, E. B.	Request of mother, Louisa Pitts. Farming. Of color
Eddins, William	8Jan1867	13 yrs on 1Sept1866	Bearden, L. J. E.	Farming. Orphan. Of color
Eddins, Nabo	8Jan1867	11 yrs on 10Aug1866	Thornton, James M.	Farming. Orphan. Of color
Evans, S. L.	4Feb1867	21 yrs on 10Feb1877	Isom, James	Orphan. Cancelled 2Sept1867
Savery, Edward	18Feb1867	11 yrs on 1Jan1867	Bailey, Cullen	Farming. Of color
Rutledge, Thomas	4Mar1867	12 yrs on 25Dec1866	Nicks, A. T.	Farming. Of color
Alexander, John	1Apr1867	9 yrs on 1Jan1867	Carey, James H.	Farming. Of color. Released 7Aug1877
Alexander, Stanuss	3June1867	12 yrs	Alexander, S. S.	Farming. Of color
Alexander, Jude	3June1867	10 yrs	Alexander, S. S.	House wifery. Of color
Whitaker, Benjamin	3June1867	12 yrs on 8Apr1867	Whitaker, Newton	Farming. Of color
Whitaker, Judith	3June1867	10 yrs on 10Feb1867	Whitaker, Newton	Cook, washer & farming. Of color
Daniel, Mary E.	1July1867	5 yrs	Bryan, B. B.	House wifery. Of color
Dunly, John W.	1July1867	9 yrs on 22Jan1867	Twitty, P. L.	Farming. Orphan. Apprenticeship completed & bond cancelled 3Feb1879
Kerchaval, Quilla	2July1867	12 yrs	Neil, Virginia E.	Housewifery. Orphan. Of color. On 6Aug1867 Quilla refuses to live with Neil. Cancelled 2Sept1867
Evans, George W.	5Aug1867	7 yrs	Wiles, Charles	Farming. Orphan
Brown, Jack	2Sept1867	17 yrs on 25Nov1867	Bearden, Alfred	Farming. Orphan. Of color

Name	Date	Age	Master	Remarks
Kerchaval, Quilla	2Sept1867	13 yrs on 1May1867	Green, N. O.	Housewifery. Orphan. Of color. Green selected by Quilla through next friend, Alcy Kerchavall
Evins, Samuel L.	2Sept1867	8 yrs on 10Feb1867	Wiles, Charles	Farming
Price, Elija	7Oct1867	14 yrs	Douglass, E. S.	Farming
Price, James	4Nov1867	12 yrs	Cole, L. L.	Farming. On 13Jan1876 Cole released from duty to educate James due to "a very weak and feeble mind"
McMullen, James	18Nov1867	6 yrs this date	Brysen, J. H.	Farming. Of color
Abernathy, C. V. T.	2Dec1867	7 yrs on 7Feb1868	Emmons, S. M.	Farming
Abernathy, R. S.	2Dec1867	11 yrs on 7Jan1868	Emmons, S. M.	Farming
Hobbs, John A.	3Feb1868	4 yrs on 12Jan1868	Arendall, Jesse H.	Farming
Gregory, Jack	3Feb1868	Abt 10 yrs	Pitts, Joel G.	Farming. Of color
Thornton, Isaac	1Feb1869	8 yrs on 15June1868	Thornton, James M.	Farming. Of color
Thornton, Jane	1Feb1869	5 yrs on 10May1868	Thornton, James M.	Cooking & housekeeping. Of color
Sanders, William	1Feb1869	10 yrs on 1Feb1869	McGee, James P.	Farming. White
Eslinger, Harrison	2Aug1869	12 yrs on 2Aug1869	Leatherwood, B. B.	Farming. Of color
Clounch, James	7Feb1870	15 yrs on 18Jan1870	Wright, James B.	Farming. Father, James Clounch, Sr, consents. Sister, Jennie, adopted this date by W. J. Stegall. Mother a lunatic in aylum
Buchanan, John W.	7Feb1870	12 yrs	Montgomery, W. M.	Farming
Clounch, George W.	7Feb1870	12 yrs	Thorenton, William A.	Farming. See James Clounch
Clounch, Allice	7Feb1870	6 yrs	Thorenton, William A.	Housekeeping. See James Clounch
Haney, James	11Mar1870	10 yrs in March1870	Anderson, John	Farming. Haney's receipt for items due at completion of apprenticeship dated 12Mar1881, filed 5Apr1881
Thurman, Thomas Franklin	2May1870	7 yrs on 7Nov1870	Whitaker, Mark D. S.	Farming. Son of Frank A. Thurman, Dcd
Gracie, Wesley	5Sept1870	10 yrs on 1Sept1870	Bonner, Jack	Farming. Of color
Gracie, Fannie	5Sept1870	8 yrs on 1July1870	Bonner, Jack	Of color. Cooking, washing, etc
Kean, John	6Feb1871	8 yrs	Stewart, George	
Abbot, Sarah E.	9Feb1871	12 yrs on 25Dec1870	Wilson, Robert W.	Housekeeping

Name	Date	Age	Master	Notes
Kirkland, Martin	6Mar1871	6 yrs on 29Aug1871	Oliver, Asa	
Taylor, Rufus	15Apr1871	6 yrs on 2July1871	Carter, William E.	Farming. Of color
Taylor, Dillar	15Apr1871	3 yrs in Dec1871	Carter, William E.	Housekeeping. Of color
McWhorter, G. W.	28Apr1871	11 yrs on 4Nov1871	Johnson, A. B.	Farming
Grace, Wesley	10Aug1871	11 yrs on 1Sept1871	Bonner, Jack	Farming. Of color. Rebound with new surety
Oaks, William Henry	12Oct1871	7 yrs on 30Apr1871	Becket, William M.	Farming
Pigg, William	6Nov1871	6 yrs on 13Oct1871	Turney, J. B.	Farming
Pamplin, James	22Nov1871	13 yrs on 23Nov1871	Badget, J. R.	Farming. Of color
Pamplin, Niel	23Nov1871	10 yrs on 23Nov1871	Ship, H. N. F.	Farming. Of color
Pamplin, Sharper	25Nov1871	5 yrs on 25Nov1871	Newman, J. M.	Farming. Of color
Gracy, Francis	14Dec1871	9 yrs on 1July1871	Bonner, Jack	Housekeeping. Of color. New surety
Gracy, Wesly	14Dec1871	11 yrs on 1Sept1871	Bonner, Jack	Farming. Of color. Rebound with new surety
Neal, Archabald	12Jan1872	12 yrs on 1Sept1871	McDonald, Anna	Farming. Of color
Cleavland, Mary S. J.	4Apr1872	8 yrs on 4Apr1872	Beavers, W. S.	Housekeeping
Fannie	23Apr1872	8 yrs on 1June1872	Allen, Mary C.	Housekeeping. Of color. Record indexed as Fannie Stonebreaker
Hays, Senia	27Apr1872	10 yrs	Allen, John	Housekeeping. Of color
Denison, Willliam	6May1872	12 yrs on 28Mar1872	Sugg, F. J.	Farming
Cooley, Andy	19Aug1872	7 yrs on 1June1872	Street, J. G.	Farming. Of color
Cooley, Ed	19Aug1872	8 yrs on 1Dec1872	Blacknoll, George R.	Farming. Of color
Gracy, Fannie	12Nov1872	10 yrs on 7July1872	Bonner, Jack	Housekeeping. Of color
Gracy, Wesly	12Nov1872	11 yrs on 1Sept1872	Bonner, Jack	Farming. Of color
Hankins, Ann	8Feb1873	8 yrs in April 1873	Hatcher, John W.	Housekeeping. Of color

Name	Age	Master	Notes
Sanders, James	11yrs on 19Sept1873	Beavers, W. S.	Farming
Goodrich, Charles	6 yrs	Stegall, E. B.	Farming. Of color
Sanders, David H.	8 yrs on 4Mar1873	Wells, Mary A.	Until 18 yrs. Farming. Cancelled 6Aug1877. Wells dead
Edmondson, Polley Ann	Abt 11 yrs	Edmondson, Maggie (Miss)	House keeping. Of color
Rosebrough, W. H.	15 yrs on 15May1875	Bostick, A. C.	Farming. White
Jones, Merrett	12 yrs in Sept1875	Landess, B.	Brick making. Of color
Thurman, Jasper	7 yrs in July1876	Holman, J. W.	Over objections of mother, Lucinda Thurman. Farming. White
Clem, George M.	10 yrs on 23Oct1876	Smith, J. F.	Farming. White
Clem, Jasper N.	13yrs on 21Sept1876	Smith, L. H.	Farming. White
Reese, Mansfield Andrew Jackson	12 ys	Little, Samuel	Farming. White
Sanders, David H.	14 yrs in March 1877	Harris, Theodore	Orphan. Farming. White
Bearden, Andrew	16 yrs on 1July1878	Jenkins, N. M.	Farming. Of color
Small, Henry	12 yrs in August1878	Small, H. P.	Farming. Of color
Unnamed male	7 yrs in March 1878	Rowell, J. T.	Farming. Of color
Oak, John	12 ys	Brady, Daniel J.	Farming. White
Pryor, Elvisa	8 yrs in April 1881	Pryor, Anna	Household affairs. Of color

Marshall County

Name	Date	Age	Master	Notes
Woody, E. J.	6Feb1837		Cleek, James	Taken from index of minutes
Winsett, N. G.	6Feb1837		Cleek, James	Taken from index of minutes

117

Name	Date	Age	Master	Notes
Park, James A.	6Mar1837	5 yrs	Harris, James	Orphan
Park, William M.	6Mar1837	4 yrs	Harris, James	Orphan
Collins, Nancy	5June1837	10 yrs	Ramsey, Samuel	Orphan
Winsett, James W.	7Aug1837	15 yrs	Cummings, Thomas	Blacksmith
Sanders, Dicey	2Oct1837	11 yrs	Bigger, James	
Selph, Martha E.	6Nov1837		Hedley, Noah	
Selph, David	6Nov1837		Hedley, Noah	
Mays, John	6Nov1837	7 yrs	William, Esq, Peter	
Springer, James	4Dec1837	9 yrs	Davis, William	
Arnold, William	1Jan1838	15 yrs	Davis, Joseph	
Wolf, William	1Jan1838	15 yrs	Dryden, Robert M.	
Logan, David M.	5Mar1838		Cummings, Thomas	
Selph, Martha E.	2Apr1838	7 yrs	Irwin, John R.	
Selph, David	2Apr1838	4 yrs	Irwin, John R.	
Wolf, Charles H.	1Oct1838		Dryden, Robert	Orphan
Reed, James	5Nov1838	13 yrs	Park, James P.	Orphan
Dalton, Isom	1Apr1839	12 yrs	Weaver, John	
McIntyre, Jane E.	7Oct1839		Orr, John	
Archey, Hosea	7Oct1839	11 yrs	McDowell, Gideon	Cancelled 4Jan1842
McIntye, Benjamin F.	7Oct1839	7 yrs	Cumming, Eunen	
Parrish, Mary K.	7Apr1840	11 yrs	Gibson, Joseph N.	
Parrish, Garland	7Apr1840	8 yrs	Parrish, Eaton	
May, Nancy	6Oct1840	8 yrs	Gideon, Daniel	Prob child of Cyntha Mays 6Apr1840
Mays, David	6Oct1840	8 yrs	Swan, Alexander H.	Prob child of Cyntha Mays 6Apr1840
Archer, Hosea	4Jan1842	13 yrs	Fisher, William D.	
Pickens, Margaret E.	4July1842	9 yrs	Calvert, William	Orphan
Pickens, Ann J.	4July1842	11 yrs	Hudson, Young M.	Orphan
Pickens, Mary E.	4July1842	7 yrs	Hudson, Young M.	Orphan

Name	Date	Age	Bondsman	Notes
London, Joseph W.	4July1842	10 yrs	London, Amos	Orphan
Wood, William	5July1842	14 yrs	Thomason, George W.	Orphan
Self, David H.	2Jan1843	9 yrs	Coffer, Allen	Orphan
Dowd, Cornelious J.	3July1843	10 yrs	Jackson, Isaac P.	
Dowd, Charles P.	3July1843	16 yrs	Hart, Joel	
Fox, Margaret	3July1843	10 yrs	Davis, Samuel	On 5Jan1852 bond cancelled. Margaret now 18 yrs
Mayes, David	3July1843		Collins, John	
Mays, Nancy	3July1843		Collins, John	
Alford, John	2Oct1843	10 yrs	Coldwell, John	
May, Thomas	4Nov1844	15 yrs in Feb next	McCaslin, Branson	Orphan
Phillips, Charles	6Jan1845	16 yrs	Burgess, Willis	
Wright, Joel G.	7Jan1845	13 yrs	Wiiie, Robert	
Archy, Hosea	7Jan1845		Hill, William B.	
May, David	8Apr1845		Fisher, William D.	
May, Nancy	8Apr1845		Thompson, Aaron	Until 21 yrs
Herrald, James W.	7July1845	12 yrs	Steel, John	
May, David	8July1845		Foysett, David	Until 21 yrs
Fry, Susan	8July1845		Wilks, Josiah	
Alvis, George	6Apr1846	14 yrs	Lee, John L.	Orphan
May, William Thomas	6July1846	16 yrs	Roand, Henry	Orphan
Tyree, Susan	7July1846	14 yrs	Hill, John	Spinster. Until 21 yrs
May, David	7July1846	Abt 13 yrs	Hughes, William	
Cook, Sarah	5July1847	8 yrs	Hawkins, John	Orphan of John Cook, Dcd 1Nov1847*
Hearld, James	5July1847	14 yrs	Smith, Andrew	
Walker, Brooks	3July1848	3 yrs	Perry, Keeble	Orphan
Luna, Joseph	3July1848	10 or 11 yrs	Landess, H. H.	Orphan
Walker, Doctor Gitton	3July1848	6 yrs	Wysong, Andrew J.	Orphan
Cooper, Mainlins	6Nov1848	12 yrs	Baumman, John B.	Yellow boy. Tanning
Cook, Sarah	6Aug1849	Abt 11 yrs	Hawkins, John D.	Dau of John Cook, Dcd
Knowis, Isaac	7Oct1850	13 yrs	Barns, William	Orphan. Farming
Knowis, David	7Oct1850		Lillard, John J.	Orphan

Name	Date	Age	Master	Notes
Cook, Sarah	4Nov1850		Morris, James L.	Orphan
Gant, William M.	6Oct1851	10 yrs	Nichols, Joshua	Orphan
Parnell, Archibald	5Apr1852		Harris, John J.	Farming
Gant, Jackson	5Apr1852		Brawly, Gaston	Farming
Parnell, Archibald	5Apr1853	14 yrs	Kerr, Willis A.	Orphan. Saddler
Banks, Elijah	3Oct1853		Bethune, Elzathun	Of color
Bugg, Joseph D.	8Aug1854		Chadwell, James B.	Harness making
Banks, Elijah	3Apr1855		Burthoon, Betsy	Of color
Shurpt, William Thomas	2July1855	Abt 4 yrs	Stallions, Ezekial	
Banks, Alfred	3Mar1856		Finley, John E.	Of color
Tucker, Franklin	7Apr1856	13 yrs on 26Oct1855	Lee, J. L.	Of color. Cavinet workman
Little, Augustine	6July1857	Abt 11 yrs	Moore, William G.	Orphan. Farmer. Heir of Zachariah Little, Dcd. Sibs George, Francis, Lydia & James ordered brought to court
Boliver, Emmit	4Jan1858	Abt 11 yrs last Oct	Wilkes, Edward H.	Of color. Blacksmith
Mantlow, James W.	5Apr1858	13 yrs 11 mo	Kirkland, James	Orphan
Hill, James	4Oct1858	14 yrs	Luna, Wright	Orphan. Farming
Bugg, James C.	4Jan1859	8 yrs on 1Jan1859	Garrett, Elisha	Orphan. Farmer. Consent of mother, Louisa Bugg
Shephard, L. D.	2May1859	Abt 9 yrs	Wilson, Edward E.	Farmer
Bugg, John B.	7Nov1859		Ewing, James D.	Farmer. Son of William Bugg, Dcd, consent of mother. Age 21yrs in 1866 8Apr1867*
Little, James	3Dec1860	Abt 12 yrs	Weaver, Thomas	Orphan
Morris, Joseph	7Jan1861	9 ys	Perry, Richard B.	Orphan. Farmer
Little, Thomas M.	4Mar1861	6 yrs on 11Aug next	Brown, Basil	Orphan. Farmer. Canc 2Dec1872
Pearce, John D.	2Sept1861	Abt 12 yrs	Hay, Jeremiah	Orphan
Harriet Louisa	3July1865	10 yrs	Hardison, Thomas	Of color. Orphan. Housekeeper & spinster
James	7Aug1865	6 yrs	Moore, Thomas D.	Of color
Williams, Callie	4Dec1865	9 yrs	Waters, Josiah N.	Of color
Phillips, Monroe	4Dec1865	27May1851	Phillips, Horatia M.	Of color. Canc 6Nov1871* Master Dcd. Monroe gone

Name	Date	Age/Birth	Owner	Remarks
Phillips, Thomas	4Dec1865	15Nov1852	Phillips, Horatia M.	Of color. Canc 6Nov1871* Master Dcd. Thomas gone
Phillips, Joseph	4Dec1865	18Mar1854	Phillips, Horatia M.	Of color. Canc 6Nov1871* Master dead
Phillips, Hannah	4Dec1865	2Oct1856	Phillips, Horatia M.	Of color. Canc 6Nov1871* Master dead
Phillips, Giles	4Dec1865	5Apr1858	Phillips, Horatia M.	Of color. Canc 6Nov1871* Master dead
Phillips, Harriett	4Dec1865	10July1859	Phillips, Horatia M.	Of color. Canc 6Nov1871* Master dead
Phillips, Samuel	4Dec1865	27May1861	Phillips, Horatia M.	Of color. Canc 6Nov1871* Master dead
Phillips, Alice	4Dec1865	10July1862	Phillips, Horatia M.	Of color. Canc 6Nov1871* Master dead
Collins, Washington	2Jan1866	14 yrs on 1Jan1866	Edwards, Andrew J.	Of color
Collins, Sylvia	2Jan1866	12 yrs on 1Jan1866	Phillips, Horatia M.	Of color
Collins, Ben	2Jan1866	10 yrs on 1Jan1866	Phillips, Horatia M.	Of color
Collins, Elizabeth	2Jan1866	5 yrs on 1Mar1865	Phillips, Horatia M.	Of color
Collins, Disa	2Jan1866	3 yrs on 15Nov1865	Phillips, Horatia M.	Of color
Collins, Charles	2Jan1866	2 yrs on 7Apr1865	Phillips, Horatia M.	Of color
Bowdon, Van	2Jan1866		Bowdon, T. N.	Of color
Davis, Georgia	13Jan1866	11 yrs on 13Jan1866	Davis, N. S.	Of color. Male
Hutton, Elijah	5Feb1866	8 yrs	Hutton, J. W.	Of color
McRady, Napoleon	5Feb1866	8 yrs in Feb1866	McRady, Joseph A.	Of color
McRady, Ann	5Feb1866	8 yrs in Feb1866	McRady, Joseph A.	Of color
Johnson, Charles	5Feb1866	8 yrs	Johnson, J. T.	Of color
Johnson, William	5Feb1866	4 yrs	Johnson, J. T.	Of color
Meadows, Robert	5Feb1866	9 yrs next Dec	Meadows, Solomon	Of color. Unhealthy
Meadows, Jennie	5Feb1866	7 yrs next Aug	Meadows, Solomon	Of color
Hayes, Valentine O.	5Mar1866		Hoyle, Peter	Farming
Evans, Tennessee	9Apr1866	12 yrs on 29Mar1866	Evans, John A.	Of color
Jim	7May1866	10 yrs	Duncan, W. M.	Of color
Felix	7May1866	11 yrs	Duncan, W. M.	Of color
Charles	12May1866	13 yrs	Adams, Robert L.	Of color. Consent of Charles
Wilson, John	4June1866	10Mar1855	Wilson, E. E.	Of color
Wilson, Nelson	4June1866	10Mar1857	Wilson, E. E.	Of color

Name	Date	Age	Master	Notes
Wilson, George	4June1866	10Feb1862	Wilson, E. E.	Of color
London, Martha	2July1866	11 yrs	London, John	Of color. On 1Feb1869 released to reputed father, Jerry Duncan
London, Albert	2July1866	5 yrs	London, John	Of color. Annulled 5June1871, John London dead
Oakley, Susanna	6Aug1866	4 yrs	Oakley, Elizabeth M.	Of color
Oakley, John	6Aug1866	Abt 6 yrs	Oakley, Elizabeth M.	Of color
Stone, Bose	3Sept1866	7 yrs	Stone, Wiley F.	Of color. Orphan. Farmer
Stone, Ellick	3Sept1866	9 yrs	Stone, Wiley F.	Of color. Orphan. Farmer
Hardison, George	1Oct1866	9 yrs on 10June1866	Gray, J. S.	Of color
Stone, Sarah	1Oct1866	10 yrs on 1Oct1866	Stone, W. R.	Of color
Stone, Ange	1Oct1866	8 yrs on 1Oct1866	Stone, W. R.	Of color
Rainey, Kitty	1Oct1866	10 yrs on 1Oct1866	Rainey, Stephen W.	Of color
Rainey, Caroline	1Oct1866	8 yrs on 1Oct1866	Rainey, Stephen W.	Of color
Liggett, Dennis	5Nov1866	10 yrs on 15June1866	Liggett, William A.	Of color. Cancelled 10Jan1867*
Hill, female	5Nov1866	7 yrs on 10Apr1866	Hill, John R.	Of color
Unnamed female	3Dec1866		Finley, James	Of color
Williams, Sarah	12Dec1866	12 yrs on 12Dec1866	Bowdon, Thomas N.	Of color. Cancelled 27Dec1866. Appealed
McClure, Emma	27Dec1866	12 yrs on 15May1866	McClure, Robert G.	Of color
McClure, Sallie	27Dec1866	10 yrs on 10Aug1866	McClure, Robert G.	Of color
McClure, Franklin	27Dec1866	8 yrs on 15Mar1867	McClure, Robert G.	Of color
Williams, Sack [Sarah]	27Dec1866	13yrs on 10June last	Ewing, James S.	Of color
Ewing, William	7Jan1867	15 yrs on 7Jan1867	Ewing, R. C.	Of color
Ewing, Finus	7Jan1867	13 yrs on 7Jan1867.	Ewing, R. C.	Of color
Ewing, Aaron	7Jan1867	10 yrs on 7Jan1867	Ewing, R. C.	Of color

Name	Date	Age	Guardian	Notes
Ewing, Calvin	7Jan1867	7 yrs on 7Jan1867	Ewing, R. C.	Of color
Ewing, John	7Jan1867	4 yrs on 7Jan1867	Ewing, R. C.	Of color
Liggett, Jim	7Jan1867	9 yrs on 15Dec1866	Cundiff, J. C.	Of color
Williams, Mittie	10Jan1867	6 yrs on 10Jan1867	West, Esq, Moses C.	Of color
Welch, James	10Jan1867	13 yrs on 21Aug1866	Welch, James W.	
Welch, David	10Jan1867	11yrs on 11June1866	Welch, James W.	
Welch, John	10Jan1867	9 yrs on 20Mar1866	Welch, James W.	
Welch, Nathanial	10Jan1867	7 yrs on 1Aug1866	Welch, James W.	
Welch, Lucy	10Jan1867	15yrs on 11June1866	Welch, James W.	
Hunter, Matilda	4Feb1867	7 yrs on 25Dec1866	Hunter, E. W.	Of color. Consent of mother
Hunter, June	4Feb1867	5 yrs on 26Aug1867	Hunter, E. W.	Of color. Consent of mother
Caruthers, Edney	6May1867	10 yrs on 15Mar1867	Murrey, Thomas A.	Of color
Caruthers, Elizabeth	6May1867	7 yrs on 20Aug1867	Murrey, James J.	Of color
Orman, Lucy	1July1867	14 yrs on 1July1867	Orman, Sarah F. (Mrs)	Of color
Hughs, Jessee	7Oct1867		Larue, John W.	Of color. On 6Feb1868 Angeline Towler asks for son's return. Denied 2Mar1868
Thompson, Burrel	7Oct1867	14 yrs on 7Oct1867	Thompson, Ewing D.	Of color
Lavender, William	8Oct1867	10 yrs on 8Oct1867	Cock, Jurrett	Of color
Isaac A.	4Nov1867		Carpenter, John & Martha E.	All of color
Jonathan A.	4Nov1867		Carpenter, John & Martha E.	All of color
Sarah C.	4Nov1867		Carpenter, John & Martha E.	All of color
Boyd, Samuel	2Dec1867	10 yrs on 2Dec1867	Boyett, J. B.	Of color
Harris, John	3Feb1868	6 yrs on 3Feb1868	Harris, William L.	Of color

Name	Date	Age	Master	Notes
Bryant, Jefferson N.	3Feb1868	14 yrs on 15Jun1868	Rone, George W.	Consent of Bryant
Moore, Eileck	2Mar1868		Fitzpatrick, S. W.	Of color. Farmer
Buchannan, Charley	6July1868	6Apr1862	Buchannan, William	Of color. Has the scrofula badly
Buchannan, John	6July1868	1May1860	Buchannan, William	Of color. Very weakly boy
Buchannan, Ruth	6July1868	3Aug1858	Buchannan, William	Of color. Stout girl
Pickins, Nannie	7Dec1868	10 yrs on 24July1867	Pickins, David B.	Of color
Ewing, Calvin	4Jan1869	9 yrs on 4Jan1869	Ewing, James V.	Of color
Ewing, John	4Jan1869	6 yrs on 4Jan1869	Ewing, James V.	Of color
Yowell, Henry	5Apr1869	5 yrs on 20Mar1869	Yowell, William R.	Pauper. Of color. On 15Apr1869 Green Medaris & Henry Yowell ask the bond be cancelled. Denied. Appealed to Circuit Court
Ogilvie, Dnira	14Oct1869	12 yrs on 1Oct1869	Wilson, Abram	Both of color
Buchanan, Hattie	7Dec1869	9May1865	Buchannan, William	Of color. Mother never married, now dead
Buchanan, Bud	7Dec1869	30July1867	Buchannan, William	Of color. Mother never married, now dead
Lancaster, Cinda	7Feb1870	15Jan1865	Leonard, John M.	Of color. Bond rejected, proper notice not given
Boaz, Tennessee M.	4Apr1870	4 yrs on 4Apr1870	Evans, John A.	Female
Noblett, John	5Sept1870	14 yrs 6 mo	Foster, G. W.	
Noblet, Jacob	13Sept1870	6 yrs on 18Nov1870	Ewing, Samuel D. (Dr)	Pauper from poor farm 5Sept1870. Canc 4Nov1872
Noblet, Jimmie	13Sept1870	4 yrs on 6July1871	Chump, John W.	Pauper from poor farm 5Sept1870
Shurron, Albert L.	4Oct1870	5 yrs on 4Jan1870	Russell, Martha E. N. (Miss)	Of color. Pauper
Lancaster, Lucinda	4Oct1870	6 yrs on 10Apr1870	Leonard, John M.	Of color
Noblett, James	11Oct1870	4 yrs on 6July1870	Peacock, Sarah (Mrs)	Of color. Pauper
Rives, Robert	11Oct1870	5 yrs	Collins, James W.	Of color?
Enasly, Finis	6Feb1871	10 yrs on 15Mar1870	McGahey, Alfred	Of color. Pauper
Williams, Louisa Allice	6Mar1871	10 yrs this day	Collins, Elisha	Of color. Pauper 6Feb1871

Name	Date	Term	Name	Notes
London, Albert	5June1871	10 yrs on 5June1871	London, Enoch	Of color
Bryant, Susan	6Nov1871	12 yrs in Aug1871	Bryant, Alexander	Of color
Bryant, Robert	6Nov1871	10 yrs in Aug1871	Bryant, Alexander	Of color
Crutcher, Mack	6Nov1871	9 yrs on 1Sept1871	Wilkinson, Mack	Of color
Phillips, Jo [Joseph]	6Nov1871	17 yrs on 13Mar1871	Phillips, W. R.	Of color
Phillips, Giles	6Nov1871	12 yrs on 5Apr1871	Phillips, W. R.	Of color
Phillips, Hannah	6Nov1871	15 yrs on 2 Oct1871	Phillips, W. R.	Of color
Phillips, Samuel	6Nov1871	10 yrs on 5May1871	Phillips, Robert L.	Of color
Phillips, Harriet	6Nov1871	12 yrs on 10July1871	McCanless, S. H.	Of color
Phillips, Alice	6Nov1871	9 yrs on 3July1871	Hill, J. H.	Of color
Scisco, John L.	2Jan1872	9 yrs on 24Mar1872	Hopper, H. H.	
Scisco, Nancy P.	2Jan1872		Hopper, H. H.	
Scisco, James W.	2Jan1872		Hutton, Thomas C.	
Power, William Edward	4Mar1872	Abt 15 yrs	Taylor, William M.	
Power, James L.	4Mar1872	12 yrs	Taylor, William M.	
Oneal, John M.	4Mar1872	16 yrs on 18Dec1871	Oneal, M. T.	Of color
Hardison, Andy	6May1872	7 yrs on 1Apr1872	McLean, Samuel	Of color
Noblin, Jacob	4Nov1872	8 yrs on 18Nov1872	Duncan, Abb M.	Aka Jacob Noblett & Jacob Nobless. Canc
Harris, Albert	4Nov1872	9 yrs on 15Oct1872	Harris, Sr, Hiram	Of color
Little, Thomas M.	2Dec1872		McClary, Allen L.	Prior indenture to Basil Brown cancelled
Moon, Jim	8Jan1873	12 yrs on 25Dec1872	Ezell, James Bal	Of color
Jackson, Ellen	3Feb1873		Blackwell, A. J.	
Noblett, Jacob	8Apr1873		Boyett, Jessee	Canc 10Apr1874
Hunter, Clementine	12Aug1873		Hunter, Maggie	Of color
Hunter, Charly	2Sept1873	9 yrs on 10Oct1872	Hunter, James B.	Of color

Name	Date	Age	Master	Notes
Hunter, William H.	2Sept1873	6 yrs on 18Sept1873	Hunter, James B.	Of color
Woods, Mary	2Sept1873	10 yrs on 1Oct1872	Woods, F. B.	Of color
Florence, Lydia	3Nov1873	9 yrs on 15Mar1873	Moore, James B.	
Brecheen, Kirk	3Nov1873	9 yrs on 1Jan1874	Collins, William F.	Of color. Given to Collins by Kirk's mother on her death bed, according to G. B. & Mary Dysart
Edwards, Arthur	3Nov1873	4 yrs on 15Oct1873	Davis, Amos C.	
McLean, Winnie	19Jan1874	10 yrs on 19Jan1874	McLean, Olmstead	Both of color
Vaughn, Thomas	2Feb1874	12 yrs on 2Feb1874	Brown, James W.	Of color
Riner,	2Mar1874	7 yrs on 1Feb1874	Hall, W. W.	Male. Consent of mother
Riner, William N.	2Mar1874	12 yrs on 12May1873	Davis, Sam	Consent on mother
Parks, Thomas	2Mar1874	12 yrs on 2Mar1874	Fields, R. E.	
Orr, John	2Mar1874	11 yrs on 1Sept1873	Bell, James W.	Of color
Moore, Nathan	2Mar1874	10 yrs on 2Mar1874	Gill, Jo J. S.	Of color. Mother of unsound mind
Noblett, Jacob	10Apr1874	6 yrs on 18Nov1870	Leonard, John	
Street, James	14Apr1874	9 yrs on 5June1874	Taylor, James M.	Of color
Street, William	14Apr1874	4 yrs on 6June1874	Taylor, James M.	Of color
Cunnigham, Mariah	7July1874		Leonard, John	Of color. Consent of mother, Lucy Cunnigham
Nunley, Francis M.	7June1875	14 yrs on 2Dec1875	Fox, M. A.	Rescinded on 5Sep1876, complaint of mother, Delilah Nunley
Bryant, Jim	2Aug1875	12 yrs	Bryant, J. W.	Of color
Cook, Lucy	3Nov1875	6 yrs	Long, James J.	Of color
Hinson, Warren	6Nov1875	13 yrs	Rone, George W.	
Nix, Edward	7Feb1876	5 yrs in June1876	Cowden, N. W.	
Holt, Nancy	5June1876	8 yrs in Feb1876	Ezell, Hugh F.	Of color. Request of mother before her death, says Amanda Holt. Consent of child

Name	Date	Age	Master	Notes
Bowden, Oscar	4July1876	5 yrs	Armstrong, J. B.	Of color
Clevenger, George	14Aug1876	11 yrs	Fox, Anderson	Of color
London, Abner	5Feb1877	Abt 16 yrs	Bryant, M. R.	Of color
Cunningham, Jimmie	5Mar1877	4 yrs in Dec last	Prosser, W. A.	Female
Jones, William	3Mar1880	4 yrs in May1880	Allen, George H.	Of color
Childs, Nettie	5Sept1881	7 yrs in March1881	Richey, Frank	Both of color
Childs, Carrie Ann	5Sept1881	9 yrs	Richey, Frank	Both of color
Crutcher, William	3Nov1884		Wilson, E. E.	Orphan of Mat. Crutcher, Dcd
Crutcher, Oliver	3Nov1884		Wilson, E. E.	Orphan of Mat. Crutcher, Dcd
Crutcher, John	3Nov1884		Wilson, E. E.	Orphan of Mat. Crutcher, Dcd
Crutcher, James P.	3Nov1884		Wilson, E. E.	Orphan of Mat. Crutcher, Dcd
Crutcher, Annie	3Nov1884		Wilson, E. E.	Orphan of Mat. Crutcher, Dcd
Green, Liphus	14Dec1886		Crutcher, R. P.	Minor heir of Liphus Green, Dcd. Both parents deceased
Green, Lena	14Dec1886		Crutcher, R. P.	Minor heir of Liphus Green, Dcd. Both parents deceased
Green, Arthur	14Dec1886		Crutcher, R. P.	Minor heir of Liphus Green, Dcd. Both parents deceased
Green, Cassie	14Dec1886		Crutcher, R. P.	Minor heir of Liphus Green, Dcd. Both parents deceased
Green, Balaam	14Dec1886		Crutcher, R. P.	Minor heir of Liphus Green, Dcd. Both parents deceased
Green, Garfield	14Dec1886		Crutcher, R. P.	Minor heir of Liphus Green, Dcd. Both parents deceased

Maury County

Name	Date	Age	Master	Notes
Harrison, Henry B.	21Dec1809	16 yrs	Orr, Joshua	
Farrisseque, Sally	3Mar1810	13 yrs	Campbell, William	Knit & sew
Vought, Stephen	21June1810	8 yrs on 2Sept	Voorheiz, William & Peter	Sadler
Vought, Nathan	21June1810	10 yrs on 13Aug last	Pursell, James	Cabinet maker
Robinson, Benjamin	17Sept1811	3 yrs 6 mo	Davis, Micajah C.	Orphan. Blacksmith
Buckham, Dolly	21Sept1812		Rutledge, James	
Russell, John H.	21Sept1812		Dickey, George M.	Maltreatment alleged by Richard Russell 24Feb1815. Disallowed 15May1815
Forni, Thomas	22Dec1812		Beaty, James	For four years. Carpenter

Name	Date	Age	Master	Notes
McCain, Archibald McCorcle	21Sept1813	3 yrs 6 mo	Kenedy, John	Orphan
Graden, Alexander	21Sept1813	4 yrs	Long, William C.	Orphan. 21Dec1813*
Dorrell, Rebecca	23Sept1813	12 yrs	Elliott, John P.	Orphan
Dorrell, Elizabeth	23Sept1813	10 yrs	Jones, Samuel	Orphan
Thompson, David Smith	20Dec1813	5 yrs on 5Nov1813	Chapilier, Samuel	Until 20 yrs. Orphan. Shop joiner
Clardy, Benjamin	22Feb1814	Abt 14 or 15 yrs	Uzzell, Elisha	Orphan
Hays, Andrew C.	25Feb1814	Bet 14 & 15 yrs	Walker, James	Orphan. Until 20 yrs
Hays, D. Augustin C.	25Feb1814	12 yrs	Walker, James	Orphan. Until 20 yrs
Gardner, Harriet	17May1814	10 yrs	Neeley, Andrew	Until 21 yrs. Orphan. Housewifery
Russell, William	20May1814	11 yrs 6 mo	Pearcell, James	House carpenter
Walbridge, Porter	26Nov1814	15 yrs on 9Mar1814	Uzzell, Elisha	Orphan. Hatter
Allington, Thomas	20Feb1815	4 1/2 yrs	Garrard, Thomas	Orphan. Stonemason
Berryman, Samuel	15May1815	2 yrs	Chun, William	Orphan. Farmer
Duffil, John	22Aug1815	6 yrs on 17Feb1815	Russell, David	Orphan. Farmer
Mitchell, Clary	19Feb1816	11 yrs	Hardin, Swan	Farming
Mitchell, Peter	19Feb1816	4 yrs	Hardin, Swan	Farming. Canc 21Jan1828* Of color?
Mitchell, Lucy	19Feb1816	2 yrs	Hardin, Swan	Spinning. Until 21 yrs
Kinamore, Isaiah	20Feb1816		Wallace, William	House carpenter
Russell, William S.	22Feb1816		McKnight, Samuel B.	Sadler
Napier, Mary Smith	20May1816		Smith, Benjamin	
Napier, Samuel Shelton	20May1816		Smith, Benjamin	
Lumpkin, George	20May1816	Going on 13 yrs	Wallace, William	Orphan. House carpenter. Resc 25May1816. On 27May1816. Wallace apppt'd guardian
Lumpkins, John Moore	20May1816	10 yrs	Pearsell, James	Orphan. House carpenter. Rescinded 25May1816. On 27May1816 William Wallace appointed guardian
Lumpkin, George	25May1816		Pearsell, James	House carpenter
Lunpkin, John	25May1816		Pearsell, James	House carpenter
Hodge, John	19Aug1816	14 yrs	Thompson, Benjamin	Sadler
Hoge, James	21Aug1816	9 yrs on 13Nov next	Wallace, William	House carpenter

Name	Date	Age	Master	Occupation / Notes
Hoge, Miles	21Aug1816	7 yrs on 25Dec last	Wallace, William	House carpenter
Hoge, George	21Aug1816		Persell, James	House carpenter
Hoge, James	18Feb1817		Jarcy, James	
Holt, William	20Feb1817		Taylor, James	Shoemaker
Modgelin, Elijah	20Feb1817		Patterson, Luke	Blacksmith
Skelly, Sparkman	20May1817		Duckworth, John	Farmer. Cancelled 18Aug1817
Skelly, Samuel	20May1817		Duckworth, John	Farmer. Cancelled 18Aug1817
Smith, Berryman	21May1817		Turner, Buford	Taylor
Rice, Jr, Ebenezer	18Aug1817		Rice, Sr, Ebenezer	Farmer
White, Rueben	21Aug1817		McIntire, Duncan	Taylor. Cancelled 16Apr1821
Johnson, Joseph	22Aug1817		Voorhies, William	Saddler. Cancelled 21July1823, as Joseph Johnston
Holt, William	22Aug1817		Holt, Edmund	Shoemaker
Nappier, James C.	21Nov1817	Abt 12 yrs	Smith, James N.	Orphan. Farmer
Nappier, John S.	21Nov1817	Abt 10 yrs	Smith, James N.	Orphan. Farmer
Hunter, Terrel	26Jan1818		Vorhies, P. J.	Saddler
Muse, Mary Ann	26Jan1818	9 ys last June	Mack, John (Esq)	Base begotton child of Kuncy? Muse 12Jan1818
Muse, Henry G.	26Jan1818	7 yrs last June	Purnel, James	House carpenter. Prob son of Kuncy Muse 12Jan1818
Muse, Betsy Ann Polin?	26Jan1818	4 yrs last July	Rush, Andrew	Base begotton child of Kuncy? Muse 12Jan1818
Lee, James Madison	26Jan1818		White, George	Orphan. Saddler
Mayberry, David	26Jan1818	14 yrs	Isham, Arthur F.	Orphan. Farming
Kaen, William	20Apr1818		Wilkins, James	Orphan. Silversmith. Canc 30Oct1822, as McKean
Churchwell, William	20July1818	8 yrs	Helm, Merideth	Orphan. Tanner & curryer
Graden, James	27July1818	10 yrs	Beaty, John	Orphan. Cabbinet workman
Ray, Robert	19Oct1818	14 yrs on 4June past	Lamaster, John W.	Blacksmith
Ray, Jesse	19Oct1818	13 yrs in june last	Lamaster, John W.	Blacksmith
Estis, Edwin C.	26Oct1818		Hodge, John	Bound by Buford & Sarah A. Turner
Russell, Robert	18Jan1819		Wilkes, Minor	Saddler. Cancelled 21Oct1822
Hardy, David	19Apr1819		Pickens, Matthew G.	Stone mason. Cancelled 15Oct1821. Pickens moving away
Richardson, Samuel	19Apr1819	10 yrs	Huston, Samuel	Farmer
Walker, James	19Apr1819	Abt 17 yrs	McCord, Alison	Wheelwright

Name	Date	Age	Master	Notes
Hardy, William Nixon?	19Apr1819		Bills, Jonathan D.	Farmer
Rily, John	26Apr1819		Dillon, Charles R.	Painter
Churchwell, Messer?	25Oct1819	13 yrs	Helm, Meredith	Tanner & currier
Richardson, Wiley	25Oct1819	13 yrs on 13Sept last	Dickey, George	Orphan. House carpenter
Shelton, Washington	24Jan1820	Abt 9 yrs	Voorhies, William	Sadler. Cancelled 17Apr1827
Hodge, James	24Jan1820	Abt 7 yrs	Sandford, James T.	Farmer. Cancelled 24Apr1820
Hodge, James	24Apr1820		Renfro, William	Farmer
Henderson, George Washington	24Apr1820		Drake, Edward	Farmer
Kelsey, Samuel A. P.	15Jan1821		Gill, John	For three years. Blacksmith
Choat, Thompson	22Jan1821		Campbell, William	Cancelled 15Apr1822
Graham, Green	16Apr1821		Walker, John	Cabinet workman
Woolard, Henry	23Apr1821		Mitchell, John	Cooper
Woolard, Alfred	23July1821		Woolard, Silas	Shoemaker
Woolard, Noah	23July1821		Woolard, Nathaniel	Shoemaker
Hardy, David W.	15Oct1821		Bills, Jonathan D.	Farming
Hammocks, Daniel	15Oct1821		Davis, James	Farmer
King, Terry	?		Wilkins, James	Cancelled 15Oct1821
Nancy	22Oct1821		Neely, Andrew	
Fey	22Oct1821		Neely, Andrew	
Jim	22Oct1821		Neely, Andrew	
Dick	22Oct1821		Neely, Andrew	
Jane	22Oct1821		Neely, Andrew	
Unnamed child	22Oct1821		Neely, Andrew	
Jacobs, Joseph	21Jan1822		Ackins, William	Farmer
Scott, James Newton	15Apr1822		White, George	Sadler. Cancelled 26July1824
Russell, Robert	21Oct1822		Stone, Thomas	
Brinkley, Weslly H.	28Oct1822		Clark, Thomas D.	Shoemaker

Name	Date	Age	Master	Occupation / Notes
Vaught, Thornton	28Oct1822		Hart, Joseph	Tanning
McKain, William	28Oct1822		Voorhies, Peter J.	Saddler
Hoskins, Leonard	21Apr1823		McKewn?, John	House carpenter
Hudson, John	28Apr1823		Lowden, John	Saddler. Canc 23Oct1826
Chauves, Joseph	28Apr1823		Long, Nicholas J.	Farmer. Mulatto
Patterson, William	21July1823		Crawford, Alexander	Of color
Patterson, Betsy Caroline	21July1823		Crawford, Alexander	Of color
Bowen, Noraney	21July1823		Walker, Griffith	Cancelled, as Lora A. Bowen, 22Oct1827
Bowen, John	21July1823		Walker, James	Ordered returned to court 23Oct1826
McKissick, Alfred	28July1823	8 yrs on 17May last	McKissick, Robert	Orphan. Cooper
Scott, Richard	28July1823	14 yrs on 8Oct1822	Uzzell & Kirkpatrick	Orphan. Hatter
Binum, Mose Patterson	20Oct1823	16 yrs next March	Allison, B. B.	Taylor
Long, Anderson	27Oct1823		Johnston, Alexander	Farmer
Callihan, Polly	27Oct1823	Abt 5 yrs	Steele, John	Housewife
Callihan, Edward	27Oct1823		Millroy, John	
Callihan, Eleanor A.	27Oct1823		Millroy, John	
Smith, Benjamin	19Jan1824		Crafton, John B.	
Webb, Hopson	19Jan1824		Hart, Joseph	Tanner
Woolard, Henry	26Jan1824		Woolard, Silas	
Howard, Parminas	26Jan1824		Ward, Hezikiah	Carpenter
Radford, Jesse	19Apr1824		Candle, William	Farmer
Stewart, Sophia	26Apr1824	11 yrs 11 mo	Haynes, John S.	Orphan
Stewart, John	26Apr1824	14 yrs 8 mo	Webb, John	Orphan. Cabinet maker
Forsyth, John L.	19July1824	14 yrs on 1Jan1824	Kaskay, Robert	Orphan. Sadler
Forsyth, John L.	24July1824		Caskey, Robert	On 27July1829 Caskey ordered to send John to school 6 mo & stop service in saddling
Robison, John	26July1824	In 19th year	Smoot, John N.	Bound for 2 yrs 5 mo. Tanning & currying
Wilson, Andrew	26July1824	Abt 6 yrs	Good, David	Farmer
Robinson, John	26July1824	Abt 19 yrs	Smoot, John N.	Tanning
Green	26July1824	Abt 7 mo	Hooden?, S.	Farming. Of color
Alfred	26July1824	Abt 2 yrs	Hooden?, S.	Farming. Of color

Name	Date	Age	Master	Notes
Brown, William C.	?		Wilkins, James	Indenture (date?) cancelled 26July1824 on petition of James Brown
Forsyth, Green L.	18Oct1824	12 yrs	Murphy, Nathaniel G.	Orphan. Cabinet maker
Loving, Tennessee	25Oct1824	9 yrs	Smith, John	Orphan boy
Loving, Henry	25Oct1824		Loving, K. M.	
Loving, David	25Oct1824		Johnson, James W.	Cabinet maker
Smith, Caroline	25Oct1824	3 yrs	Yancy, William	Child of Winney Smith. Of color
Smith, June	25Oct1824	1 mo	Yancy, William	Child of Winney Smith. Of color
Smith, Betsy	25Oct1824	2 yrs	Yancy, William	Child of Sally Smith. Of color
Smith, Amy	25Oct1824	8 mo	Yancy, William	Child of Sally Smith. Of color
Smith, Selvey	25Oct1824	18 mo	Yancy, William	Child of Betty Smith. Of color. Canc 2Oct1837 & rebound under name Sylva
Radford, William	17Jan1825	Abt 13 yrs	Williams, Isaac H.	Orphan. Stonemason
Dickey, Alfred	17Jan1825	Abt 14 yrs	Johnson,	Orphan. Cabinet maker
America	23Apr1825		Chadwell, David	Of color. Canc 23Jan1826
Henry	23Apr1825		Chadwell, David	Of color. Canc 23Jan1826
Nancy	23Apr1825		Chadwell, David	Of color. Canc 23Jan1826
Erwin	23Apr1825		Chadwell, David	Of color. Canc 23Jan1826
Cranford, Jr., William	25Apr1825		Christopher, William	House carpenter. William Cranford Sr. a surety
Owen, William	18July1825	9 yrs on 20Dec last	Slauter, Francis	Gunsmith
Buck, Elijah	25July1825		Johnson, James W.	Cabinet maker
Haney, Jesse	25July1825	16 yrs in Nov1825	McMurry, Joseph	
Billy	25July1825	Abt 14 yrs	Hardin, Swan	Indian boy. Farmer
Lowder, Judy	17Oct1825	Abt 13 yrs	Record, Sherwood P.	Orphan. Spinster
Johnson, Churchwell	17Oct1825	15 yrs last March	Johnson, James W.	Cabinet maker
Harriet	24Apr1826		Chapel, Dick	Of color. Free or slave status unclear
Dickey, Alfred	24July1826		Eubanks, George	Ink smear obscures full names, age etc
Bucks, Elias	24July1826	19 yrs on 1April last	Eubanks, George	Orphan. Cabinet making
Smith, Salley	24July1826	18 yrs	Yancy, William	Of color. Order of Apr1825 entered this date

Name	Date	Age	Master	Notes
Smith, Betsy	24July1826	16 yrs	Yancy, William	Of color. Order of Apr1825 entered this date
Green, Williford	16Oct1826	14 yrs in June1826	Evans, Jessee U.	Orphan. Blacksmith. A prior (unrecorded?) indenture with William Lytle cancelled. Cancelled 15Jan1827
Hudson, John	23Oct1826	15 yrs in Apr1826	Knight, Carlisle W.	Tanning & currying. Orphan
Bugg, Jacob	23Oct1826	12 yrs	Gray, James	Orphan
Howard, Parminas	23Oct1826	Abt 17 yrs	Thomas, Phineas	Orphan
Wilson, Thomas	15Jan1827		Crowder, Nathaniel	
Smith, Williford Green	15Jan1827		Moore, Isaac	See Williford Green
Hudson, John	15Jan1827	Abt 15 or 16 yrs	Knight, Carlisle W.	Duplicate entry
Bowen, Lora A.	22Jan1827		Selsinger, Andrew	Selsinger her stepfather
Harris, Nathaniel	22Jan1827	15 yrs	White, James N.	Saddler
Loving, Henry	22Jan1827	8 yrs	Mack, John	Until age 16 yrs, then to be returned to court. Indenture completed?
Hudson, John	17Apr1827	Abt 16 yrs	Knight, C. W.	Farmer. Duplicate entry
Hardison, Alex	17Apr1827	Abt 10 yrs	Alexander, A. B.	Cabinet workman
Stewart, Andrew	17Apr1827		Ballifont, Joseph	Orphan. Formerly bound to David Love, now dead
Bigley, Thomas	17Apr1827	15 yrs	Eubanks, George	Cabbinett workman
Smith, Catherine	17Apr1827	Abt 1 yr last Xmas	Rodgers, Jacob	Of color. Dau of Sally Smith
Shelton, Washington	17Apr1827	Abt 16 yrs	Ketchum, Levy	Brickmason
Owens, Samuel	16July1827	9 yrs on 3Mar1827	Slaughter, Francis H.	Orphan. Gunsmith
Whortan, Andrew Jackson	16July1827		Webb, Gray P.	Taylor. Cancelled Oct1829*
Hodge, Gabriel L.	17July1827		Hill, J.	Bound by Sally Hodge
Deel, Wesley	17July1827	Abt 17 yrs	Alexander, A. B.	Cabinett workman
Muse, Abraham	21Jan1828	17 yrs	Shelton, L. R.	Tailor
Peter	28Jan1828	Abt 18 yrs	Helm, Meredith	Of color. Carpenter. Probably Peter Mitchell, formerly bound to S. Hardin. Canc Oct1828
Dial, Wyatt Hawkins	28Jan1828		Robinson, Bennett	
Dial, Mary M.	28Jan1828		Robinson, Bennett	
Willson, Benjamin	21July1828	Abt 14 ys	Johnson, Thomas P.	Orphan. Tanner & currier
Berryman, Allen	21Oct1828	Abt 14 yrs	McAdams, Samuel	Farmer
Sutton, Robert	21Oct1828	Abt 6 yrs	Mills, Gideon	

Name	Date	Age	Master	Notes
Peter	28Oct1828		Hudspeth, Thomas	For 3 yrs. Farmer
Higlin, James	28Oct1828	4 yrs	Webster, Jonathan	
Woodard, William P.	28Oct1828	16 yrs	Knight, C. W.	Tanner
Deel, Wilford	Jan1829	Abt 16 yrs	Webber, George E.	Tanning
Deel, Bluford	Jan1829	Abt 16 yrs	Webber, George E.	Tanning
Lister?, Hugh	April1829	Abt 11 yrs	Neeley, Andrew	
Winters, George	April1829		Smith, J. T.	
Horton, Andrew	April1829	Abt 13 yrs	Herndan, Joseph	Cabinet trade
Pulse, James	20July1829	Abt 16 yrs	Watson, Jonathan	Cabinet workman
Gifford, William	20July1829		Hill, Isaac H.	Bound by father, William Gifford
Hodge, Gabriel	20July1829			Indenture between Isaac H. Williams & Isaac H. Thomas [sic]. Proven by John R. Hill. Cabinett maker
Smith, Green	27July1829	Abt 18 mo	Johnson, Cadar	Of color
Bynum, Lard S.	Oct1829		Goff, Thomas J.	Tailor
Emeline	Oct1829		Porter, H. B.	Daughter of Betsy Smith
Styles?, William	March1830	Abt 8 yrs	Johnson, Joshua W.	Taylor
Holmes, Thomas	March1830	Abt 13 yrs	Hardison, Charles	Farmer
Groves, Joseph	Sept1830	15yrs on 13June1831	Shields, John N.	
Thomas	Sept1830	Abt 3 yrs	Ervin, Christopher	Farming. Of color. Child of ___ Smith
Foster, Albert	Sept1830	Abt 15 yrs	Helm & Phillips	Tanner
Richardson, Presly C.	Sept1830	Abt 17 yrs	Nicholson & Estes	Printer
Renfro, Angeline	18Mar1830	Abt 8 yrs	Mack, John	Put in care of court Oct1829. Cancelled 13Dec1830
Renfro, Elisabeth	18Mar1830	Abt 5 yrs	Mack, Robert	Put in care of court Oct1829
Bailey, Francis Ann	13Dec1830	16 mo	Gunter, John	Spinster
Renfro, Angeline	13Dec1830		Rogers, Samuel P.	
Unnamed boy	13Dec1830	Abt 3 yrs	Shockley, Ephraim	Of color
Coleman, William	14Mar1831	11 or 12 yrs	Kilpatrick, Benjamin M.	Farmer. Duplicate entry. Canc 19Dec1831 & returned to grandfather Baucomb

Name	Date	Term/Age	Rankin, Robert	Notes/Trade
Beattie, William	20June1831	11 yrs		Cabinet making. Canc 6Nov1837. Rankin neglecting his duty toward William
Ferrill, Nelson	20June1831	15 yrs in March 1832	Hart, Joseph	Tanner
Burns, Milton	29June1831	19 yrs	Little, William	Blacksmith
Alderson, Larkin	19Sept1831		Read, John W.	
Sutton, Mary J.	12Dec1831	Abt 4 yrs	Osburn, John	
Ferril, John	19Dec1831	Between 9 & 10 yrs	Lytle, William	Blacksmith
Coleman, Daniel	?		Brown, William	Indenture cancelled 19Dec1831. Returned to grandfather Baucomb
Cook, Elbert	19Dec1831	11 yrs abt 1Jan1832	Skipworth, Peyton? H.	Spinning & ?
Cook, Willis H.	19Dec1831		Johnson, Joshua W.	Talor
Cook, George W.	19Dec1831		Moore, James W.	Tailor
Jim	12Mar1832	5 yrs in Nov1832	Vorhees, William	Of color. Child of free Sally, now living with Vorhees
Calvin	12Mar1832	2 yrs in July1832	Vorhees, William	Of color. Child of free Sally, now living with Vorhees
Lod, Thomas	12Mar1832	17 yrs on 11Mar1832	Fergeson, William O.	Tailor
Draper, John	18June1832	Abt 16 yrs	Lytle, William	Blacksmith. Mulatto 11June1832
Cole, William	18June1832	Abt 10 yrs	Kuff, Thomas	Carpenter
Love, Wilson D.	18June1832	8 yrs on 1Aug	Ramsey, David	
Gidon T.	17Sept1832	Abt 13 yrs	Moore, James W.	Orphan. Tayloring
Childress, Robert	17Sept1832	18 yrs on 1Mar1832	Dillon, Charles R.	Orphan. Painting
Llewellin, Joseph	17Sept1832	5 yrs	Brown, Gabriel	Orphan. Farmer
Cates, John	17Sept1832	8 yrs in January last	Shelton, James R.	Orphan. Tailoring
Butler, John	17Sept1832	17 yrs on 8Jan1833	Shelton, James R.	Tailor
Steele, Aron	18Mar1833	16 yrs on 8Aug1833	Orr, Thomas	Tanner
Steele, Eli	18Mar1833	18 yrs on 17Feb1834	Nance, Joseph	Cabinet maker
Steele, Franklin A.	18Mar1833	13 yrs on 23Nov1833	Campbell, Samuel F.	Tailoring
Steele, William C	18Mar1833	8 yrs on 12Nov1833	Black, Amzi	Farmer

Name	Date	Age	Master	Notes
Steele, Mary	18Mar1833	10 yrs on 19Apr1833	Moore, Samuel	Moore is grandfather
Steele, John	18Mar1833	4 yrs on 23Feb1834	Moore, Samuel	Moore is grandfather
Forbes, James	18Mar1833	10 or 11 yrs	Kennedy, Thomas	Brickmaker & plasterer. Canc 16June1834. To father
Cook, Willis H.	10June1833	Abt 6 yrs	Estes, Henderson	Gunsmith
Duke, Benjamin	10June1833	12 yrs	Farris, John T.	Saddler
Alexander, Cyrus C.	9Sept1833	Abt 7 yrs	Alexander, Absolom A.	Farmer
Furr, Nancy	10Sept1833		Rogers, John	Spinster. Mulatto
Woodard, John W.	10Sept1833	14 yrs on 19July1833	Woodard, William P.	Tanner & currier
Lovel, William	9Dec1833	Abt 11 yrs	Anderson, John W.	Carpenter. Cancelled 14Sept1835
Lovel, Edward	9Dec1833	Abt 7 yrs	Anderson, John W.	Carpenter. Canc 14Sept1835, as Edmond
McGraw, Cynthia A. Celia	9Dec1833	Abt 8 yrs	Ewings, Andrew	Spinstress
Derrons, Hiram	10Mar1834	Abt 13 yrs	Bond, John B.	Saddler
Pearce, John	11Mar1834	Abt 17 yrs	Ridly, John T.	Waggon maker
Tom	9June1834	Abt 6 yrs	Lytle, William	Blacksmith. Of color. Canc 1July1839. Aka Green Smith. To mother, Winifred Smith, moving to Fayette Co
Cooke, Noah	10June1834	Abt 7 yrs	Rod, Anderson	Farmer
Ferrill, Nelson	10June1834	Abt 16 yrs on 1Jan1834	Helm, Meredith	Tanning
Calvin	15Sept1834	7 yrs	Neelly, Andrew	"Yellow boy"
Westbrook, Rufus M.	8Dec1834	Abt 6 yrs	Guthrie, Jacob F.	Canc 4Oct1847. Rufus then a soldier in Mexico. Name of apprentice taken from cancellation entry
Love, Decator	8Dec1834	Abt 11 yrs	Kendrick, Thomas	Kendrick promised to make him his heir
Maberry, Thomas	8Dec1834	Abt 15 yrs	Lawhorn, William	Black smith
Jackson, Thomas	9Dec1834		Woolard, Nathaniel	Farmer
Ham, Henry	9Dec1834	Abt 17 yrs	Graham, Dudley J.	Cotton gin maker
Bobbitt, James	9Mar1835	Abt 17 yrs	Thompson, James A.	Saddler
Lovel, William	14Sept1835	Abt 11 or 12 yrs	McKey, Joel L.	Blacksmith
Lovel, Edmond	14Sept1835	Abt 9 or 10 yrs	McKey, Joel L.	Blacksmith

Name	Date	Age	Bound to	Notes
Forgeson, George	15Sept1835	Abt 14 yrs	Johnson, Thomas P.	Tanner
Willie, Cyrus	15Sept1835	Abt 17 yrs	Johnson, William A.	Farmer
Mayes, Lydda	15Sept1835	Abt 7 yrs	Wiggs, Rigdon	Spinster. Until age 21. Prob bastard daughter of Cynthia Mayes 17Mar1834
Mayes, Sarah	15Sept1835	Abt 7 yrs	Watson, William	Until 21 yrs. Prob bastard daughter of Cynthia Mayes 17Mar1834
Fields, Oren	14Mar1836		Fields, Jr, William	Printer
Estes, Claudius	21Mar1836	Abt 19 yrs	Gayle, Matthew W.	Mill wright
Cooke, Burton	21Mar1836	Abt 15 yrs	Jennings, William J.	Tanner & currier
Patterson, John	4July1836	b. 27March1824	Thomas, Jonas E.	Of color. Farmer
Patterson, Mary	4July1836	b. 15May1828	Thomas, Jonas E.	Spinstress. Of color
Patterson, Catharine	4July1836	b. 15April1826	McManus, Jonathan	Spinstress. Of color
Patterson, Narcissa	4July1836	b. 20Aug1835	McManus, Jonathan	Spinstress. Of color
Patterson, Margaret	4July1836	b. 15Feb1833	Mayson, Joseph	Spinstress. Of color
Patterson, Julia	4July1836	b. 15Feb1833	Dugger, William W.	Spinstress. Of color
Lowder, William	5Sept1836	Abt 16 yrs	Blackburn, John C.	Carpenter
Margaret	5Sept1836	Abt 3 yrs	Mason, Joseph	Of color. Cancelled 5Dec1836
Julia	5Sept1836	Abt 3 yrs	Dugger, William W.	Of color
Tuckness, Gilbert	7Nov1836	Abt 14 yrs	Bond, John B.	Saddler. Cancelled 1Oct1838. Green Graham apptd administrator of estate of Felix F. Tuckness 1Oct1838
Miller, William	9Nov1836	Abt 10 yrs	Thompson, Silas D.	Saddler
Miller, Francis M.	9Nov1836	Abt 4 yrs	Thompson, Silas D.	Saddler
Miller, Martha J.	9Nov1836	Abt 14 yrs	Dale, Adam	Housekeeper
Miller, Susan C.	9Nov1836	Abt 8 yrs	Ament, Thomas W.	Housekeeper. Canc 6July1840
Collins, Lafayette K.	9Nov1836	Abt 17 yrs	Thompson, James A.	Saddler. Cancelled 8Feb1837
Margaret	5Dec1836	Abt 3 yrs	Dugger, William W.	Of color. On 7Oct1851 Dugger allowed to remove Margaret to Henry Co. Apprenticeship to expire Dec1854
Sellers, Eli	8Feb1837	Abt 15 yrs	Bynum, Chesly P.	Saddler
Lusk, William J.	6Mar1837		Faris, John T.	
Katharine	3Apr1837	Abt 11 yrs	McManus, Jonathan	Of color. Cancelled 6Nov1843, as Catharine Patterson
Narcissa	3Apr1837	Abt 2 yrs	McManus, Jonathan	Of color. Cancelled 6Nov1843, as Narcissa Patterson

Name	Date	Age	Master	Notes
Mays, Sarah S.	1May1837	Abt 8 yrs	Crutchfield, Jesse	
Thomas, William	5June1837	Abt 12 yrs	Crofford, Alexander C.	
Fergusson, Eliza Emily	3July1837	Abt 8 yrs	McFadden, Margaret	Prob dau of John Forgusson 21Mar1836*
Maberry, Willis	4Sept1837		Lawhorn, William	
Ferguson, William F.	4Sept1837	Abt 11 yrs	Johnson, Thomas P.	Tanner & currier. Prob son of John Forgusson 21Mar1836*
Amy	2Oct1837	Abt 14 yrs	McMurry, Joseph	Of color
Sylva	2Oct1837	Abt 14 yrs	Bingham, James	Previously bound as Selvey Smith to William Yancy
Miller, Francis	6Nov1837	Abt 8 yrs	Moore, James W.	Tailor. Alias Francis Collins. Cancelled 7Mar1842*. To be delivered to Green Duke
Durham, Presly	6Nov1837	14 yrs	Barns, Almon L.	Carpenter & joiner. Son of Ila Durham, Dcd 7Aug1837*
Smith, Celia	6Nov1837	Abt 6 yrs	Rogers, Jacob	Of color. Spinstress
Smith, Green	6Nov1837	Abt 7 yrs	Rogers, Jacob	Of color. Farming
Smith, Rufus	6Nov1837	Abt 3 yrs	Rogers, Jacob	Of color. Farming
Miller, William	6Nov1837	Abt 14 yrs	Phillips, Lemuel J.	Tanner & currier. Alias William Collins
Fields, Oren	6Nov1837	Abt 13 yrs	Vaught, Nathan	Carpenter
Smith, Emaline	6Nov1837	Abt 11 yrs	Porter, Hugh B.	Of color
Neeley, Martha J.	3Sep1838	Abt 9 yrs	Higgins, Michael	
Kirkpatrick, Plummer W.	3Dec1838	Abt 15 yrs	Vaught, Nathan	Until 20 yrs
Simpson, Thomas	3Dec1838		Faris, John T.	Sadler
Stone, William J.	7Jan1839	16 yrs	Johnson, Thomas P.	Tanner & currier
Huson, David	7Jan1839	Abt 14 yrs	Graham, R. & S.	Tailor
Morris, William P.	1Apr1839	Abt 9 yrs	Uzzell, Elisha	With consent of father, George C. Morris
Hood, Margaret	1July1839	Abt 5 yrs	Rail, Richard	
Brown, Richard S.	1July1839	Abt 15 yrs	Bailey, Augustus D.	Until 20 yrs
Cooke, Willis H.	5Aug1839	Abt 14 yrs	Estes, Henderson	Gun smith
Cooke, Noah J.	5Aug1839	Abt 13 yrs	Holeman, Leonidas	Shoe & boot maker
Bowmer, James	7Oct1839	Abt 13 yrs	Warren, John D.	Saddler
Mitchell, Samuel	7Oct1839	Abt 10 yrs	Bynum, Andrew J.	Of color. House carpenter. Canc 2Mar1840*, petition of Clara Mitchell

Name	Date	Age	Bondsman/Witness	Remarks
Woodson, Frank	2Dec1839		Cobal, Terry H. & Houston, Russel	Of color. Son of Cuffy Woodson, Dcd 4Nov1839. Canc 4Feb1851*
Listen, Calvin	3Feb1840		Neelley, John C.	Of color
Nicholson, Ruth	2Mar1840		Bradshaw, Eli G.	
Parrish, Joseph	6Apr1840	Abt 9 yrs	Steele, William D.	
Mitchell, Samuel	4May1840	Abt 9 yrs	Mahon, Thomas	
Woodson, Lucinda	6May1840		Wingfield, Lucy	Milener. Of color. Dau of Cuffy Woodson, Dcd 4Nov1839
Smith, Betsey	6May1840		Pantel, Ankey Y.	Of color. Housekeeping
Dale, Thomas	3Aug1840	Abt 17 yrs	Vaught, Nathan	
Hudspeth, Louisa	3Nov1840	Abt 11 yrs	Hudspeth, Thomas	Orphan. Canc 1Mar1841. Dau of James Hudspeth, Dcd 1Mar1841
Whitfield, William	5Jan1841	Abt 5 yrs	Whitfield, James G.	
Smith, Sylva	5Jan1841	19 yrs	Kilpatrick, Thomas J.	Of color
Smith, William	5Jan1841	1 yr	Kilpatrick, Thomas J.	Of color. Son of Sylva Smith
Lawrence, Miles	6Sept1841	Abt 7 yrs	Kilpatrick, Thomas J.	Tanner & currier
Cunningham, William W.	4Oct1841	14 yrs on 29Feb1842	King, William	Farmer. Orphan
Parten, John H.	6Dec1841	Abt 12 yrs	Mills, William A.	
Smith, Henry	1Aug1842	2 yrs 6 mo	Mohon, Thomas E.	Farmer. Of color
Letsinger, Andrew J.	1Aug1842	Abt 14 yrs 5 mo	Sowell, Peyton & Wilkins, John A.	Orphan. Tanner & currier
Letsinger, George W.	1Aug1842	Abt 10 yrs	Sowell, Peyton & Wilkins, John A.	Orphan. Tanner & currier
Sellers, Robert J.	2Aug1842		Dunagan, John C.	Orphan. Saddler
Simpson, Thomas S.	6Sept1842		Jordon, John A.	Orphan. Carpenter. Consent of mother
Lawrence, Sarah	6Mar1843		Rowe, Johnson	Orphan of Joseph Lawrence, Dcd 3Oct1842
Churchwell, Holbert	7Mar1843	Abt 15 yrs	Chalk, William R.	Orphan
Smith, Aaron	17Aug1843		Johnson, Thomas P.	Tanner
Gordon, John W.	17Aug1843		Sowell, Peyton & Wilkins, John A.	Tanner
Mitchell, James Polk	17Aug1843		Mahan, Thomas E.	Of color

Name	Date	Age	Master	Notes
Patterson, Adeline	?		McManus, Jonathan	Indenture cancelled 6Nov1843. Of color
Patterson, Narcissa	?		McManus, Jonathan	Indenture cancelled 6Nov1843. Of color
Patterson, Catharine	?		McManus, Jonathan	Indenture cancelled 6Nov1843. Of color
Patterson, Narcissa A.	6Nov1843		Price, Francis	Of color. Canc 2Dec1851
Dorell, Edward	6Nov1843	Abt 4 yrs	Morrow, James	Wagon maker
Patterson, Catharine	6Nov1843		Ridley, Georgia M.	Of color
Jonas	2July1844	Abt 7 yrs	Harrison, Alfred M.	Farmer. Of color
Arnold, William	7July1845	10 yrs on 17Feb next	Gardner, Britain	Req of Mary Ann Arnold, mother. Farmer
Nellums, Daniel	4Aug1845	Abt 8 yrs	Huey, James H.	Orphan
Nellums, Nancy M.	4Aug1845	Abt 9 yrs	Johnson, Wiley	
Nellums, George W.	4Aug1845	Abt 16 yrs	Cayce, Henry	Orphan
Simpson, Thomas W.	1Sept1845	18 yrs	Jordon, John A.	Orphan. House carpenter
Nellums, Sarah A.	3Nov1845	12 yrs	Tucker, Abram	Orphan
Smith, William James	1June1846		Hodge, Asa B.	Farmer. Of color. Rebound 5Dec1848
Johnson, Nimrod	1June1846	9 yrs on 4Nov1846	Irvine, James D.	Orphan. Farmer. Canc 3Mar1850. Irvine dead
Morlam, John R.	6July1846	18 yrs	Jones, Willie	Farmer. Consent of mother, Jenkins
Blackburn, Jane	7Sept1846	13 yrs on 13May1846	Benner, Henry E.	Orphan. Cons of mother. Canc 2Apr1849, as Frances J., request of father, Eli Blackburn
Bowman, John	4Dec1846	12 yrs	Hardison, Asa	Orphan. Canc 1Apr1850. John a runaway
Johnson, Jefferson	6Jan1847		Jackson, Mark	Orphan. Farming
Johnson, Croton	6Jan1847		Jackson, Mark	Orphan. Farming
Johnson, William S.	1Mar1847	12 yrs on 25Dec1846	Tate, William C.	Orphan. Farming
Kerr, Crotilda E.	3May1847		Kerr, Andrew M.	Orphan. Grandchild of Andrew M. Kerr
Kerr, Andrew Moderal Walker	3May1847		Kerr, Andrew M.	Orphan. Grandchild of Andrew M. Kerr
John	4May1847	Abt 11 yrs	Lankford, John B.	Of color. Blacksmith. Son of Viney. Canc 6Dec1853. Lankford broke
Stringfellow, Sarah S.	6July1847		Bynum, Chesley P.	Orphan. Milliner

Name	Date	Age	Bound to	Remarks
Johnson, Mary J.	6July1847	13 yrs this day	Bynum, Chesley P.	Orphan. Milliner
Chapman, Milus Gardner	6Mar1848	6 yrs	Perry, Powell	Orphan. Farmer. Son of Elizabeth Chapman (or Chatman) 4Jan1848. Canc 3Sept1849
Chapman, Taylor R.	6Mar1848	10 yrs	Fleming, Thompson	Orphan. Farmer. Son of Elizabeth Chapman (or Chatman) 4Jan1848. Canc 6Jan1857. Bad behavior & neglect of duties
Barlow, James	1May1848	13 yrs	Luckett, William C.	Orphan [sic]. Shoe making. Father William Barlow 4Mar1850
Barlow, William	1May1848	11 yrs	Luckett, William C.	Saddle tree making. Canc 3June1850 at request of father, William Barlow
Letsinger, George W.	1May1848	14 yrs	Wilkins, John A. & Hamilton, John B.	Orphan. Tanner. Cancelled 1Jan1849. Apprentice's surname from cancellation entry
Stringfellow, Columbus	1May1848	15 yrs	Keesee, Thomas W. & Turpin, T. W.	Orphan. Coach & carriage making
Blackburn, James	5June1848	11 yrs	Sellers, James Y.	Orphan. Farmer. Cancelled 2Apr1849, request of father, Eli Blackburn
Stewart, Alexander	3July1848	16 yrs on 10Apr1848	Brandon, Charles	Of color. House carpenter
Hood, Walter C.	5Sept1848	Abt 7 yrs	Taylor, Thomas	Orphan. Canc 4Dec1860, request of Hood
Smith, William James	5Dec1848	8 yrs on 25Aug1848	White, Reuben	Of color. Previously bound to Asa B. Hodge. 6Oct1859* Canc 6May1861. "Bill" to enter the Army of Tennessee as a servant
Redding, William H.	5Feb1849	15 yrs on 2May1849	Garrett, Stephen J.	Orphan. Farmer. Cancelled 2Sept1850
Redding, Thompson J.	5Feb1849	Abt 9 yrs	Redding, Thompson P.	Orphan. Farmer
Redding, Thomas J.	5Feb1849	Abt 11 yrs	Redding, Thompson P.	Orphan. Farmer. Cancelled 2Sept1850
McKay, Sarah Elizabeth	5Mar1849	6 yrs	Shelton, James R.	Seamstress. Of color. Consent of mother, Vina
Smith, Green	6Aug1849	19 yrs on 7Nov1849	Campbell, John A.	Of color 1July1850*
Celia	6Aug1849	18 yrs	Allen, Robert B.	Of color. Housekeeping. Canc 4Mar1850
Granville	6Aug1849	2 yrs	Allen, Robert B.	Of color. Farming. Son of Celia. Cancelled 4Mar1850
[Smith], Robert	6Aug1849	8 yrs	Underwood, Edward	Of color. Farming. Canc 1Oct1849,* request of mother, Sally. Underwood appealed. Back to Underwood on 1Apr1850. Canc 6Jan1852
Chapman, Milas G.	3Sept1849	7 yrs in March1849	Foster, Jonathan	Orphan. Farming. Cancelled 4Oct1852

Name	Date	Age	Master	Notes
Celia	1Apr1850	Abt 18 yrs	Hardeman, Thomas	Of color
Randal	1Apr1850	Abt 3 yrs	Hardeman, Thomas	Of color. Son of Celia
Harrison [Johnson], Nimrod P.	1Apr1850	14 yrs in Dec1850	Harrison, Hugh C.	Orphan. Cancelled 1Dec1851. Runaway
Sally	6May1850	9 yrs	Alley, Albert R.	Housekeeping. Of color. As Sarah Jane Smith, cancelled 1July1850 for maltreatment. 4June1850*
Smith, James Anthony	3June1850	2 yrs on 31July1850	Mahon, Thomas E.	Of color. Assent of mother
Smith, William Caswell	3June1850	b. 21Apr1850	Mahon, Thomas E.	Of color. Assent of mother
Barlow, William A.	3June1850	12 yrs in March1850	Reaves, Robert A.	Father William Barlow 4Mar1850* Cancelled 6Jan1853, Reaves having moved to Dickson Co with Barlow. Rebound there
Lowry, Samuel	1July1850	17 yrs	Black, Samuel S.	Orphan
Thadeus	2July1850	11 yrs	Jordan, Laban	Of color. Child of Lucy
Jim	2July1850	< 11 yrs	Jordan, Laban	Of color. Child of Lucy
Sarah	2July1850	< 11 yrs	Jordan, Laban	Of color. Child of Lucy
Ben	2July1850	< 11 yrs	Jordan, Laban	Of color. Child of Lucy
Woot	2July1850	< 11 yrs	Jordan, Laban	Of color. Child of Lucy
Smith, Sarah J.	3July1850		Porter, William R.	Of color. Cancelled 8Oct1850
Redding, Thomas J.	2Sept1850	10 yrs	Burke, Franklin A. (Esq)	
Bomer, John	2Sept1850	Abt 16 yrs	Holden, Norflet R.	Saddler. Cancelled 6Sept1852
Briant, William	2Sept1850	9 yrs	Gray, James	Orphan
Gilmore, Benjamin F.	2Sept1850	13 yrs	Davis, Ephraim	Orphan. Cancelled 6Sept1852
Smith, Sarah Jane	8Oct1850		Wood, William	Of color
Purcell, Francis	3Dec1850		Cross, Robert & Kuhn, Edward	Orphan. Coach or carriage smith
Mitchell, Benjamin	9Jan1851	6 yrs	Timmons, Squire H.	Farmer. Of color
Mitchell, Sarah	9Jan1851	8 yrs	Rainey, W. S.	Housekeeping. Of color. Canc 5Dec1856
Mitchell, Thaddeus	9Jan1851	13 yrs	Scott, William	Farmer. Of color. Cancelled 3Mar1856. Scott dead
Mitchell, Susan	9Jan1851	7 yrs	Scott, William	Canc 3Mar1856. Scott dead
Mitchell, James	9Jan1851	11 yrs in Nov1850	Harrison, Hugh C.	Brick mason. Of color. Canc 7Feb1854 as Jim Mitchell

Name	Date	Age	Owner	Notes
Smith, Mary Jane	6May1851	7 yrs on 18Jan1851	Shelton, James R.	Request of mother. Seamstress. Of color
Jordan, Ann	1Sept1851	11 yrs	Moore, James T.	Orphan. Housekeeper
Barlow, James	1Sept1851	Abt 18 yrs	Trousdale, James W.	Farmer
Hunt, Joseph D.	2Nov1851	11 yrs	Stricklin, Thomas A.	Rough workman in wood. Of color
Hunt, Mary Jane	2Nov1851	12 yrs	Stricklin, Malinda L.	Housekeeping, sewing etc. Of color
Eliza	2Nov1851	18 yrs	Merritt, William	Housekeeping. Of color
Patterson, Narcissa A.	2Dec1851		Stockard, William P.	Housekeeping. Of color. Cancelled 6Sept1854, as Narcissa being hired out by Stockard
Watts, John W.	5Jan1852	13 yrs	Willis, C. W.	Orphan. Farmer. Cancelled 2Oct1855
[Smith], Robert	6Jan1852		Melton, William	Farmer. Of color. 1Oct1849*
Hurt [Hunt], Joseph D.	7Dec1852	Abt 12 yrs	Stricklin, Malinda L. (Miss)	Blacksmith. Of color
Sandy	7Feb1853	Abt 9 yrs	Porter, William R.	Farmer. Of color. Cancelled 6Aug1861. Porter dead
Pharo	8Mar1853	Abt 7 yrs	Thurman, A. S.	Indenture requested in will of Marry Thurman. Dcd. Formerly her slave
Mitchell, John	5Sept1853	8 yrs	Loftin, Alfred	Of color. Request of mother, ___ Mitchell
Henry	6Oct1853	Abt 10 yrs	Renfro, James S.	Of color. Son of Martha Mitchell. 7Oct1857*
Lucy	6Oct1853	Abt 8 yrs	Renfro, James S.	Of color. Dau of Martha Mitchell 7Oct1857*
Edmond	6Oct1853	Abt 6 yrs	Renfro, James S.	Of color. Son of Martha Mitchell. 7Oct1857*
Amanda	6Oct1853	Abt 4 yrs	Renfro, James S.	Of color. Dau of Martha Mitchell 7Oct1857*
John	6Dec1853	Abt 17 yrs	Southen, William F.	Body servant. Of color. Previously bound to John B. Lankford
Sarah	4Jan1854	4 yrs on 11Apr1854	Shadden, William	Of color
Leonidas	4Jan1854	2 yrs in March1854	Shadden, William	
Mitchell, James	7Feb1854	13 yrs on 1Jan1854	Harrison, Hugh C.	Farmer. Of color
Sorrel, Edward	2May1854	14 yrs on 7May1854	Hoffman, E. C.	Farmer
Mitchell, Lucien	4Sept1854	1 yr 9 mo	Denton, Corda	For 19 ys. Farmer. Of color
Mitchell, William	4Sept1854	10yrs on 1Sept1854	Denton, Corda	For 19 yrs. Of color
Mitchell, Sally	4Sept1854	14 yrs on 4Sept1854	Denton, Corda	For 7 yrs. Seamstress. Of color
Mitchell, George	4Sept1854	8 yrs on 1Sept1854	Denton, Corda	For 13 yrs. Farmer. Of color

Name	Date	Age	Master	Notes
Mitchell, John	4Sept1854	12 yrs on 1Sept1854	Denton, Corda	For 9 yrs. Farmer. Of color
Patterson, Narcissa A.	6Sept1854		Cook, John M.	For 1 yr 11 mo. Of color
Stewart, Chelonus	2Oct1854		Rucker, James H.	For 4 & 5/12 yrs. Of color
Stewart, Lilburne	2Oct1854		Rucker, James H.	For 8 yrs 3 mo. Of color
Stewart, Samuel	2Oct1854		Collier, William M.	For 12 & 3/4 yrs. Of color
Stewart, Laura	2Oct1854		Walker, Sarah	For 14 yrs 3 mo. Of color
Lambert, John T.	2Oct1854		Brandon, John L.	For 7 & 1/2 yrs. Father dead. Cancelled 6Dec1858 at request of Lambert, now nearly 18 yrs old
Lambert, William S.	2Oct1854		Holt, Calvin H.	For 9 yrs 9 mo. Father dead. Mother unable to support. Cancelled 6Dec1858, Lambert having left Holt
Lambert, Andrew J.	2Oct1854		Brandon, John L.	Father dead, mother unable to support him
Stewart, Elizabeth	3Oct1854		Forgey, F. C.	For 11 yrs 8 mo
Humphrey, Louisa J.	3Oct1854		Baker, Mary	Orphan. For 13 yrs or until she marries
Humphrey, Mary E.	3Oct1854		Baker, Robert	Orphan. For 11 yrs or until she marries. Seamstress & house keeper
Stewart, Sarah	6Nov1854		Riveer, William	For 1 yrs 22 mo [sic]. Of color. Housekeeper & seamstress
Huggins, Robert	6Nov1854		Olds, James	Orphan. For 8 yrs. Farmer
Cull, Reece	4Dec1854	4yrs on 1Jan1855	Thomas, Jonas E.	For 17 yrs. Farmer. Of color. Cancelled 5Nov1856. Thomas dead
Coffee, Mary	4Dec1854	2 yrs on 10June1855	Craig, John F.	Bastard. Mother assents. For 19 yrs
Kessell, Samuel A.	7May1855	14 yrs on 10Jan1855	Drake, Benjamin F.	Father dead. For 6 yrs 8 mo. Harness maker. Son of Mary Ann Holt, or Holtson
Baughan, John Henry	15Jan1856	15 yrs on 22Jan1856	Kent, William K.	For 6 yrs. Orphan. House painter
Mitchell, Susan	3Mar1856	Abt 12 yrs 1Jan1856	Scott, Ann (Mrs)	For 8 yrs 10 mo. Housekeeper. Of color

Mitchell, Thadeus	3Mar1856	Abt 18 yrs 1Jan1856	Scott, Ann (Mrs)	Farmer. Of color. Cancelled 4Aug1856
Goodwin, Henry H.	11Apr1856	16 yrs on 28July1856	Drake, Benjamin F.	For 4 yrs 3 mo 17 d. Orphan. Coach & carriage painter
Mitchell, Thadeus	4Aug1856	Abt 18 yrs 1Jan1856	Timmons, Squire H.	
Cull, Reece	5Nov1856	Abt 6 yrs 1Jan1857	Erwin, William H.	For 15 yrs. Cancelled 4Oct1859. Erwin dead
Mitchell, Sarah	3Dec1856	Abt 14 yrs 9Jan1857	Ashton, James H.	Of color. For 7 yrs 38 d. Housekeeping
Russell, Thomas A.	1June1857	Abt 10 yrs 5Mar1857	Priest, John M.	Motion of Payton Russell. Cabinet maker.
Mitchell, Sarah	3June1857	Abt 14 yrs 9Jan1857	White, James M.	Housekeeping. Of color
Funderburk, George	4Oct1858	Abt 10 yrs 1Dec1858	Ashton, John	For 11 yrs. Farmer. On 9Jan1861 George reported ill, unable to work. Ordered to court
Whitaker, Caroline	7Feb1859	Not quite 11 yrs	Wood, William	For 10 yrs. Of color. Housekeeper. In behalf of her mother, George, her uncle, objects, is overruled and appeals to Circuit Court. Canc 3Apr1866, Caroline having left Wood
Whitaker, Lewis	7Feb1859	Abt 8 yrs	Blackwood, William	For 13 yrs. Of color. Farmer. In behalf of his mother, George, his uncle, objects, is overruled and appeals to Circuit Court
John Samuel	2May1859	Abt 10 yrs 16Mar1859	McDonald, Malcom	For 10 yrs 10 mo. Farmer. Of color. Mother dead. Canc 9Jan1867. Taken by father
Matilda Jane	2May1859	Abt 9 yrs 26June1859	McDonald, Malcom	For 12 yrs. Housekeeper & seamstress. Of color. Mother dead. Canc 9Jan1867. Taken by father
Eliza Ann	2May1859	Abt 5 yrs 16Dec1858	McDonald, Malcom	For 15 yrs. Of color. Mother dead. Canc 9Jan1867. Taken by father
Nancy Caroline	2May1859	Abt 7 yrs 26Feb1859	McDonald, Malcom	For 13 yrs 9 mo. Housekeeper & seamstress. Of color. Mother dead. Canc 9Jan1867. Taken by father
Mary Rebecca	2May1859	Abt 2 yrs 27Feb1859	McDonald, Malcom	Housekeeper & seamstress. Of color. Canc 9Jan1867. Taken by father

Name	Date	Age	Master	Notes
Coleman, Bridget	7June1859	Abt 6 yrs 25Dec1859	Irvine, Elizabeth	For 11 yrs. Parents dead. Housekeeper & seamstress. Cancelled 9June1859, request of Martin Coleman, her uncle. To his care
Cull, Reece	4Oct1859	Abt 9 yrs 1Jan1860	Erwin, Angeline	Farmer. Of color
Johnson, Wiley	6Feb1860	Abt 14 yrs 13Nov1859	Watson, James T.	Fro 7 yrs. Orphan. Wagon maker
Liston, Alice	6Mar1860	Abt 5 yrs 15Oct1860	Erwin, Jemimia A.	For 15 yrs. Of color. Housekeeper & seamstress
Chaffers, Nichols J.	7May1861		Daly, Jones	For 11 yrs 6 mo. Of color
Sandy	6Aug1861	17 yrs 6 mo	Porter, Sarah E.	For 3 yrs 6 mo. Farmer. Of color
McFall, Samuel	2Jan1866	Abt 12 yrs 2Jan1866	McFall, David D.	Farmer. Of color. Without father or mother
McFall, Betty	2Jan1866	Abt 9 yrs 2Jan1866	McFall, David D.	Housekeeper. No father or mother. Of color
Kittrell, Frank	2Jan1866	Abt 10 yrs 2Jan1866	Kittrell, Jacob H.	Farmer. Of color. Without father or mother
Kittrell, Vina	2Jan1866	Abt 6 yrs 2Jan1866	Kittrell, Jacob H.	Housekeeper. No father or mother. Of color
Embrey, Calvin	2Jan1866	Abt 10 yrs 2Jan1866	Bridges, Wiley J.	Farmer. Of color. Without father or mother
Embrey, Allice	2Jan1866	Abt 8 yrs 2Jan1866	Bridges, Wilbourn J.	Housekeeper. No father or mother. Of color
Dodson, Samuel	2Jan1866	Abt 10 yrs 2Jan1866	Dodson, Pawl W.	Farmer. Of color. Without father or mother
Harlan, Thomas	2Jan1866	Abt 10 yrs 2Jan1866	Harlan, Benjamin	Farmer. Of color. Without father or mother
Harlan, Moses	2Jan1866	Abt 12 yrs 2Jan1866	Harlan, Benjamin	Farmer. Of color. Without father or mother
Crosby, Horace	3Jan1866	Abt 8 yrs 3Jan1866	Crosby, Thomas J.	Farmer. Of color. Without father or mother
Crosby, Medora	3Jan1866	Abt 13 yrs 3Jan1866	Crosby, Thomas J.	Housekeeper. No father or mother. Of color
Webster, Dallas	3Jan1866	Abt 13 yrs 3Jan1866	Webster, Margaret R.	Farmer. Of color. Without father or mother
Alexander, Beckey	3Jan1866	Abt 7 yrs 3Jan1866	Alexander, Jr, E. C.	Housekeeper. No father or mother. Of color

Name	Date		Employer	Remarks
Alexander, Jane	3Jan1866		Alexander, Jr, E. C.	Housekeeper. No father or mother. Of color. Badly diseased from exposure
Alexander, Catherine	3Jan1866	Abt 4 yrs 28Jan1866	Alexander, Jr, E. C.	Housekeeper & farmer. Of color. No father or mother
Alexander, Thomas	3Jan1866	Abt 10 yrs 3Jan1866 / Abt 12 1/2 yrs today	Alexander, Jr, E. C.	Farmer. Of color. Without father or mother. Cancelled 5Jan1870. Thomas long gone
Minor, Robert	5Feb1866		Smithson, John S.	For 9 yrs
Smithson, Robert	5Feb1866		Jones, Wiley	For 16 yrs
West, Henry	5Feb1866		Kittrell, Thomas M.	For 10 yrs
Kittrell, Santa Anna	5Feb1866		Kittrell, Robert H.	For 9 yrs
Harris, Roxana	5Feb1866		Harris, Thomas A.	For 10 yrs
Miller, Flossa	5Feb1866		Miller, E. M.	For 10 yrs
Miller, Robert	5Feb1866		Miller, E. M.	For 15 yrs
Miller, Dora	5Feb1866		Miller, E. M.	For 15 yrs
Miller, Lucius	5Feb1866		Miller, E. M.	For 9 1/2 yrs
Harrison, Hannah	5Feb1866		Bingham, Samuel H.	For 12 yrs
Kennedy, Peter	5Feb1866		Kennedy, Albert A.	For 9 yrs
Kennedy, James	5Feb1866		Kennedy, Albert A.	For 9 yrs
Kennedy, Stewart	5Feb1866		Kennedy, Albert A.	For 15 yrs
Webster, Martha	5Feb1866		Webster, Mary Ann H.	For 14 yrs
Webster, Anna	5Feb1866		Webster, Mary Ann H.	For 11 yrs
Webster, Cicero	5Feb1866		Webster, Mary Ann H.	For 14 yrs
Webster, James	5Feb1866		Webster, Mary Ann H.	For 10 yrs
Webster, Low	5Feb1866		Webster, Mary Ann H.	For 5 yrs
Webster, Serhey	6Feb1866		Webster, G. P.	For 12 yrs. Of color
Cathey, Scipio	5Mar1866		Cathey, James	For 9 yrs. Of color. Canc 3Apr1871. Absconded to parts unknown
Hunter, Nancy	5Mar1866		Hunter, W. G. J.	For 8 1/2 yrs. Of color. Canc 22Apr1876, Nancy refusing to serve further, demands pay
Polk, Simon	5Mar1866		Polk, Rufus K.	For 7 yrs. Of color

Name	Date	Age	Master	Notes
Stratton, Judy	5Mar1866		Stratton, John H.	For 10 yrs. Of color. Cancelled 16June1877, Judy refusing to remain with Stratton
Shaw, Martha	3Apr1866		Shaw, Ebenezar	For 16 yrs. Of color
Shaw, Billy	3Apr1866		Shaw, Ebenezar	For 10 yrs. Of color
Goodloe, Joan	3Apr1866		Goodloe, Dabney M.	For 10 yrs. Of color
Ashton, James	7May1866	11yrs abt 25May1866	McKelvie, John	Farmer. Without father or mother
Crutcher, Fanny	4June1866	Abt 11 yrs	Sheppeard, James M.	For 7 yrs. Of color
Gordon, Rufus	6Aug1866	Abt 10 yrs 6Aug1866	Gordon, William O.	For 11 yrs. Of color. Canc 5Aug1867. Taken by Eldrige Gordon & Albert Webb, of color
Rickets, Samuel	1Oct1866	Abt 7 yrs 1Oct1866	Rickets, Robert D.	For 14 yrs. Of color. Consent of mother
Johnson, Herman	2Oct1866	Abt 14 yrs 1Jan1867	Johnson, David	For 7 yrs. Of color
Cross, Jane	6Nov1866		Ewell, Richard S & Luzinka C.	Orphan. For 6 yrs. Housekeeping
Cross, Sarah	6Nov1866		Ewell, Richard S & Luzinka C.	For 4 yrs. Housekeeping
Cross, Charles	6Nov1866		Ewell, Richard S & Luzinka C.	For 13 yrs. Farmer
Huey, William	3Dec1866	9 yrs on 3Dec1866	Huey, James H.	For 12 yrs. Farmer. Of color
Biffle, Adam	3Dec1866	12 yrs	Biffle, William	For 9 yrs. Farmer. Of color
Hagan, Mariah	3Dec1866	6 yrs	Hunter, W. G. J.	For 12 yrs. Housekeeping. Of color
Hagan, Mary Jane	3Dec1866	10 yrs	Hagan, James W.	For 8 yrs. Housekeeping. Of color. Cancelled 5May1869
Hoge, Abraham	3Dec1866	11 yrs	Hoge, Lucy A.	For 10 yrs. Farmer. Of color
Cecil, Jane	3Dec1866	Abt 9 yrs	Cecil, James H.	For 9 yrs. Housekeeping. Of color
Roberts, Melvina	8Jan1867	12 yrs	Jones, Charles G.	For 6 yrs. House keeper. Of color
Hardison, Rachael C.	9Jan1867	12 yrs on 4Apr1867	Hardison, William W.	For 6 yrs. Housekeeper. Of color. Cancelled 1June1868, Rachael having left Hardison

Name	Date	Age	Guardian	Notes
Hardison, George C.	9Jan1867	7 yrs 28Oct1859 [sic]	Hardison, William W.	For 14 yrs. Farmer. Of color
Loftin, Jane	9Jan1867	Abt 14 yrs 9Jan1867	Loftin, Shadrack	For 4 yrs. Housekeeper. Of color. Cancelled 2Feb1869, Jane never having come to Loftin's control
Bryant, Myra	4Feb1867	Abt 10 yrs	Bryant, Robertson	For 8 yrs. Housekeeper. Of color
Reed, Cicero	4Feb1867	Abt 13 yrs	Perry, Richard B.	For 8 yrs. Farmer. Of color. Cancelled 3Feb1868
Campbell, Aaron	5Feb1867	Abt 15 yrs	Smith, Dilcy	For 6 yrs. Orphan. Farmer. Cancelled 2May1870. Aaron uncontrollable
Summerel, Julius	3June1867	14 yrs	Craig, Frank B.	For 7 yrs. Farmer. Of Color
Watkins, Joseph	2July1867		Frierson, Alexander	For 10 yrs. Both of color. Farmer
Watkins, Ben	2July1867		Frierson, Alexander	For 8 yrs. Both of color. Farmer
Watkins, Littleton	2July1867		Frierson, Alexander	For 13 yrs. Both of color. Farmer
Jenkins, Harriet	2July1867		Kennedy, William C.	For 12 yrs. Of color. House keeping
Cathy, Sarah Alice	5Aug1867		Cathy, Martha L.	For 7 yrs. House keeping. Of color. Cancelled 6Sept1869
Byers, John W.	5Aug1867		Byers, Nancy	For 15 yrs. Farmer. Of color
Kennedy, Mary	5Aug1867		Kennedy, George A.	For 5 yrs. House keeper. Of color. Cancelled 6Sept1869
King, Elizabeth P.	5Aug1867		Sowell, Jane C.	For 7 yrs. House keeper. Of color
Moore, Matilda	2Sept1867	Abt 12 yrs 22Feb1855 [sic]	Moore, James T.	For 5 1/2 yrs. House keeper. Of color. Cancelled 2Aug1869
Moore, Sarah Jane	2Sept1867	Abt 10yrs 27Feb1867	Moore, James T.	For 7 1/2 yrs. House keeper. Of color. Cancelled 2Aug1869
Turner, Philip	3Sept1867	Abt 9 yrs 3Sept1867	Harris, Henry	For 11 yrs. Farmer. Of color
Fogleman, Jane	3Sept1867	Abt 4 yrs 3Sept1867	Gillespie, Ninean C.	For 14 yrs. Housekeeper. Of color
Wainwright, Hadly	3Sept1867	Abt 5 yrs 3Sept1867	Gillespie, Ninean C.	For 16 yrs. Farmer. Of color
Hayes, Edward	8Oct1867	Abt 15 yrs	Hayes, Davis K.	For 6 yrs. Of color. Canc 8Oct1872, as Edmund. Ran away
Blackwell, Negly	2Dec1867	Abt 4 yrs 2Dec1867	Ogelvie, Richard H.	For 17 yrs. Farmer. Of color
Blackwell, Henry	2Dec1867	Abt 12 yrs 2Dec1867	Ogelvie, Richard H.	For 9 yrs. Farmer. Of color
Blackwell, Lucius	2Dec1867	Abt 10 yrs 2Dec1867	Ewing, F. J.	For 11 yrs. Farmer. Of color

Name	Date	Age	Master	Notes
Tidwell, Charles	7Jan1868	Abt 13 yrs 7Jan1868	Walker, Albert	For 8 ys. House carpenter. Of color
Kittrell, Frank	7Apr1868	Abt 8 yrs 3 mo	Kittrell, Agnes D.	For 8 yrs 3 mo. Farmer. Of color. Canc 22Apr1876. Frank in State Prison
Kittrell, Viney	7Apr1868	Abt 8 yrs 9 mo	Kittrell, Agnes D.	For 10 yrs 3 mo. Housekeeper. Of color. Canc 22Apr1876, Viney refusing to serve
Cross, David	3Aug1868	Abt 10 yrs 3Aug1868	Bond, William M.	For 8 yrs. Farmer. Canc 4Apr1871. Left the state & fled to parts unknown
Roberson, Rufus Scott	2Nov1868	10 yrs this day	Sellers, William C.	For 11 yrs. Neither father nor mother to support him. Farmer. Of color
Litzey, Alfred	2Nov1868	Abt 15 yrs 2Nov1868	Kilpatrick, N. B.	For 6 yrs. Orphan. Farmer. Of color
Pollard, Dee	2Mar1869	Abt 11 yrs 2Mar1869	Potts, James	For 10 yrs. No father or mother. Boot & shoe maker. Orphan of Joseph Pollard, Dcd 4Jan1872, Dcd 4Jan1872, Dcd 4Jan1872. 5Feb1872* Canc 6Feb1872
Pepper, Calvin	3May1869		Holcomb, T. H.	For 5 yrs. Farmer. Of color
Hagan, Mary Jane	5May1869	Abt 12 1/2 yrs	Kirk, William P.	For 5 1/2 yrs. House keeping. Of color. Cancelled 6June1870
Boaz, Matthew	7June1869	6 yrs on 28Feb1869	Scott, Samuel W.	For 14 yrs. Orphan. Farmer
Fox, Jane	7July1869	15 yrs on 10May1869	Harrison, Benjamin	For 2 yrs 10 mo. House keeper. Orphan
Foster, Willis	7Sept1869	Abt 15 yrs	Foster, Jackson	For 6 yrs. Both of color. Farmer
Oakly, Ellick	5Oct1869		Oakly, Lewis	For 7 yrs. Both of color
Oakly, Rachel	5Oct1869		Oakly, Lewis	For 7 yrs. Both of color
Greenfield, Lewis	7Mar1870		Dorsett, T. J.	Of color
Dobbins, Lucius	6June1870		Witherspoon, Riley	For 7 yrs. Farming. Witherspoon of color
Cheatham, Mary	12Sept1870		Cheatham, Thomas	For 8 yrs. House keeping. Of color
Cheatham, Rachel	12Sept1870		Cheatham, Thomas	House keeping. Of color
Boman, Anna M.	5Dec1870		Jones, G. W.	For 16 yrs. House keeping
Wright, Jerry	5Dec1870		Stone, J. M. C.	For 9 yrs. Farming

Lee, Henry	6Dec1870		Easley, William	For 8 yrs. Farming
Houghf, Willis	3Jan1871		Houghf, Agnes	For 12 yrs. Farmer
Brown, William	7Feb1871		Miller, John A.	For 14 yrs. Farmer
Vanderver, Emma	6Mar1871		Richardson, Elizabeth W	Without parents or estate
Johnson, Jefferson	7Mar1871		Sparkman, John T.	For 8 yrs. Without parents or estate
Leggett, Mary	3Apr1871	Abt 11 yrs 1Aug1871	Rogers, S. M.	For 10 yrs. Consent of mother. Of color
Moore, Charles	?		Pillow, Albert	Aka Charles Tidwell. Both of color. Canc 3Apr1871. Taken by mother, Emeline Moore
Thomas, Alice	1May1871		Thomas, R. P.	Until age 21. Orphan. Of color. Cancelled 13Jan1877, Alice having left
Partee, William	5June1871		Partee, Phill	Orphan. Assent of mother. All of color
Lavender, William Thomas	3July1871		Wrenn, Thomas W.	Illegitimate child of Sarah Lavender, who consents
Stewart, Brown	7Aug1871		Walker, Thomas M.	For 3 yrs. Black smith. Of color. Mother excepts. Appealed to Circuit Court by Wesley Church, husband of the mother
Gregory, Kattie	11Dec1871		Sellers, W. C.	For 4 yrs. Orphan. Of color
Brown George	4Jan1872		Kinzer, Mary	Minor of Mary Brown, Dcd
Brown, Sydney	4Jan1872		Kinzer, Mary	Minor of Mary Brown, Dcd
Davis, Ritta	5Feb1872		Gordon, J. C.	For 10 yrs. Orphan. Of color
Mackey, George	5Feb1872		Holcolmb, T. H.	For 9 yrs. Of color
Parson, Henry	4Mar1872	8 yrs on 3Mar1872	Foster, R. S.	For 13 yrs. Of color. 3Apr1872*
Frierson, Adison	1Apr1872		Bullock, Rufus	Orphan. Both of color
McHenry, Granville	5Aug1872		Walker, J. F.	For 8 yrs. Orphan. Canc 2Sept1872
McHenry, Granville	2Sept1872		Joyce, W. W	Orphan
Hoge, Allice	2Sept1872		Hoge, G. S.	For 7 yrs. Orphan
Hoge, Walter	2Sept1872		Hoge, G. S.	For 7 yrs. Orphan
Miller, Thomas	7Oct1872		Thompson, M. S.	For 11 yrs from 4Feb1872. Orphan. Of color
Hancock, Ervin	9Oct1872		Hurt, W. S.	For 7 yrs. Canc 2June1873
Hancock, Josie	9Oct1872		Billington, J. M.	For 11 yrs
Allen, Ellen	4Nov1872		Allen, Harriet	Orphan
Wiley, Rose	8Jan1873		Akin, Walter	For 8 yrs. Orphan

Name	Date	Age	Master	Notes
Crowell, David	5May1873		Shannon, D. J.	For 8 yrs. Orphan. Farmer
Floyd, Martha H.	7July1873		Frierson, Leon	Orphan. House girl
Lochridge, Jeff	7Oct1873		Parks, J. C.	For 12 yrs. Farming
Lochridge, Dilcy	7Oct1873		Parks, J. C.	For 15 yrs
Thornton, Ellen	5Jan1874		Hunt, F. M.	No means of support. No one to care for her
Greenfield, Berry	5Jan1874		Dorsett, T. J.	For 16 yrs
Greenfield, Jennie	5Jan1874		Dorsett, T. J.	For 16 yrs
Nolen, William	6Jan1874		Matthews, W. H.	For 16 yrs
Reaves, Barney	2June1874	Abt 12 yrs	Howard, J. W.	
Tilford, John	7Dec1874		Tye, W. M.	For 10 yrs. Orphan
Stewart, Charles	7Dec1874		Estes, Daniel	For 12 yrs. Orphan
Thompson, James C.	1Feb1875	Abt 5 yrs	Bingham, J. J.	For 16 yrs. Orphan
Johnson, William	7June1875		McGibbins, William	For 15 yrs. Orphan. Of color. Cancelled 14Apr1879, Willie having left McKibbin [sic]
Dean, Anderson	7June1875	12 yrs	Harris, Jesse	Orphan. Of color. Cancelled 25Feb1878, Dean having left Harris
Dean, Mollie	7June1875	10 yrs	Harris, Jesse	Orphan. Of color
Dean, Houston	7June1875	6 yrs	Harris, Jesse	Orphan. Of color
Dean, Clementine	7June1875	4 1/2 yrs	Harris, Jesse	Orphan. Of color
Bowen, Will	14June1875		Bowen, A.	For 17 yrs. Orphan. Of color
Moore, David	30Oct1875		Butler, Lawson	For 16 yrs. Orphan. Of color
Black, William	3Apr1876	12 yrs	Hickman, James C.	For 9 yrs. Orphan. Of color
Black, Alphonzo	3Apr1876	4 yrs	Hickman, James C.	For 17 yrs. Orphan. Of color
Black, John	3Apr1876	6 yrs	Hickman, A.	For 15 yrs. Orphan. Of color
Henderson, Sallie	3Apr1876	5 yrs	Fleming, R. G.	For 16 yrs. Orphan. Of color
Anderson, James	4Apr1876	13 yrs	Jennings, James W.	For 8 yrs. Orphan. Of color
Webster, Harry	7Aug1876		Webster, Wash	For 16 yrs. Abandoned child, in care of Webster since infancy. Of color
Cheairs, Celie	12Aug1876		Cheairs, Charles	For 5 yrs. Orphan. Of color

Name	Date	Term	Bound to	Notes
Smith, Richard	26Aug1876		Lockridge, Rebecca	For 8 yrs. Orphan. Of color
Thomas, Missie	6Nov1876	9 yrs	Thomas, R. P.	For 12 yrs.Orphan. Of color
Blanton, Alfred	6Aug1877	8 yrs	Shannon, W. J.	For 13 yrs. Orphan
Watson, William	29Oct1877		Stone, J. W.	Farmer. Mother consents. Father not supporting
Thompson, Gabriel	?		Thompson, M. S.	Canc 1Mar1878, Gabriel having left. Of color
Brown, Dora Ann	4Mar1878	4 yrs	Scribner, Rebecca Ann	Daughter of John Brown, who fails to support
Rollicoffer, Jr., Elizabeth	16Mar1878		Rollicoffer, Elizabeth	For 17 yrs
Pruett, Walter	1July1878	8 yrs	Kennedy, W. C.	For 13 yrs. Orphan
Pruett, John	1July1878	6 yrs	Kennedy, W. C.	For 15 yrs. Orphan
Nicholson, Dolly	23Sept1878		Bostrick, W. E.	For 10 yrs. Of color
Jackson, William	?		Mack, London	Cancelled 12Oct1878, Will having left
Jackson, Forrest	?		Mack, London	Cancelled 12Oct1878, Forrest having left
Hendley, Hugh	4Nov1878		Harris, J. W.	For 11 yrs. Orphan
Partee, Benjamin	2Dec1878		Partee, Jacob	For 17 yrs. Abandoned. Of color
Carter, William	24Nov1879		Sellers, W. C.	For 8 yrs. Farmer. Of color

Montgomery County

Name	Date	Term	Bound to	Notes
Burchett, John	?		Corben, Charnell	Orphan. Cancelled 24Sept1806
Burchett, John	24Sept1806		Ellsworth, John	Orphan of Elias Burchett, Dcd
Unnamed male	25Sept1806		Brawner & West	Tanning. Of color
Caroline	25Sept1806		West, George A. & Polly	Needlwork. Of color
Johnson, William	14Apr1807		McCorkle, Abraham	Orphan. Black smith
Brown, John	?		Lockert, James (Esq)	Orphan of Hannah Brown. Canc 15Apr1807
Brown, John	16Apr1807		Drake, Timothy	Orphan of Hannah Brown. Taylor
Harris, John	?		Drake, Timothy	Orphan of James Harris, Dcd. Cancelled 16Apr1807
Anderson, Timothy	22Mar1808	Abt 7 yrs	Drake, Josiah G.	Orphan
Mills, Griffin	24Mar1808		Harris, Hugh	
Izzle, Thomas	20Dec1808		Bradshaw & Wilson	For 3 yrs. Orphan. Hatter
Chumney, Mary	22Mar1809		Small, Henry	Orphan
Arnold, Price	27June1809	17 yrs	Lynes, Samuel	Sadler
Tyre, Connsil	18Apr1810		Mitchel, Michael	Bound by mother, Elizabeth Tyre. Cabinet house joiner

Name	Date	Age	Master	Notes
Chumbley, Nancy Boyd	17July1810		Hay, Leonard	Orphan of John Chumley [sic]
Irwin, Ester	16Apr1811	Abt 16 yrs	Willis, Elisha	Orphan. Dau of Ester Erwin, white. Mulatto*
Sims, Barnet	18Apr1811		Williams, James	Taning & currying
Culbertson,	22Oct1811		McCorkle, Abraham	Forename not given. Orphan of John Culbertson, Dcd. Blacksmith
Sims,	22Oct1811		Lee, John	Forename not given. Orphan of James Sims, Dcd. Tanner & currier
Sims, Francis	23Apr1812		Lee, John	Orphan of Clabourn Sims, Dcd. Tanner & curryer
Washer, James	22July1812	2 yrs 6 mo	Hale, Jedediah	Bastard child of Caty Washer, a single woman. Farmer
Harper, Elizabeth	21Apr1814	10 yrs	Nelson, Elizabeth	Orphan. Spinster
Washer, Flemship	18July1814		Hutchison, John	Bound by mother, Elizabeth Rhineheart
Puckett, Peter	18Oct1814		Lytaker, Peter	Blacksmith
Humphries, Louisa B.	17Jan1815		Brigham, James H.	Orphan of Richard Humphries
McCawmick, Berry	19Jan1815		Lister, James	Cooper
Walker, James	16Oct1815		Williams, James	Tanner & currier
Walker, William	16Oct1815		Killebrue, Edwin	Farmer
White, William	17Oct1815		Purdue, Howell	Orphan of Davis White. Farmer
White, Mathew	17Oct1815		Purdue, Howell	Orphan of Davis White. Farmer
McCormack, Heydon	16Apr1816		Lytaker, Peter	Blacksmith
Keneday, Dempsey	16July1816		Carter, Robert	Cutler. Bound by guardian, Robert Barnes, by Deed of Indenture
Kerr, Thompson	18July1816		McLean, Charles D. & Norvell, Joseph	Orphan of William Kerr, Dcd. Printer
Wilkinson, Samuel M.	23Oct1816		Caldwell, John	Orphan of George Wilkinson, Dcd. Shoe & boot maker
Tonage, Margaret Grimes	25Oct1817		Groves, George	Orphan of Polly Tonage. Spinstress
Hightower, Harriet	21Oct1817		Groves, George	Orphan of Polly Tonage. Spinstress
McCormack, Berry	22Oct1817		Baxter, James	
Ellen	23Jan1818		Bailey, Charles	Cancelled 22Jan1819. Orphan

McCormack, Berry	25Apr1818	Lynes, Samuel & Lyons, William J.	Bound by guardian, James Baxter, by Deed of Indenture
Steele, William	20July1818	Patton, John	Taylor
Melton, John	22July1818	Dougherty, Dennis	Orphan of Jacob Melton. Tanner
Neblett, Thomas	22July1820	McFall, Samuel	Heir of Francis Neblett, Dcd. Carpenter. Bound by Deed of Indenture
Melton, Noah	21Oct1820	Allbright, John	Drawing out iron. For 3 yrs, by Deed of Indenture
Smith, Anthony	21Oct1820	Allbright, John	Drawing out iron. For 3 yrs, by Deed of Indenture
Cate,	15Jan1821	Nixon, George	Female. Bound by mother, Polly Cate, by Deed of Indenture, until 21 yrs
Lesuce, Cladius	26Jan1822	Warfield, Laban	Orphan. Black smith
Steele, William	26Jan1822	Searcy, Robert	Orphan
Neblett, William	26Jan1822	Adams, Richard	Farming. Cancelled 24Oct1823 by consent of mother, Nancy Vaughan, formerly Nancy Neblett, and of Adams
McCutcheon, John	15July1822	Boyd, Walter	Orphan of Valentine McCutcheon, Dcd. Taner
McCutcheon, Robert	15July1822	Boyd, Walter	Orphan of Valentine McCutcheon, Dcd. Taner
Sanders, Raner?	20July1822	Lynes, William J.	Female orphan of Lucy Sanders. House servant. 18July1822*
Compery, John	20July1822	Curry, William	Orphan of Francis Compery. House carpenter. 18July1822* 26Oct1822*
Compery, Rufus	20July1822	Simmons, Matthew D.	Orphan of Francis Compery. House carpenter. 18July1822*
Compery, Robert	20July1822	Persise, John B.	Orphan of Francis Compery. Hatter. 18July1822.* On 26Oct1822 returned to father by court
Wages, James	20July1822	Pellam, C. H.	Brick mason
Bryan, Warran	21Oct1822	Bryan, Hardy	Farming
Dunn, John	21Oct1822	Grant, Samuel	Orphan of Benjamin Dunn. Black smith
Bonds, William	21Apr1823	Rogers, Alexander M.	
Taylor, Louisa	26Apr1823	McClure, Robert	
Mann, Samuel	21July1823	Roach, John	Orphan of Robert Mann, Dcd.
Jones, Isaac	26July1823	Ogalsby, Daniel	Orphan of Isaac Jones, Dcd

Name	Date	Age	Master	Notes
Lowry, William	19Jan1824	14 yrs	Barbee, Horace	Illegitimate son of James Trousdale
Morris, George C.	24Jan1824		Laird, David	Bound by father, George C. Morris. Tailoring
Cato, Mary	24Jan1824		Smith, James N.	Orphan. 5Jan1846.* Bound by Sterling Neblett, Esq
Taylor, Louisa	23Apr1824		Peterson, Isaac	Orphan
Walk, Isaiah	17July1824		Patton, John	Orphan
Walker, William	17July1824		Persise, John B.	Orphan
Martin, Morgan L.	20July1824		Philips, Richard B.	Canc 20Apr1825. Orphan. Printing
Martin, Seth	20July1824		Laird, David	
White, Mathew	19Oct1824		Persise, John B.	Orphan of David White
White, William	20Oct1824		Curry, William	Orphan of David White
Bonds, William	?		Walker, Herbert	Canc 17Jan1825. Walker paid $8 by court
Washer, Flemons	18Apr1825		Bristoe, Samuel	Gun smith
Wash, James	18July1825		Grace, Solomon	Son of Caty Wash
Company, John	18July1825		McFall, Samuel	Son of Francis Company
Munns, John	19Jan1827		Watkins, Isham L.	Has a brother, Charles 23Apr1824. Cancelled 26July1828
Ferrell, Vincent	16Apr1827		McFall, Samuel	
Hatch, Benjamin	16Apr1827		Glasgow, William	Cancelled 24Jan1829
Ferrell, John	16Apr1827		Collins, George H.	
Crutchfield, Richard	26Apr1828		Root, Chester	Tailoring
Vale, Caty	22July1828		Berry, Leynard	
Munns, Charles	?		Watkins, Isham L.	Cancelled 26July1828
Munns, Charles	26July1828		Brooks, James	Cancelled 20Oct1828, as was bound against consent of acting guardian
Munns, John	26July1828		Samuel Gala__ & Co.	Son of Charles Munns. Until Christmas 1829
Munn?, Charles	20Oct1828		Thomas, Joseph	Tight binding
Munn?, Charles	20Oct1828		Thomas, Joseph P.	Tight binding. Consent of acting guardian
Lafayette, John Wyat	21Oct1828		Newell, William	Of color
Melissa	21Oct1828		Newell, William	Of color

Name	Date	Bound to	Notes
Wiggins, Polly	27Oct1828	Smith, Thomas	Bastard child of Winny Wiggins 23Oct1828. Cancelled 25Jan1831 for abuse. To grandfather, William Niggins [sic]
Wiggins, William	27Oct1828	Smith, Thomas	Bastard child of Winny Wiggins 23Oct1828. Cancelled 25Jan1831 for abuse. To grandfather, William Niggins [sic]
Hatch, Benjamin	24Jan1829	Root, Chester	Tailoring
McCulchen?, Henry	26Jan1829	Collins, Robert & George H.	Tight binding. Brick laying
Cocke, Stephen	25Apr1829	McMoran, Robert	
Peterson, Basil	27Apr1829	Woods, John	
McCulchen, Charles E.	31Oct1829	Collins, George H. & Robert	Brick laying
Smith, Fielding	19Apr1830	Rudolph, George	
Greggs, Samuel	19Apr1830	Halaway, William	Until 16 yrs. Of color.
Bedford, Thomas	19July1830	McMorder?, Robert	Taning
Johnson, Stephen	19July1830	McMorder?, Robert	Taning
Tennessee, Bellfield	24July1830	Brown, James	
Riley, James	24July1830	Brown, James	
Marion, Francis	24July1830	McCall, Samuel	
Archy	24July1830	Brown, Joshua	Son of Mrs Elizabeth Heathcocke. Of color
McGehee, Henry	24July1830	Vick, Nathan	On 23July Pyrant McGehee, Jr ordered brought to court to be bound
Henseley, James	18Oct1830	Peachey, P.	Shoe making
Bridgewater, Chesley	18July1831	Black, George W.	
Rye, James	14Jan1832	Brown, Joshua	
Rye, Levi	21Jan1832	Williams, John N.	
Hall, William Orville	24July1832	Thomas, Joseph P.	Son of Lucky Hall 21July1832
Sears, Isaac	25July1832	Lamberth, Thomas	Orphan 21July1832
Hall, Milton James	25July1832	Black, George W.	Son of Lucky Hall 21July1832. Cancelled 23Oct1832
Wiggins, Mary	25July1832	Lamberth, Thomas	Child of Winny Wiggins 21July1832

Name	Date	Age	Master	Notes
Bonds, Lucinda Morton [Milly]	25July1832		Harbour, Mildred	Illegitimate child of Crusy Bonds 21July1832. Milliner. Cancelled 26Oct1833
Bonds, John Nickerson	25July1832		Thomas , Joseph P.	Illegitimate child of Crusy Bonds 21July1832
Hall, Milton	23Oct1832		Brown, Mathren P.	Making & laying brick. Son of Lucky Hall 21July1832
Reasons, Quintus	21Jan1833		Hail, John W.	Tailor
Benton, Lewis	28Jan1833		Nelson, Robert & H.	Blacksmith
Robinson, William Francis Asbury	20July1833		Black, George W.	Cabinet making
Sears, Isaac	20July1833		McCan, James	Stone mason
Seers, Isaac	21Oct1833		Hail, John W.	Tailor
Bunten, John D.	26Jan1835		Hail, William	Farming. On 19Jan1835 John & James Bunton ordered brought to court to be bound. Cancelled 5Dec1836
Smith, John	24Oct1835		Lockhert, Eli	
Green, Elias Marion	24Oct1835		Powers, Barney B.	
Green, Henderson	24Oct1835		Davidson, Alfred	
Smith, Louisa	26Oct1835		Harbour, Mildred	
Rhodes, Josephus	2May1836		Johnson, Aquilla M.	Taning
Canady, Thomas H.	6June1836		Shoemaker, George J.	
Rye, Harrison	6June1836		Hoskins, Josiah	
Darnell, James	4July1836		Stagner, John	
Darnell, Jeffries	4July1836		Stagner, John	
Darnell, Sampson	4July1836		Stagner, John	
McDaniel, Mary	1Aug1836		Bright, Andrew J.	Infant of James McDaniel, Dcd. Cancelled 5Sept1836
McDaniel, Mary	5Sept1836		Everett, Bennett	Until 21 yrs
Bunten, John	5Dec1836		Orgain, William D.	Farming
Jones, Eli	6Feb1837	Abt 8 yrs	Jones, James	Blacksmith. Of color
Rye, Levi	5Feb1838		Williams, Joseph B.	

Name	Date		Notes
Rye, Harrison	5Nov1838	Connelly, J. T.	Tayloring
Hathcock, Archer	3Dec1838	Bradley, William	Of color
Harris, Asa Brunson	3Dec1838	Hail, John W.	Tayloring
Harris, George	3Dec1838	Hail, John W.	Tayloring
Ray, William	5Feb1839	McDuff, James	Brick laying. Son of Thomas Ray*
Ray, Paschal	5Feb1839	Steele, Moses	Farming. Son of Thomas Ray*
Ray, Elizabeth	5Feb1839	Allen, William H.	Dau of Thomas Ray*. May not have been formally bound. Entry unclear
Mickle, John G.	4Mar1839	Donaldson, William	
Sears, Isaac	4Mar1839	Simmons, Matthew D.	
Wray, Drury	5Aug1839	Jones, James	On 2July1839 Thomas, Martha, Sally & Drury Wray sent to poor house
Ray, Thomas J.	3Dec1839	Cherry, Lemuel	Orphan. Taken from poor house. See "Wray" above
Clark, John	6Jan1840	Roberts, Collins H. & R. W.	Carpenter
Tucker, Robert	2Nov1841	Bradley, William	Orphan. Bricklaying. Son of James Tucker, Dcd 1Nov1841*
Tucker, Alexander	2Nov1841	Bradley, William	Orphan. Bricklaying. Son of James Tucker, Dcd 1Nov1841*
Mitchell, Jacob	6Dec1841	Cook, V. S.	Of color. On 5July1852, now 21 yrs & planning to leave state, given evidence of freedom. 5' 7" bright complexion, curley black hair, eyes greyish cast, lower end of left ear bit off, 15 small scars on left side of the belly just above the navel
Cato, Mary	5Apr1842	Jackson, John	5Jan1846*
Harris, Asa Brunson	8Nov1842	Loughran, John	
Harris, George	8Nov1842	Loughran, John	
Bradshaw, Samuel B.	2Jan1843	Marshall, Honea (or Horace) D.	
Furguson, Samuel	3July1843	Newel, Joseph	With Nancy Furgurson, ordered to court from custody of Thomas Sills 3Apr1843
Ransdale, John E.	4Sept1843	Knott, John W.	
Chavis, Francis	8Mar1844	Davis, Maris?	

159

Name	Date	Age	Master	Notes
McGuire, Adaline	8July1844		Moss, W. D.	Destitute orphan. Mother died on 4th instant. Probable child of Mary McGuire 7Oct1844* Cancelled 3Mar1835
McGuire, James	8July1844		Moss, W. D.	Destitute orphan. Mother died on 4th instant. Probable child of Mary McGuire 7Oct1844*
McGuire, Nancy Adaline	3Mar1845	6 yrs	Jackson, Isaac	On motion of W. D. Moss. Orphan. Cancelled 2June1845
McGuire, Nancy A.	2June1845		Foster, John F.	Orphan
Robertson, Nicholas	3Mar1846		Hobbs, John M.	Tinner. Consent of father, John Robertson
Johnson, Benjamin F.	4Mar1846	14 yrs	Dorris, H. P.	Orphan
McGuire, James	4May1846		Foster, John F.	Orphan
Beanans, Ethel L.	5May1846		Hobbs, John M.	Dau of Jesse Beanans, Dcd. 2Mar1846. Consent of Joseph S. Statue, Guardian
Cato, Jane	8Dec1846		Gafford, James M.	Orphan. Of color. 5Jan1846*
Hicks, Henry	9Jan1847	15 yrs	Majors, Robert W.	Orphan. Of color
Walker, William	1Feb1847		Turner, M. G.	
Johnson, Martha Ann	2Mar1847		Smith, Mitchel	Orphan. Left on the wharf some days ago by a man calling himself William Rogers
Johnson, Mary Ann	2Mar1847		Smith, Mitchel	Orphan. Left on the wharf some days ago by a man calling himself William Rogers
Johnson, Mary Jane	6Apr1847		Watson, J. R.	Orphan. Cancelled 8Feb1859. Watson no longer in county. Mary Jane, now abt 15 yrs, selects Jacob B. Little as her guardian
Martin, Margaret	3May1847	3 yrs	Macklin, Resdin?	Orphan
Robertson, Thomas	6Dec1847		Beavins, William E.	Canc 3July1848, request of John Robertson, father of Thomas
Spencer, James T.	6Dec1847	11 yrs	Mays, Richard	Orphan. Cooper
Coleman, George W.	2Apr1849		Shelton, Creal	For 10 yrs. Farming
Hamilton, William	3July1849		Bradly, P. T.	Son of Garrett Hamilton, Dcd. Mother sick & destitute. Sister not bound. 3Sept1849* On 1Oct1849 Ellen Hamilton sent to poor house

Name	Date	Age	Bound to	Notes
Hamilton, John Henry	3July1849		Bradly, P. T.	Son of Garrett Hamilton, Dcd. Mother sick & destitute. Sister not bound. 3Sept1849* On 1Oct1849 Ellen Hamilton sent to poor house
Hamilton, William	7Jan1850		Sheppard, Lewis	?Son of Thomas Hamilton 3Sept1849
Hamilton, John	7Jan1850		Sheppard, Lewis	?Son of Thomas Hamilton 3Sept1849
Elizabeth	5Aug1850	1 yr	Foster, H. B.	Of color
Shadoin, John M.	2Dec1850		Leone, J. M.	Sadler. Orphan. Consent of mother.
Bumpass, Gebidee	2Dec1850		Bumpass, William	Blacksmith. Son of Catharine Bumpass, declared a lunatic this date and ordered to asylum in Nashville 7Jan1851
Baker, Richard D.	13Jan1851	Abt 9 yrs	Hale, John W.	From the 7th district. Stewartships bar keeping. John D. Baker ordered to court and brought by sheriff 3Feb1851. On 7Apr1851 sheriff reports the father has returned and the mother declines any further action
Boyd, Elizabeth C.	6Oct1851	Abt 11 yrs	McDermit, Nancy	Abandoned by father, Richard Boyd, and mother
Barrett, Samuel P.	5Jan1852	4 yrs	Wood, John D.	Canc 3Oct1853 as Samuel Houston Barrett. Record of Circuit Court in case of Henry Harris & wife Matilda vs John D. Woods read. Taken by mother, Matilda Harris
Barrett, William	5Jan1852	5 yrs	Wood, John D.	Canc 3Oct1853, as William Dallas Barrett. Record of Circuit Court in case of Henry Harris & wife Matilda vs John D. Woods read. Taken by mother, Matilda Harris
Capps, Nancy L.	2Feb1852	10 yrs	Bayliss, Burrell	Orphan. Bound at insistance of her friend & sister, Josephine Capps. Cancelled 5Sept1853. To Josephine
Hamilton, Ellen	2Feb1852	Between 10 & 11 yrs	Pruett, T. B.	Orphan. Cancelled 1Mar1852. Ellen unable to work. Sent to poor house
Gooch, John A.	2Feb1852	10 yrs	Luter, William E.	Orphan. Cancelled 1Aug1853. Returned to mother by order of Attorney General
Shepherd, William	1Mar1852	13 yrs	Cooper, Levi	Orphan
Harrison, William H.	1Mar1852		Rineheart, Andrew	At request of mother, Henrietta G. Walker
Spencer, Frank	6Apr1852	8 yrs	Blount, Archibald	Orphan

Name	Date	Age	Master	Notes
Clark, C. B.	4Oct1852		Clark, Margarett	Male. Permission of Elizabeth Clark, mother. Placed in her care by Circuit Court. Cancelled 6Dec1852. Margarett now married to G. W. Sampson, petitioner
Lowenhart, Henry	6Dec1852		Lundsberg, W	Orphan. Nephew of Lundsberg
Lowenhart, Leopold	6Dec1852		Lundsberg, W	Orphan. Nephew of Lundsberg
Lowenhart, Bernard	6Dec1852		Lundsberg, W	Orphan. Nephew of Lundsberg
Baker, Elizabeth Eleanora	4July1853	Under 16 yrs	Smith, James S.	By petition of sister, Matilda Patterson. Abandoned by father, Isham Baker. Mother dead* Cancelled 5Sept1853. To Matilda
Baker, Aaron S.	4July1853	Under 16 yrs	Paccand, Ferdinan	Farming. By petition of sister, Matilda Patterson. Abandoned by father, Isham Baker. Mother dead*
McGreggor, Lucinda Catharine	5July1853	Under 16 yrs	Fratch, Jacob	Until 21 yrs. Granddaughter of Isham Baker. Has a brother, Joseph H. 4July1853*
Arnold, John	5Dec1853	11 yrs	Dilling, W. H.	Orphan
Jeanes, Nancy	6Mar1854	6 yrs	Ginning, John	Seamstress. Daughter of Carter Jeanes
Jeanes, Robert	6Mar1854	3 ys	Dillen, John	Farmer. Brother of Nancy Jeanes
Foster, John	3Apr1854	12 yrs	Nesbitt, Samuel	Orphan
Shadonin, John	7Aug1854	Over 14 yrs	Boatwright, B. W.	Orphan. Bound at John's request. On 6Sept1855 John permitted to move to Texas with A. M. Anderson, partner of Boatwright
Potter, Shelby Henry	10Nov1854		Nix, John	Illegitimate son of Polly Potter. Taken from custody of Jessee Baggett. Cancelled 4Dec1854, as Henry Shelby Potter. Mother able to provide. 9Dec1854*
Maden, Walter D.	1Jan1855	13 yrs	Hunter, Allen	Orphan. Farmer
Humphrey, Paralee	7May1855	Abt 15 mos	Anderson, Elizabeth	Paralee a lunatic. Deserted by mother, Mary Humphrey. Both Elizabeth & the father of color. Illigitimate. County to support*
Lemmons, John W.	8Mar1856	12 yrs	Grand, Joseph	Orphan

Name	Date	Age	Bound to	Notes
Black, Almira (Elmira)	?		Williams, Daniel C.	Petition to release indenture filed 3Feb1857, by next friend, R. R. Malone. Dismissed 3Mar1857. Of color
Black, Sarah Jane	?		Williams, Daniel C.	Petition to release indenture filed 3Feb1857, by next friend, R. R. Malone
Black, G. W.	?		Williams, Daniel C.	Petition to release indenture filed 3Feb1857, by next friend, R. R. Malone
Jarnagan, Jasper Newton	5July1858	12 yrs	Hinson, Thomas H.	Orphan
Riter, William	8Feb1859	Abt 17 yrs	McReynolds, W. S.	Orphan. Carpenter. Consent of mother, Malinda Riter. Sibs Charles, John & Polk Riter 10Apr1858
Barrett, William H.	1Oct1860	Abt 11 yrs	Wood, Alexander	Orphan. Of color
Barrett, Samuel	1Oct1860	Abt 14 yrs	Edlin, James	Orphan. Of color
Bush, Andrew I.	14June1865		Elder, Reuben	Both of color
Caldwell, William	16Dec1865		Caldwell, S. A.	Orphan. Farmer. Of color. Canc 31Jan1866. Mother, Elizabeth Mcfall, able to support
Marable, Benjamin	16Dec1865		Marrable, J. H.	Orphan. Of color
Marable, Catharine	16Dec1865		Marrable, J. H.	Orphan. Of color. Cancelled 28June1869, as Kitty Marable. Mother now able to support
Leavell, Nicholas	13Jan1866		Leavell, N. K.	Of color
Leavell, Florence	13Jan1866		Leavell, N. K.	Of color
Williams, Nely	13Jan1866		Williams, Mary W.	Of color
Williams, Diisy	13Jan1866		Williams, Mary W.	Of color
Burress, Charles	10Feb1866	Under 14 yrs	Burress, David	Orphan. Of color
Burress, Henry	10Feb1866	Under 14 yrs	Burress, David	Orphan. Of color
Burress, Hester	10Feb1866	Under 14 yrs	Burress, David	Orphan. Of color
Williams, Clara	7Mar1866		Williams, Sarah A.	Of color
Williams, Nicy	7Mar1866		Williams, Sarah A.	Of color
Williams, Ellin	7Mar1866		Dunlop, Mattie	Of color
DeWyer, Lucy A.	7Mar1866		Baston, Lyaergus	Abandoned by father
Williams, Jacob	2Apr1866		Williams, R. B.	
Harris, Jacob	7Apr1866		Wickam, S. G.	

163

Name	Date	Age	Master	Notes
Wain, Mary	4June1866		Middleton, John	On application of her mother, Mrs Wain. Cancelled 3Oct1871
Benson, George	11Aug1866		Crozier, C. W. (Dr)	Consent of George. Of color
Trice, James Simon	8Jan1867		Trice, Wiley	Base born. Wiley & James of color. Mother unable to provide
Trice, Mary Ann	8Jan1867		Trice, Wiley	Base born. Wiley & Mary Ann of color. Mother unable to provide
Reed, Cornelius	8Jan1867		Reed, John C.	No parents to care for him. Of color. Cancelled 3Oct1871, as Neil Read
Cook, Charley	24Apr1867		Rice, Daniel	Both of color. No parents to care for him
Wright, Eugene	24Apr1867		Wright, Frances	Both of color
Dortch, Burton	29Apr1867		Dortch, Lewis	Both of color
Ogden, Albert	18May1867		Ogden, Betsey	Both of color
Grier, Sarah	19Aug1867		Brunson, J.	Orphan
Grier, Mary	19Aug1867		Brunson, J.	Orphan
Martin, William	11Jan1868		Henry, G. A.	Of color
Crotzer, Jane	6May1868	8 yrs	Bryan, Caleb	Until 17 yrs. Of color
Jones, Dixie	20Jun1868	7 yrs	Sims, George	Male. Of color
Jones, Victoria	20Jun1868	12 ys	Sims, George	Of color
Dabbs, Nancy P. J. E.	7Sept1868	11 yrs	Mallory, James H.	Consent of mother, Mary A. M. Annis & her present husband, Charles L. Annis. Cancelled 7Sept1870
Ramsey, Jane	12Oct1868		Norfleet, R. H.	Orphan
Garrett, Willis	15Dec1868	13 yrs	Thomas, Robert W.	Of color. Cancelled 3Oct1871
Parks, Florence	4Jan1869	10 yrs	Parks, L. P.	Of color. Entry also refers to her as Florence Hicks
Steele, Andy	19Jan1870	10 yrs	Allen, G. P.	Until age 16. Farming. Of color
Raimey, Washington	1May1871	12 yrs	Raimey, S. D.	Until 18 yrs
Raimey, Prince	1May1871	10 yrs	Raimey, S. D.	Until 18 yrs
Fry, Willy	4Mar1872		Fry, Jack	Mother an improper person to care for him
Baker, Alexander	29Nov1873	4 yrs	Stewart, Thornton	Both of color. Mother consents.
Black, Jordan	22Oct1874	Of tender years	Black, John G.	Both of color. Child requires constant medical attention. Mother, D___ Black, a prostitute, allowed to visit

Name	Date	Age	Master	Notes
Smith, Tilman	28Aug1875	15 yrs	Williams, James	Orphan
Nipper, James	2May1876		Trotter, J. K.	
Leavell, Columbus	9Oct1876		Taylor, W. L.	Consent of father, Dick Leavell
Quarles, Thomas	11Oct1876	10 yrs	Martin, S. W.	Of color

Moore County

Name	Date	Age	Master	Notes
Simmons, Almeda	5Jan1875	7 yrs on 31Jan1875	Edens, Samuel	Illegitimate child of Mary Elliott, who consents
Edens, Elmira J.	3Dec1877	11 yrs	Bobo, W. P.	Orphan

Overton County

Name	Date	Age	Master	Notes
Upton, William	7Oct1844	14 yrs	Bauman, Samuel	Orphan. Farmer
Upton, Louis	7Oct1844	12 ys	Bauman, Samuel	Orphan. Farmer
West, Teletha Adalane	5May1845	11yrs on 28Sept next	Tompson, George M.	Orphan. Housewifery
Williams, Nancy	7July1845	8 yrs	Crawford, Thomas	Orphan
Elder, Manira Jane	1Sept1845	6 yrs	Elder, William	
Brown, William	6Apr1846	8 yrs on 9June	Officer, John	Orphan. Farmer. To mother, Melind[a] Brown, free woman of color, on 1Mar1847
Ledbetter, Joseph	6July1846	10 yrs on 13Oct next	Hayter, William K.	Orphan. Farmer
Grace, Ambroes M.	2Nov1846	3 yrs	Grace, Cyrus	Orphan. Tanning
Jack	7Dec1846	Abt 18 yrs	Turner, William	Orphan. Farming
Brown, Eleneal Gust Roles	7Dec1846	5 yrs	Warthen, James C.	Orphan. Cancelled 1Oct1849 for maltreatment. To care of Archible Grissom
Alley, Margaret Jane	7Dec1846	11 yrs	Gore, George W.	Orphan. Prior indenture in Dec1841 with John Kennedy cancelled
Odle, Washington V.	4Jan1847	6 yrs	Sulivan, Edward	Orphan. Farming
Odle, James A.	4Jan1847	11 yrs	Chowning, Burrel G.	Orphan. Farming

Name	Date	Age	Master	Notes
Odle, Nancy	4Jan1847	10 yrs	Carlisle, William	Orphan. Business common to females
Warren, John	5Apr1847	2 yrs	Warren, Greenberry	Orphan. Farming
Yelton, William R.	3Jan1848	16 yrs on 29Aug next	Yelton, John P.	Orphan. Farmer
Chafin, George W.	7Feb1848	Abt 19 mo	Goolsby, Wade	Orphan. Farmer
Yelton, John L.	7Feb1848	9 yrs on 23July1848	Johnson, Daniel C.	Orphan. Farmer
Yelton, Susan E.	3Apr1848	Abt 11 yrs	Peek, William M.	Orphan. Dau of Barnet Yelton 6Mar1848. Taken to White Co by Peek. John Norris, Guardian. Order to return her 2July1849. Bond rescinded 3Sept1849
Richardson, Barby L.	5June1848	2 yrs on 26Mar last	Grace, T. R.	Orphan. Housewifery
Richardson, Elbert S.	5June1848	4 yrs on 15May last	Grace, T. R.	Orphan. Tanner
Ally, Samuel B.	2Oct1848	6 yrs next Sept	Looper, Antony C.	Orphan. Farmer. Son of Mary Ally 7Aug1848*
Riddle, Adeline	2Oct1848	4 yrs last Sept	Looper, Antony C.	Orphan. Housewifery
Ally, Elizabeth	2Oct1848	Abt 12 yrs	Sewell, Benjamin C.	Orphan. Housewifery. Dau of Mary Ally 7Aug1848*
Ally, James	2Oct1848	4 yrs on 16Feb1849	Bledsoe, Jesse G.	Orphan. Farmer. Son of Mary Ally 7Aug1848*
Sims, William	6Nov1848	3 yrs in July1848	Poor, William	Orphan. Farmer
Ally, John	6Dec1848	8 yrs	Kennedy, John	Orphan. Farmer. Son of Mary Ally 2Oct1848. 7Aug1848*
Scribner, Sarah Ann	?		Scribner, Green	Previously bound. Rescinded 4June1849, Sarah having left
Alley, Joseph	3Sept1849	3 yrs on 7Dec next	Smith, Martin K.	Orphan. Carpenter
Ray, George	5Nov1849	7 yrs on 15Oct last	Maxwell, J. M.	Orphan. Farmer
Nations, Isaac J.	1May1854	13 yrs on 1Jan last	Sells, David	Orphan
Ally, Elizabeth			Carmack, George W.	Canc 5June1854. Elizabeth of unsound mind
Foster, Rebecca E.	7Aug1854	b. 12Oct1845	Thompson, George M.	Orphan
Laughery, Walker	5Sept1854	7 yrs last March	Lane, Noah W.	Bastard free boy of color, born of Polly Laughery, white. Polly lewd etc and in jail*
Harris, Marion	?		Looper, Jr, Magness	Indent canc 6Nov1854. Father came home
Harris, Samuel	?		Looper, Samuel N.	Indent canc 6Nov1854. Father came home
Harris, Abraham	?		Ray, Magness	Indenture cancelled 6Nov1854. Father came home
Ross, Robert Emery	1Jan1855	Near 7 yrs	Kennedy, John	Farmer. Bound by mother, Nancy Driskill Genieve Ross, on 18Dec1854. Abandoned by husband & destitute. 6Nov1854*

Name	Date	Age	Master	Notes
Whitehead, William J.	5Feb1855	12 yrs on 18Oct last	Matthews, John F.	Orphan. Farmer
Whitehead, Robbert A.	5Feb1855	9 yrs on 2Feb1855	Matthews, John	Orphan. Farmer
Harrison, Samuel	2Apr1855	9 yrs on 18Dec1854	Smith, Jr., B. W.	Orphan
Harrison, James M.	2Apr1855	11 yrs on 18Dec last	Davidson, B. R.	Orphan
Harrison, Margaret E.	2Apr1855	7 yrs in Feb1854	Smith, Thomas M.	Orphan
Medlock, Mallard	2Apr1855	4 yrs on 10Aug next	Dillon, William T.	Orphan
Crawford, William H.	5June1855	15 yrs last March	Hickey, Obadiah	Orphan
Harrison, Alexander	6Aug1855	8 yrs in Feb1855	French, Samuel W.	Orphan
Nations, Thomas	6Aug1855		Ledbetter, William	Orphan
Skimahorn, Martha	5Nov1855	2 yrs last August	Knight, Joseph W.	Orphan. Prior bond with Gabert Pritchett 6Nov1854 cancelled (page missing)
Stacy, James	4Feb1856	5 yrs on 28May1855	Boman, E. F.	Orphan
Randolf, Benjamin	4Mar1856	5 yrs	Neely, Robert	Orphan. Farmer
Garrett, George	7Apr1856	3 yrs next August	Brown, William R.	Orphan
Foster, Rebecca Elizabeth	2June1856		Quarles, John	
Foster, Leorah T.	2June1856		Yates, Emerson	
Benton, Franklin	7July1856	15 yrs on 7July1856	Eldridge, Jesse	Orphan
Franklin, James	7Sept1856	Abt 3 yrs	Fluty, William	Orphan
Morris, Margaret	7Sept1856	2 yrs on 30June1856	Morris, William B.	Until age 21 yrs. Illeg dau of Thomas Carr & Simantha Morris. Dcd. 8Oct1856*
Garratt, George	5Dec1857	4 yrs 4 mo	Gainwell, J. C.	Of color. Child of Polley Garratt
Maples, Susan	6Sept1858	5 yrs	West, Enoch	Domestic affairs
Maples, Levi	6Sept1858	10 yrs	Carr, Thomas	Farming
Daugherty, C. P.	1Nov1858	7 yrs on 3July1858	Davis, William	Farming
Daugherty, William T.	1Nov1858	4 yrs on 17Mar1859	Davis, William	Farming
Boswell, Samuel	4Jan1859	13 yrs	Carr, Hilery P.	Orphan. Farming
Monroe, Vandever	4Jan1859	9 yrs on 27June next	Pritchett, Gabbert	Orphan. Farming
Skimnehorn, Elizabeth	6Nov1854		Pritchett, Gabbard	Bond executed in past cancelled (again)
Stover, Baily	6June1859	Abt 12 yrs	Collins, Overton	Farmer
Murry, Andy	1Aug1859	4 yrs 6 mo	Reeves, Hardy P.	Of color. Farmer. Abandoned by mother

167

Name	Date	Age	Master	Notes
Upton, Lewis C.	3Sept1860	7 yrs next mo	Huddleston, S. H.	Farmer
Hargrove, Milton	1Oct1860	13 yrs in Dec next	Owen, Edward L.	
Hargrove, William	1Oct1860	8 yrs in Nov next	Baker, William	
Upton, Malisa J.	4Mar1861	9 yrs	Thompson, R. J.	
Emaly	1July1861	b. 12Aug1850	Looper, S. H.	Until 18 ys. Of color. Child of Joseph & Julia*
Joseph	1July1861	b. 29Sept1852	Looper, S. H.	Of color. Child of Joseph & Julia*
Esabll	1July1861	b. 19June1855	Looper, S. H.	Until 18 ys. Of color. Child of Joseph & Julia*
James Maddison	1July1861	b. 7Feb1859	Looper, S. H.	Of color. Child of Joseph & Julia*
Hall, Joseph	4Nov1861	16 yrs on 26Apr last	Ray, W. N.	
Upton, Lewis	2Dec1861	Abt 7 yrs	Davis, Thomas B.	
Swift, McDonald	7Jan1862	9 yrs on 5Dec1861	Chapin, William P.	Farmer. Ordered returned to mother, Phebe Swift, 1Dec1862
Swift, William	7Jan1862	Abt 7 yrs	Chapin, William P.	Farmer
Black, Wesly	5Nov1866	10 yrs	Hall, William L.	Of color
Jacob	5Nov1866	8 yrs	Hall, William L.	Of color
Joshua	5Nov1866	7 or 8 yrs	Neeley, T. J.	Of color
John	5Nov1866	Abt 5 yrs	Neeley, T. J.	Of color
Unnamed male	7Jan1867	Abt 12 yrs	Dale, William	Of color
Malissa	7Jan1867	Abt 10 ys	Davis, M. W.	Of color
Arms, William V.	2Dec1867	11 yrs	Martin, Ruth	Orphan. Farming
Whitehead, James	2Dec1867	9 yrs	Boier, James	Orphan. Farming
Sullivan, Wiley	5Apr1869	13 yrs	Sullivan, Nancy	Orphan. Farming. 6June1871 Nancy deceased
Sullivan, Nancy	5Apr1869	11 yrs	Sullivan, Nancy	Orphan. Farming. 6June1871 Nancy deceased
Hooper, Nancy E.	4Oct1869	4 yrs	Davis, Thomas B.	Orphan. Housekeeping
Looper, Jane	6Dec1869	5 yrs	Garrett, Jacob	Of color. Housekeeping
Eldridge, William D.	6Dec1869	4 yrs	Garrett, Elizabeth	Orphan. Farming
Brum, Green	7Feb1870	13 yrs	Stinson, Aaron	Orphan. Farming
Busby, George Stanton	2Nov1870	9 yrs	Andrews, H. C.	Minor without a guardian
Dickerson, Thomas A.	?		Bilbrey, Isaac	A prior indenture cancelled 4Sept1871
Daugherty, Benjamin	2Jan1872	13 yrs	Cain, J. L.	Orphan. Farmer. Consent of his friends

Name	Date	Age	Master	Notes
Stout, William	5Aug1872	8 yrs	Allred, Theophilus	Farmer. Father & mother both dead. Minor heir of Thomas Stout, Dcd. Allred apptd guardian 2Sept1872
Harrison, Daniel	2Dec1872	8 yrs	Carr, Eliza Jane	Orphan. Farmer. Consent of mother
Brown, Andrew J.	3Feb1873	10 yrs	Copeland, T. J.	Orphan. Farmer. Abandoned by father. On 4Feb1873 Elizabeth Brown ordered to be cared for by Lard Hammock
Brown, Franklin	3Feb1873	8 yrs	Hammock, Lard	Orphan. Farmer. Abandoned by father. Ordered returned to court 5July1875*. On 4Feb1873 Elizabeth Brown ordered to be cared for by Hammock.
Eldridge, Charley	5May1873	9 yrs	Eldridge, James	Of color. Farmer. Orphan, abandoned by father & mother
Beasly, William A.	1Sept1873	3 yrs on 8Aug1873	Cannon, Benjamin	Orphan. Farmer. Consent of mother
Boswell, Lydia	3Nov1873	2 yrs	Little, John	Orphan. Housewifery. Consent of mother
Wilson, George	4May1874	Abt 8 yrs	Speck, Polly	Orphan. Farmer. Forsaken by parents
Norris, Jackson	3Aug1874	4 yrs on 8July1874	Looper, Sr, Magness	Orphan. Farmer. Cancelled 1Mar1875
Pitman, William	3Aug1874	Abt 9 yrs	Looper, Joseph	Orphan. Farmer
Cooper, George	1Mar1875	6 yrs	Little, John	Orphan. Farmer
Brown, Franklin	6Sept1875	11 yrs on 10Aug1876	Bilbry, Dawson	Orphan. Farmer
Hollows, William	3Apr1876	13 yrs on 1Mar1876	Cannon, John	Orphan. Farmer. Rescinded 1May1876
Hollows, Andrew	3Apr1876	15 yrs on 1Mar1876	Finley, R. J.	Orphan. Farmer. Rescinded 1May1876
Brown, John	2Apr1877	11 yrs on 5May1876	Lawson, S. R.	Orphan. Farming
Hollers, Sarah	7May1877	13 yrs on 1July1877	Cumings, Thomas	Father dead. Mother poor & of bad character, gives consent. Returned to mother, Pattie Hallers, 2Aug1880
Harp, J. R.	3Nov1879	9 yrs on 5Apr1879	Yelton, R. P.	Orphan. Farming

Perry County

Name	Date	Age	Master	Notes
Mary Zilpa Ann	6May1867	7 yrs	Rouquier, Edward	Of color
Alison, Francis Marion	1Mar1869	12 yrs	Dyer, C. C.	Abandoned by father, mother unable to provide. Farming
Alison, John Morgan	1Mar1869	5 yrs	Dyer, C. C.	Abandoned by father, mother unable to provide. Farming
Rouquier, Joe	3May1869	10 yrs	Johnson, Joseph	Destitute of father or mother
Rouquier, Betty	3May1869	8 yrs	Johnson, Joseph	Destitute of father or mother

Name	Date	Age	Master	Notes
Rouquier, Mitt	3May1869	17 mo	Johnson, Joseph	Destitute of father or mother
Skaggs, Joe	4Oct1869	10 yrs	Skaggs, Melinda	Orphan. Farming
Skaggs, Ann	4Oct1869	8 yrs	Skaggs, Melinda	Orphan. Housekeeping
Crowell, John	1Aug1870	7 yrs	Barber, R. B.	Consent of John. Without father. Abandoned by mother. Farmer
Harris, Martha J.	5Dec1870	4 yrs	Morgan, Elizabeth	Orphan. Housekeeping
Harris, Sarah R.	5Dec1870	2 yrs	Morgan, Elizabeth	Orphan. Housekeeping
Jackson, Thomas	2Oct1871	11 yrs	Greer, Henry	Orphan. Farming
Gray, William	6Jan1873	10 yrs	Morgan, W. L.	Orphan. 2Feb1874*
Gray, William Henry	2Mar1874	11 yrs	Morgan, J. L.	Orphan
Fidler, Harvey	7Apr1874	9 yrs on 12Feb next	Wilsdorf, E. L.	Orphan. Abandoned by mother
Ogwin, James	7Apr1874	15 yrs on 24Mar last	Patry, A.	Abandoned by father. Farmer
Ogwin, John R.	7Apr1874	8 yrs on 1Nov last	Patry, A.	Abandoned by father. Farmer
Dowdy, Thomas	7Apr1874	15 yrs on 6May1874	Hinson, E. L.	Without father or mother. Farmer
Kingkade, Mark Alexander	7Dec1874	7 yrs in Jan1874	Kittrell, B. C.	Consent of mother, Hannah S. Kingkade
Kingkade, James Calvin	7Dec1874	5 yrs on 1Jan1874	Land, E. A.	Consent of mother, Hannah S. Kingkade
Kingkade, William. G.	5Jan1875	7 yrs on 28Feb1874	Godwin, R.	Until 21 yrs. Consent of mother, Hannah S. Kingkade. Housewife [sic]
Carroll, George	1Mar1875	15 yrs next October	Dodson, M. A.	Consent of Carroll. Farmer

Robertson County

Name	Date	Age	Master	Notes
Murphey, Patrick	18Apr1797		Crocket, William	Orphan of Patrick Murphey, Dcd. Cancelled 15Jan1798. From Montgomery Co & has property inventoried there. To mother
Murphey, Peggy	18Apr1797		Crocket, Jane	Orphan of Patrick Murphey, Dcd. Cancelled 15Jan1798. From Montgomery Co & has property inventoried there. To mother
White, Elisabeth	23Aug1799		McIntosh, Charles	
Chambers, Elisabeth	24Apr1801		Norris, Sr, Thomas	

Name	Date	Name	Notes
Crow, James	19Oct1801	Hunt, James	Cancelled 6Nov1804. To mother, Mary Crow. Hunt dead.
Haggard, Edmond	19Jan1802	Jones, Jesse	House carpenter
Haggard, John	19Jan1802	Jones, Jesse	House carpenter
Rogers, John	19Jan1802	Rogers, Isham	Hatter
Tucker, Peggy	20Oct1802	Simmons, Charles	Samuel, John & Riggs Tucker, children of John Tucker, Dcd also mentioned this date*
Tucker, Nancy	20Oct1802	Philips, Joseph	Samuel, John & Riggs Tucker, children of John Tucker, Dcd also mentioned this date*
Tucker, Sarah	20Oct1802	Tucker, Silas	Samuel, John & Riggs Tucker, children of John Tucker, Dcd also mentioned this date*
Tucker, Henry	20Oct1802	Tucker, Silas	Samuel, John & Riggs Tucker, children of John Tucker, Dcd also mentioned this date*
Tucker, Phebe	18Jan1803	Elmon, Traviss	Daughter of John Tucker, Dcd. Cancelled 6Nov1804. To mother, Jane Engleman.
Childress, John	21Oct1803	Pinkley, Daniel	
Childress, Jacob	7Feb1804	Pinkly, Jacob	
Emson, William	6Aug1804	Biggs, Elijah	
Emson, Rebekah	6Aug1804	Biggs, Elijah	
Emson, Calib	6Aug1804	Hall, Dickeson	
Leeland, George	6Nov1804	Browner, Peter	
Tucker, John	4Aug1805	Varnon, Nehemiah	Son of John Tucker, Dcd 20Oct1802*
Childress, Joseph	6May1806	Fry, Henry	Orphan
Tucker, Riggs	8May1806	Fiser, Henry	Son of John Tucker, Dcd 20Oct1802*
Robins, Samuel	6Oct1807	Tucker, Samuel	Son of John Robins, Dcd
Robins, John	6Oct1807	Tucker, Samuel	Son of John Robins, Dcd
Robins, Betsy	6Oct1807	Tucker, Elisabeth	Daughter of John Robins, Dcd
Robins, Polly	6Oct1807	Tucker, Elisabeth	Daughter of John Robins, Dcd
Latham, John	7Apr1809	Pauly, William	
Adams, John	12Nov1810	Skinner, Jesse	Orphan of William Adams, Dcd
Adams, Allen	12Nov1810	Skinner, Jesse	Orphan of William Adams, Dcd
Huckaby, Thomas	12Nov1810	Young, Abraham	

Name	Date	Age	Master	Notes
Unnamed	14Aug1811		West, George A.	Bound by John Johnson
Cozeans, John Bartley	9Aug1813		Earheart, Abraham	Orphan. Making guns
Swann, Edward	9Aug1813		Wilson, Cornelius	
Wills, John	13Feb1815	12yrs on 16June next	Brown, George G.	
McGraw, Uriah	13Feb1815	8 yrs on 4May next	Brown, George G.	
Short, Martin	13Feb1815	8 yrs	Spearman, Joshua	
Short, Jefferson	13Feb1815	10 yrs	Ewbanks, Martin	
Brooks, Funny West	14Aug1816		Paine, Thomas	Male
Martin, Augustin	11Nov1816	12 yrs in Jan next	Green, Jesse	Waggon making. Cancelled 12Nov1816
Goodman, James Stewart Brown	12Nov1816	7 yrs on 7April next	Belamy, Elisha	Sadling
Page, George	12Nov1816	13 yrs on 14Feb next	Crocket, William	Blacksmith
Artes, James Ransam	12May1817		Fox, Linus	Farming
Artes, Susanna	12May1817		Fox, Linus	Spin, weave & sew. House business
Young, William	14May1817		Gosham, William B.	Tanning & curring
Boon, John	11May1818		Paisley, Samuel	Saddling
Boon, William	11May1818		Hall, Corban	On 19Feb1820 ordered brought to court to investigate his treatment
Sanders, Sidney	11May1818		Parter, Alexander B.	
Lazarus, Penny	9Nov1818		Freeman, Matthew	Dau of William Woody. Canc 14Nov1818 as Penny Nazara. To mother
Ousler, Orlander	10May1819		Elliott, Benjamin	Until 20 yrs
Johnson, Elizabeth	14Feb1820		Johnson, John	Until 21 yrs or marries
Hopkins, Ruthy	14Aug1820		Harrison, Reuben	
Traughbor, Henry	?		Tremble, John	Orphan. Blacksmith. Cancelled 19Aug1820
King, Jane	13Nov1820	Abt 10 yrs	Cheatham, Anderson	
Artis, Rachel	13Aug1821	b. 10Feb1818	Fox, Zines	House business. Of color 7Dec1840*
Artis, Eliza	13Aug1821	b. 1Oct1819	Fox, Zines	House business. Of color 7Dec1840*

Name	Date	Age	Master	Notes
Artis, Hardy	13Aug1821	b. 15May1821	Fox, Zines	Farming business
Harper, Sally	12Nov1821	8 yrs last August	Green, Asa	
Morris, Washington	17Nov1821	Abt 13 yrs	Binkley, Jacob	Orphan. Farming & distillery business
Alexander	11Mar1822	Abt 11 yrs	Williams, Christopher	Farming. Of color
Gima?, Jackson	11Mar1822	Abt 8 yrs	Bigbee, John J.	Orphan. Could be Jackson Ginn
Edward, Elizabeth	11Mar1822	5 yrs	Williams, Jr, Thomas	
Dixon, William W.	16Mar1822		Kirk, John H.	Orphan. Bricklaying. Cancelled 13Feb1824
Robertson, William	12May1823		Cox, Lewis	Orphan
Hoffman, James	11Aug1823		Lewis, James	Orphan. Under name of James Lewis previously bound to George G. Brown 15May1823
Robertson, Joseph	10Nov1823		McIntosh, Benjamin	Orphan
Walker, George	14Nov1823		Mefferd, George	Orphan
Farmer, William Henry	10May1824	Abt 8 yrs	Ury, Robert	Orphan
Darr, Henry	9Aug1824	Abt 10 yrs	Elliott, Benjamin	Cabinet business*. Cancelled 8Aug1831
Williams, David	13Nov1824	16 or 17 yrs	Chapman, Jr, Daniel	Orphan. Taning
Darden, Joshua	18Feb1826	16 yrs	Gunn, Pinkney	
McGraw, Archer	8May1826		Nicholson, Granville	Orphan. Farming. Cancelled 9Feb1829
Goodman, James	8May1826		Bryan, William P. P. C.	Orphan. Cabinett business
Robert	14Aug1826		Benson, Philis	Both of color
Turner, James	14Nov1826	11 yrs on 10Jan next	Williams, William	Orphan
Warran	12Feb1827	Abt 6 yrs	Gardner, Henry	Of color
Krantz, John	12Feb1827	9 yrs on 6Jan last	Carr, Arthur	Cancelled 9Feb1829
Krantz, Michael	16Feb1827		Gunn, Pinkney	Orphan
Krantz, Joel	16Feb1827		Farmer, Thomas	Orphan
Gin, Thomas	16Feb1827		McMillen, John	Orphan
Love, Amanda E.	11Feb1828		Williams, Green	Daughter of Catherine Love, who was let out to Kindred Miles. Sibs William & Emeline 16Nov1827*
Robertson, William	9Feb1829	Abt 16 yrs	George, James N.	Orphan
Gardner, John	9Feb1829	Abt 14 yrs	Hughs, Richard E.	Orphan
McGraw, Archibald	9Feb1829	Abt 17 yrs	Morris, Even	Orphan

Name	Date	Age	Master	Notes
Bain, George W.	9Feb1829		Ferguson, Elizabeth	Orphan
Krantz, John	11May1829		Perry, Josiah	Orphan
Bunton, William R.	11May1829		Elliott, John R.	Orphan
McGraw, Mary	11May1829		Felts, Hardy	Orphan. Canc11Feb1833
William	14Aug1829	4 yrs on 24Jan last	Covington, Nicholas	Of color
Earle, William H.	9Nov1829	Abt 3 yrs	Derham, Zechariah	Cancelled 12Nov1829
Thompson, Washington	10Aug1830	Abt 14 yrs	Lattimer, William	Orphan
Thompson, John	10Aug1830	Abt 11 yrs	McCallen, James	Orphan
Holman, Daniel David	10Aug1830	Abt 13 yrs	Henly, Charles R.	Orphan. Tayloring. Cancelled 12May1832
Saunders, Lawson	14Feb1831		Hunter, Matthew R.	
Harris, Edmund	14Feb1831	Abt 10 yrs	Harris, Thomas W.	
Darr, Henry	8Aug1831	Abt 17 yrs	Elliott, Benjamin	Orphan. Farming
Farmer, Wesley	13Feb1832	15 yrs on 10Mar next	Perry, William S.	Orphan
McGraw, Mary	11Feb1833	Abt 12 yrs	Morris, Evin	Orphan. Housewifery
Krantz, John	15Feb1833		Gunn, Pinkney	Orphan. Tanning & currying
Bush, Granderson	16May1833	Abt 5 yrs	Villines, William	Farming. Of color
Bush, Irrena	16May1833	Abt 8 yrs	Chowning, John	Housewifery. Of color
Hammer, Milly	12Aug1833	Abt 8 yrs	Benson, William	Orphan
Karr, William	15Aug1833	14 yrs	Johnson, William H.	Orphan. Cabinett business
Edwards, Viney	10Feb1834	Abt 14 yrs	Pitts, Bartley	Orphan
Witt, James Harvey	12May1834	4 yrs on 12Mar last	Philips, Preston D.	Orphan. Cancelled 15Aug1834. To care of mother, Marthena Summers
Read, Hugh Thomas	10Nov1834	14 yrs in Feb last	George, James W.	Orphan. Blacksmithing
Forester, Nancy	10Nov1834	Abt 5 yrs	Pementer, Malachi	Housewifery
Winn, William J.	11May1835	9 yrs on 20Aug next	Baldry, John S.	Cancelled 6June1836
Alvice, Walter	2May1836	10 yrs	Chism, Jr, Obadiah	Orphan
Chapman, Thomas	2May1836	9 yrs	Redfern, John	
Chapman, Sally	2May1836	4 yrs	Redfern, John	

Name	Date	Age	Master	Notes
Garner, James Monroe	4July1836	3 yrs in Jan last	Pride, David	Orphan
Derham, Silas Herndon	1Aug1836	9 yrs on 22Oct next	Jones, Thomas	Orphan
Hampton, William	3Oct1836	Abt 12 yrs	Kirby, Miles	Orphan. Saddling
Chapman, Elbert	2Oct1837		Braden, Daniel P.	Braden also apptd guardian of Elbert, an heir of Benjamin Chapman, Dcd
Irvine, Biard?	2April1838		Binkley, Hiram B.	
Ward, Adeline	7May1838		Owen, Zadoc	Voided same day. Returned to mother
Ward, John	7May1838		Owen, Zadoc	Voided same day. Returned to mother
Wilson, Millberry	7May1838		Wilson, William	
Wilson, Tillberry	7May1838		Wilson, William	
Francis, William	7May1838		Hiett, Isaac	Cancelled 6Aug1838. Returned to mother, Mrs. Martha Francis
Adams, Samuel	7May1838		Skinner, Hannah	
Luter, Adeline Frances	5Jan1840		Luter, Benjamin W.	Taken from possession of John Wynn for mistreatment. 2Dec1839*
Hart, John Etter	1Mar1841		Hart, Barnaby	Orphan
Osbin, John Wesley	5Apr1841	Abt 10 yrs	Parker, David H.	Consent of father. Cancelled 4July1842 by agreement with father, Joseph Ausburn/Ousburn
Easley, Francis P.	5Apr1841	Abt 12 yrs 5 mo	Holman, David D.	Tailoring
Pepper, Leander	2May1842		Chowning, John	
Sprouce, Richard	6June1842		Dorres, Robin B.	Heir of Thomas Sprouce, Dcd
Campbell, Thomas	5Dec1842		Holeman, D. D.	
Hankins, Elizabeth	6Nov1843	6 yrs	Harper, Asa	Orphan
Evans, Louisa	5Feb1844	2 yrs	Parker, Jr, Felix	Of color
Evans, Charlotte	5Feb1844	3 mo	Parker, Jr, Felix	Of color
Ewing, John A.	5Jan1846	10 yrs last July	Griffin, Reuben	Orphan
Rose, William	5Oct1846	10 yrs on 4Aug last	Anderson, James	Orphan
Rose, Polly	5Oct1846	9 yrs on 4Oct present	Anderson, James	Orphan
McIntosh, Allen	7Oct1846		Ayres, William	Orphan
Menees, Oliver C.	7Oct1846		Fyke, Mathew V.	Orphan

Name	Date	Age	Master	Notes
Menees, William H.	7Oct1846		Fyke, John P.	Orphan
Morris, John	1Mar1847	10 yrs next April	Farmer, Samuel	Orphan. Child of George C.Morris Dcd
Benton, William	3May1847		Sprouse, T. G.	Son of R. Benton
Whiting, William H.	3May1847		Dorris, Robertson	
Morris, Mary	3May1847		Harper, Asa	Child of George Morris, Dcd 5Apr1847
Utley, Gloster	7June1847		Winfield, Jo E.	Child of Piety? Utley, of color, who consents
Utley, Lemuel	7June1847		Winfield, Jo E.	Child of Piety? Utley, of color, who consents
Bush, Carter?	4Oct1847		Stark, Jo C.	Consent of mother, Delila Bush
Monroe, J.	1Nov1847	14 yrs on 8Jan last	Conrad, George C.	Mulatto. Free born
Rose, Elizabeth	7Feb1848		Anderson, James	
Dulin, Wesley	7Feb1848		Menees, T. J.	
Dulin, Thomas	7Feb1848		Hall, Joshua	
Murphey, John C.	7Feb1848		Izer, Jay	
Ewing, John A.	6Mar1848	Nearly 13 yrs	Kelly, Greenberry	Orphan
Dulin, George	7Aug1848	Abt 11 yrs	Baldwin, Abram	Orphan son of J. G. Dulin
Hellerbrand, Simpson	4Feb1850	Abt 11 yrs	Chapman, John	
Holland, Richard M.	4Feb1850		West, Thomas L.	On 4Mar1850 John L. Yates chosen guardian of Margaret Holland (>14 yrs) and other minor children of Thomas Holland, Dcd
Holland, Rebecca F.	4Feb1850		West, Thomas L.	On 4Mar1850 John L. Yates chosen guardian of Margaret Holland (>14 yrs) & other children of Thomas Holland, Dcd. Canc 4Aug1856, with Yates' consent
Hawkins, William	3June1850		Bracy, Thomas W.	Orphan
Monsor?	7Oct1850	18 yrs	Conrad, Nancy N.	Mulatto
Dulen, James W.	6Jan1851	16 yrs in April next	Binkly, A. J.	
Bush, Louisa	1Sept1851	Abt 12 yrs	Phillips, W. W.	Of color. Child of Delila Bush 5Nov1850*
Jones, William Thomas	1Sept1851	15 yrs last August	Warren, Lucas?	Orphan
Bush, Jane	2Sept1851		Turner, John	Of color. Child of Delila Bush 5Nov1850* 3Nov1851*
Bush, Elizabeth	2Sept1851	Abt 2 yrs	Turner, John	Of color. Child of Delila Bush 5Nov1850* 3Nov1851*. Cancelled 8Mar1855

Name	Date	Age	Bound to	Notes
Bush, William	2Sept1851	Abt 8 yrs	White, Iredell	Of color. Child of Delila Bush 5Nov1850* 3Nov1851*
Bush, John Calvin	2Sept1851	Abt 6 yrs	Henry, John M.	Of color. Child of Delila Bush 5Nov1850* 3Nov1851*
Jackson, Reuben D.	2Aug1852		Jackson, L. M.	Orphan
Whiting, Charles	6Sept1852		Whiting, Elisha	Orphan
Snow, Samuel	6Sept1852		McCormack, Joseph	Orphan
Whiting, Synthia J.	6Sept1852		Jackson, John B.	Orphan
Richards, Joseph G.	4Oct1852		Parker, John C.	Orphan
Richards, Joseph G.	6June1853	14 yrs on 30May1854	Fowler, E. C.	Orphan
Whiting, Charles	5Dec1853		Dorris, Marley	Orphan
Whiting, Synthia J.	5Dec1853		Dorris, Marley	Orphan
Bush, Elizabeth	8Mar1855		Hutcheson, John S.	Of color
Harrison, George	6Apr1857	15 yrs in March 1857	Reeder, Jonathan	Until 18 yrs. Orphan
Reeves, James	5Apr1858	6 yrs	Morris, Jane	Until 15 yrs. Abandoned by father, J. J. Reeves. Mother, Mary A. Reeves, has fits. Appealed to Circuit Ct by father 10Apr1858 as Rhoda Jane Reaves
Reeves, Mary Frances	5Apr1858	3 yrs	Morris, Jane	Until 15 yrs. Abandoned by father, J. J. Reeves. Mother, Mary A. Reeves, has fits. Appealed to Circuit Ct by father 10Apr1858.
Rust, Washington L.	4Jan1859	11 yrs	Simmons, G. W.	Until 18 yrs. Orphan
Whiting, G. W.	7Mar1859		Edson, J. B.	
Warren, Samuel G.	1Oct1860	7 yrs on 2Feb1860	Cole, M. S. (Dr)	Orphan. Mother unable to support
Garth, Florence	7May1866		Garth, W. C.	Of color. Bond to D. D. Holman, U. S. Ag't
Fort, Anderson	7May1866		Fort, E. A.	Of color. Bond to D. D. Holman, U. S. Ag't
Lovell, William	7May1866	10 yrs	Babb, James	
Woodard, James	8Jan1867	9 yrs	Woodard, James	Of color. Bond to D. D. Holman, U. S. Ag't
Shannon, Manda	8Jan1867	13 yrs	Woodard, James	Of color. Bond to D. D. Holman, U. S. Ag't
Villines, Henry	2Sept1867	7 yrs	Villines, William	Of color
Villines, Rebecca	2Sept1867	10 yrs	Villines, William	Of color
Fort, Dick	3Feb1868	7 yrs on 15May1868	Fort, T. E.	Of color. Orphan

Name	Date	Age	Master	Notes
Taylor, Amanda	4Feb1868	7yrs 25Dec1866[sic]	Taylor, J. B.	Of color. Orphan
Taylor, Burrel	4Feb1868	5 yrs on 25Dec1868	Taylor, J. B.	Of color. Orphan
Scoggin, Thomas	5Oct1869		Scoggin, William	Of color. Orphan
Scoggin, Buck	5Oct1869		Scoggin, William	Of color. Orphan
Demumbram, Richard	5Dec1870	11 yrs	Barr, Isaac	Without father or mother. Canc 3Dec1877*
Darden, Monroe	6Dec1870	10 yrs	Darden, George W.	Without father or mother. Of color. Annulled 3Oct1871, G. Darden having left Tennessee
Wilson, Robert	2Feb1874		Owen, J. W.	
Williamson, Joseph T.	6Sept1875		Herring, Stephen	
Sanders, John	1Nov1875		Connell, J. T.	
Maberry, William	8Feb1876		Wilson, J. W.	
Careless, W. E. C.	6Mar1876		Burney, William L.	
Williams, Francis	5June1876		Smith, Levi	Of color
Strange, John S.	6Nov1876		Mason, E. C.	
Strange, Sarah A.	6Nov1876		Braswell, William	
Strange, George J.	6Nov1876		Braswell, William	
Strange, Samuel V.	6Nov1876		Braswell, William	
Strange, Albert B.	6Nov1876		Braswell, J. H.	
Leffew, James	7May1877		Groves, Wiley	
Willis, Henry	3Sept1877		Smith, Martin	Both of color. Cancelled 3Dec1877, as Henry Hart
Willis, Jo	3Sept1877		Smith, Martin	Both of color. Canc 3Dec1877, as Jo Hart
Smith, Mary Ann	6Nov1877		Moore, William	
Hart, Jo	3Dec1877		Moore, Lewis	Both of color
Hart, Henry	3Dec1877		King, John	Both of color
Allen, William N.	5May1879		Head, Robert	Request of mother, Mrs. Sallie Allen
Allen, Susan M.	5May1879		Head, Robert	Until 21 yrs. Req of mother, Mrs. Sallie Allen
Gunn, J. E.	1Dec1879		Gunn, E. W.	Consent of J. E.
Harrison, Katie	2Aug1880		Martin, D. A.	
Hassell, Sallie	1May1882	13 yrs in Nov1881	Fort, E. L.	Of color

Rutherford County

Name	Date	Age	Master	Notes
Rogers, Isam	7Oct1805	Abt 10 yrs	Rogers, Isam	Hatter
Philips, George	9July1806		Jetton, Robert	Bound by father, William Philips
Stage, Richard	6Oct1808	Abt 4 yrs	McIntosh, Lochlin	Until 20 yrs
Callahan, Daniel	3Apr1809		Miller, John	Bound by mother, Margret Callahan
Carr, Samuel	4Apr1809	Abt 18 yrs	Wood, John	Orphan. Bound for 2 yrs 9 mo
Marlin, James	2Jan1810		Oliphant, James	Orphan. Bound by Thomas Marlin
Burnett, William	9Oct1811	Abt 9 yrs	Nance, Isaac	Mulatto
Gregory, John G.	8Apr1812	14 yrs	Ross, James	Orphan
Gregory, Nancy M.	8Apr1812	10 yrs	Ross, James	Orphan
Gregory, Mildred E.	8Apr1812	6 yrs	Ross, James	Orphan
Gregory, Wright S.	8Apr1812	8 yrs	Fulton, John	Orphan
Miller, Alfred	7July1812		Statler, Abraham	Hatter
Scott, Charles	13July1814	Abt 10 yrs	Thompson, Gideon	Blacksmith
Nicholl, Anny	10Oct1814	Abt 5 yrs	Yerbys, Averett	James Tucker (or Rucker), from whom Anny was taken, objects & appeals to Circuit Court 12July1814
Phelps, Jackson	15Oct1814	Abt 5 yrs	Phelps, Zadoch	Now in possession of Daniel Phelps. Cancelled 21Apr1817
Vaught, Malinda	9Jan1815	Abt 6 yrs	Wilson, Samuel	
Vaught, Matilda	9Jan1815		Cowan, Nancy	
Walker, John	10July1815	Abt 14 yrs	Roberts, George	Boot & shoe maker
Phillips, Louisa	9Oct1815		Hayes, Adam	
Reynolds, Richard	9Oct1815		Lilly, Noah	
Williams, Daniel	11Oct1815		Wilson, Samuel	
Dabusk, Tempy	13Oct1815		Berry, Elizabeth	
Wright, Nancy	13Oct1815	9 yrs	Holden, Sr, Charles	
Wright, George	13Oct1815	6 yrs	Potts, Thomas	Rescinded 15Apr1822
Wright, Lucy	13Oct1815	4 yrs	Holden, Sr, Charles	
Wright, Elizabeth	13Oct1815	12 yrs	Adcock, Barney	
Dodd, Polly M.	8Apr1816	14 yrs	Johnson, Henry	

179

Name	Date	Age	Master	Notes
Brown, Fayette	19July1816	Abt 18 yrs	Seaton, George	Orphan. Hatter. Cancelled 21Oct1816
Perry, Jesse	14Oct1816	Abt 10 yrs	Curlee, Calvin	
Watson, Thomas	14Oct1816	Abt 8 yrs	Curlee, Calvin	
Brown, Samuel	21Oct1816	17 yrs on 6Feb next	Niles, Charles	Orphan
Vardell, Thomas	20Jan1817	Abt 16 yrs	Lewis, Samuel	Shop joiner
Hicks, Jefferson	22Jan1817		Nichols, Joshua	
Vardell, Moore J.	24Jan1817	13 yrs on 17Aug next	Jones, Amza	Minor heir of John Vardell, Dcd. Saddler. 14Apr1817*
Nelson, Benjamin	17Apr1817	b. 23Jan1801	Jetton, John L. & Robert	
Nelson, Joseph W.	17Apr1817	b. 1Jan1803	Davidson, Jessee	
Phelps, Jackson	21Apr1817		McGibbs, Miles	
Owen, John Smith	21July1817	Abt 6 yrs	Montague, John & Thomas	
Owens, David	21July1817	Abt 17 yrs	Ganaway, Burwell	
Vardell, Moore Johnson	21July1817	Abt 13 yrs	Niles, Charles	
Wood, Jessee	21July1817	Abt 17 yrs 6 mo	Reed, Lemuel	
Nichols, Ann	21July1817	Abt 8 yrs	Williamson, Rowling	
Twidwell, Polly	13Oct1817	Abt 7 yrs	McKelvy, William	
Wright, James	19Oct1817		McMurry, William	
Miller, Austin	24Oct1817	Abt 17 yrs	Trott, Henry	
White, John	16Mar1818		Allen, Henry	
Kelly, Abner	15Mar1819	Abt 17 yrs in Jan last	Niles, Charles	
Perry, James H.	15Mar1819	Abt 5 yrs	Curlee, Cullin	
Robinson, Hugh	14June1819		Robinson, David I.	
Hicks, William	18June1819		Gardiner, John S.	
Watts, James	21June1819		Bole, James	
Carter, Lucy	21June1819		Smoot, Wyatt	Spinstress. On 20Dec1819 released to care of Allen McNiece

Name	Date	Age	Name (2)	Notes
Waddle, Samuel	21June1819		Watkins, Thomas G.	Taylor
Cox, William	13Sept1819	Abt 12 yrs	Niles, Charles	
Morris, Daniel	13Dec1819		Pollan, Robert	
Butler, William I. C.	13Dec1819		Weatherspoon, John	
Morris, James	13Dec1819		Johnson, Larkin	
Little, Susan	13Dec1819		Pollan, Robert	
Porter, John	14Dec1819	Abt 15 yrs	Finger, John	Orphan
Butler, Henry B. F. G.	14Dec1819	8 yrs	McKnight, Elam	Orphan
Butler, Tobias	14Dec1819	11 yrs	McKnight, Richard L.	Orphan
Johns, Jack H.	20Dec1819		Jamison. Henry D.	
Johns, Madison	20Dec1819		Jamison. Henry D.	
Bell, Obediah C.	20Dec1819		Sublett, George A.	
Quarles, Alexander R.	21Mar1820		Jetton, John L.	Tanner
Williams, Leonard	28Mar1820		Patton, James	Saddler
Curtis, John Madison	28Mar1820		Patton, Samuel	Cabinet maker. Canc 24July1826. Not being taught trade as required. To mother
Johns, Frederick	28Mar1820		Patton, Samuel	Cabinet maker
Biggs, Jason	1Apr1820		Jetton, Robert	Tanner
Pate, William	19June1820		Warren, Peter	
Stags, Richard	19June1820		Posey, William S.	
Smith, William	23June1820		Davidson, Jessee	
Gibson, Levander	29Sept1820		Jetton, John S.	
Smith, David	28Dec1820		Roach, Stephen	Tanner
Watson, Aley	18June1821		Morrison, William	Canc 10Sept1821. Morrison leaving county
Watson, Aley	10Sept1821		Bowles, James	
Whitworth, Zititha	10Sept1821		Whitworth, Margaret	
Smallage, Jethro	10Sept1821		Dickson, John	
Moore, Jefferson	12Sept1821		Bevans, James	
Wood, Spencer	15Apr1822		Wood, John	
Fevers, Moses	23Apr1822		Gilliam, William	Blacksmith. A prior indenture with Portland I. Curlee cancelled. Curlee excepted

Name	Age	Date	Master	Notes
Renshaw, Elijah		15July1822	Elam, Edward	
Wright, George		21Jan1823	Vinson, William	
Abel, William		27Jan1823	Jones, Samuel	Tailor. Rescinded 19July1824
Singleterry, Charles		27Jan1823	Rawlston, George	Cabinet maker. Son of Nancy Singleterry 20Jan1823
Pybus, James		27Jan1823	Statler, Abraham	Hatter
Arbuckle, Rawlston		21Apr1823	Woodruff, John	Taylor
Edwards, Joseph		28Apr1823	Barker, Willis	Shoe & boot making
Hutton, Claiborne		28Apr1823	McKirnon, John & Butcher, Solomon	Hatter
Smith, William		22July1823	McKirnon, John & Butcher, Solomon	Hatter
McCutchen, Jason		27Oct1823	Jones, John	House carpenter
Brashear, Nathan		27Oct1823	Jones, John	House carpenter
Blanton, Albert G.		19Jan1824	Cooper, John	
Gasaway, John		27Jan1824	Cooke, Hezekiah G.	
Wilkinson, John		21Apr1824	Sublett, George A.	Printer
Abel, Reuben		?	Newgent, William H.	Indenture rescinded 19July1824
Blanton, James		19July1824	Niles, Charles	Saddler
Blanton, Thomas		19July1824	Blanton, Benjamin	Black smith
Morris, Mary		19July1824	Hoover, Matthias	Until 14 yrs
Span, Thomas W.		18Oct1824	Gardner, Samuel G.	Saddler
Tucker, Thomas		18Oct1824	Anderson, Miles	Carpenter
Wright, William		17Jan1825	Tatum, Hollawell	
Matthews, Joseph		17Jan1825	Elliott, James	Mill right
Crownover, James		17Jan1825	Brally, Levi	Cabinet maker
Cooke, Wyatt		17Jan1825	Jones, George	Tanner
Harrison, William		18Apr1825	Sloss, Joseph	
Cooke, John		18Apr1825	Brandon, William W.	House carpenter
Tucker, Caswell		17Oct1825	McEwen, Alexander	Blacksmith

Wade, Jeremiah	17Jan1826	Elliott, William	Mill wright
Suggs, Moses	17Apr1826	Stephens, William	Farmer
York, John	22Apr1826	Holmes, Henry	Bound 17Apr1826. On 17July1826 Holmes ordered to show cause why indenture should not be cancelled
York, Jane	22Apr1826	Holmes, Henry	Bound 17Apr1826. On 17July1826 Holmes ordered to show cause why indenture should not be cancelled
Arbuckle, William	28July1826	Campbell, Peter	Tailor
McLin, Willie	16Oct1826	McLin, Godfrey	Shoemaker
Hazlett, Melzy?	20Oct1826	Gilliam, William	Blacksmith
Tucker, Thomas	22Jan1827	Hutchinson, William M.	Blacksmith. Canc Oct1827, as John Tucker
Hazlett, Lawson H.	17Apr1827	Jamison, Henry D.	Saddler
Nance, Isham	16July1827	Smith, James M.	
Carter, William	16July1827	Overall, Abraham	Overall apptd guardian of Catey, Polly, Anne, John & Rachel Carter, minor heirs of John Carter, Dcd. 20Aug1828
Cook, John	15Oct1827	Ratliff, Joseph	
Cook, Nancy	15Oct1827	Ratliff, Joseph	
Burton, Morris G.	15Oct1827	Ralston, George	Cabinet maker
Trott, George	17Oct1827	Bowman, Jr., Samuel	Tanner
Moore, Milly	18Oct1827	Bivins, James	
Pybass, Nathaniel	31Jan1828	Bolles, Reuben	Taylor
Oliver, Pleasant	19May1828	Cowan, Varner D.	Saddler
Oliver, Edmund	20May1828	Jones, John	Minor heir of George W. Oliver, Dcd
Powell, Martha Anne	18Aug1828	Stout, John	Until 21 yrs
Vaughan, Lemuel	26Aug1828	Newgent, William H.	
Hogwood, Thomas	17Nov1828	Bone, James	Tanner
Hager, Elizabeth	17Nov1828	Cutrell, Charles	
Screws, James H.	16Feb1829	Bowman, Samuel	Tanner
Screws, Nathan	16Feb1829	Freeman, Oswell	Carpenter
Peck, Thomas R.	24Feb1829	Gilliam, William	Blacksmith
Simmons, Thomas	25Feb1829	McDowell, James	Carpenter
Nance, Isham	26Feb1829	Bone, James	Tanner

Name	Date	Age	Master	Notes
Aldridge, Betsey	18May1829		Smotherman, John	
Peyton, William H.	21May1829		Fisher, Edward	Cabinet maker
Peyton, Benjamin A.	21May1829		Jamison, Henry D.	Saddler
Douglas, Luther	18Nov1829		Davis, Charles L.	Of color
Douglas, Luther	19Feb1830		Parrish, William G.	Of color. A prior indenture with Jonathan Currin cancelled
Bates, Thomas G.	24Feb1830		Jones, John	
McFarlin, John	24Feb1830		Gilliam, William	Black smith
Wright, Thomas	17May1830		Wright, Reuben	Cancelled 15Nov1830. Reuben is brother of Thomas
Anderson, Clinton	22May1830		Campbell, Peter	Jailor
Hogwood, Thomas	15Nov1830		Allison, Hugh H.	Tanner
Bobbett, Thomas T.	21Feb1831		Davis, James B.	Saddler
Tucker, William	21Feb1831		Jordan, David	
Hogwood, Alexander	21Feb1831		Ball, William T.	Shoe maker
Harris, Wyley	24Feb1831		Elliott, William	Mill right
Pearson, Thomas	26Nov1831		Gilliam, Jesse	Black smith. 22Nov1831*
Pearson, William M.	26Nov1831		Campbell, Peter	Tailor. 22Nov1831*
Pearson, Samuel	26Nov1831		Jamison, Henry D.	Saddler. 22Nov1831*
McNamer, Milton	25Feb1832	16 yrs	Jamison, Henry D.	Sadler
Hazlett, John G.	20Aug1832	18 yrs on 8Jan1833	Davis, James B.	Sadler
Floyd, Josiah W.	19Nov1832		Fanner, Bailey W. & Jetter, Rufus	Tailoring
Robbins, James H.	19Nov1832		Kirkpatrick, Thomas	Saddler
Farmer, Samuel	19Nov1832		Fowler, Thomas	Farmer
McLanahan, John T.	18Feb1833		Hill, Isaac	Shoe & boot maker
Johns, James	18Feb1833		Fletcher, Jeremiah W.	Brick layer
Rouse, Hiram	18Feb1833		Howland, John F.	
Allard, James	18Feb1833		Cheshier, John	
Elam, John	19Feb1833		Jamison, Henry D.	Saddler
Farmer, Susan	20Feb1833		Soape, William	

Name	Date	Master	Notes
Pearson, William	21Feb1833	Jetter & Fanner	Tailoring
Robbins, Atkinson	22Feb1833	Thompson, Nimrod	Tannering
Ivey, William T.	22Feb1833	Davis, James B.	Saddlering
Rouse, Joseph	23Feb1833	Richardson, Thomas	
Robins, Atkinson D.	20May1833	Kirkpatrick, Thomas	Saddler. Kirkpatrick also apptd guardian of Atkinson, Elmina Ann, and Atalanta Ann Robins, heirs of Thomas Robbins, Dcd
Robbins, Almira	21May1833	Dickson, Enos H.	Canc 5Dec1836. Dickson's wife dead
Jones, Gaston	21May1833	Smith, Samuel	Saddler
Ford, Merinda M.	19Aug1833	Fuqua, William	
Ford, William	19Aug1833	Conelly, John W.	
Namer, Milton M.	21Aug1833	Thomas, Wilson	Saddler
Ford, Nathan	22Aug1833	Goodloe, Morris H.	
Furgason, Rittenhouse	18Nov1833	Overdeer, Jacob	Hatter
Robbins, Hull	17Feb1834	Kirkpatrick, Thomas	Saddler
Bobbett, John	17Feb1834	Keeble, Edwin A. & Warren, Peterson G.	Printing
Blanton, George W.	18Aug1834	Blanton, James	Saddler
Ford, Pleasant	19Aug1834	Blanton, James	Saddler. Cancelled 7Aug1837, Blanton having sold his shop
Finney, Thomas	17Nov1834	Clements, Louis F.	Cotton gin making. John Shelton apptd admin of estate of Andrew Finney, Dcd
Finney, Addison	17Nov1834	Clements, Louis F.	Cotton gin making. John Shelton apptd admin of estate of Andrew Finney, Dcd
Anderson, Christopher C.	20Nov1834	Statler, Samuel	Until 15Feb1838. Hatter
Aldredge, Jessee	21Nov1834	Anglin, Samuel	Until 16 yrs.
McLanahan, Robert	16Feb1835	Killen, Henry	Gun smith. Rescinded 17Aug1835
Covington, James A	17Feb1835	Davis, James B.	Saddler
Covington, Joseph A.	17Feb1835	Thomas, Wilson	Saddler
Pearson, Samuel	19Feb1835	18 yrs on 20Nov1834	Thomas, Wilson	Saddler
Bailey, James	19Feb1835	12 on 25Dec1834	Thomas, Wilson	Saddler

185

Name	Date	Age	Master	Notes
Champbell, Hardy	18May1835		Gilliam, James	Black smith
Gum, William	21May1835		Blanton, James	Saddler
Moore, Talitha	16Nov1835		Davis, Barbary	
Soape, William	16Nov1835		Knox, Joseph	
Soape, George	16Nov1835		Roberts, Cyrus L.	
Soape, Betsey Ann	16Nov1835		Roberts, Cyrus L.	
Owen, Dempsey	16Nov1835		May, Joseph	
Crouse, Elizabeth	16Nov1835		Crouse, Spencer	
Kittrill, Samuel	17Feb1836		Parrish, Samuel L.	Tailoring
Hatfield, William R.	17Feb1836		Parrish, Samuel L.	Tailoring
Burton, Henry S.	6June1836		Goodloe Jr, Henry	Orphan
Smith, Thomas	6June1836	15 yrs	Doak, Nelson	Orphan. Doak a Wilson Co resident
Broyls, Mathias	5Dec1836		Broyls, Mathias	Until 20 yrs
Broyls, Jemima	5Dec1836		Broyls, Mathias	Until 20 yrs
Broyls, Polly Ann	5Dec1836		Broyls, Mathias	Until 20 yrs
Broyls, Mathias	5Dec1836		Broyls, Mathias	Until 20 yrs
Hatton, James	5Feb1837	11 or 12 yrs	Irons, Augustus	Orphan
Pugh, John	1May1837		Ridly, Jr, James	
Pugh, Thomas	1May1837		Leonard, Frederick	Canc 7Mar1842. Leonard not teaching Pugh farming business. Pugh gone to Wilson Co 5Apr1842. 4Sept1843*
Bernard, Walter	1May1837		Ralston, George	
Coving[ton], James M	1May1837		McLin, William E.	
Covington, William M.	1May1837		Thomas, Wilson	
Barber, Joel	7Aug1837		Goodloe, Morris H.	Son of Joel Barber 1May1837, 6Feb1837*
Stephens, Thomas	7Aug1837		Fields, Richard	
Ford, Pleasant	7Aug1837		Carter, Hiram & Mosby, Fountain C.	Saddling
Guill, Thomas S.	4Dec1837		Arnold, Henry S.	Blacksmith
Manuel	1Jan1838	15 yrs	Ruswurm, John S.	Of color

Name	Date	Master	Notes
Jack	1Jan1838	Ruswurm, John S.	Of color
Major	1Jan1838	Ruswurm, John S.	Of color
Mcnamar, Jonathan B.	5Feb1838	Shanklin, G. W & R. D.	
Davis, William	5Feb1838	Mullins, John	
Taylor, Elcany W.	6Aug1838	Scoggins, John	
Anderson, George	1Oct1838	Johnson, Daniel H.	
Hailey, Margaret C.	1Oct1838	Henderson, Green T.	
Alexander, James	2Oct1838	Shanklin, Gordon W.	Tanning
Puckett, William R.	4Dec1838	Shanklin, Gordon W.	Saddling
Hughes, Thomas	8Jan1839	Shanklin, Gordon W.	Tanning
Hailey, Martha A.	1Apr1839	Webb, James E.	Canc 1July1839. Martha a lunatic, sent to poor house
Furgerson, William	1Apr1839	Thomas, Wilson	Saddler
Cooper, Samuel	3June1839	Low, William	
Moody, David	3Aug1839	Read, Peter	
Covington, James M.	2Sept1839	Shanklin, R. D. & G. W.	Saddling
Griffin, Andrew J.	3Feb1840	Shanklin, Gordon W.	
Griffin, James M.	3Feb1840	Shanklin, Gordon W.	
Bradford, Charles	7Apr1840	Thomas, Wilson	
Jack	7Apr1840	Butler, William S.	Of color
Mary	6July1840	Shanklin, Gordon W.	Of color
Elizabeth	6July1840	Shanklin, Gordon W.	Of color
Watts, William	6July1840	Brown, Richard	
Owen, James	3May1841	Shanklin, Gordon W.	
Furgerson, Anderson J.	2Aug1841	Warren, John	
Bobbett, William	5Apr1842	Warren, John T.	Tanner
Coleman, Joseph S.	5June1843	Martin, Amzi	Cancelled 3Dec1855. Martin dead. Coleman now 17 y/o, wants to learn a mechanical trade
Wallace, William	4Sept1843	Hall, Randol	
Pugh, Thomas	4Sept1843	Walker, John W.	
Browder, John	4Sept1843	Ridley, James	
Sparks, Thomas	6Nov1843	Kelton, Samuel	

187

Name	Date	Age	Master	Notes
Bailey, George W.	5Feb1844		McElroy, Andrew W.	Has sibs John, Hugh, James & one other 1Jan1844*
Street, Walter	5Feb1844		Arbuckel, Ralston	
Daughtry, Tyler	3Mar1845		Flemming, A. J.	
Hewitt, Henry W.	?		Shanklin, R. D.	Indenture cancelled 4Aaug1845
Taylor, Joseph N.	4Aug1845		McCullough, William W.	
Denney, Francis	7Sept1846		Haynes, William A.	
Graves, James R.	2Nov1846		Coleman, James	
Puckett, William P.	7Dec1846		Fletcher, Granderson	?Heir of Charles Puckett, Dcd. 5June1854*
Bussey, George W.	7Dec1846		Flemming, Andrew J.	
Hall, John	7Dec1846		Pope, Hardy	
Albert	4Oct1847		Allen, William H.	Of color. Canc 4Feb1857, as Albert Daniel. Mistreatment. To be returned to Rutherford Co
Littleton	4Oct1847		Allen, William H.	Of color. Canc 4Feb1857 as Littleton Daniel. Mistreatment
Robert	4Oct1847		Allen, William H.	Of color. Canc 4Feb1857, as Robert Daniel. Mistreatment. To be returned to Rutherford Co
Louisia	4Oct1847		Allen, William H.	Of color
Winney	4Oct1847		Allen, William H.	Of color
Sinclair, Elizabeth J.	4Jan1847		Hampton, John C.	
Crosthwait, James	3Apr1848		Leath, Marcus H.	Orphan. Request of William Crosthwait. Canc 6Jan1851. To Crosthwait's custody
Fuller, William	2Apr1849		Fuller, Thomas	Orphan. 1Mar1852*
Singlen, Allan J.	7May1849		Floyd, James A.	Orphan
Ray, James	3Sept1849		Lewis, Andrew J.	
Hall, Alfred P.	1Oct1849		Pitts, William	Orphan
Summers, Joseph	4Feb1850		Summers, George D.	Orphan
Sharber, William C.	4Feb1850		Primm, John G.	Heir of John Sharber, Dcd. 5July1852*
Sharber, John E.	4Mar1850		Primm, Thomas M.	Heir of John Sharber, Dcd. 5July1852*
Bryant, Cynthia Ann	2Sept1850		Herod, Jane	Orphan
Hunt, James M.	2Sept1850		Parrish, Thomas L.	Consent of father, John W. Hunt

Name	Date	To Whom	Age/Term	Remarks
Primm, Sarah	1Sept1851	Primm, John G.		Orphan. Canc 6Oct1851. Bad treatment. To mother, Mrs. Nancy Primm
Primm. John W.	1Sept1851	Primm, John G.		Orphan. Canc 6Oct1851. Bad treatment. To mother, Mrs. Nancy Primm
Primm, Judith A.	1Sept1851	Primm, John G.		Orphan. Canc 6Oct1851. Bad treatment. To mother, Mrs. Nancy Primm
Primm, William	1Sept1851	Primm, John G.		Orphan. Canc 6Oct1851. Bad treatment. To mother, Mrs. Nancy Primm
Primm, Jarvis S.	1Sept1851	Primm, Jarvis		Orphan
Patton, John A.	7Mar1853	McManner, William M.		Orphan. Canc 6Mar1854. To mother, Eliza Patton, at her request
Summers, Josephus	2May1853	White, Robert G.		Orphan
Ferriss, Joseph	3Nov1856	Adkerson, John H.		Until 18 yrs
Daniel, Littleton	4Feb1857	Jordan, E. J.		For 2 yrs. Mulatto
Blair, John	7Sept1857	Blair, James W.	4 yrs	Until 18 yrs. Farming
Washington	6Jan year?	Allen, J. G.		Canc 6Dec1858.
Anthony	6Jan year?	Allen, J. G.		Canc 6Dec1858. Placed under the "guardianship & protection" of J. B. Lasater
Washington	6Dec1858	Lasater, J. B		Until 6Dec1860
Petty, Joseph	6Aug1860	Caffey, Medford		Until 18 yrs. Orphan. Agriculture
Petty, Thomas	6Aug1860	Caffey, Medford		Until 18 yrs. Orphan. Agriculture
Cruch, Edwin.	18Jan1866	Daniel, George	15 yrs on 1Jan last	FB. Farming
Duffer, Dock	9Mar1866	Keeble, H. P.	14 yrs on 4July last	FB. Consent of mother, Louisa Duffer
Mathis, Solomon	19Mar1866	March, Moses	15 yrs	FB. Farming. Mathis of Franklin Co
Bentley, Andrew	16Apr1866	Lawing, J. J.	7 yrs on 1Jan last	FB. Cabinet making
Willis, William	18Apr1866	Lawing, J. J.	11 yrs on 1Jan last	FB. Farming
Florida, Rebecca	24Apr1866	Manson, J. E.	9 yrs on 1Jan last	FB. Housework
Jones, Frank	24Apr1866	Holden, F. C.	6 yrs on 1Jan last	FB. Farming
Washington, George	24Apr1866	Adkinson, John H.	12 yrs on 1Jan last	FB. Farming
Daniel, Melvin	24Apr1866	Daniel, Richard	12 yrs on 1Jan last	FB. Farming
Lytle, Frank	10May1866	Hall, John Lewis	13 yrs on 1Jan last	FB. Blacksmithing

189

Name	Date	Age	Master	Notes
Spence, Rosa	11May1866	9 yrs on 1Jan last	Spence, John	FB. Housework. Until 19 yrs
Tyler, Amanda Elizabeth	19May1866	10 yrs on 1Jan last	Goodlow, Coleman	FB. House & needle work
Sarten, Nancy	7Aug1866		Nevel, Hampton	Mother, a free woman of color, dead
Sarten, John	7Aug1866		Nevel, Hampton	Mother, a free woman of color, dead
Armstrong, Bill	3Sept1866		White, Frank	Of color
Sharp, Frank	4Sept1866	10 yrs	Sharp, William P.	Of color. Canc 6Oct1866, request of father, James Smith
Sharp, Horace	4Sept1866	12 yrs	Sharp, William P.	Of color. Canc 6Oct1866, request of father, James Smith
White, William	1Oct1866		White, M. A. F.	Of color
Cook, Jack	1Oct1866		Love, John R.	Of color
Hollis	2Oct1866		Davis, Luckett	Of color
Bell, R. E.	4Feb1867		Adkerson, John H.	Of color. On 4Oct1870 Adkerson ordered to answer charge of maltreatment by R. B. Bell
Ingram, Prince	4Feb1867	10 (or 16) yrs	Miller, T. W.	Of color
Jordan, Edmund	6May1867		Brown, Parthenia	Of color. Legibility poor
Robison?, Frederick, 3 male children of	1July1867			Of color. Illegible
Baird, Benjamin	6Oct1868	14 yrs	Baird, J. M.	Of color
Baird, Ruth	6Oct1868	9 yrs	Baird, J. M.	Of color
Rily, Henry Brown	6Apr1869	9 yrs	Weakley, Hick	Consent of mother
Rily, Louisa F.	6Apr1869	7 yrs	Weakley, Hick	Consent of mother
Walden, Thomas	3May1869		White, Henry	Consent of father. Of color
Ward, Ella	2Aug1869	11 yrs	Bowman, Charles	Consent of child. Of color
Ward, George	2Aug1869	9 yrs	Bowman, Charles	Consent of child. Of color
Lynch, Melvina	4Sept1869	11 yrs	Lynch, Owen E.	Consent of child. Of color
Bell, Mary Ann Elizabeth	4July1870	14 yrs	Brantly, E. T.	
Ivy, Delia	1Aug1870	4 yrs	Tilford, H. W.	Of color
Wilson, Tom	6Sept1870		Jarnett, S. S.	Of Color
Arnold, Moses	4Oct1870		Arnold, Moses	Both of color
Arnold, Julian Elizabeth	4Oct1870		Arnold, Moses	Both of color

Name	Date	Age	Name	Notes
Ridley, Calo	4Oct1870		Ridley, Charles L.	Of color
Armstrong, G. W.	6Mar1871		Jernigan, Jesse	
Jones, Edmund	6Mar1871		Overall, Aaron	Both of color
Mappin, Charles	8Mar1871		Hartwell, John A.	Of color
Austin, Samuel	8Aug1871	10 yrs	Baxter, R. Z.	Of color
Miles, Laura	9Aug1871	9 yrs	Hicks, W. D.	Of color
Hoover, Samuel Odis	4Sept1871	5 mo	Hoover, Isaac	Both of color
Baugh, Tom	5Oct1871	9 yrs	Baugh, Mary Ann (Mrs)	Of color
Haley, Fannie	4Dec1871	10 yrs	Haley, P. B.	Of color
Valentine, Emiline	1Jan1872	6 yrs	White, B. N.	Of color
Ross, Pat	5Feb1872	6 yrs	May, Thomas	Both of color
Robinson, Jimmie	6Feb1872	12 yrs	Bolles, C. A. (Mrs)	Of color
Hendrix, Peyton	4Mar1872	14 yrs	Kelly, E. B.	Of color
Finney, Benjamin Martin	3Apr1872	15 yrs	Smith, Walter	Both of color
Finney, Abraham Martin	3Apr1872	14 yrs	Smith, Walter	Both of color
Armstrong, Jeff Davis	6May1872	11 yrs	Carter, P. A.	
Watson, Albert	5June1872	9 yrs	Eaton, T. T.	Of color. Canc 3Sept1872. Albert ran off
Williams, Edna	6Aug1872	6 yrs	McDonald, G. W.	Consent of Mary Williams, mother. Of color
Watson, Albert	3Sept1872	9 yrs	Moore, D. D. (Dr)	Of color. Request of Albert. Canc 3Aug1874. Moore leaving Tennessee
Wilson, Andrew	4Sept1872	14 yrs	Barber, John H.	Of color
Wilson, Fanny	4Sept1872	7 yrs	Henderson, William P.	Of color
Foster, Jim	4Nov1872	4 yrs	Dunnaway, Cumbey	Both of color
Butler, Anna	5Dec1872	10 yrs	Hallyburton, Mary H.	Of color
Crockett, Matilda	3June1873	11 yrs	Kirkman, Lewis	Both of color
Ruben, Fredric	4Nov1873	14 yrs	Lowe, Alfred P.	A prior indenture with E. Rosenfeld canc
Garratt, Green	2Feb1874	3 yrs	Youngblood, Isaac	Of color
Garratt, Simon	2Feb1874	6 yrs	Youngblood, Isaac	Of color
Garratt, Henry	2Feb1874	9 yrs	Youngblood, Isaac	Of color
Garratt, L. M.	2Feb1874	12 yrs	Youngblood, Isaac	Of color
Payne, Elana?	2Feb1874	10 yrs	Allen, W. N.	Male. Of color

Name	Date	Age	Master	Notes
Moore, Anna	7Sept1874	11 yrs	Moore, John T.	Of color
Moon, William	7Apr1875	8 yrs	Moon, Eliza	Of color
Scruggs, Oscar	7June1875	12 yrs	Scruggs, William	Of color
Scruggs, William	7June1875	8 yrs	Scruggs, William	Of color
Billings, James	4Jan1876	6 yrs	Todd, C. W.	White
Petty, Dennis	7Mar1876	9 yrs	Adams, J. M.	White
Turner, William	7Aug1876	12 yrs	Taylor, N. R.	White
Nations, Charlie	5Feb1877	7 yrs	Lyon, N. J.	Blacksmith & farmer
Neal, John P.	5Feb1877	15 yrs	Coleman, Jesse	Abandoned by father. Coleman is Grandfather
Neal, Susan E.	5Feb1877	11 yrs	Coleman, Jesse	Abandoned by father. Coleman is Grandfather
Reed, Mary	6Feb1878	13 yrs	Ross, W. A.	Of color
Howland, Welcome	4Nov1878	5 yrs	Murray, H. W.	White
Tucker, William	5May1879	8 yrs	Henderson, William T.	Of color. Cons of mother, Chainey Swafford
Webster, Mary	2June1879	15 yrs	Russell, Martha W.	Of color
Brewer, Wakefield	4Aug1879	9 yrs	Johnson, B. J.	Orphan. Of color
Lyon, Stephen	1Sept1879	13 yrs	Lowe, A. P.	Of color
Collier, Elen	5Nov1879	8 yrs	Ransom, W. A.	Of color
Settle, John	1Dec1879	10 yrs	Anderson, H. I.	Of color
Waters, Elizabeth	3Dec1879	7 yrs	Anderson, Charles W.	Of color
Waters, Robert	3Dec1879	10 yrs	Haynes, E. F.	Of color
Bullock, Asbury	4Mar1880	12 yrs	Jordan, M. B.	Until 18 yrs. Of color. Without father or mother. Consent of Asbury
Bullock, William	4Mar1880	8 yrs	Jordan, W. M.	Until 18 yrs. Of color. Without father or mother. Consent of William
Bullock, John E.	4Mar1880	10 yrs	Boehms, Joseph A.	Until 18 yrs. Of color. W/O father or mother. Consent of John
Jones, Babe	6July1880	4 yrs	Jones, A. B.	Illegitimate. Abandoned by mother. Of color
Jones, Cass	6July1880	3 yrs	Jones, A. B.	Illegitimate. Abandoned by mother. Of color
Haynes, Mary	7July1880	8 yrs	Hicks, James S.	Orphan. Of color
Lyon, Ann	7Dec1880	5 yrs	Lyon, J. P.	Of color. Without a father. Mother deranged

Smith County

Name	Date	Age	Master	Notes
Sutton, Polly	22Sept1801	Abt 7 mo	Sutton, John	Foundling. Original name unknown. 18Mar1801*
Craggot, Robert	23Sept1801	Abt 4 yrs	Barton, Benjamin	Orphan
Craggot, Peter	23Sept1801	Abt 10 yrs	Hibits, James (Esq)	Orphan
Hall, Reubin	23Dec1802	Abt 6 yrs	Dyer, Joel	Blacksmith
Billiff, Vallentine	23Dec1802	Abt 16 yrs	Greer, Andrew	
Hall, Margarett	23Dec1802	Abt 9 yrs	Johns, Isaac	
Short, Isaac	11Sept1804		Binion, John	Sadler
Stinkard, Mary	8Mar1808		Dale, Adam	Orphan. Guardianship terminated 5Sept1810. Of age
Thomason, Polly	6June1808		Payne, Benjamin	For 8 yrs. Orphan
Stinkard, William	5Dec1808		Williams, Morgan	Sadler. Previously bound to Lewis Johnson. On 7Sept1808 maltreatment alleged. Ordered taken from Johnson
Turney, Hopkins Lacy	6Sept1809		Cochran, John	Taylor. Son of Peter Turney, Dcd
Moss, John	8Mar1810		Moore, William	
Morris, Daniel	4June1810		Moore, William	Orphan. Printer
Bush, Moltan?	3Dec1810		Cawley, William	
Pinkley, Asa	7Dec1810		Smith, Jessie	Orphan
Handy, Vicey	7Dec1810		Smith, Jessie	
Smith, John	4Mar1811		Maden, Thomas	Black smith. Smith also choses Maden as guardian
Greson, Lydia	4Mar1811		Canter, Zachariah	Canc 27Sept1813
Grissom, Lydia	27Sept1813		Pendarris, William	
Carr, Peggy	29Sept1813		Chitwood, Pleastant	Canc 15Nov1819
Carr, Molly	29Sept1813		Chitwood, Pleastant	Canc 15Nov1819, as Matty Carr
Watkins, William	15Feb1814		Watkins, Joel M.	
Watkins, Overton	15Feb1814		Watkins, Joel M.	
Calhoun, Nelly	8Aug1814		Grisham, Peter	"Article of Agreement"
Whaley, James	12Aug1816		Williams, Silas W.	Sadler
Belew, Richard	10Nov1816		Liggon, William	Orphan. Millwright

193

Name	Date	Age	Master	Notes
Carr, Patsey	15Nov1819		Fare, Jonathan	Orphan
Mathewson, Daniel	15Nov1819		Harvey, Jr, John	Bound by John & Margaret McKinnie
Wilbourne, Thomas	15Nov1819		Brevard, Alfred A.	Orphan
Bright, Nelly	14Feb1820		Jeller, John	Orphan. Cancelled 5May1823, as John Tawler (master)
Johnson, Tempe	21Feb1820		Mills, James	Orphan
Smith, Spencer	21Feb1820		Parrott, Thorpe	Orphan
Unnamed	8May1820		Dillon, Daniel	Bound by Martin & Polly Holland
Brown, Mary Ann	8May1820		Roark, Asa	
Brown, Polly W.	8May1820		Teder, Elizabeth	
Goodan, John	8May1820		Lawler, John	Orphan. Cancelled 18Feb1821
Harrell, Asa	15May1820		Bowen, Jeremiah	Orphan
McClellan, Alfed	14Aug1820		Farmer, Philip	Orphan
Mobias, Elizabeth	14Aug1820		Farmer, Philip	Orphan. Canc 12May1823, as Phillip Parmer
Hare, Samuel	14Aug1820		Ballew, James	Orphan
Barton, John	13Nov1820		Durant, Thomas & Bantell, John	Orphan
Uhles, Frederick J.	13Nov1820		Uhles, Sr, Frederick J.	Orphan
Duke, Nimrod W.	20Nov1820		Moore, Benjamin	
Duke, Matthew	20Nov1820		Ralph, Thomas	
Payne, George	12Feb1821		Cornwell, Silas C.	Consent of David Hogg, Guard. 14May1821*
Goodin, John	18Feb1821		Mason, John	Orphan
Spivey, Thomas S.	18Feb1821		Mason, John	Orphan
Bush, Asa Martin	14May1821		Lyon, John	Of color. A prior indenture with Thomas R. Short cancelled
Bush, Asa Martin	21May1821		Lyon, John	Of color. Duplicate recording
Anderson, Albert Gallatin	21May1821		Raulston, James G.	Orphan
McClellan, Nancy	21May1821		Collins, Joseph	Orphan
McClellan, William	21May1821		Collins, Joseph	Orphan
Calibreath, Betsey	13Aug1821		Ellis, William	Orphan
Juniper, Sally	13Aug1821		Terry, Peter	Orphan

Name	Date		Name	Notes
Juniper, George Granderson	13Aug1821		Terry, Peter	
McKinney, Greenberry	13Aug1821		Brandon, Harrison	Orphan
Mobias, Charles F.	17Feb1822		Smith, William	Orphan
Garrison, Patsey	13May1822		Fite, John	Orphan
Garrison, Lucretia	13May1822		Evans, Joseph	Orphan
Garrison, Agnes	13May1822		Turner, Robert	Orphan
Jumper, Frank	12Aug1822		Terry, Peter	Orphan
Calbreath, William	4Nov1822		Bratton, Thomas	Orphan
Calbreath, Sally	4Nov1822		Atkinson, Elias	Orphan
Borom, William	5May1823		Parris, Obadiah	Orphan
Bright, Nelly	5May1823		Lyon, John	Orphan
Culbreath, Polly	1Dec1823		King, Samuel	Orphan. Cancelled 9Mar1825. Polly now 14 yrs, may choose her own master
Jones, Armstead	28Feb1825		Uhls, Richard	
Kitterell, William	7Mar1825		Jackson, Thomas	
McKinger, Greenberry	30May1825		Pankey, Uzzi	Orphan
Mulsan, Roby	22Aug1825		Douglass, Ila	Orphan. Of color. Canc 29Aug1825
Fellon, William	22Aug1825		Chapman, Daniel	
Mulsan, Rob	29Aug1825		Mosser, Samuel	Orphan. Of color
Strickland, David A.	4Mar1826		Linch, David	Orphan
Strickland, John	4Mar1826		Denton, James W.	Orphan
Justice, William	24Nov1828		Dale, Adam	Orphan
Witt, Morris	2Mar1829		Smith, Daniel	
Lewis	25May1825		Pate, Stephen	Of color
Bush, Irena	14June1829		Cochran, Simeon	Of color
Bush, Grandison	14June1829		Cochran, Simeon	Of color
Huchison, Sally	14June1829		Scruggs, Archibald	
Huchison, Daniel	14June1829		Scruggs, Archibald	
Buchinsan?, William	14June1829		Adcock, James	Orphan
Smith, Spencer	29Nov1829		Smith, Dennis	

Name	Date	Age	Master	Notes
Buck, Samuel	22Feb1830		Haynie, William	Mulatto. On 22Nov1830 an affidavit by Amy Haynie relating to the freedom of Buck ordered recorded
Tines, West	1Mar1830		Batton, Daniel	Orphan. Canc 24May1830. To mother
Franks, Joseph	23Aug1830		Lancaster, Dabney	Orphan. Cancelled 23May1831
Brown, Joseph	23May1831		Dillon, George W.	Orphan
Tyree, Abner C.	30May1831		Tyre, Thomas J.	Orphan
Stafford, Martha	28May1832		Carman, Archibald	Orphan. Annulled 4June1832
Mariah	3Sept1832		Wooten, Benjamin	Of color
Nelson	3Sept1832		Wooten, Benjamin	Of color
Richards, Walter	25Feb1833		Raymon?, David L.	
Edmond	25Feb1833		Evans, Onesimus	?Of color. Cancelled 4March1833
McKinney, Andrew	26Aug1833		Holloway, Henry	Orphan
Edmond	26Aug1833		Evans, Onesimus	Orphan
Starkey, James	25Nov1833		West, M. S.	Orphan
Gains, Polly	26Nov1833		Lyle, Stephen B.	Orphan. Bound to Lyle in Jackson Co February 1822. Now residing in Smith Co
Gains, Adaline	26Nov1833		Lyle, Stephen B.	Orphan. Bound to Lyle in Jackson Co February 1822. Now residing in Smith Co
Gains, Fletcher	26Nov1833		Lyle, Stephen B.	Orphan. Bound to Lyle in Jackson Co February 1822. Now residing in Smith Co
Gains, Washington	26Nov1833		Lyle, Stephen B.	Orphan. Bound to Lyle in Jackson Co February 1822. Now residing in Smith Co
Mourning	26Aug1834		Hutchison, William	Of color
Hutchison, William	24Nov1834		Beaty, William	Orphan
Justin, Henry	1Dec1834		Rison, Richard	Orphan
Mason, William A.	25Feb1835		Brevard, Alfred A.	Orphan
Walker, Robert	25May1835		Upton, Nancy	Orphan. Of color
Richards, John	24Aug1835		West, Thomas W.	
Suten, John	4July1836		Dillon, William B.	

Apprentice	Date	Age	Master	Notes
Nelson, William	4July1836		Dillon, William B.	
Chapman, William	1May1837		Bramer, John	Orphan
Chapman, Elizabeth	1May1837		Bramer, John	Orphan
Palmer, William	5June1837		Bridges, Joseph	Orphan. Taken from Bridges by William's father on 8Jan1841. Indenture cancelled
Paschal, Jackson	7Aug1837		Gullick, Jonathan	
Unnamed	7Aug1837		Farr, Jonathan S.	
Bandy, Jamison	5Mar1838		Bandy, Thomas	
Jackson, Andrew	5Feb1839		Stevens, John	Cancelled 2Aug1841
Beterworst, Adira	5Feb1839		Stevens, John	
Hunter, Henry	4Nov1839		Goard, Ruben	
Smith, John	7Sept1840		Smith, Isaiah	
Alison, Elizabeth	6Dec1841		Shomake, James	
Allison, Linus	6Dec1841		Martan?, Washington	
Allison, Frances Jane	3Jan1842		Glover?, G. T.	Cancelled 6Oct1845. To mother, Tabitha Allison. Glover leaving county
Rigsby, Lawson	7Feb1842		Herod, William	Orphan
Smith, John	4July1842		Black, David	Cancelled 2Nov1846
Hickman, Simon W	9Nov1842		Hickman, Stephen	
Hickman, Amalia S. A.	9Nov1842		Hickman, Stephen	
Penell, Washington	3Jan1843		Gee, John M.	
Whitehead, John	2Oct1843		Bridges, Joseph	
McGray, James	4Nov1844	15 yrs	Anderson?, Dorcas	7Oct1844*
McGray, And_	4Nov1844	12 yrs	Anderson?, William P.	
Hawkins, John R.	4Nov1844		Denny?, L. D.	
Orren, William	6Jan1845		Stevens, M.	Orphan
Buck, Samuel	5May1845		Webb, Ross	A prior indenture to Nelson Thornton cancelled
Allen, William James	5Jan1846		Ward, Nathan	
Allen, John D.	5Jan1846		Donell?, Thomas?	
Allen, Joseph F.	2Feb1846	Abt 10 yrs	Washburn, W.	Cancelled 5Feb1849
Grigsby, George	7Dec1846		Smith, F. M.	Orphan

Name	Date	Age	Master	Notes
Gillispie, James A.	4Apr1847		Smith, Jonathan H.	Orphan
Denham, Elizabeth	4Apr1847		Man, Timothy W.	Orphan
Denham,	4Apr1847		Man, Timothy W.	Orphan
Unnamed	6June1848		Brown, David	
Owens, David T. M.	4Sept1848		Smith?, William M.	
Allen, Joseph F.	5Feb1849		Allen, Benton	
Mitchell, Henry A.	5Feb1849		Gregory, Milton	On 7June1859 Mitchell's suit against Gregory to recover his payment due at completion of apprenticeship successful
Lucas, James E.	7May1849		Corley, Matthew	
Unnamed	6Aug1849		Washer, Thomas	
Muckleray, Francis	8Jan1850		Waitten?, Thomas W.	Of color
Allen, David L.	?		Turner, Wilson	Indenture cancelled, Allen having been bound to Willian H. George in Wilson Co
Prescott, William	5Aug1850		Cheek, William H.	
Hankins, Rowland	6Jan1851		Newly, Rowland W.	Newly ordered to post apprentice bond
Lucas, James E.	3Feb1851		Gill, Francis P.	
Gregston, George W.	7Apr1851		Jackson, A. T.	
Chapman, Isaac G. B.	1Sept1851	6 yrs	Cheek, Ephrain	Orphan. Farmer. Lost bond refiled 1Apr1867
Ball, John J.	5Apr1852		Burdin, John B.	Canc (as John Jasper Ball) 6Nov1855, having been bound in Wilson Co to C. C. Rutherford
Rice?, Linus? C.	6Sept1852		Coggins, Jeremiah C.	Apprentice name poorly legible
Pepper, Richard	4Oct1852		Jenkins, Obediah	
Braswell, Thomas	1Nov1852		Lancaster, Thomas	
Jones, Mary	2May1853		Baugh, William	
Lamb, Malinda J.	5Dec1853		Heynie, William	Also refered to as Malinda J.Land
Creasy, Josephus	6Mar1854		Smith, L. A.	
Jackson, Thomas	6Mar1854		Nowls, John S.	A prior indenture to William Suit cancelled
Hicks, James R.	6Feb1855		Minton, Joel W.C.	
Roberts, James	5Nov1855		Smith, Abner	

Name	Date	Age	Master	Notes
Lee, John	?		Weatherford, William B.	Indenture cancelled 7Nov1859. Weatherford about to leave state
Gass, Fountain E. P.	6Mar1860		Hughes, Leandrew	Orphan of Joseph Gass, Dcd
Jones, Thomas	1Apr1861		Massey, George W.	Taken from Eliazer Smith, former master, for bad treatment
Conditt, Betty	5Feb1866	10 yrs	Conditt, James M.	FB. Orphan
Conditt, Joseph	5Feb1866	8 yrs	Conditt, James M.	FB. Orphan
Conditt, Wilson	5Feb1866	4 yrs	Conditt, James M.	FB. Orphan
Conditt, Richmond	5Feb1866	2 yrs	Conditt, James M.	FB. Orphan
Saddler, Sam	10Feb1866	8 yrs	Beasley, Jessee	FB. Bound by mother, Marry Saddler
Saddler, John	10Feb1866	5 yrs	Beasley, Jessee	FB. Bound by mother, Marry Saddler
Saddler, Jeaner?	10Feb1866	10 yrs	Cooper, T. W.	FB. Bound by mother, Marry Saddler. Female. Until 21 yrs
Jones, John T.	5Oct1866	14 yrs	Crawell, M. M.	Farming. Abandoned child of John Jones. A prior indenture to G. W. Massey cancelled
McClelland, Harriett	12Dec1866	12 yrs	McClelland, Sampson	Abandoned. Farming. Of color
McClelland, Lettica	12Dec1866	9 yrs	McClelland, Sampson	Abandoned. Farming. Of color
McClelland, Ben	12Dec1866	8 yrs	McClelland, Sampson	Abandoned. Farming. Of color
Kyle, Jane	2Sept1867	Abt 7 yrs	Smith, Charles B.	Orphan of Hugh B. Kyle. Dcd
Kyle, Hughella	2Sept1867	Abt 5 yrs	Smith, Charles B.	Orphan of Hugh B. Kyle. Dcd
Hargus, Solomon	1Sept1873	9 yrs	Barrett, John M.	Mother without a husband, consents. Farming
McCall, Caldwell	3Sept1877		Pate, S. H.	Without father, mother, or means. Of color

Stewart County

Name	Date	Age	Master	Notes
Massada, Nathaniel	19Oct1807		Cook, Archibald	Orphan
Smith, Jeremiah	27Jan1809	16 yrs	Williams, John	Orphan. Bryant Oneal apptd guardian. Guardians apptd for Polley & Jenny Smith this date. One of 3 sons of Thomas Smith, Dcd. 26Apr1809* John Smith the third
Smith, Solloman	27Jan1809	20 yrs	Gatlin, James	Orphan. Farming. Guardians apptd for Polley & Jenny Smith this date. One of 3 sons of Thomas Smith, Dcd. 26Apr1809*
Collier, William	3Aug1812		Martin, Sr, George	Orphan. Cancelled 4Aug1812. To mother

8

Name	Date	Age	Master	Notes
Weston, Sarah	3Aug1813		Bowers, James	
Weston, Sally	3Aug1813		Bowers, James	
Russell, Jordan	4May1814		Bowers, James	
Cato, Rufus	2Aug1814	15 yrs	Cato, Burwell	Mulatto
Haggard, West Noel	7Nov1814		Bradford, Alsey	Orphan
			Haggard, Sr, William	Alias West Noel Lancaster. Consent of mother, Polly Lancaster
Lancaster, Crisianna	9Nov1814	Abt 3 yrs	Clark, Abram	Consent of mother, Sarah Lancaster
Guill, Armstead	5May1817	15 yrs	Gray, James	Hatter. Consent of mother, Elizabeth Guill. Sibs Sally Ann, Nancy & William 6Aug1816, 7May1817
Guill, Vincent	5May1817	13 yrs	Gray, James	Hatter. Consent of mother, Elizabeth Guill. Sibs Sally Ann, Nancy & William 6Aug1816, 7May1817
Branson, David	2Feb1819		McKinney, Ewing	Saddling
Sanders, Elijah	1Nov1819		Bingham, Martin	Farming. Son of Rebecca Sanders
Sanders, Enoch	1Nov1819		Bingham, Martin	Farming. Son of Rebecca Sanders
Berry, Simeon	7Aug1820		Skinner, Nathan	
King, Judith	6Nov1820		McCain, John	Until 21 yrs
King, Joshua	6Nov1820		Pinner, John	
Rataree, James	7May1821	15 yrs	English, Stephen	
Rataree, Thomas	7May1821		Gray, Thomas	Orphan son of James Rataree, Dcd
Sanders, Elijah	3Nov1823		Sanders, Rebecca	
Sanders. Enoch	3Nov1823		Sanders, Rebecca	
Taylor, Harriett	7Nov1823	In18th year	Cooper, Robert	Of color
Ford, Sally	3May1824		Hambleton, James	Orphan. Bastard child of James Ford
Cain, William	3May1824		Weston, Frederick	Orphan. Farming
Cain, John	3May1824		Weston, Frederick	Orphan. Farming
Ford, Sarah	3May1824		Hambleton, James	
Williams, Polly	2Aug1824		Miller, William	
Taylor, Harison	1Nov1824		Blanton, Richard	Of color
Black, Lowry	5Nov1828		Wimberly, Joseph P.	Orphan

Name	Date	Bound to	Notes
Black, Moses	5Nov1828	Wimberly, Joseph P.	Orphan
McGee, Elbert	5Nov1828	McGee, Adam	Orphan
Stalls, Samuel	?	Kingston, William	Indenture canc on 6Nov1828. 2Aug1830*
Slaughter, William	2Feb1829	McLoud, Malcomb	
William	4May1829	Bingham, John	Of color
Robertson, Henry	4May1829	Manning, Willis	
Slaughter, William	4May1829	Brown, Jane	Orphan
Newbery, Sally	4May1829	Andrews, Drewry	Orphan
Johnson, Edmond	2Nov1829	Owens, Robert	Orphan
Cherry, Monroe	2Nov1829	Stancill, John	Orphan
Black, Alexander	1826-27	Kimberly, George	Previously bound by Lurina Black, mother, now married to John Kersey, who, on 1Feb1830, requests that indenture be cancelled. Denied. Kimberly gives security 5May1830
Johnson, Edmond	3Aug1830	Acree, Edward	Orphan
Bennet, Samuel	1Nov1830	Alsbrook, John	Orphan. Farming
Bennet, Risden	1Nov1830	Alsbrook, John	Orphan. Farming
Johnson, William	2May1831	Downs, John	Orphan
Black, Lucinda	6Feb1832	Walker, Robert	Of color
Loary, Henry J.	6Feb1832	Jones, Wiley B. H.	Orphan
Scott, James	6Feb1832	Kelly, Benjamin	Orphan
Watson, Samuel	5Nov1832	Thompson, Augustis	Orphan
Collins, William W.	5Nov1832	Collins, Hanah	Hanah is mother of William
Brown, Robert	8May1833	Outland, Briant	Orphan. Cancelled 5May1834. Robert taken by his father
West, Moses	4Nov1833	Sidebottom, Fielding L.	Orphan. Sadling. Cancelled 1Feb1836*
West, John	4Nov1833	Sidebottom, Fielding L.	Orphan. Sadling
West, George	4Nov1833	Morris, Jesse	Orphan
Stalls, William	?	Taylor, Benjamin W.	Orphan. Indenture canc 4May1834. James Stalls to keep William at County expense
Newbery, Henry	5May1834	McDaniel, Mac	Orphan
Drury	5May1834	Harris, Susan	Orphan
Frunk, Westley	4Aug1834	Willin, Abitha	Orphan

Name	Date	Age	Master	Notes
Slaughter, Duncan M.	3Nov1834		McCloud, Roderick	
Black, Mary Jane	3Nov1834		Wimberly, Levi	Orphan
Black, William	3Nov1834		Wimberly, Levi	Orphan
Jackson, Byrum	4May1835		Crosswell, Nimrod	Orphan
Johnson, William	4May1835		Priestley, Philander	Orphan. Cancelled 4Aug1835
Stokes, Uriah George	2Nov1835		Etheredge, William	
Butler, Sally	2Nov1835		Winters, Nathan A.	Until 21 yrs
Johnson, William	1Feb1836		Bass, Norflet	Orphan
Jobe, William	2Feb1836		Griffin, Joseph	
Smith, George B.	2May1836		Thomas, Nathan	
Scott, James	3Oct1836		Parchment, John	
Johnson, Edmond	?		Taylor, Benjamin	Mistreatment alleged 7Nov1836* 5June1837*
McCollum, Jesse	6Feb1837	Abt 12 yrs	Skinner, Johnathan	
Black, Jackson	3Apr1837		King, Henry	
Black, Rebecca	3Apr1837		King, Henry	Until 21 yrs
Black, Julian	2Oct1837	7 yrs	Rogers, David	Of color
Black, Elizabeth	2Oct1837	8 yrs	Wall, John	Of color
Duffell, Benjamin F.	6Nov1837		Dawson, Elisha	
Black, Perry	6Nov1837		Taylor, Armsted	Of color. Canc 7Jan1839. Taylor leaving county.
Duffell, Joseph W.	6Nov1837		Gillaspie, William	
Smith, John N.	April1838		Findly, Luke D.	Cooper
Smith, William H.	April1838		Findly, Luke D.	Cooper
Black, Perry	7Jan1839		Pinner, John	Of color. Pinner ordered to bring child to court 1July1839. Cancelled & returned to mother, Rebecca Black, 6Apr1840
Wallace, Harriett	4Mar1839	10 yrs	Brandon, Wesly	
Rushing, John	6Jan1840		Martin, Jeremiah G.	Orphan of Clement Rushing, Dcd. Farming. Mark Rushing appt'd guardian 2Mar1840
Rushing, William	6Jan1840		Martin, Jeremiah G.	Orphan of Clement Rushing, Dcd. Farming. Mark Rushing appt'd guardian 2Mar1840

Name	Date	Age	Master	Notes
Gray, Henry	6Jan1840		Western, William T.	Consent of mother
Gray, Mary	6Jan1840		Western, William T.	Consent of mother
Black, Jackson	6Sept1841		McGee, William H.	Of color
Smith, Josiah	7Feb1842		Brandon, Nathan	For 20 yrs
Black, Rebeckah Ann	5Jun1842		King, Pennina	Until 21 yrs
Butler, Mahala	3Oct1842		Winters, Nathan A.	Until 21 yrs. Cancelled 5Feb1844
Butler, Merina	3Oct1842		Winters, Nathan A.	Until 21 yrs
Page, Henry	1May1843		Ellis, William H.	Orphan
Black, Catherine	5Feb1844		Goodrich, A.	Of color
Robertson, Henry	3Mar1845		Denson, Reuben	
Robertson, Memari	3Mar1845		Denson, Reuben	Female
Cunningham, Stephen T.	?		Manning, Tapley M.	Abuse alleged 6Oct1845. Indenture cancelled & boy returned to parents
Miles, Christopher L.	3Nov1845		Leeland, Sterlin B.	Tayloring
Fowler, David	8Apr1846		Gray, Peter F.	Of color
McCrutcher, Mary	6July1846		Gentry, Jefferson F.	Of color
Washer, Rebecka	7Dec1846		Gray, Martin J.	Alias Rebecka Fowler. Of color. Orphan. Canc 5Apr1847. To mother, Marjay Washer
Black, Amanda	1Feb1847		Wimberly, Mary	Until 21 yrs. Canc 5Apr1847, as Amanda Catherine. To mother, Melvina Elmore
Mills, George W.	1Mar1847	8 yrs	Williams, John S.	Orphan
Heath, Franklin C.	7Jan1850		Graham, Samuel	Orphan
Heath, Henry C.	7Jan1850		Graham, Samuel	Orphan
Black, John	3June1850		Williams, Danil C.	
Black, Richard	3June1850		Williams, Danil C.	
Black, William	3June1850		Williams, Danil C.	
Lancaster, Richard L.	3Feb1851		Williams, Joseph	
Henry	3Feb1851		Chambers, James	Of color. Cancelled 7Mar1853
Doty, Nancy	8Apr1851	8 yrs	Lankford, Leander	
Black, Sally	7July1851		Williams, Daniel C.	Of color
Finlay, William	3Nov1851		Bishop, Joseph	Of color

Name	Date	Age	Master	Notes
Finlay, George W.	3Nov1851		Bishop, Joseph	Of color
Finlay, Sally Eliza	3Nov1851		Ellis, William	Of color
Heath, Nancy Jane	1Mar1851		Jobes, James P.	
Busby, Martha E.	5July1852		Trinkle, Henry	Of color
Finlay, William	2Aug1852		Finlay, James	Of color
Finlay, George W.	2Aug1852		Finlay, James	Of color
Henry	7Mar1853		Gately, Thomas W.	Of color
Black, Robert	7Mar1853	12 yrs	Bates, Joseph B.	Abandoned by mother 7Feb1853
Black, Mary	7Mar1853	6 yrs	Atkins, Thomas M.	Until 21 yrs. Abandoned by mother 7Feb1853
Pass, Robert N.	5Apr1853		Darr, Andrew J.	Orphan. Son of Dicy Pass 5Oct1852*
Pass, Frances	5Apr1853		Darr, Andrew J.	Orphan. Dau of Dicy Pass 5Oct1852*
Doty, Nancy	5June1854		Manning, Mathew	Orphan
Curry, George	5June1854	10 yrs	Johnson, Abner	Son of Benjamin & Betsey Curry. Siblings Caroline & Maranda 6May1854
Cathon, John M.	3July1854		Lee, Samuel	
Dixson, Ephraim	3July1854		Kirksey, John	
Jordan, Wesly	4Dec1854		Stacker, Samuel	Of color
Jordan, Metilda	4Dec1854		Stacker, Samuel	Of color
Brewer, Richard	8Apr1856	7 yrs	Crockarell, Barnet	Of color
Word, John	4Aug1856	6 yrs 5 mo	Crick, John	
Knight, Thomas	3Nov1856		Pugh, W. H. A.	Orphan
Brown, Manda	1Dec1856	5 yrs	Martin, S. W.	Of color. Consent of mother
Brown, Danil	1Dec1856	4 yrs	Martin, S. W.	Of color. Consent of mother
Brown, William	1Dec1856	3 yrs	Martin, S. W.	Of color. Consent of mother
Brewer, Henry	7Jan1857	3 yrs	Rolls, J. S.	Of color
Norris, Nancy C.	4May1857	6 yrs	Brigham, James W.	Servant. Of color
Keet, Elizabeth	1June1857		Thompson, Oliver T.	Of color
Gooden, James P.	7Sept1857	10 yrs	Boyd Joel	Orphan

Name	Date	Age		Name	Notes
Brewer, Sandy	6Oct1857	9 mo		Stewart, Thomas H.	Of color
Burris, Nancy	2Nov1857	9 yrs		Parker, Laban	Servant. Orphan
Morehead, William	3May1858	4 yrs		Parchmen, James W.	Of color
Bullock, George	3Jan1859	13 yrs		Williams, Isaac	
Brewer, Henry	4Jan1859	5 yrs		Caldwell, G. W.	Of color
Weaver, Allen	7Feb1859	9 yrs		Cathey, George	Orphan
Combs, Fredonia	4Jan1860	15 yrs		Settle, Hamelton	Servant. Of color
Fowler, David	6Aug1860			Gray, Mary (Mrs)	Of color
Bridges, James T.	2Oct1860	7 yrs 8 mo		Barr, Alexander H.	Of color
Lancaster, William P.	4Feb1861			Kelly, Elisha	
Hester, Alexander	4Feb1861			Gillum, E. W.	
Hankins, Joseph	8Oct1861	7 yrs		Breeden, James	
Norris, John	3Oct1865	10 yrs 9 mo 3 d		Barr, Martha	Of color. Canc 1Apr1867
Floyd, James	3Oct1865	10 yrs 9 mo 18 d		Barr, Martha H.	Of color. Canc 1Apr1867
Menart	6Nov1865			Carter, B. N.	Of color. Canc 1Apr1867
Carter, Eddy	6Nov1865			Carter, B. N.	Of color. Female. Canc 1Apr1867
Scott, Winfield	6Nov1865			Carter, B. N.	Of color. Canc 1Apr1867
Moore, Satty	6Nov1865			Moore, Thum	Female
Doty, James	6Nov1865			Parchiner, J. T.	
McAuley, Jane	4Dec1865	10 yrs		Downs, Benjamin	Of color. Canc 1Apr1867
Parchman, Ella	4Dec1865	6 yrs		Parchman, Jesse	Of color. Canc 1Apr1867
Parchman, Mary	4Dec1865	10 yrs		Parchman, Jesse	Of color. Canc 1Apr1867
Parchman, Neely	4Dec1865	4 yrs		Parchman, Jesse	Of color. Female. Canc 1Apr1867
Parchman, Lizza	5Dec1865			Parchman, Jacob H.	Of color. Canc 1Apr1867
Parchman, Dora	5Dec1865			Parchman, Jacob H.	Of color. Canc 1Apr1867
Parchman, Bell	5Dec1865			Parchman, Jacob H.	Of color. Canc 1Apr1867
Parchman, Dennis	5Dec1865			Parchman, Jacob H.	Of color. Canc 1Apr1867
Bogard, Emely	5Dec1865				Of color. Canc 1Apr1867
Bogard, Randle	5Dec1865				Of color. Canc 1Apr1867
Bogard, Samuel	5Dec1865				Of color. Canc 1Apr1867
Bogard, Rose Ann	5Dec1865				Of color. Canc 1Apr1867

Name	Date	Age	Master	Notes
Bogard, Arthur	5Dec1865			Of color. Canc 1Apr1867
Bogard, Vina	5Dec1865			Of color. Canc 1Apr1867
Ellis, Lewis	5Dec1865		Ellis, W. H.	Of color. Canc 1Apr1867
Ellis, George	5Dec1865		Ellis, W. H.	Of color. Canc 1Apr1867
Ellis, Telemicus	5Dec1865		Ellis, W. H.	Of color. Canc 1Apr1867
Ellis, Fellis?	5Dec1865		Ellis, W. H.	Of color. Canc 1Apr1867
Ellis, James	5Dec1865		Ellis, W. H.	Of color. Canc 1Apr1867
Ellis, Charles	5Dec1865		Ellis, W. H.	Of color. Canc 1Apr1867
Ellis, Sallie	5Dec1865		Ellis, W. H.	Of color. Canc 1Apr1867
Ellis, Ellen	5Dec1865		Ellis, W. H.	Of color. Canc 1Apr1867
Landy, Barrum	5Dec1865		Landy, Edward	Of color. Canc 1Apr1867
Moore, John	5Dec1865		Moore, John D.	Of color. Canc 1Apr1867
Blanton, Pollard	5Dec1865		Wofford, W. G.	Of color. Canc 1Apr1867
Blanton, Alabama	5Dec1865		Blanton, J. R.	Of color. Female. Canc 1Apr1867
Blanton, James	5Dec1865		Jameson, J. S.	Of color. Canc 1Apr1867
Williams, Tommy	2Oct1866	10 yrs	Williams, Burrel	Female
Boswell, Jackson	3June1867	11 yrs 3 mo 3 d	Boswell, Hiram	
Ramsey, George	4Nov1867	7 yrs	Barford, James	
Hicks, Jesse	7June1869	11 yrs 6 mo	Vinson, J. C.	White. On 6Dec1869 suit seeking to cancel indenture rejected. On 3Aug1874 permission granted to remove to Illinois with Jesse
Hester, Leander	2Aug1869		Dillard, Newton	Both of color
Lane, Elizabeth	6Sept1869	7 yrs	Landy, Edward	Canc 2Nov1874. Lizzie to mother's custody*
Hardeson, Louisa	4Jan1870	6 yrs	Vickers, Thomas M.	Servant
Travis, Sam	2May1870	14 yrs	Dinkins, Robert	Servant. Of color
Melton, Robert M.	2May1870	10 yrs	Boswell, G. W.	Servant
Melton, William R.	2May1870	7 yrs next July	Boswell, G. W.	Servant
Bussel, Albert	5Sept1870	8 yrs	Cooly, W. M.	Servant. Of color
Presley, William Thomas	2Jan1871	12 yrs	Campbell, Joseph	Servant

Name	Date	Age	Master	Notes
Askew, William	6Feb1871	4 yrs	Askew, D. O.	Servant. Of color
Ramsey, George	6Feb1871	10 yrs	Stone, W. J.	Servant
Kelly, William Henry Burton	1Jan1872	9 yrs on 22Nov1871	Bruton, W. M.	Servant. A duplicate entry made next day
Ramsey, George	1Apr1872	12 yrs	Stone, Richard	White
Wilson. G. W.	2Dec1872		Wilson, James	Servant. Orphan of John Wilson. Dcd
Wilson, William	2Dec1872		Wilson, James	Servant. Orphan of John Wilson. Dcd
Bailey, Rebecca	3Feb1872		Crook, T. J.	Orphan of Henry Bailey, Dcd
Bailey, Finesse	2June1873		Herndon, R. M.	Orphan son of Henry Bailey, Dcd
Hogan, Cordelia T.	2Feb1874	7 yrs	Marshall, W. R.	Orphan
Ramsey, George	5Oct1874		Bradford, W. C.	
Aaron, Charles	5Apr1875	17 yrs	Bruton, W. M.	Servant
Hollister, Seymour	4Sept1876		Gault, Carrie D. (Miss)	Orphan. Servant. Of color
Hollister, Charley	4Sept1876	3 yrs	Gault, Carrie D. (Miss)	Orphan. Servant. Of color
Hollister, Ida	4Sept1876	6 yrs	Gault, Carrie D.	Orphan. Servant. Of color
Clements, Read	6Aug1877		Phippen, Charles	Orphan. Of color
Coleman, Royal	6Aug1877		Phippen, Charles	Orphan. Of color
Black, Viola	3June1878	Abt 5 yrs	Dunbar, W. L.	Alias Chick. Of color
Hollister, Seymour	2Sept1878	Abt 10 yrs	Hollister, Hellen	Of color
Hollister, Charles	2Sept1878	Abt 5 yrs	Hollister, Hellen	Of color
Hollister, Idah	2Sept1878	Abt 7 yrs	Hollister, Hellen	Of color
Bussell, George	6Oct1879	Abt 16 yrs	Free, W. R. J.	Orphan. Of color
Bussell, Lewis	6Oct1879	13 yrs	Free, W. R. J.	Orphan. Of color
Sampel, G. W.	2Feb1880		Jones, F. A.	Orphan
Sampel, A. J.	2Feb1880		Jones, F. A.	Orphan

Sumner County

Name	Date	Age	Master	Notes
Searcy, Richard	9Apr1787		McKain, James	Orphan. McKain also apptd guardian
Price, William	9Apr1787		Hardin, John	Orphan. Price to receive 200 Ac in Sumner Co when free
Searcy, John	9Apr1787		Hardin, John	Orphan
Searcy, Reubin	9Apr1787		Hardin, John	Orphan

Name	Date	Age	Master	Notes
Jinnings, Henry	7Jan1794		Cantril, Stephen	Orphan of Joshua Jinnings. Hatting.
Brooks, William	7Jan1794		Betts, Zachariah	Tanning & currying of leather
McClelan, Andrew	4Apr1796		Murphy, John	
Moore, Samuel	4Apr1796		Murphy, John	
Aflick (or Aslick), John	3Apr1797		Thomas, William	Orphan
White, John Witt	2July1798		Rather, James	Orphan
Grisham, Harris	2Oct1798		Kennedy, William	Wheel wright
Wall, Simon	8Jan1799		McKnight, Alexander	Blacksmith. Son of Peane? Wall, Dcd. On 3July1799 chose James Cryer as guardian
Wall, Hugh	8Jan1799		Wilson, Thomas	Farming. Son of Peane? Wall, Dcd. Brother of Simon Wall 3July1799
McAdams, Samuel	8Jan1799		Sample, William	Bound by father, Joseph McAdams
Parmer, Daniel	2July1799		Cooper, Christopher	Blacksmith
Parmer, Wilson Lee	2July1799		Cooper, Christopher	Blacksmith
Howel, William	17Jan1800		Gilespie, John	Cabinet trade. Orphan of Edward Howell, Dcd
Mullins, George Washington	5Jan1801		Bradley, John	Hatter
Jones, Mary	7Jan1801		Anderson, Matthew	Dau of Joyce Jones, free woman of color
Young, William	7Jan1801	1 yr	Bush, George	Orphan
Jones, Isham	7Jan1801		Seawell, William	Son of Joyce Jones, free woman of color
Jones, Moses	7Jan1801		Cryer, John	Son of Joyce Jones, free woman of color
Jones, Edmund	7Jan1801		Baker, Isaac	Son of Joyce Jones, free woman of color
Jones, Vina	7Jan1801		Hannum, Jonathan	Dau of Joyce Jones, free woman of color. Cancelled 8July1801
Jones, Vina	8July1801		Huginor Hogin, Edward	Dau of Joyce Jones, free woman of color
Jarod	9July1801		Seawell, Jr, Benjamin	Of color. House carpenter
Bunckley, Jonathan	7Oct1801		Callahan, James	Orphan. House carpenter
Candler, Ann	5Apr1802		White, Archibald	Orphan. Sewing, spinning, knitting, weaving
Turner, Samuel	5Apr1802		Garrett, William	Orphan. Taylor
Etheridge, Godfrey	5July1802		Adam or Odam, Moses	Sadler

Name	Date	Master	Notes
Morrish, Moses	7July1802	Winchester, William	Cabinet trade. Canc 22June1804. "Defect of genius to acquire said art"
Morrish, Catey	7July1802	Hall, William	
Morrish, Newburn	7July1802	Hall, William	
Morrish, Nelley	7July1802	Harrison, James	
Bowyer or Boyce, Pleasant	4Oct1802	Miller, Frederick	Farming
Williams, William	6Oct1802	Piper, Samuel	
Parsons, John	5July1803	Perry, Rolls	Orphan. House carpenter
Houch, George	20Mar1804	Stuart, John	Orphan. Wheel right
Weathers, Patsey	20June1804	Weathers, John	
Morrish, Moses	22June1804	Winchester, James	Orphan. Miller
Williams, William	17Sept1804	Pewatt, John	Orphan
Turner, Betsey	20Sept1804	Miers, Eandier	
Mitchell, Stephen	20Sept1804	Moss, Thomas	Orphan. Wheelright
Donoho, Isaac	18Dec1804	Simpson, James	Orphan. Tanning & currying leather
Zeigler, John	19Dec1804	Shackleford, Thomas	Orphan. Bricklaying
Jones, William	18Mar1805	Clark, Joseph	Orphan
Lowry, William	19June1805	Catron, Christly	Orphan. Farmer
Lowry, Reuben	19June1805	Catron, Christly	Orphan. Farmer
Edwards, John	21June1805	Spooner, John	Orphan. Cabinet maker. Orphan of John Edwards, Dcd
Brown, John	22Mar1808	Pendergrass, John	Taylor. Data from cancellation 13Mar1810
Webb, John	21June1808 18 yrs	Draper, Joshua	Orphan. Blacksmith
Melton, Andrew	12Sept1808 12 yrs	McGuin, Thomas	Orphan
McClung, Peggy	12Sept1808 8 yrs	Duty, George	Orphan
Melton, Thomas	12Sept1808 15 yrs	Foster, David	Orphan
Young, Thomas	12Sept1808 9 yrs 6 mo	Harper, Summers	Orphan. Stone mason & bricklayer
Rosber, John	23Sept1808 15 yrs	Blythe, Samuel K.	Orphan. Nailer
Jarrett	14Mar1809 13 yrs	Steele, Robert	Of color
Jossy, John E.	24Mar1809 14 yrs 4 mo	Truett, John B.	Orphan. Shoe & boot maker
Morrish, Caty	12June1809	Crook, Eiben	Orphan

Name	Date	Age	Master	Notes
Morrish, Neubern	12June1809		Crook, Eiben	Orphan. House carpenter
Benthall, Enos	13Sept1809		McCall, William	Orphan. Hatting
Moore, Timothy	21Sept1809		Hall, George	Orphan. Tanning & currying
Asbrooks, William Wilson	11Dec1809	13 yrs on 6th inst	Parker, Daniel	Orphan
Asbrooks, Nancy	11Dec1809	11 yrs in Mar1810	Gambling, James	Orphan. Canc 15Sept1812
Brown, John	13Mar1810		Youree, Patrick	
House, William	16Mar1810		Scurry, Thomas	Orphan. Hatter
Latimer, Nathaniel	10Sept1810	17 yrs	Latimer, Joseph	Orphan. Farmer. Prior binding to Richard Cope cancelled
Wilkerson, Joel	10Sept1810	9 yrs 8 mo	Allen, Rhodam	Orphan. Cooper
Starks, Lucy	13Dec1810		Trumbo, Ambrose	On 9Dec1811 ordered returned to court. Trumbo dead
Gardner, William	11Mar1811		Patton, David	Shop joiner & cabinet maker
Kennedy, William	12Mar1811		Hall, George	
Phipps, Charles	12Mar1811		Turner, Martin	
Byrum, Jeremiah	13Mar1811	16 yrs	McCorkle, James M.	Orphan. House carpenter. Prior binding to William Seawell cancelled
Horner, James	9Dec1811		Wynne, Peter	Orphan. Taylor
Byrum, Moses	11Mar1812		Blythe, Samuel K.	Blacksmith
Bloodworth, James	13Mar1812	14 yrs	Seevia, Jacob	Orphan. Sadler
Douglass, Alfred	10June1812	8 yrs	Reid, George	Orphan
Groom, William	15Sept1812	15 yrs	Herndon, Cornelius	Orphan
Smith, Benjamin	16Sept1812	9 yrs	Smith, William	Orphan. Saddler
Smith, Rebecka	16Sept1812	11 yrs	Cloar, Absolam	Orphan
Johnson, Thomas Ross	16Sept1812	7 yrs on 17Aug1811	Holley, Jonathan	Bound by father, George Johnson, on 30Mar1811. 17Sept1812*
Johnson, John	16Sept1812	5 yrs on 5May1811	Holley, Jonathan	Bound by father, George Johnson, on 30Mar1811. 17Sept1812*
Downs, William May	16Dec1812	17 yrs on 12Aug next	Lambeth, William	Orphan. Horn comb making
Powell, Starkey	12July1813	6 yrs	Winham, Stephen	Orphan. Shoe & boot making

Apprentice	Date	Term	Master	Notes
Douglass, Luvena	13Oct1813	4 yrs	Boyles, Robert	Orphan
Young, Thomas			Harper, Lummus	A prior indenture cancelled 1Mar1814
Parmelton, Maria	1Mar1814		Blakemon, Thomas	Orphan
Melton, Andrew	3Mar1814		Bull, Richard	Prior binding to Thomas McGuire cancelled
Parker, William	3Mar1814	11 yrs	Woodall, Christopher	Orphan
Mallard, John	24May1814		Mallard, Joseph	Farming
Duty, Henry	24May1814		Black, John	Orphan of George Duty, Dcd. Gunsmith. Cancelled 30May1816
Duty, Philip	24May1814		Anderson, Samuel	Orphan of George Duty, Dcd. Cabinet & Joiner trade
Stafford, Patsey	22Aug1814	10 yrs	Hansbrough, Daniel	Orphan
McNeely, Betsey	29Nov1814	11 yrs	Barr, William	Orphan
McNeely, Polly	29Nov1814	9 yrs	Barr, Hugh	Orphan
McNeely, Sarah	29Nov1814	3 yrs	Barr, Patrick	Orphan
Moon, William	3Dec1814	16 yrs	Stewart, John	Orphan. Carpenter house joiner
Gunsalls, David	19Feb1815	16 ys	Jennings, John	Orphan. Sadling
Trapenanfearey, Philip	28Feb1815	15 yrs	Dugger, Leonard	Orphan. Shoemaking
McNeely, Robert	28Feb1815	7 yrs	Barr, Hugh	Orphan
Adams, Lewis	23May1815		Scurry, Thomas	Orphan. Hatter
Morris, Ann	23May1815		Green, Daniel John	Orphan
Adams, Eli	23May1815		Stalcup, James	Orphan. Blacksmith
Branton, Abel	24May1815		Davis, Nathan	Orphan
Tinsley, Tipton	2Aug1815		Turner, William	Orphan. Farming
Kettle, Sally	28Nov1815	11 yrs	Bledsoe, William L.	Orphan
Bloodworth, Alexander	30Nov1815	6 yrs next April	McAdams, William	Orphan
Allen, William	1Mar1816		Henderson, Charles	Orphan of Porter Allen, Dcd. Cabinet workman
Allen, David	2Mar1816		Given, Edward	Orphan of Porter Allen, Dcd
Allen, Thomas	2Mar1816		Given, Edward	Orphan of Porter Allen, Dcd
Allen, Lytle	2Mar1816	19 yrs on 8Oct next	Frack, Henry	Orphan. House carpenter
Allen, David	2Mar1816	6 yrs	Given, Edward	Orphan of Porter Allen, Dcd
Allen, Thomas	2Mar1816	6 yrs	Given, Edward	Orphan of Porter Allen, Dcd
Holt, Greaf	27May1816	19 yrs on 1Feb next	Smith, John	Orphan. Blacksmith

Name	Date	Age	Master	Notes
Simpson, Elisha	27May1816	9 yrs on 25Dec next	Higgins, Bernard	Orphan. Spinning
Rice, John	27May1816	17 yrs on 1Mar last	Turner, John	Orphan. Cabinet making
McNeely, Asa	28May1816	7 yrs on 14Jan next	Hodge, William	Orphan. Hodge also apptd guardian
Benthall, Laban	31May1816	14 yrs on 25Feb last	McCall, William	Orphan. Hatter
Hood, Alexander	31May1816	18yrs on 25June next	Stamps, John	Orphan. Making & laying of brick
Reddett, Starkey	28Aug1816	14 yrs	Byrns, John	Orphan. Shoe making. Son of Theophilus Reddett, Dcd. Elijah Rutledge apptd guardian 17May1819. 20Nov1820*
Wilson, Zauhuis?	29Aug1816	17 yrs	Stamps, John	Orphan. Brick laying
Keith, Bennett J.	29Aug1816	17yrs on 27Sept last	Bell, John	Orphan. Taylor
Benthall, Daniel	29Aug1816	16 yrs 5 mo	Henderson, Charles	Orphan. Cabinet making
McNeeley, Aaron	25Nov1816	17 yrs 3 mo	Crocket, William	Orphan. Tanning & currying
Loury, William	26Nov1816	18 yrs next March	Loury, James	Orphan. Hatting
Loury, Reuben	26Nov1816	17 yrs next March	Loury, James	Orphan. Hatting
Williams, William	26Nov1816	17 yrs next July	Uzzle, Jourdan	Orphan. Hatting
Clary, Vachel	30Nov1816	17 yrs	Bell, John	Orphan. Male
Carter, James A.	26May1817		Fleming, Beverly	Orphan. Wheelwright
Dean, Thomas	26May1817		Bell, John	Orphan. Taylor
Unnamed male	26May1817	10yrs on 12Nov next	Jackson, Craven	Orphan. Plastering
Pulford, David	15Feb1819	14 yrs	Outlaw, John C.	Orphan. Book keeping
Ellis, Simeon	22Feb1819	9 yrs	Crocket, William	Orphan. Tanning & currying
Cheek, Randel	17May1819	14 yrs next March	Kyser, Philip	Orphan. Cooper
Lassley, Malcom	18May1819	13 yrs 13th this mo	Hutcheson, Alexander	Orphan. Cabinet maker
Morris, Thomas	24May1819		Hassell, Joudan & Grayor, James M.	Sadler
Jones, Daniel	16Aug1819	10 yrs	Hutcheson, Alexander	Orphan. Cabinet making. On same date Hutcheson apptd administrator of estate of Isaac Jones, Dcd

Name	Date	Term/Age	Master	Notes
Jones, John	16Aug1819	7 yrs	Hutcheson, Alexander	Orphan. Cabinet making. On same date Hutcheson apptd administrator of estate of Isaac Jones, Dcd. 10Feb1828* Indenture & guardianship canc 11Aug1829* 19Aug1829*
Hall, William	17Aug1819		Metlock, William	Orphan, Farming. Indent signed 14Feb last
Atkins, William	23Aug1819		Byrn, John	Shoe & boot maker
Warner, Reuben	23Aug1819		Byrn, John	Shoe & boot maker
Carter, Delilah	15Nov1819	5 yrs last Aug	Ragan, James	Orphan
Lyttle, Betsey	21Feb1820		Johnson, Richard	Orphan
Lyttle, Nancy	21Feb1820		Johnson, Richard	Orphan
Lyttle, Polley	21Feb1820		Johnson, Richard	Orphan
Little, William	21Feb1820	3 yrs next April	Parrish, Benjamin	Orphan. Farming
Bloodworth, Melinda	21Feb1820	6 yrs 15 days	Turner, Philip	Orphan
Unnamed male	21Feb1820		McReynolds, Joseph	Carpenter
Roster, Thomas	22Feb1820	18 yrs on 12Nov1819	Stewart, John	Orphan. Carpenter & joiner
Roster, George	22Feb1820	18 yrs on 12Nov1819	Stewart, John	Orphan. Carpenter & joiner
Wells, Austin	25Feb1820		Harrison, Richard	Orphan. Farming & currying
Morrison, John	29Feb1820	17 yrs on 16Sept last	Stamps, John	Orphan. Making & laying of brick
Morrison, Samuel	29Feb1820	15 yrs on 16Sept last	Stamps, John	Orphan. Making & laying of brick
Stilts, Moses	15May1820	8 yrs	Groves, Allen	Orphan. Cooper
Bloodworth, Betsey	15May1820	8 yrs on 6Feb last	McReynolds, Joseph	Orphan. 22May1820*
McFarland, Thomas	22May1820	15 yrs on 10Apr last	Given, Joseph	Orphan. Farming. 28Feb1820*
McFarland, Archibald	22May1820	12 yrs on 12Apr last	Given, Joseph	Orphan. Farming. 28Feb1820*
Proctor, Alfred	21Aug1820		Holt, Henry	Of color. Blacksmith
King, George	28Aug1820		McLin, John	Of color. Blacksmith
Stapleton, Martha	28Aug1820	7 yrs	Donnell, Thomas	Of color
Briganer, John	28Aug1820	14 yrs	Dicky, James	Orphan. Taylor

Name	Date	Age	Master	Notes
Choat, Preston	20Nov1820	9 yrs	Harrison, Richard	Orphan. Tanning & currying
Allen, Ira N.	27Nov1820		Henderson, Charles	Orphan. Cabinet maker
Pyle, William	26Aug1822	18 ys	Winham, Robert	Orphan. Shoe & boot making
Proctor, Alfred	26Aug1822	Abt 8 yrs	Outlaw, John C.	Orphan. Tavern keeping
Pyle, Ford	26Aug1822	17 yrs	Winham, Robert	Orphan. Shoe & boot making
Tarver, Jourdan	8Aug1825	16 yrs	Stewart, John	Orphan. House carpenter
Smith, Hobson	9Aug1825	18 yrs	Stewart, John	Orphan. House joiner & carpenter
Burton, Lewis	17Nov1825	17 yrs 9 mo	Crocket, William	Orphan. Tanner & currier
Tavern [Tarver?], Patsey	13Feb1826	6 yrs	Wright, William	Orphan. Housewifery
White, William	20Feb1826	13 yrs	Bell, John	Taylor
Wynn, Valia Coste	21Feb1826	18 yrs	Knight, James	Plaistuer
Bryann, William	8May1826	17yrs on 12June next	Schabell, John F.	Orphan. Taylor
Cloar, William	12May1826	16 yrs	Chappell, Robert	Orphan. Cabinet business
Ornstreet, William	14Aug1826	14 yrs	Bean, Alfred M.	Orphan. Blacksmith
Brasher, Zachariah	14Aug1826	15 yrs	Tyler, Stephen	Orphan. Blacksmith. Rescinded 21Aug1826
Lasseter, Eliza	15Aug1826	9 yrs	May, Baley	Orphan. Housewifery. Cancelled 17Nov1828
Lasseter, Clarissa	15Aug1826	6 yrs	Lasseter or Lawrence, Robert	Housewifery
Shoemake, Polly	21Aug1826	12 yrs	Bell, William	Housekeeping. With brother, Eli, taken from father, Pearcy Shoemake 18Aug1826
Shoemake, Eli	21Aug1826	8 yrs 5 mo	Stewart, John	House carpenter. With sister, Polly, taken from father, Pearcy Shoemake 18Aug1826. Canc 18Feb1829. To reputed father, John White
White, Iredale	13Nov1826	14 yrs	McKoin, James L.	Orphan. Cabinet business
Brothers, William	14Nov1826	6 yrs	Evans, Cornelius	Orphan. Brick layer & stone mason
Berry, Henry S.	14Nov1826	15 yrs	Schabell, John F.	Orphan. Taylor
Nickens, Laurence B.	20Nov1826	14 yrs	Martin, Peter H.	Orphan. Sadler
Taylor, Mary	20Nov1826	7 yrs	Anderson, Phoebe	Orphan. Housekeeping
Taylor, John	20Nov1826	11 yrs	Parker, John	Orphan. Farming

Taylor, Marcus	20Nov1826	10 yrs	Parker, William	Orphan. Farming
Taylor, William	20Nov1826	15 yrs	Hallaway, James	Orphan. Farming
Taylor, Moses	20Nov1826	3 yrs	White, Thomas	Orphan. Farming
Green, Parris	13Feb1827	18yrs on 17Sept next	Dillion, Daniel	Orphan. Tanner, currier & dresser of leather
Bloodworth, Thomas	19Feb1827	19 yrs	Griffin, John	Blacksmith
James	19Feb1827		Stealy, John M.	Of color. Tanner
Tadlock, Sally	20Feb1827	10 yrs	Jourdan, Thomas	Illegitimate child. Housewifery
Ragan, Isaac Jesse	15May1827	1 yr	Tilly, Wiley	Orphan. Farming
Turnage, Shelby	21May1827	15 yrs	Grooms, John	Orphan. Shoemaker
Whitson, Steptner [Stephen?]	17Nov1827	15 yrs in May last	Stewart, John	Orphan. House carpenter & joiner
Whitson, Leonard	17Nov1827	13 yrs in Jan last	Stewart, John	Orphan. House carpenter & joiner
Ragsdale, Thomas	19Nov1827	15 yrs	Sanders, William	Orphan. Tanner & currier of leather
Starks, John	19Nov1827	17 yrs on 9May last	Arnold, Ebenezer	Orphan. Blacksmith
Nickins, Elizabeth	19Nov1827	11 yrs in March last	West, Robert	Orphan. Housekeeping. Canc 10Nov1829
Vaughan, Joel	24Nov1827	14 yrs on 25Apr last	Robertson, Elijah	Orphan. Farmer
Jones, Jackson	13Feb1828	9 yrs	Winham, William	Of color. Shoe maker
Murry, Alfred	14Feb1828	16 yrs	Martin & Henly	Orphan. Sadler. For 4 yrs from last Christmas
Jones, Dotia	14Feb1828	7 yrs	Winham, William	Of color. Housekeeping, weaving etc
Barber, Thomas	21Feb1828	15 yrs	Winham, Robert	Orphan. Shoe & boot maker
Justice, Adison	12Aug1828	7 yrs in Dec last	Justice, Mark	Orphan. Farming
Ferrell, Alsey	10Nov1828	18 yrs next Feb	Arnold, Ebenezer	Orphan. Blacksmith
Lassater, Eliza or Maliza	17Nov1828	12 yrs & 9 mo	West, John	Housekeeping & weeving
Carr, Harrison Jackson	17Nov1828	15 yrs	McKoin, James L.	Orphan. Cabinet workman
Bloodworth, John	18Nov1828		McKoin, James L.	Cabinet workman. Cancelled 23Feb1831
Jackson, Eleanor	17Feb1829	Abt 9 yrs	Hudson, James	Orphan. Housekeeping
Jones, Edmund	18Feb1829	Abt 14 yrs	Pyle, Joshua	Of color. Silversmith
Jackson, James	21Feb1829	14 yrs	Laudordale, John	Orphan. Farmer
Stewart, William Morgan	11May1829	4 1/2 yrs	Arnold, Ebenezer	Of color. Blacksmith
Brady, Reuben	12May1829		Bernard, Elisha	Son of Betsey Brady. Farming
Brasier, Isaac	12May1829		Wood, Henry A.	Son of Martha Brasier. Farming

Name	Date	Age	Master	Notes
Glover, Harriet	10Aug1829	6 mo	Montgomery, Stephen	Of color. Housekeeping, weaving etc
Handershott, George Washington	9Nov1829	16 yrs	Crocket, William	Orphan. Tanner & currier of leather
Nickens, Elizabeth	10Nov1829	13 yrs	Love, William	Orphan. Housekeeping, weaving, sewing etc
Shewmake, Zaritha	16Nov1829	14 yrs	Markham, Sabrina	Orphan. Housekeeping & weaving. 17Aug1829*
Emmury, John	19Nov1829	16 yrs	Stewart, John	Orphan. House carpenter
Emmury, William	19Nov1829	18 yrs	Stewart, John	Orphan. House carpenter. Exp 15Mar1832
Frazor, Martin	15Feb1830	16 yrs	Joiner, Hugh	Until 20 yrs. Orphan. Making patent spinning machines
Frazor, Danal Jones	15Feb1830	14 yrs	Joyner, Hugh	Until 20 yrs. Orphan. Making patent spinning machines
Williams, Elijah	16Feb1830	13 yrs	Freeman, James	Until 20 yrs. Orphan. Brick mason
Holmes, Thomas	12May1830	10 yrs in Feb last	Martin, William	Orphan. Shoe maker & farmer. Alias Thomas Butler
Loman, Caroline	10Aug1830	10 yrs next Feb	Gregory, Pembleton	Orphan. Housekeeping, weaving etc
Slater, Edward	20Aug1830	15 yrs on 19Mar last	Saffarrous, Danal	Orphan
Taylor, Alfred	?		Collins, John G.	A prior indenture cancelled 15Nov1830
White, Hardy	21Feb1831	13 yrs in June next	McKoin, James L.	Orphan. Cabinet workman
White, Alfred	21Feb1831	10 yrs on Jan next	Bell, John	Orphan. Taylor
Harris, John D.	22Feb1831	13 yrs on 25Mar next	Lauderdale, Samuel H.	Orphan. Farming
Shoemake, Henry	22Feb1831	12 yrs	Simpson, Benjamin F.	Orphan. Blacksmith
Loman, Frances	22Feb1831	Abt 6 or 7 yrs	Simpson, Benjamin F.	Of color. Housekeeping
Hollis, William	10May1831	11 yrs	Gray, Benjamin & Gray, Charles H.	Orphan. Winsor chair making & painting
Sharlock, William	8Aug1831	14 yrs	Taylor, Alexander K.	Orphan. Farming
Alexander, Edwin	10Aug1831	Abt 13 yrs	Warner, J. L.	Orphan. Tayloring
Alexander, Joseph	10Aug1831		Warner, J. L.	Orphan. Tayloring
Holmes, Martin Thomas	15Nov1831	11 yrs in Feb last	Martin, James L	Orphan. Saddler & farrier. Alias Thomas Butler. Cancelled 2Oct1837
Wells, James	21Nov1831	16 yrs in Jan next	Solomon & Harrell	Orphan. Hatter
Ferguson, Edward	20Aug1832		Simpson, B. F.	Orphan. Cancelled 6Sept1836. Edward disabled from a white swelling on the leg. Data from cancellation entry

Name	Date	Term	Surety	Notes
Butler, John	10Feb1835	11 yrs	Davis, Samuel	Orphan. Blacksmith
McCorkle, Eliza	10Feb1835	7 yrs	Meador, Joseph G.	Orphan. Housekeeping, spinning, weaving
Patton, William	17Feb1835	15 yrs on 24Apr next	Bell, John	Orphan. Taylor
Rogers, David	12May1835	17 yrs on 14Apr last	Alexander, Josiah A.	Orphan. House carpenter
Cummins, Mary Jane	12May1835	14 yrs in Aug next	Stalcup, Elijah	Orphan. Housekeeping. One of three daughters of Lucinda Cummins (in poor house) 17Feb1835. 11Aug1835*
Cummins, Sarah Jane	11Aug1835	14 yrs in Aug last	Stalcup, Barbery	Apparantly corrected entry. Elijah now surety
Jackson, George W.	11Aug1835	15 yrs on 28Apr last	Potts, Robert M.	Orphan. Sadler
Rodgers, Enos	11Aug1835	19 yrs in May last	Foster, John B.	Orphan. House carpenter
Clark, Charles W.	13Nov1835	11 yrs on 6Feb next	Warner, Jacob L.	Orphan. Tailor
Barns, Jackson	9Feb1836	8 yrs	Hunt, George G.	Orphan. Blacksmith. Canc 6June1836*
Tovnor, Joseph	6June1836	15 yrs	Turner, William	Orphan. Making hats
Coleman, Alfred	6June1836	15 yrs 3 mo	Gray, B. & C. H.	Orphan. Chair making & painting
Cook, John	6June1836	12 yrs	Dilliard, Gabrial	Orphan. Boot & shoe maker. 10Nov1835*
Clark, William E. W.	6June1836	13 yrs	Bell, John	Taylor
Bloodworth, Chapman	7June1836	17 yrs	Pincham, Peter	For three yrs & six mos. Blacksmith
Martin, Zachariah	5July1836	14 yrs 7 mo	Turner, William	Orphan. Hatting
Phillips, Thadeus	1Aug1836	17 yrs 7 mo	Burtrand, Joseph N.	Orphan. House painting
Harvey, Mathew	7Nov1836	15 yrs 20 days	Solloman, William	Orphan. Hatting
Lewis, Edward	3Jan1837		Douglass, Y. N.	For seven years
Neely, Isaac	6Feb1837	16 yrs	Renn, C. G.	Orphan. House carpenter
Winston, John	6Feb1837	11 yrs	Pincham, Peter	Orphan. Carriage making
Pitt, Alfred	6Feb1837	17 yrs on 5 Aug1836	Warner, J. L.	Taylor
Ray, James C.	7Aug1837		Renn, C. G.	Deed of indenture. Orphan
Martin, Zachariah	4Sept1837	16 yrs on 7June last	Foster, John B.	House carpenter. On 5Mar1838 an order to cancel & rebind crossed out
Homes, Thomas	2Oct1837	17 yrs last Feb	Pursley, Daniel O.	Orphan. Tanner. Alias Thomas Butler
Lomax, William	2Oct1837	14 yrs	Gray, Ben	Orphan. Chair making & painting
Stanley, John	2Oct1837	Abt 7 yrs	Webb, James G.	Orphan. Brick making & laying

Name	Date	Age	Master	Notes
Sanley, Jane	6Nov1837	12 yrs	Combs, William	Orphan
Johnson, Robert	4Dec1837	Abt 9 yrs	Staley, Oscar	Orphan. Tanning
Johnson, Nathaniel	4Dec1837	Abt 11 yrs	Staley, Oscar	Orphan. Tanning
Bradley, John Carrol	4Dec1837	6 yrs on 12Mar1831!	Skein, Keenan T.	Tanning. For 14 yrs 9 mo 14? days. Entry crossed out
Silvers, Alsey	1Jan1838	12 yrs	Bugg, Bob	Orphan. House carpenter. Canc 7May1839
Megee, William	5Feb1838		Morrison, John	Brick laying
Stewart, James	5Feb1838		Wren, C. G.	House carpenter
Martin, Zachariah	5Mar1838	16 yrs	Johnson, Austin	Orphan.
Jackson, Andrus	5Mar1838	14 yrs	Barrow, Bartholomew	Orphan. Blacksmith
Gillespie, Gideon	7May1838		Kelly, Warren	Until age 15 yrs
Kilbuck, Washington	6Aug1838	17 yrs	Stewart, John	Carpenter & joiner
Cluck, Martha	3Oct1838	Nearly 14 yrs	Jenkins, Thomas	Orphan. Housewifery
Dickerson, William	7Jan1839	16 yrs 8 mo	Solomon, William	Orphan. Hatting
Toomy, James	1Apr1839		Alexander, James	House joiner & carpenter
Rutherford, Rachel	1Apr1839		Starky, Sellah	Of color. Housewifery
Silvers, Alsey	7May1839		Wallan, John	Blacksmith. 1Aug1842*
McGraw, Jacob	8Oct1839		Caldwell, Hardy	Agriculture
Duke, Samuel	6Jan1840	16 yrs	Hiett, Lewis	Orphan. Making cotton spinning machinery
Newton, Joshua	1Mar1841	8 yrs	Yourie, Alexander P.	Illegitimate child. Farming
Hodges, Mary	1Mar1841	4 yrs 6 mo	Hardin, Joseph	Orphan. Housewifery
Arnold, Luiza Elizabeth	6June1842	7 yrs in Jan next	King, Samuel	Orphan. Housewifery
Hill, Issabella	3Oct1842	12 yrs	Busby, James H.	Orphan. Housewifery. Dau of Nancy Hill 6June1842*
Lovell, Mahala	3Oct1842	9 yrs on 29July last	Fleming, Robert	Illegitimate child. Housewifery
Hill, Rhoda Adaline	7Nov1842	7 yrs 6 mo	Nimmo, William	Orphan. Housewifery. Dau of Nancy Hill 6June1842*
Hill, Elizabeth Jane	7Nov1842	9 yrs 6 mo	Strather, George	Orphan. Housewifery. Dau of Nancy Hill 6June1842*
Vanhook, Hiram	7Nov1842	13 yrs	Frack, A. J.	Orphan. House carpenter
Handyshell, Jacob J.	6Feb1843	16 yrs on 8Mar next	Handyshell, George W.	Orphan
McKent, Robert J.	6Mar1843	17 yrs	Bertrand, Joseph N.	Orphan. House & sign painting

Name	Date	Age	Master	Notes
Jonnegin, Granville	5Aug1844	18 yrs	Shephard, I. D.	Orphan. Tailoring
Henly, Patrick L.	7Apr1845	18 yrs last July	Bertrand, Joseph N.	Orphan. House & sign painting
Stark, Alexander	4Aug1845	11 yrs on 2nd inst	Winham, William	Orphan. Wool carding. Canc 1Sept1851. Restored to guardian, William Walton. William Stark apptd guardian 6Dec1852*
Stark, John	4Aug1845	13 yrs on 8June last	Nokes, E. B.	Orphan. Sadling
Bates, Almarinda	6Oct1845	6 yrs on 25Sept1845	Lowman, David	Orphan. Housewifery
Lawrence, Richard	2Feb1846	13 yrs	Love, Hiram	Orphan. Blacksmithing
Winham, William B.	4May1846	11 yrs 8 mo	Pearson, Calvin W.	Orphan. Farming. Minor of Mary Winham Canc 6Oct1846
Winham, William B.	6Oct1846		Moore, Samuel W.	Farming
Bloodworth, John Wesly	1Mar1847	4 yrs	McAdams, Alfred	Orphan. Agriculture & farming
Bowler, Sarah	3May1847	13 yrs	Cloar, Hubert	Orphan. Housewifery
Hadley, Nella	7June1847	14 yrs	Robb, W. D.	Orphan. Of color. Housewifery
Hadley, Clinton	7June1847	12 yrs	Robb, W. D.	Orphan. Of color. Agriculture & farming
Ellis, Mary Jane	6Sept1847	5 yrs	Hicks, Thomas	Orphan. Housewifery
McKey, John	6Dec1847	9 yrs	Link, Jr, William	Of color. Farming
Ellis, Mary Jane	4Apr1848	6 yrs	Hart, William	Orphan. Housewifery
Marshall, William H.	1May1848	8 yrs on 20Aug next	Key, Napoleon B.	Orphan. Farming.
Marshall, Ezekial	1May1848	7 yrs on 15Aug next	King, Joseph	Orphan. Farming
Kelly, John	6Nov1848	12 yrs	Judd, John W.	Orphan. Brick making. Canc 1Jan1849
Mills, James T.	6Aug1849	16 yrs	Glover, James	For three yrs. Printer
Wiley, George A.	?		Key, Napoleon B.	A prior indenture cancelled 6Aug1849
Gillespie, Gideon	7Aug1849	15 yrs	Thomas, William W.	Orphan. Tailoring
Ellis, Jane	5Nov1849	8 yrs	McDaniel, Fountain L.	Of color. Housewifery
Goode, Harriet	4Feb1850	9 yrs	Warner, Reuben T.	Orphan. Of color. Housewifery
Goode, Lorenzo	4Feb1850	11 yrs	Guild, J. C.	Orphan. Of color. Blacksmithing
Goode, John	5Feb1850	5 yrs	Daughtry, Joel H.	Orphan. Of color
Weaver, Samuel	4Mar1850	5 yrs	Norvell, Robert	Orphan. Farming
Kelly, John	2Apr1850	16 yrs	Johnson, George W.	Orphan. Farming
Webb, William	3June1850	7 yrs	Durham, James	Orphan. Canc 7Apr1851. Restored to mother, Adaline Webb

Name	Date	Age	Master	Notes
Webb, James	3June1850	12 yrs	Durham, James	Canc 7Apr1851. To mother, Adaline Webb
Duke, Abagel	7Jan1851		Thomas, William W.	Of color. Abandoned by father. Mother dead. Until 18 yrs
Duke, Talbot	7Jan1851		Thomas, William W.	Of color. Abandoned by father. Mother dead
Duke, Mary	7Jan1851		Solomon, William	Of color. Abandoned by father. Mother dead
McKey, John [or McKay]]	6Sept1852		Goostree, James W.	Of color. Until 18 yrs. Cancelled 8Aug1854. Goostree no longer in brick molding trade
Key, Elizabeth	8Mar1853		Davis, John L.	Abandoned by father
Key, John F.	8Mar1853		Davis, John L.	Abandoned by father
Cokley, Charles	7Nov1853	12 yrs on 27Apr last	Leath, William	Parents dead
Cokley, John	7Nov1853	10 yrs	Leath, William	Parents dead
Bandy, Amanda	5Dec1853	9 yrs	Austin, James	Dau of Marcus Bandy, Dcd* 5Sept1853*
Bandy, William T.	5Dec1853	7 yrs	Briley, James	Son of Marcus Bandy, Dcd* 5Sept1853*
Bandy, Larkin	5Dec1853	5 yrs	Williams, Benjamin	Son of Marcus Bandy, Dcd* 5Sept1853*
Bandy, Howard	5Dec1853	11 yrs	Bandy, Woodford	Son of Marcus Bandy, Dcd* 5Sept1853* Woodford also administrator of estate of Marcus S. Bandy, Dcd. A fifth child is Isaac
Warren, John	2May1854	17 yrs in Dec last	Jones, Michael	Of color
McKay, John	8Aug1854	16 yrs in Oct next	Henley, William	Orphan. Of color. Until 18 yrs. Brick moulding
Drake, Laura Ann	2Oct1854	10 yrs	Bartholume, J. B. C.	
Odle, William C.	5Mar1855		Pryor, Allen L.	
Calloway, John	3Dec1855		Richardson, William	Orphan. Of color. Blacksmith. 6Nov1855* Canc 7Nov1860. Abandoned by Richardson
Reed, James	8Apr1856	11 yrs	Reed, William	Orphan
Riddle, William	7July1856	6 yrs	Smart, John N.	Orphan
Riddle, John	1Sept1856	10 yrs	Ellis, Isaac	Orphan
Stanton, Martha	6Jan1857	4 yrs on 12May last	Banon, James C.	Orphan
Anderson, George W.	4July1859	12 yrs on 20Mar last	Hanner, James A.	Orphan. Farmer. Canc 6Feb1860. Carried off by father
Withers, Sarah B.	4July1859		Moody, Bennet	Orphan
Sadler, Elijah	6Feb1860	13 yrs	Stone, N. H.	Orphan. Farmer

Name	Date	Age	Guardian	Notes
Rippy, Sally	2June1860	1 yr	Cooper, F.	Orphan
Rippy, Josiah	2July1860		Davis, John L.	
Rippy, Amanda J.	2July1860		Davis, John L.	
Rippy, Eli	6Aug1860	13 yrs	Nimmo, J. A.	Orphan
Caloway, John	7Nov1860	Abt 15 yrs	Barnes, Alex	Of color. Farmer
Mayes, Jackson	12Nov1860	12 yrs	Hollis, James M.	Farmer. Cancelled 23Sept1865
Miller, Jacob	5Dec1860	15 yrs	Durham, Jonathan	Until 18 yrs. Tanner
Sadler, Richard	8Apr1861	12 yrs	Gourley, John	Farming. Canc 13Nov1865. John Gourley now dead. Samuel Gourley chosen guardian by Richard
Sarah	26Dec1865	9 yrs	Lovell, J. C.	Orphan. Of color
Luke	26Dec1865	6 yrs	Lovell, J. C.	Orphan. Of color
Tin	2Jan1866	11 yrs	Bantin, J. C.	Female. Of color. Motherless & abandoned
Wesley	2Jan1866	8 yrs	Bantin, J. C.	Of color. Motherless & abandoned
Dempsey	2Jan1866	6 yrs	Bantin, J. C.	Female. Of color. Motherless & abandoned
Unnamed male	2Jan1866	4 yrs	Bantin, J. C.	Of color. Motherless & abandoned
Edmond	6Jan1866	11 yrs	Bullock, David P.	Of color. Canc 8Aug1878*. Whereabouts ?
John	6Jan1866	9 yrs	Bullock, David P.	Of color. Canc 8Aug1878*. Whereabouts ?
Henry	6Jan1866	5 yrs	Bullock, David P.	Of color. Canc 8Aug1878*. Whereabouts ?
Daniel Jackson	6Jan1866	3 yrs	Bullock, David P.	Of color. Canc 8Aug1878*. Whereabouts ?
Hannah	6Jan1866	1 yr	Bullock, David P.	Of color. Canc 8Aug1878*. Whereabouts ?
Timothy	6Jan1866	14 yrs	Bullock, David P.	Of color. Canc 8Aug1878*. Whereabouts ?
Nancy	9Jan1866	14 yrs	Turner, James N.	Of color. Consent of mother, Julia Bullock
Sally	16Jan1866	11 yrs	Frazor, Theophilus	Orphan. Of color
James	16Jan1866	13 yrs	Harper, William	Orphan. Of color
Cynthia Ann	16Jan1866	6 yrs	Harper, William	Orphan. Of color
Savely, Fanny	30Jan1866	8 yrs	Savely, Wesley	Of color
McFaddin, Mary	3Feb1866	12 yrs	Rigsby, R. J.	Of color
Andrew	26Feb1866	11 yrs	Roney, Benjamin	Of color. Rec by Freedmen's Bureau
Allen	26Feb1866	9 yrs	Roney, Benjamin	Of color. Rec by Freedmen's Bureau
Stalker, Cyrus	26Feb1866	7 yrs	Lawrence, L. W.	Orphan. Of color. Rec by Freedmen's Bureau
Margaret	26Feb1866	10 yrs	Patterson, John	Of color. Rec by Freedmen's Bureau

221

Name	Date	Age	Master	Notes
Ben	26Feb1866	8 1/2 yrs	Patterson, John	Of color. Rec by Freedmen's Bureau
George	26Feb1866	6 yrs	Patterson, John	Of color. Rec by Freedmen's Bureau
Violet	26Feb1866	4 yrs	Patterson, John	Of color. Rec by Freedmen's Bureau
Jane	26Feb1866	3 yrs	Patterson, John	Of color. Rec by Freedmen's Bureau
George	5Mar1866	9 yrs	Durham, A. M.	Orphan. Of color. Rec by Freedmen's Bureau
Levinia	5Mar1866	10 yrs	Simpson, W. C.	Orphan. Of color. Rec by Freedmen's Bureau
Charity	5Mar1866	12 yrs	Simpson, W. C.	Orphan. Of color. Rec by Freedmen's Bureau
Tennessee	5Mar1866	8 yrs	Frazor, W. J.	Female. Of color. Recommended by Freedmen's Bureau. Cancelled 14Mar1866
Bettie	7May1866	9 yrs	Dobbins, Franklin	Of color
James	22May1866	11 yrs	Whitworth, W. H.	Born a slave of William Hutchison
Charlotte	22May1866	Abt 9 yrs	Whitworth, W. H.	Formerly the slave of Dr. William Lawrence
Andrew Jackson	22May1866	8 yrs	Watson, Thomas S.	Of color. Abandoned by mother. Formerly owned by Watson
Hatton, Jim	6July1866	14 or 15 yrs	Peyton, Baile	Of color. Mother dead. Father out of county
Franklin, Smith	6July1866	14 yrs	Peyton, Baile	Of color. Father dead. Mother either dead or somewhere in the South, where she was sold many years ago
Peyton, Minerva	18Aug1866	b. 20Feb1854	Peyton, Emily F.	Of color. Dau of Cali, a deaf & dumb woman
Ellanora	18Aug1866	10 or 11 yrs	Frazor, James	Orphan. Of color. Formerly owned by Frazor
Susan	18Aug1866	7 or 8 yrs	Frazor, James	Orphan. Of color. Formerly owned by Frazor
Goss, Harry	12Oct1866	10 yrs	Goss, J. D.	Of color
Goss, Lucy	12Oct1866	9 yrs	Goss, J. D.	Of color
Ferrell, Harriett	6Nov1866	15 yrs	Ferrell, B. F.	Of color. Cancelled 24Dec1867
Ferrell, Winnie	6Nov1866	13 yrs	Ferrell, B. F.	Of color. Cancelled 24Dec1867
Ferrell, Lucy	6Nov1866	12 yrs	Ferrell, B. F.	Of color. Cancelled 24Dec1867
Myra	26Nov1866	b. 29Oct1853	Bernard, John	Of color. Formerly belonged to Bernard
John	26Nov1866	b. 15Mar1855	Bernard, John	Of color. Formerly belonged to Bernard. Canc 3June1867. Parents dead. Aunt, from Cincinnati, OH, carried child off
Henry Buchanan	26Nov1866	b. 15Sept1856	Bernard, John	Of color. Formerly belonged to Bernard. Canc 3June1867. Parents dead. Aunt, from Cincinnati, OH, carried child off

Name	Date	Age	Bound to / Parent	Notes
Pleasant	26Nov1866	b. 15Feb1859	Bernard, John	Of color. Formerly belonged to Bernard. Canc 3June1867. Parents dead. Aunt, from Cincinnati, OH, carried child off
Yateman	26Nov1866	b. 15Feb1860	Bernard, John	Of color. Formerly belonged to Bernard. Canc 3June1867. Parents dead. Aunt, from Cincinnati, OH, carried child off
McMurry, John Booker	3Dec1866	Abt 8 yrs	Littleton, John A.	Of color
Lewis, Willis	24Dec1866	Abt 8 yrs	Lewis, J. M.	Orphan. Of color. On 2Sept1869 Lewis allowed to remove Willis to Macon Co., TN
Smith, John	31Dec1866	9 yrs	Latimer, George E.	Orphan. Of color. Canc 10Mar1870. Jones uncontrollable
Cunningham, Robert	23Jan1867	Abt 14 yrs	Peyton, Balie	Of color. Came from South Carolina when quite small. Parents status unknown to him
Sanderson, Lou	4Feb1867	Abt 7 yrs	Franklin, Sarah F. (Mrs)	Of color. Mother dead, father in Virginia
Roper, Anthony	9Feb1867	Abt 11 yrs	Roper, John Y.	Orphan. Of color
Durham, Mary Caroline	1Apr1867	b. 5May1860	Durham, Jonathan	Of color. Mother dead. Father consents
Durham, John Wesley	1Apr1867	b. 6Jan1863	Durham, Jonathan	Of color. Mother dead. Father consents
Durham, Henry	1Apr1867	Abt 11 yrs	Durham, J. G.	Of color. Mother dead. Father consents
Haynes, Lettie	4Nov1867	11 yrs last April	Haynes, Maria E.	Of color. Mother dead. Father's whereabouts unknown
Jones, Eli	8Jan1868	11 yrs	Bennett, R. A.	Of color
Creasy, Thomas	2Mar1868	11 yrs on 14Feb1868	Carr, John D.	Orphan, son of Thomas Creasey, Dcd. Canc 5Aug1871 Thomas having runaway July1871
Covington, Henry	27Apr1868	13 yrs	Ellis, Thomas	Son of Amanda Valines (or Covington) Dcd
Foster, Wilver	4May1868	13 yrs	Frankin, A. C.	Orphan. Son of Simon & Maggie Foster, Dcd
Simmons, George	4Nov1868	10 yrs	Simmons, Alexander W.	Orphan. Son of Simmons [sic]
Trible, Elvis Huston	6Nov1868		Groves, Bennett	Cancelled 31July1872, Trible having left
Kearley, Samuel	16Nov1868	7 yrs	Kearley, John B.	Son of Charles & Harriett Kearley
Rickman, Lucy	19Dec1868	9 yrs	Rickman, Francis E. (fe)	Orphan. Lucy also called Fanny in entry
Clark, Essex	6Sept1869	2 yrs	Trimble, Porter	Both of color. Cancelled 12Apr1873
Hodges, Isaac L.	4Oct1869	12 yrs	Moss, W. F.	Father & mother dead
Hodges, Ezekial	6Dec1869	8 yrs	Davis, Davis D.	Father & mother dead. Cancelled 13Nov1875
George	17Jan1870	10 yrs	Tompkins, Joel M.	Of color. Mother assents. Father dead
Ben	17Jan1870	12 1/2 yrs	Tompkins, James S.	Of color. Mother assents. Father dead
Shute, Kittie	1Mar1870	13 yrs	Jackson, Nancy A.	Of color. Father & mother dead

Name	Date	Age	Master	Notes
Violet	2Mar1870	8 yrs	McConnell, N. W.	Of color. Father dead
Bush, Shelton	11Apr1870	12 yrs	Johnson, Jesse H.	Of color. Mother dead. Abandoned by father
Scott, Columbus	2May1870	15 yrs	Wyatt, D. C.	Father & mother dead
Scott, Morgan	2May1870	2 yrs	Wyatt, D. C.	Father & mother dead
Baker, Elisabeth	6June1870	10 or 11 yrs	Joyner, James H. (Dr)	Of color. Cancelled 8Nov1870. Not likely to become a charge on the county
Margaret	5Sept1870	14 yrs	Smith, R. H. M.	Of color
Stone, Samuel	30Sept1870		Stone, W. P.	Father & mother dead
Beck, Frank	31Oct1870	15 yrs	Raulston, Harriet R. (Mrs)	Of color. Canc 17May1871. Moving to another county. To be bound there
Drane, Gilbert	28Nov1870	14 yrs	Drane, Thomas H.	Of color
Drane, Granville	28Nov1870	10 yrs	Drane, Thomas H.	Of color
Parker, John W.	5Aug1871		Barns, Alexander	Without father or mother
Rice, James	15Nov1871		Cook, Thomas J.	Father & mother dead
Frazier, Jonas	20Mar1872	Abt 14 yrs	Frazier, John	Of color
Walton, Ann	14Dec1872		Hassell, M. J.	Orphan. Of color
Solomon	26Mar1873	Abt 10 yrs	Dye, D. B. F.	Father & mother dead. Of color
Clark, Essex	12Apr1873	Abt 6 yrs	Watkins, Monroe	Of color
Franklin, Washington	16Jan1874	14 yrs	Franklin, John W. (Dr)	Until 20 yrs. Of color. Without father or mother
McGee, Maria	24Jan1874	8 yrs	Walker, L. W.	Without father or mother
Lucus, Martha	16Mar1874	8 yrs	Heermans, S.	Of color
Williams, Violet	30Sept1874	Abt 10 yrs	Franklin, James	Orphan. Of color
Davis, Samuel	1July1875	Abt 3 yrs	Newton, J. C.	Of color. Abandoned by parents
Durham, Charlie	16Oct1875	Abt 8 yrs	Corkran, W. L.	Until 19 yrs. Orphan
Hodges, Ezekial	13Nov1875		Tuttle, John A.	Change of master requested by Hodges
Brinkley, Martha	22Jan1877		Brinkley, E. W.	Of color
Smart, John	13Feb1877	Abt 12 yrs	Buck, E. B.	Cancelled 24Jan1878. Runaway
Andrews, John B.	17Mar1877		Potete, Andrew	Orphan
McMahon, Mary	21June1877	Abt 8 yrs	Watkins, Lucy (Mrs)	Canc 25Aug1878. Returned to mother

Name	Date	Age	Master	Notes
McClellan, Ollie	26June1877	Abt 6 yrs	Mills, Dicy J.	Until 20 yrs. Orphan. Of color
Amos, Henry	5Sept1877	Abt 2 yrs	Gooseberry, Mary	Of color
Patterson, John	26June1878	Abt 7 yrs	Chenault, Colby	
Reeves, Belle	9Nov1878	Abt 11 yrs	Crunk, J. B.	Orphan. Of color. Male

Van Buren County

Name	Date	Age	Master	Notes
Kelly, John	1June1840	Abt 17 yrs	Moore, Jr, Samuel	On motion of Joseph Cummings, Jr, a prior indenture in White Co with Sanford Medley cancelled
Hopkins, Jr, William	7Nov1842	10 yrs	More, William	
Hopkins, Jesse	7Nov1842	7 yrs	Moore, David	Cancelled 5Aug1844
Hopkins, Sally	7Nov1842		Mitchell, Robbert S.	Cancelled 5Feb1844
Hopkins, Hanah	7Nov1842		Cummings, William B.	Nancy & Elisabeth Hopkins to be brought to court next term. 2Jan1843*
Creeley, Angaline	1May1843	5 yrs	Love, Legrand C.	
Creeley, Isaac T.	1May1843	2 yrs on 23Sept last	Love, Legrand C.	
Creeley, Emeline	5June1843	7 yrs	Stewart, John	Cancelled 1June1846
Hopkins, Sally	5Feb1844	Abt 15 yrs	Sparkman, William	
Hopkins, Jesse	5Aug1844		Earles, Nathan	
Hopkins, Hannah	5Aug1844	7 yrs	Sparkman, George	
Grantham, Pleasant Lensara	7Apr1845	3 yrs on 7Sept1845	Lawson, James	
Creely, Emeline	1June1846		Reese, Solomon	
Creely, Marion	3Apr1849	16 yrs last November	Gillentine, M. T.	Son of Lavisa Crealy 3July1848
Crealy, William	7May1849		Maston, William C.	3Apr1849*
Female, Unnamed	6Aug1849	13 yrs	Lockhart, Eanock	Orphan
Crain, Mason	7Mar1853		Clark, John E.	Father, Jesse Crain, a pauper 4Apr1853
Crain, Emily	7Mar1853		Crain, Axes?	Father, Jesse Crain, a pauper 4Apr1853
Crain, Sarah L:	7Mar1853		Wommack, James	Father, Jesse Crain, a pauper 4Apr1853
Jeffers, William	7Mar1853		Charles, Sullivan?	
Crain, Moses	Sept1854	19 yrs	Crain, Axies? (fe)	

Name	Date	Age	Master	Notes
Phillips, Simon	Sept1854	7 yrs	Wood, Mortimer	Cancelled 5Nov1855
Creley, William	1Oct1855		Steakley, William L.	
Lane?, Sarah M.	1Oct1855		Simons, B. L.	
Phillips, Simon	5Nov1855	9 yrs	Billingsly, John M.	
Hais, John	7Jan1856		Yates, John	Has sibs Sarah, Matissa, Amanda & one other 3Dec1855
Hais, Amanda	7Jan1856		Yates, Larking	Has sibs Sarah, Matissa, John, & one other 3Dec1855
Sailors, Samuel	1Mar1858	5 yrs	Brock, Jesse	Orphan. Farming. Bond recorded June1858
Jeffers, Grundy	6Feb1860	4 yrs	Sparkman, James	Orphan
Carroll, Lucinda	8Jan1867		Foresyth, Henry	Orphan. 5March1866*
Jane	March1867	Abt 12 yrs	Worthington, William	Orphan. Of color
Annanias	March1867	Abt 9 yrs	Worthington, William	Orphan. Of color
Cummings, Thomas	1April1867	9 yrs	Cummings, W. B.	Orphan. Farming. Of color
Sparkman, Mary C.	1July1867	Abt 9 yrs	Sparkman, Bryant	Canc 5Aug1872 as Catherine Sparkman. To G. W. Sparkman. Minor heir of Solomon Sparkman 5Aug1872. As Mary G. Sparkman to James Worthington 3Feb1873
Sparkman, Thomas W.	1July1867	Abt 7 yrs	Sparkman, Bryant	Canc 5Aug1872. To G. W. Sparkman. Minor heir of Solomon Sparkman 5Aug1872. To James Worthington on 3Feb1873
Sparkman, Martha A.	1July1867	Abt 5 yrs	Sparkman, Bryant	Canc 5Aug1872, as Dorsey Sparkman. To G. W. Sparkman. Minor heir of Solomon Sparkman 5Aug1872. To James Worthington on 3Feb1873
Sparkman, Samuel M	1July1867	Abt 3 yrs	Sparkman, Bryant	Canc 5Aug1872. To G. W. Sparkman. Minor heir of Solomon Sparkman 5Aug1872. To James Worthington on 3Feb1873
Neal, Isabel	2Dec1867	13 yrs on 15Oct1867	Worthington, Samuel	Orphan
Neal, John	2Dec1867	11 yrs on 18July1867	Worthington, Samuel	Orphan
Neal, Charles	2Dec1867	11 yrs on 18July1867	Worthington, Samuel	Orphan
Myres, Frank	7Sept1868	10 yrs	Myres, James B.	Farming. No father or mother. James is GF
Myres, Joseph	7Sept1868	8 yrs	Myres, James B.	Farming. No father or mother. James is GF

Edwards, James	6Apr1869	13 yrs	Stewart, John	Of color
Hascue, James	1Aug1870	12 yrs	Haston, W. C.	Abandoned by parents. Of color
Brymer, Henry	6Sept1870	8 yrs in August1870	Hillis, L. H. (or H. L.)	Orphan. Cancelled 2Oct1871
Hash, Manda	3Oct1870	7 yrs on 3Oct1870	Rodgers, D. C.	Abandoned. Mother unable to provide. Of color
Crutcher, Henry	2Jan1871	6 yrs	Tash, Daniel A.	Consent of mother, Eliza Crutcher, who is unable to provide. Of color
Griffith, Sciatha	3July1871	2 yrs	Childress, Joseph	
Brymer, Henry	2Oct1871	8 yrs in August1870	Forsythe, W. H.	Orphan
Sparkman, George W.	6Nov1871	Abt 13 yrs	Johnson, Squire	Orphan. Cancelled 2Feb1874. Johnson dead
Minnis, Marian	6Oct1873	Abt 16 yrs	Johnson, G. B.	Orphan. Male
Sparkman, George W.	2Feb1874	Abt 15 yrs	Johnson, Lavina	Orphan. Canc 3Dec1877 as George W. Sparkman, Jr, consent of both
Louvall, Charles	7Jan1878	10 yrs on 9Apr1878	Cummings, JoDeny	
Louvall, Edny	7Jan1878	8 yrs on 2Aug1878	Drake, Carter	Male
Hillis, Murph	2Feb1880	Abt 9 yrs	Russell, Thomas	
Corder, Jimmy	2Apr1883		Curtis, Aaron	

Warren County

Name	Date	Age	Master	Notes
Jones, Mary	5Aug1850	13 yrs 11 mo	Haynes, G. W. (Esq)	Orphan. Previously bound to William Ruder
Youngblood, James M.	7Oct1850		Cummings, Jr, William	Orphan
Youngblood, William W.	7Oct1850		Starkey, Isaiah	Orphan
Brooks, Larkin K.	3Mar1851	12 yrs 1 mo 3 d	Hill, E. L.	
Reynolds, Jesse M.	2Feb1852		Coppinger, David	Orphan. Resc 2Oct1854. Son of Saraah Reynolds
Reynolds, A. D. (fe)	2Feb1852		Coppinger, David	Orphan. Rescinded 2Oct1854. Dau of Saraah Reynolds
Reynolds, David Washington	6Sept1852	11 yrs	Patrick, William	Resc 2Oct1854. Child of Saraah Reynolds
Bright, Thomas	1Aug1853		Miller, Filander D.	Orphan
John	3Oct1853	13 yrs	Springs, Thomas B.	Orphan. Of color
Poppy	3Oct1853	11 yrs	Springs, Thomas B.	Orphan. Of color
Laura	3Oct1853	5 yrs	Springs, Thomas B.	Orphan. Of color
Dennis	3Apr1854	7 yrs	Hayes, William	Of color

Name	Date	Age	Master	Notes
Medley, Thomas	1854		Hopper, William	Orphan. Rescinded 7Aug1854
Tosh, William	7May1855		Snipes, Britton W.	Indenture terms affirmed 4Mar1867. Snipes dead. "Tash" not yet 21 yrs old
Whitlock, Benjamin	4June1855	14 yrs	Gording, James	Orphan
Tosh, Martin V.	2July1855		Biles, Jonathan	
Annis, Mary	2July1855		McGregor, Phip	
Annis, Henry	2July1855		McGregor, Phip	
Mitchell, Saluda Ann	3Dec1855		Pearson, Solamon	Pages numbered wrong
Annis, Ive	5May1856		Sites, J. M.	Free boy
Annis, Laura	5May1856		Hardin, Daurathy	Free girl
Byars, William H. H.	4Aug1856		Garth, Jessee T.	
Fowler, Thomas	1Dec1856		Kell, Thomas	
Lanis, Thomas	1Dec1856		Cope, James S.	
Williams, William L.	5Jan1857		Fossett, Abel P.	
Byers,	6Jan1857		Stubblefield, John S.	Cancelled 6Dec1858
Annis, Frances	1June1857	7 yrs	Cartwright, William J.	Orphan. Of color
Fults, John	6July1857		Scott, Levy	
Harry	1Feb1858		Clarke, J. P.	Of color
Female, Unnamed	7June1858		Hennessee, P. S.	Of color
Female, Unnamed	7June1858		Hayes, H. Y.	Of color
Jones, Richard	6Dec1858		Greer, A. P.	Orphan
Kitchens, James Alexander	6Dec1858		Bell, James M.	Cancelled 5Aug1867. Kitchens gone
Taylor, Nicey	7Feb1859		Mazey, Solamon	On 6Dec1858 Frances, Isaah, Emica & Mary Taylor ordered brought to court
Taylor, Isaah	7Feb1859		Moffets, G. P.	On 6Dec1858 Frances, Isaah, Emica & Mary Taylor ordered brought to court
Taylor, Mary	7Feb1859		Moffets, Aaron	On 6Dec1858 Frances, Isaah, Emica & Mary Taylor ordered brought to court
Rey, Margaret	7Mar1859		Bess, Bazel	

Name	Date	Age	Master	Notes
Rey, Henry	7Mar1859		Clendenon, Jackson	
Fults, John	7Mar1859		Scott, Cooper	Bound at request of parents
Medley, Thomas	5Dec1859		Wilcher, A. T.	Orphan
Edington, Joseph	6Feb1860		Morton, Moses	Orphan
Ridinger, Martha Ann	6Aug1860		Rains, J. G.	Orphan. Probably dau of Adaline Ridinger 7Jan1861*
Medley, James	3Sept1860		West, William C.	Orphan
McCorcle, Cyntha	4Feb1861		Turner, Henry	Orphan
Ridinger, Jane	4Mar1861		Gray, R. A.	Orphan. Dau of Adaline Ridinger, living 3 mi west of Morrison 7Jan1861*
Annis, Sam	4Nov1861	6 yrs	Harding, George	Child of Matilda Annis, free woman of color. Cancelled 6July1869, child having left
Annis, Clerrisa	4Nov1861	3 yrs	Harding, George	Child of Matilda Annis, free woman of color. Cancelled 6July1869, child having left
Annis, Andrew	4Nov1861	1 yr	Harding, George	Child of Matilda Annis, free woman of color. Cancelled 6July1869, child having left
Orthelia	3Feb1862		Poindexter, J. W.	Of color
Crockett	7July1862	Abt 4 yrs	Griswould, N. W.	Of color
Coonrod, Paul	2Jan1866		Lane, Bright	Both of color. Blacksmith
Templeton, Eliza H.	2Jan1866		Paine, Mary L.	Of color
Bruster, George	7May1866		Bruster, O. F.	Orphan. Of color
Carden, Colombus	2July1866		Hill, B. J.	Orphan. Of color.
Manning, John	3Sept1866	Abt 10 yrs	Holcombe, Malinda	
Furn, Richard	5Nov1866	6 yrs	Vanhooser, Eulysses	Orphan. Cancelled 1Dec1879. Fern absconded
Macon, John Ess	3Dec1866	Abt 7 yrs	McRamsey, Sam	
Muray, Elia Ann	3June1867	Abt 9 yrs	Clift, James	Of color. Cancelled 9Oct1867
Jones, James Ervin	5Aug1867	Abt 8 yrs	Masey (or Mazey), S. A.	Orphan. Canc 7Oct1867. Calvin Jones assessed costs
Manus, Tillman C.	4Nov1867		McLane, D. V.	Orphan. McLean [sic] died 29Apr1871. Indenture cancelled 3Oct1871
Parton, Lewis	4Nov1867	Abt 11 yrs	Ware, William N. M.	Orphan
Gains, Thomas	2Dec1867	Abt 15 yrs	Jones, Eli	Orphan
Campbelle, William	6July1868	13 yrs	Picket, John	Orphan. Of color

Name	Date	Age	Master	Notes
Smith, Hugh A.	6Sept1869	10 yrs	Ingland, Richard	Orphan
Kirk, William	7Mar1870	12 yrs	Smartt, J. P.	Orphan. Cancelled 3July1871. "John" Kirk gone
Haley, George	4Apr1870	8 yrs	Hammer, Joseph	
Macon, J. E. J.	3Apr1871	11 yrs	Ramsey, David	
Manus, Tillman C.	3Oct1871	15 yrs	Whitson, W. V.	Cancelled 5Feb1872. Manus uncontrollable
Myfield, Jack	1Jan1872		Smith, Ann	Cancelled 8Oct1872
Mayfield, Vesta	2Jan1872	13 yrs next May	Green, Sandford V.	Cancelled 5July1875. Vesta gone, won't return
Kirby, Isaac C.	5Feb1872	4 yrs on 15May next	Steakley, William S.	Orphan
Fern, Nannie J.	5Feb1872	9 yrs on 4Mar next	Farmer, Malchus	Until 21 yrs. Orphan
Mayfield, Mary	4Mar1872	Abt 10 yrs	York, G. W.	York apptd administrator of John Mayfield, Dcd. Indenture cancelled 5Apr1875
Mayfield, Martha	4Mar1872	6 or 7 yrs	Mauzy, Thomas	Orphan. Cancelled 1Nov1873. Martha uncontrollable
Mayfield, Dora	2Apr1872	Abt 4 yrs	McPhearson, Thomas	Orphan
Richardson, William	2Apr1872	16 or 17 yrs	Douglass, Joel	Orphan
Jones, Henry S.	3Mar1873	13 yrs	Finger, William P.	Orphan. Cancelled 5Oct1874. Runaway
Escue, John	7Apr1873	8 yrs	Wheeler, John D.	Orphan. Cancelled 3Nov1873
Escue, Samuel R.	7Apr1873	4 yrs	Wheeler, John D.	Orphan. Cancelled 1Dec1873 as Robert Samuel Escue
Jack	2June1873	Abt 10 yrs	Dunlap, E. S.	Orphan. Of color
Escue, John	3Nov1873	9 yrs on 15Apr1873	Garnett, J. S.	Orphan
Escue, Robert Samuel	1Dec1873	5 yrs next March	Macon, John	Orphan
Ladd, Zylpha Bell	6Apr1874	8 yrs	Mead, W. W.	Consent of mother, Mrs Ann Ladd
Ladd, Laura Jane	4May1874	13 yrs	Mead, Raman	Consent of mother, Ann Ladd
Quarles, Robert	1June1874	11 yrs	Jeffrees, J. D.	Orphan
Mazy, George Wesley	1June1874	6 yrs	Meadows, W. M.	Orphan
Mazy, Edmond	1June1874	8 yrs	Meadows, W. M.	Orphan
Beal, W. H.	5Jan1875	15 yrs	Swan, W. J.	Orphan. Contract fulfilled 2Aug1880. Swan now 21 yrs, released.
Comer, James	1Nov1875	9 yrs on 25Dec1875	Mead, George W.	Orphan. Of color. Until age 18 yrs. Cancelled 7May1877. Returned to mother

Name	Date	Age	Master	Notes
Hobbs, James	6Dec1875	10 yrs	Bullin, W. S.	Orphan. Cancelled 3Sept1877. Runaway
Escu, John	4Sept1876	11 yrs	Garnett, J. L.	Orphan. Cancelled 6Nov1876, John having run away
Escue, John	6Nov1876	11 yrs	Martin, William P.	Orphan
Philips, Sarah Luvina	1Oct1877	8 yrs	Stoner, S. M.	Orphan
Female, Unnamed	1Oct1877	7 yrs	Hill, Susan	Orphan
Scott, Elizabeth	1Oct1877	6 yrs	McDonough, F. M.	Orphan. Of color
Gowan, John Wesley	6Oct1879	Abt 9 yrs	Green, S[anford]. V.	Consent of parents, both in poor house. Cancelled 1Nov1880. Green dead
Collins, Seth	6Oct1879	Abt 12 yrs	Darnell, W. T.	Orphan. Father in poor house in Coffee Co
Outlaw, Tabitha	6Oct1879	10 yrs on 16Oct1879	Fuston, J. S.	Of color. Abandoned by father & mother. Cancelled 2Apr1883. Left, refuses to return
Dalton, Rachael	7June1880	Abt 11 yrs	Smith, Harrison	Until 21 yrs, or sooner if necessary. Orphan
Gowan, John Wesley	1Nov1880		Green, Margarett	Widow of Sanford V. Green
Bates, Jennie	1Nov1880		Green, Margarett	Orphan. Of color
Barnes, William	7Mar1881		Wagner, Sarah (Mrs)	Orphan. Of color
Barnes, George	7Mar1881		Wagner, George F.	Orphan. Of color
Rowland, Nelson	7Mar1881	13 yrs	Craven, Solomon	Illegitimate child
Taylor, Hattie Jane	5Sept1881	Abt 11 yrs	Hunt, T. J.	Of color
Lusk, Edward	5Sept1881	Abt 12 yrs	Parris, Jonathan	Of color
Collins, John W.	?		Darnell, W. T.	Indenture cancelled 7Apr1884.
Cope, Lucinda	7Mar1882	8 yrs next Aug	Towler, John W.	Of color. Consent of mother, Mollie Cope

Wayne County

Name	Date	Age	Master	Notes
Carr, Thomas J.	2Dec1848	11 yrs	Brown, George W.	Orphan of James F. Carr. Dcd. Cancelled 7July1851
Davis, Alexander	5Feb1849	b. 3Oct1844	Davis, Alexander	Orphan of John Davis, Dcd
Davis, John W.	5Feb1849	b. 26Sept1847	Davis, Alexander	Orphan of John Davis, Dcd
Cunningham, Franklin	5Mar1849	15 yrs	Philips, Absolom L.	Farmer. Abandoned by father 5+ yrs ago. Mother dead. 4Dec1848*
Cunningham, Jordan	5Mar1849	13 yrs on 30Jan past	Philips, David L.	Farmer. Abandoned by father 5+ yrs ago. Mother dead. 4Dec1848*

Name	Date	Age	Master	Notes
Atwood, William	6Nov1850	6 yrs on 11Nov1850	Cackman, Joseph	Consent of mother, Lucinda Atwood
Atwood, Mary Ann	6Nov1850	8 yrs on 6Oct last	Brewer, W. J.	Consent of mother, Lucinda Atwood
Martin, Caroline	3Mar1851		Etherage, Allen	Minor heir of John Martin, Dcd
Martin, Ben	3Mar1851		Etherage, Allen	Minor heir of John Martin, Dcd
Martin, Mary	3Mar1851		Etherage, Allen	Minor heir of John Martin, Dcd
Carr, Thomas	7July1851		Cook, Marcus	Orphan. Until 18 yrs. Consent of Carr & George W. Brown
Williams, Eliza	2Apr1855		Lutes, J. L.	
Hanes, Jasper A.	1Dec1856	11 yrs	Bickam, John	Orphan
Tilley, Elihu R.	7Apr1857	12 yrs	Rose, F. M.	
Kimbell, James D.	2June1857	13 yrs on 13June inst	Brown, William R.	Of color. Request of mother, Rachael Kimbell
Morton, Mary E.	1Feb1858	Abt 7 yrs	Tharp, A. J.	Orphan. Cancelled 2May1859
Cole, Alfred B.	?		Talley, John A.	Indenture cancelled 1Mar1858
Cole, Alfred B.	1Mar1858		Cole, Bennet	Bennet is grandfather of Alfred. Appointed administrator of Hartwell Cole, Dcd. 2Feb1857. Bennet's will probated 7Nov1859
Banks, Thomas	2Nov1858		Cypert, John L.	Farming. Illegitimate child. Mother, Katharine Banks, keeps a house of ill fame
Mourton, Mary Elizabeth	2May1859	Abt 8 yrs	Whitehead, John	
Murphy, Ephram	1Aug1859	Abt 5 yrs	Stribling, Thomas J.	Orphan. Farming
Daniels, John	7Nov1859	Abt 11 yrs	Stribling, Joseph C.	Orphan. Farming
Cole, Alfred B.	8Nov1859	5 yrs on 1Mar1860	Cole, John H.	Orphan
Daniel, Isaac	5Mar1860	Abt 9 yrs	Greesan, John L.	Orphan.
Banks, Eli	1Oct1860	Abt 15 yrs	Copeland, Joseph M.	Orphan. Mother unable to support
Banks, Marion J.	1Oct1860	Abt 6 yrs	Tackett, Joseph W.	Orphan. Mother unable to support
Banks, Jasper M.	4Mar1861	Abt 6 yrs	Tackett, Joseph W.	Orphan. Illegitimate child. Aka Marion J. Banks. Duplicate entry, bound 1Oct1860
Banks, Eiic	4Mar1861	Abt 15 yrs	Copeland, Joseph M.	Orphan. Bound 1Oct1860
Mclean?, Morris	8Jan1867		Walker, William B.	Orphan. Of color
Mclean?, Thomas	8Jan1867		Skillern, David S.	Orphan. Of color

Name	Date	Age	Bound to	Notes
Hassell, Eliza	9Jan1867		Hassell, A. T.	Of color
Murphy, Ephram	4Feb1867	Abt 13 yrs	Greesan, Henry C.	Orphan. Of color
Burns, Alexander	5Feb1867	11 yrs	Burns, W. C.	Orphan. Of color
Burns, Celia	5Feb1867	9 yrs	Burns, W. C.	Orphan. Of color
Brooks, W. B. [Wiley B.]	4Nov1867	10 yrs on 17May1867	Ross, J. W.	Mother dead. Abandoned by father. Cancelled 5July1875* Ross dead. Wiley fled
Brooks, Sarah Catherine	4Nov1867	5 yrs on 28Sep1867	Ross, J. W.	Mother dead. Abandoned by father. Cancelled 5July1875. Ross dead
Brewer, Robert	4Oct1870	Abt 7 yrs	Brewer, A. J.	Farmer. Bound until 1884. Of color. Consent of mother, Jane Brewer, of color
Huckaba, James	6Feb1871		Honeycut, J. B.	Bound by mother, Fana? Huckaba
Huckaba, Luella	7Mar1871	3 yrs on 29Apr1871	Honneycutt, J. B.	Bound by mother, Fannie A. Johnson, of Waynesboro
Cypert, Frank	4July1871	4 yrs on 1Mar1871	Lawson, M. L.	Orphan. Of color. Farming
Thompson, Charlin	4Dec1871	2 yrs on 27July1871	Throgmorton, E. B.	Farmer. No legitimate father. Mother unable to support, left the state
Castiel, Thomas	1July1872	12 yrs in Aug1872	Barker, George W.	Orphan. Farmer. Bound at request of mother
Ellison, F. M.	2Dec1872	5 yrs last July	Morris, John G.	Farmer. Abandoned by father
Shull, Lenora	3Feb1873	Abt 16 yrs	Shull, William H.	Mother dead. Not living with his father, Frank Shull, who consents. Cancelled 1Sept1873
Castiel, Thomas	7Oct1873	12 yrs in Aug1873	Barker, G. K.	Orphan. Farmer
Brooks, Sarah Catherine	5July1875	b. 28Sept1862	Ross, Mary E.	Spinster
Conaley, John J.	7Oct1878	7 yrs on 26May1878	Jones, Allen	Orphan totally abandoned
Eaton, George W.	7Nov1881	3 yrs on 30Jan1882	Mullery, Andrew	Request of mother, M. E. Eaton. Abandoned by father. Farmer. On 12Jan1885 Mullery allowed to remove Eaton to Hardin Co, TN
Porter, Ace	6Mar1882	12 yrs on 25Dec1881	Dickerson, W. J.	Son of H. C. & Sophia Porter, Dcd. Of color
Porter, Mat	6Mar1882	9 yrs in Oct1881	Carr, T. S.	Dau of H. C. & Sophia Porter, Dcd. Of color
Rose, James S.	2June1884	Abt 11 yrs	Fitts, J. W.	Taken from Poor Asylum. Mother, Eliza Rose, indigent. Farmer. Canc 4Aug1884
Rose, James S.	4Aug1884		Arnett, T. J.	See above

White County

Name	Date	Age	Master	Notes
Stuart, Betsey	16Apr1807		Johnson, William & Martha, his wife	Bound by mother, Isabell Stuart
Pool, Thomas	14Oct1807		Chisum, William	Son of Chisum and Judith Pool
Ferril, Thomas	9May1808		Ward, Jonathan	Orphan
Flynn, David	14Nov1808		Porterfield, Richard	
Bean, Hiram	16May1810	11 yrs	Shaw, Benjamin	
Risen, James Emery	18July1814	4 yrs	Coan, John E.	
Weaver, Jeremiah	20July1814	9 yrs on 15Mar1814	Catrow, Sr, Jacob	
Weaver, Elisabeth	20July1814	6 yrs on 5Jan1814	Catrow, Sr, Jacob	
Benton, James W.	18July1815		Franks, Henry	Cancelled 15Jan1821
Beatty, William	16Oct1815		Hamlett, George C.	Bound by Mahala Beatty. Canc 25July1818
Weaver, Jeremiah	16Oct1815	10 yrs on 15Mar1815	Long, George	Black smith
Weaver, Elizabeth	16Oct1815	7 yrs on 5Jan1815	Catrow, Elisabeth	
Haynes, Washington	15Apr1816	3 yrs in May next	White, John	
Morton, Lewis	15July1816	12 yrs	McKie, Benjamin	Hatting. One of six orphan children of Sarah Morton 8Sept1813
Morton, William	15July1816	10 yrs	Welch, Isaac	Farming. One of six orphan children of Sarah Morton 8Sept 1813
Martin, Polly	16July1816	8 yrs	Sweany, Daniel	?One of six orphan children of Sarah Morton 8Sept 1813
Green, Thomas	22Oct1816	7 yrs on 22Apr1816	Scoggon, Jesse	
Green, Jane	22Oct1816	4 yrs on 23June last	Scoggon, Jesse	
Johnston, Andrew	20Jan1817	6 yrs on 2nd of ?1816	Britain, William C.	Hatting
Loving, Jane	20Jan1817	3 yrs on 2Sept1816	Britain, William C.	
Jarvis, William	22Apr1817	9 yrs on 1Feb1817	Webb, David	Black smith
Tapper, William	26July1817	11 yrs on 4Oct next	Britain, William C. (Esq)	Hatting

Frisbey, Alexander	21Oct1817	Glenn, Jr, William	Cancelled 19Oct1818
Byers, John	19Jan1818	May, William	Farming. Cancelled 20Apr1818
	14 yrs on 13Apr next		
Byers, Thomas	19Jan1818	Bennett, William J.	Boot & shoe making. Canc 20Oct1818
Southerland, Mahala	19Jan1818	Rice, Daniel	Until age 15 yrs
	3 yrs on 1Sept last		
Williams, William	20Apr1818	Jones, Zachariah	
	15 yrs on 31Oct last		
Dalton, James	20Apr1818	Hailey, Jesse	Cancelled 16July1822
	12 yrs		
Shoemake, John	18Jan1819	Lee, Barnett	Mill wright. 25Oct1819* Canc by agreement of Lee and Elizabeth Shoemack 9Oct1820
	11 yrs on 1Nov1818		
Dalton, William	?	Porterfield, Richard	On 23Jan1819 William ordered brought to court, having previously been bound to Porterfield. Indenture cancelled 15Oct1821. Son of Talbot Dalton 15Oct1821
Dalton, John	?	Porterfield, Richard	On 23Jan1819 John ordered brought to court, having previously been bound to Porterfield. Indenture cancelled 15Oct1821. Son of Talbot Dalton 15Oct1821
Simpson, Samuel	19Apr1819	Turner, Randolph	For 3 yrs. Tanning & currying
	16 yrs		
Turner, Thomas	19Apr1819	Owens, James	
	6 yrs		
Simmons, William	24July1819	Sparkman, William	Cancelled 9Oct1820
	3 yrs		
Crawley, James Madison	18Oct1819	White, Woodson P.	
	11 yrs on 15Feb next		
Newman, Polly	25Oct1819	Smith, William J.	Daughter of Charles & Peggy Newman, Dcd. 19July1819*
	8 yrs on 22Oct1819		
Newman, John	25Oct1819	Lane, Turner	Son of Charles & Peggy Newman, Dcd. 19July1819*
	13 yrs on 31Aug1819		
Newman, Thomas	25Oct1819	Ashworth, George	Son of Charles & Peggy Newman, Dcd. 19July1819*
	14 yrs in Dec1818		
Newman, Danal	25Oct1819	Scoggon, Sr, John	Son of Charles & Peggy Newman, Dcd. 19July1819*
	11 yrs on 8July1819		
Wright, Aaron	10Apr1820	Hughlett, Silvester	Bound by mother, Barbara Wright
	3yrs 1mo 2d on 18Mar1820		
Eldridge, Polly	19Jan1821	Baker, Baxter	Canc 10Oct1825. Age 7 yrs on 3Sept 1825. Sally Eldridge posted bond for her support
	2 yrs		
Findley, Anderson	17July1821	Shirly, Thomas	Of color. On 21July1821 Shirly ordered to show cause why indenure should not be cancelled. 16Apr1822
	14 yrs		

Name	Date	Age	Master	Notes
Scott, James	?		Oliver, Levi	Indenture cancelled 8Apr1822*
Harris, Mary Ann	16July1822	1 yr on 8May1822	Campbell, Robert	
Newman, John	16July1822	16 yrs on 1Aug next	Hunter, William	
Finley, Loray	21Oct1822	7 yrs	Jenkins, James H.	Orphan girl of color
Griggs, Jr, Mary	?		Griggs, Sr, Mary	On 12Apr1824 order to bring bound girl canc
Cody, Sally	?		Cody, Pierce	Daughter of Burnett Cody. On 19Apr1824 Cody ordered to bring Sally to court. Previously bound to him
Underwood, Benjamin	11Oct1824	Abt 11 yrs	Rotan, William	Orphan of Seth Underwood. Sibs Brice & Thomas 21Oct1822
Findley, Anderson	18Oct1824		Mitchell, David L.	Orphan
Kerr, Levi	17Jan1825	10 yrs on 11Mar last'	Walker, John	
Dungy, Christopher	17Jan1825	11 yrs	Turner, John E.	Orphan. Alias Christopher Woodson. Son of Sarah Dungey 23Oct1824*
Dungy, Nancy	17Jan1825	5 yrs	Leftwich, Waman	Orphan. Alias Nancy Woodson. Daughter of Sarah Dungey 23Oct1824* Of color. Terms altered 3Jan1837
Dungy, William	17Jan1825	9 yrs 3 mo	Ford, John W.	Orphan. Alias William Woodson. Son of Sarah Dungey 23Oct1824* Canc 11Apr1825
Dungy, Richard	17Jan1825	6 yrs on 16May1824	Lane, Jacob A.	Orphan. Alias Richard Woodson. Son of Sarah Dungey 23Oct1824*
Gaines, James H.	17Jan1825	16 yrs 7 mo	Ursery, William	Until 19 yrs 8 mo. Saddler
Dungy, Sally	17Jan1825	2 yrs	Eastland, Thomas	Orphan. Alias Sally Woodson. Daughter of Sarah Dungey 23Oct1824*
Dungy, William	11Apr1825	9 yrs	Carey, Calford	Of color
Underwood, Brice	?		Lewis, Benjamin	Apprenticeship cancelled 11Apr1825. Orphan of Seth Underwood 21Oct1822*
Welbourne, Thomas J.	23July1825	17 yrs on 4May next	Ursery, William	Saddler. Until 20 yrs
Brinlee, Stephen	17Apr1826	11 yrs on 4May next	Howard, Peter	Black smith. Bond filed 16Oct1826
Brinlee, Asa	17Apr1826	7 yrs on 1Dec last	Lane, Jacob A.	

Name	Date	Age	Master	Notes
Brinlee, Elijah	17Apr1826	7 yrs on 1Dec last	Lane, Jacob A.	Blacksmith
Mason, Simion	17Apr1826	18 yrs	Mitchell, John G.	
Whitley, Taylor	10July1826		Whitley, Isaac	Shoemaker. Bound for one year by guardian, Isaac J. Leftwich
Hailey, Polly	16Oct1826	10 yrs	Briggs, Nathan B.	Brought to court by John Hailey, guardian
Hailey, John	16Oct1826	13 yrs	Alstad, John N.	Brought to court by John Hailey, guardian
Hailey, Eliza	16Oct1826	7 yrs	Alstad, John N.	Brought to court by John Hailey, guardian. Nathan C. Davis apptd guardian 2Apr1838
Cain, William	9Apr1827	16 yrs on 1Jan next	Eastland, Thomas	
Hailey, William	9July1827	15 yrs on 14Feb last	Britain, William C.	Hatter
Williams, John	9July1827	14 yrs on 1May last	Usery, William	Orphan, son of Elizabeth Williams, who consents. Saddling
Williams, Thomas	9July1827	16 yrs on 28May last	Eastland, Thomas	Orphan, son of Elizabeth Williams, who consents & is paid $5. Boy to receive 100 Ac of mountain land at expiration of term
Williams, Chaney N.	14July1834		Cann, James M.	Data from cancellation entry 5Nov1838
Abner, Mary Anne	12Oct1835	11 yrs	Denton, Samuel	Living with Denton & called Mary Ann Dabney on 13July1835 entry
Moore, William	19Oct1835	6 yrs 6 mo	Young, William M.	Tanning. Son of Eleanor Moore, who consents
Moore, James	19Oct1835	5 yrs 6 mo	Young, William M.	Tanning. Son of Eleanor Moore, who consents
Ledbetter, Eliza	11Jan1836	12 yrs	Anderson, Joseph	Alias Louisa Jane Ledbetter. A prior indenture with James T. Offim cancelled 6Sept1836. Returned to mother, who has married Samuel Crabtree of Warren Co.
Glenn, Jesse Alan	11Jan1836	9 yrs on 24Aug next	Lowell, Andrew	Son of Henry Glenn 19Oct1835. Orphan. Cancelled 5Mar1838* Again! cancelled 6Dec1841. Lowell leaving Tennessee
Glenn, Nancy Ann	11Jan1836	10 yrs on 20Mar next	Connor, Archibald	Daughter of Henry Glenn 19Oct1835
Mays, Creasy	11Apr1836	10 yrs	Kerr, Joseph	Dau of Nancy Mays 11Jan1836* Orphan. Prior indent with James Mayes, Jr cancelled 1Aug1836
Kerr, Ammon L.	11Apr1836	4 yrs on 29April1836	Green, Thomas	Cancelled 3Oct1836

237

Name	Date	Age	Master	Notes
Bennington, Henry	3May1836	Abt 15 yrs next fall	Yeager, Joel	Of color. On 11Apr1836 Ann Bennington also ordered brought to court. On 4Dec1843 Yeager filed receipt dated 14May1842 from Henry Bruington for horse beast, bridle etc
Finley, Anderson	1Aug1836	2 yrs on 8July1836	Jenkins, James H.	
Hopkins, Nathaniel C.	3Oct1836	13 yrs in Dec1835	Glenn, Robert B.	Orphan. Blacksmith. 7Nov1836* Cancelled 3Sept1839
Kerr, Ammon L.	3Oct1836	4 yrs on 19April1836	Herd, Joseph	Orphan. Cancelled 7Nov1836
George, Henry	7Nov1836	14 yrs	Hutson, William B.	Orphan. Mack, Patsy, and Caswell George, orphans & paupers, also ordered brought to court 3Oct1836. Canc 6Mar1837. To mother
Kerr, Ammon L.	7Nov1836	4 yrs on 19April1835	Vincents, John	Age as written
Owens, Adrian	5Dec1836	14 yrs on 14June last	Cannon, Elisha	Orphan
Anderson, John L.	5Dec1836	9 yrs on 15April last	Burden, William	Orphan. A prior indenture to Jacob Anderson cancelled
Roberts, John	5June1837	13 yrs on 24Nov1837	Scott, James	Of color. Child of Sally Roberts 1May1837*
Roberts, Lucinda	5June1837	8 yrs on 20Mar1837	Scott, James	Of color. Child of Sally Roberts 1May1837*
Dalton, Alexander	5June1837	10 yrs on 11Apr1837	Griffith, George	Orphan. Son of Elizabeth Dalton 1May1837. Cancelled 5July1841
Watkins, Edward	4Sept1837	14 yrs	Leftwich, Woman	Orphan. Bound for 5 1/2 yrs
Williams, William K.	5Feb1838	6 yrs on 29Oct1837	Young, John	Orphan. Cancelled 3Sept1838
Dawson, Ephraim	5Feb1838	15 yrs on 5July1837	Green, William G.	Orphan
Arnold, James	4June1838	11 yrs on 3June1838	Humphreys, Sr, John	Orphan
Jeffers, Amelia Ann	4June1838	7 yrs	Young, William L.	Orphan of Allen Jeffers. Until 21 yrs
Jeffers, Amarilla	4June1838	5 yrs	Young, William L.	Orphan of Allen Jeffers. Until 21 yrs
Williams, William K.	3Sept1838	6 yrs on 29Oct1837	Warren, John	Orphan
Williams, Chaney N.	5Nov1838	13 yrs on 7Jan last	Warren, John	
Dyer, Francis Marion	7Jan1839	9 yrs on 18Feb1839	Warren, Stuart	Cancelled 7Feb1842

Name	Date	Age	Master	Notes
Lourey, Matilda	4Feb1839	6 yrs on 15Mar1839	Cummings, Joseph J.	Until 21 yrs. Cancelled 5June1843
Lowry, Montgomery	5Aug1839	9 yrs on 20Nov1839	Lowry, Mark	Orphan
Worley, William Preston	2Dec1839	10 yrs on 26May1839	Clenny, James T.	Saddler. Orphan 4Nov1839. Cancelled 4Feb1840.
Breakbill, Henry	7Jan1840	16 yrs on 2May1840	Carrick, James M.	Orphan
Breakbill, William	7Jan1840	14 yrs on 5July1840	Price, John L.	
Deatherage, Bird C.	4Feb1840	16 yrs on 4July1839	Clenny, James T.	Saddler. Orphan
Worley, William Preston	4Feb1840	10 yrs on 26May1839	Bryan, Jr, William M.	Orphan
Kelly, John	?		Medley, Sandford	Indenture cancelled 6July1840 on information from Van Buren County Court
Lamb, Asa G.	4Aug1840	14 yrs this day	Roberts, Richard G. (Esq)	Taylor. Cancelled 7Feb1842
Parsons, Major	5Oct1840	5 yrs on 15Feb1841	Clark, Daniel	Cancelled 2Nov1840
Parsons, Francis Marion	5Oct1840	9 yrs on 6Feb1841	Green, Thomas	Orphan
Parsons, Sarah Ann	5Oct1840	10 yrs on 21Oct1840	Anderson, Joseph	Orphan
Parsons, Elin	5Oct1840	12 yrs on 13Apr1841	Hill, Joab	Orphan
Shelton, George	6Oct1840	5 yrs 6 mo	Tucker, William R.	Orphan, from poor house. Blacksmith
Parsons, Major	2Nov1840	5 yrs on 15Feb1841	Gamble, Andrew	Orphan. Receipt of Major Washington Passons filed 6Apr1857
Harden, Berryman	1Feb1841	15yrs on 26June1840	Lane, Jacob A.	Orphan
Harden, Henry	1Feb1841	14 yrs on 1Jan1841	Lane, Turner	Orphan
Harden, Jefferson	1Feb1841	6 yrs on 22Mar1841	Jones, Thomas	Orphan
Harden, Elizabeth	1Feb1841	8 yrs on 5 April next	Bartlett, James	Orphan
Harden, Nelly	1Feb1841	9 yrs on 15Sept1840	Jones, Thomas	Orphan. Until age 21
Dempsey, Margarett	1Feb1841	2 yrs on 26Jan1841	Green, William	Orphan twin. Until age 21
Dempsey, Sarah	1Feb1841	2 yrs on 26Jan1841	Green, William	Orphan twin. Until age 21

Name	Date	Age	Master	Notes
Howard, Thomas	1Mar1841	11yrs on 10Sept1840	Murray, Edward M.	Orphan. Saddler
Lamb, Joseph	1Mar1841	14 yrs on 1Oct1840	Clayton, William	Orphan. Printing. Cancelled 7June1841
Dalton, Alexander	5July1841	14 yrs on 11Apr1841	Bradley, Noah H.	Canc 2Mar1846
Broyles, James H.	7Sept1841	2 yrs on 23Mar1841	Mason, William	Orphan
Glenn, Jesse Allen	6Dec1841	14 yrs on 24Aug1841	Jones, Samuel	Orphan
Dyer, Francis Marion	7Feb1842	9 yrs on 9Feb1839	Thomas, Jr., Samuel	
South, Stephen	7Feb1842		Fisher, James	A prior indenture with Thomas E. Hutson cancelled
Johnson, James	7Mar1842	Abt 8 yrs	Knowles, John W.	Orphan. Cancelled 4Dec1848
Howard, John	4Apr1842	12 yrs on 21Aug1842	McConnell, James A.	Orphan
Dyer, Appollus	6June1842		Warren, Stuart	Bound by Lydia Dyer
Johnson, Thomas	4July1842	7 yrs this day	Holland, Harrison	Cancelled 2Jan1843
Lathum, John	1Aug1842	8 yrs this day	Grissum, Moses	Orphan
Johnson, Thomas	2Jan1843		Knowles, Sr., James	Orphan
Kirby, John	3Apr1843	4 yrs on 10Dec1842	Wilson, William	Orphan. Of color. Consent of mother, Rebecca Kirby 5Mar1843* Canc 5Oct1846 for maltreatment
Kirby, James Madison	3Apr1843	2 yrs on 16Apr1843	Wilson, William	Of color. Consent of mother, Rebecca Kirby 5Mar1843. Canc 5Oct1846 for maltreatment
Kirby, Mahala	3Apr1843	12 yrs in May1843	Minnis, John A.	Orphan. Mother Rebecca Kirby 5Mar1843*
Kirby, Pardima	3Apr1843	8 yrs in March last	Hutson, Isaiah	Orphan. Mother Rebecca Kirby 5Mar1843* Sister, Lucinda Kirby, pronounced an "idiot pauper," sent to poor house. Canc 3Nov1845
Lowry, Matilda	5June1843		Herd, James R.	Orphan. Until 21 yrs. Cancelled 3July1843
Lowry, Matilda	3July1843		Clayton, William	Until 21 yrs
Bruington, Jonas	4Dec1843	14 yrs	Yeager, Joel	Of color*

Benton, Clarisa Jane	6Feb1844	7 yrs on 1March next	Harlow, William J.	Orphan. Until 21 yrs. Orphan of John Benton, Dcd 2June1844*
Benton, Jesse Lewis	6Feb1844	9 yrs on 14Jan last	Volisa, James	Orphan of John Benton, Dcd 2June1844* Cancelled 4Mar1844
Benton, Jesse Lewis	4Mar1844	9 yrs on 14Jan1844	Webb, James	Orphan of John Benton, Dcd 2June1844*
Corder, Darkes A.	3June1844	11 yrs	Johnston, William C.	Until 21 yrs. Female.
Corder, Elizabeth	3June1844	4 yrs on 1May last	Yeager, James	Until 21 yrs
Dunnigin, Thomas	4Oct1844	8 yrs on 4May1845	Holder, Andrew J.	
Lowery, Simpson	8Oct1844	11 yrs	Lowery, Charles	
Manner, Levi	3Feb1845	11 yrs on 6June1845	Fraser, Thomas	Or Levi Mainyard 6Jan1845*
Warnic, Maryann Strother	3Feb1845	10 yrs in Aug1844	Bussell, John E.	Until 21 yrs
Williams, Gilbert G. W.	3Mar1845	5 yrs on 29th this mo	Howard, George D.	Orphan. 2Dec1844*
Bales, Willey	5May1845	14 yrs on 13Nov last	Bruster, Obediah F.	
Webbester, William B.	5May1845	6 yrs on 1May1845	Bailey, James	Rescinded 5June1845
Kirby, Allen	5May1845	7 yrs 11 mo	Burden, William	
Williams, John	7July1845	7 yrs	Whitley, Sharp R.	2Dec1844*
Kirby, Perdenny	3Nov1845	10 yrs on 1Mar1845	Kirby, Richard	Until age 21
Morrias?, William	2Mar1846	16 yrs on 6June next	James, John	Orphan
Dalton, Alexander	2Mar1846	19 yrs on 11Apr next	Nicholas, David	Receipt in full from Dalton recorded 2May1848
Williams, George Gilbert W.	6Apr1846	6 yrs on 29Mar last	Holder, Joel	Orphan
Benton, John	6Apr1846	7 yrs on 1May next	Hudgins, Shelby	Orphan. Cancelled 3Mar1858. To mother
Walling, Mary Jane	1June1846	Abt 5 yrs	Walling, James	Until age 21. Orphan of William Walling, Dcd. 4May1846
Kirby, John	5Oct1846	8 yrs on 10Dec next	Carrick, James	Of color
Kirby, James M.	5Oct1846	6 yrs on 6April last	Carrick, James	Of color. Cancelled 4Oct1847
Wammack, Mary Ann S.	1Feb1847	12 yrs in August next	Pistole, Stephen C.	Until 21 yrs. Cancelled 5Mar1849

Name	Date	Age	Master	Notes
Showmaker, Charles M.	1Feb1847	16 yrs on 6Mar next	Graham, Andrew	
Wineder, George	7June1847		Graham, John H.	
Kirby, Mahalle Jane	6Dec1847	16 yrs on 9 May last	Pass, John A.	Until age 21
Kirby, James M.	4Oct1847		Crawford, Robert N.	Orphan. Cancelled 2May1854
Ouinding, John P.	4Oct1847		Jackson, James	Orphan. Cancelled 2Jan1854. Jackson dead
Jeffreis, Lucinda	3Jan1848	Abt 2 yrs 6 mo	Dew, Jose C.	Of color
Hannon, Asa	7Feb1848	9 yrs on 20May next	Baker, Green H.	Orphan
Jaco, James	6Mar1848	3 yrs on 4Mar1848	Jones, James	Orphan
Scott, Mary Jane	6Mar1848	1 yrs on 12Mar1848	Jones, James	Orphan. Until age 21
Netherton, Armilda Elizabeth	1May1848	8 yrs 6 mo	Netherton, James	Until age 21. Canc 4Dec1854. To accompany mother leaving the country
Williams, Peran	8Aug1848	10 yrs on 14Nov1848	Little, Thomas G.	Orphan. 7Aug1848* Son of Elizabeth Williams
Collins, Mary Jane	8Aug1848	12 yrs on 3July1848	Little, Thomas G.	Orphan. 7Aug1848*
Collins, Feraly	8Aug1848	10 yrs on 26Mar1848	Forsythe, John L.	Orphan. 7Aug1848*
Williams, John	8Aug1848	10 yrs on 10Jan1849	Stewart, William R.	Orphan. Silversmith. Son of Elizabeth Williams 5Sept1848 7Aug1848* Cancelled 3Jun1850 for mistreatment. To mother, Polly Williams
Williams, John Lafayett	8Aug1848	12 yrs on 25May1849	Wallace, Quantian H.	Orphan. Son of Elizabeth Williams 5Sept1848 7Aug1848*
Collins, Manerva	8Aug1848	7 yrs on 11July1848	Hunter, Turner L.	Orphan. 7Aug1848*
Williams, Malissa Jane Catharine	4Sept1848	5 yrs on 19Dec1847	Rogers, John M.	Orphan. Dau of Elizabeth Williams 5Sept1848 7Aug1848* Cancelled 2Oct1849
Fox, Alvira	5Sept1848		Belcher, Bartlett	Orphan 4Sept1848
Fox, Polly Thornton	5Sept1848		Belcher, Bartlett	Orphan 4Sept1848
Williams, Andrew Jackson	5Sept1848	17 yrs on 23Mar1849	Officer, Alexander	Orphan. Son of Elizabeth Williams
Dunger, Frances	6Nov1848	8 yrs on 1Jan1849	Simpson, Eliza	Of color. Dau of Sally Dunger. A third child not bound
Dunger, William Crockett	6Nov1848	4 yrs on 1Jan1849	Herd, Joseph W.	Of color. Son of Sally Dunger. A third child not bound

Johnson, James	4Dec1848	14 yrs on 7Mar1848	Knowles, Hester C.	Orphan
Wamack, Mary Ann S.	5Mar1849	14 yrs in Aug next	Bussell, John W.	Orphan
Davis, James S.	3Sept1849	15 yrs this day	Little, John H.	Orphan
Davis, John M.	3Sept1849	11 yrs on 15Mar1849	Gillentine, John W.	Orphan
Currie, William	1Oct1849	9 yrs this day	Rogers, William W.	Son of William N. Curry 4Sept1849. Cancelled 4Mar1850
Williams, Malissa Jane Catharine	2Oct1849	7 yrs on 19Dec1849	Stanley, Henderson	Orphan
Currie, William	4Mar1850	9 yrs on 1Oct1849	Robison, Alexander C.	Orphan, son of William N. Curry 4Sept1849
Price, James M.	4Nov1850	10 yrs on 13Jan1851	Maulden, Tucker	Cancelled 5Feb1855, Price having runaway
Jeffreys, Jane	6Jan1851	5 yrs	Norman, John	Until age 18. Of color. Cancelled 4Apr1853
Kirby, Martha	3Mar1851	6 yrs on 1Jan1851	Lowrey, Vance C.	Orphan. Cancelled 1June1857
Jenkins, Altamyra	4Mar1851	4 yrs on 1Mar1851	Moore, William W.	Orphan. Of color. Cancelled 3Feb1857
Jenkins, Amanda	4Mar1851	4 yrs on 31Mar1851	Sims, Andrew J...	Orphan. Of color
Davis, Jesse Eli	7July1851	6 yrs on 4Mar1851	Webb, Jeremiah	
Huddleston, Catharine	1Sept1851	8 yrs on 19Sept1851	Brady, Patrick	Orphan
Scott, Alexander	2Sept1851	Abt 15 yrs	Carrick, John A.	Of color
Scott, David	2Sept1851	Abt 13 yrs	Carrick, John A.	Of color. Cancelled 3Apr1855, as Dock Scott. Disabled by "white swelling"
Blalock, John Wesley	1Dec1851	8 yrs on 11Mar next	Robinson, William H.	Orphan
Vaughn, William	1Mar1852	7 yrs on 1Apr1852	Herd, Joseph W.	Orphan. Cancelled 1May1854
Dale, Rufus	5Apr1852	11 yrs	Hickey, Cornelius	Orphan
Dale, Dicey	5Apr1852	9 yrs	Little, Bryan	Orphan
Dale, Weley Martin	5Apr1852	6 yrs	Bleasdale, John	Orphan
Miller, Hannah K.	5July1852	b. in June	Corly, Williamson	Orphan. Record damaged, incomplete
Jeffreys, Jane	4Apr1853	7 yrs on ?	Anderson, John B.	Record damaged, incomplete
Oxandine, John P.	2Jan1854	12 yrs on 19Mar1854	Jackson, Sarah	John Jackson, her son, security. See Ouinding, John

Name	Date	Age	Master	Notes
Bothel, Jesse	6Mar1854	10 yrs on 22July1854	Frewitt, John A.	Orphan
Vaughan, William	1May1854	9 yrs on 1Apr1854	Cantrell, Parris	Orphan. Cancelled 3Sept1855
Kirby, James Madison	2May1854	14 yrs on 6Apr1854	Carrick, John W.	Orphan. Of color
Jeffreys, Henry	2Oct1854	2 yrs last of Aug1854	Yates, Raleigh W.	Of color. Canc 4Feb1855, Yates having left the country 7Jan1856
Golden, Joshua	6Nov1854	12 yrs on 12May1855	Williams, Isaiah	
Jenkins, Darthula	5Dec1854	Abt 3 1/2 yrs	Pope, Thomas	Orphan. Of color
Brown, Sarah Ellen	5Feb1855	6 yrs on 20Dec1854	Franks, Jesse	
Brown, Noah	5Feb1855	8 yrs on 20Dec1854	Franks, Jesse	
Vaughan, William	3Sept1855		Rogers, Anderson S.	Orphan
Lowell, Leah Manerva	1Oct1855	8 yrs on 21Oct1855	Reynolds, William R.	
Lowell, Martha Eleanor Jane	1Oct1855	10 yrs on 31Aug1855	Walker, John M. B.	
Webster, Emily	1Oct1855	12 yrs on 10Dec1855	Snodgrass, Robert J.	Orphan
Ghaskey, Nancy Ann	1Oct1855	9 yrs on 25Oct1855	Little, David	Orphan
Webster, Sarah	5Nov1855	2 yrs on 5Feb next	Duncan, Thomas W.	Orphan
Webster, Martha Jane	3Dec1855	Abt 4 yrs this day	Clenny, Samuel	Orphan
Brewington, James	7Jan1856	In 17th year	Farley, Simpson	
Jeffreys, Henry	4Feb1856	4 yrs on 31Aug1856	Holland, Seabon	Of color. Cancelled 5Aug1867 with assent of mother
Bell, Eliza	9Apr1856	Abt 10 yrs this date	Glenn, Samuel R.	Orphan. Dau of Joseph Bell, taken from poor house 7Apr1856*
Bell, Josephus	9Apr1856	Abt 7 yrs this date	Glenn, Samuel R.	Son of Joseph Bell. Taken from poor house 7Apr1856*
Papous, William	1Sept1856	3 yrs on 20Mar1856	Wallis, Laban	Orphan
Southard, Andrew Jackson	1Sept1856	9 yrs on 19Feb1856	McConnell, James A.	Orphan. One of five children of Benton P. Southard 4Aug1856

Name	Date	Term	To whom	Remarks
Southard, Polk Dallas	1Sept1856	12 yrs on 9Nov1856	Southard, Micajah	Orphan. One of five children of Benton P. Southard 4Aug1856
Southard, Franklin Pierce	1Sept1856	4 yrs on 8Nov1856	Southard, Micajah	Orphan. One of five children of Benton P. Southard 4Aug1856
Southard, Sarah Emeline	1Sept1856	14 yrs on 6July1856	Southard, Micajah	Orphan. One of five children of Benton P. Southard 4Aug1856
Golden, Tilman Renshaw	6Oct1856	8 yrs on 24May1856	Irwin, Alexander P.	
Golden, John S.	6Oct1856	10 yrs on 12Feb1857	Knowles, James (Esq)	Cancelled 7July1862
Williams, Waman	1Dec1856	11 yrs on 1Feb1856	Hickey, Cornelius	Orphan
Jenkins, Altamyan	3Feb1857	10 yrs on 1Mar1857	Powers, Jacob H.	Until 18 yrs. Orphan girl. Of color
Davis, Jasper	2Mar1857	14 yrs on 10Apr1857	Franks, William	Orphan
Woodston, Huston	7Apr1857	9 yrs	Clark, Daniel	Of color. Cancelled 5Mar1866, Huston having left
Rankhorne, Peter	1June1857	5 yrs	Carrick, John M.	Of color. With Adalin Rankhorne, taken from poor house 4May1857*
Kirby, Martha	1June1857	12 yrs on 1Jan1857	Voss, Alexander	Orphan. Of color
Bell, Lean	1June1857	3 yrs last October	Arnold, Hays	Taken from poor house 4May1857
Golden, Roderick A. Delbert	3Aug1857	6 yrs on 2June1857	Knowles, William W.	Orphan
Kirby, Henry Wilson	4Jan1858	14 yrs on 28Nov1857	Snodgrass, William J.	Orphan. Cancelled 7Oct1861
Scott, Lavinia	3May1858	12 yrs on 1July1858	Camp, William E.	Orphan. Dau of Mary Scott 1Dec1857
Stewart, Josephine	3Aug1858	5 yrs on 19June1858	Hudgins, Joseph	Hudgins is reputed father of Josephine
Bell, Benjamin Franklin	3Jan1859	3 yrs on 15May1858	Belcher, Bartlett	Orphan. Cancelled 7Nov1859
Dempsy, Butch	4Jan1859	6 yrs on 24Dec1858	Snodgrass, Thomas	Of color
Dempsy, Tennessee	4Jan1859	4 yrs on 10Dec1858	Snodgrass, Thomas	Of color. Cancelled 1Mar1869, child having left
Lett, James K. P.	3Oct1859	14 yrs on 6July1859	Webb, Jr, Jeremiah	
Jeffreys, William	7Nov1859	10 yrs on 7Feb1859	Charles, Mary P.	Of color. Mary is widow of Solomon Charles, to whom William had been bound in Van Buren Co*

Name	Date	Age	Master	Notes
Bell, Benjamin Franklin	7Nov1859	4 yrs on 15May1859	Livingston, Jacob	Orphan
Stites, Joseph	5Dec1859	Abt 10 yrs	Duncan, Thomas W.	Orphan
Simmons, Melly	6Aug1860	6 yrs	Whitley, John R.	Of color
Quin, James Thomas	3Dec1860	2 yrs	McKinney, Thomas J.	
Corden, Anna	3Dec1860	2 ys	Sturn, C. T.	Of color
Haley, Jesse	7Jan1861	10 yrs on 1Mar1861	Lowry, James	Orphan. Cancelled 6Dec1869, Jesse having left
Roberts, Lucinda	4Mar1861	8 yrs	McManis, Samuel	Dau of Alsira Roberts. Completed 4Mar1872
Golden, James	2Sept1861		Knowles, James	Orphan of Hiram Golden 5Aug1861. Cancelled 7July1862
Golden, Roderick	2Sept1861		Allen, James	Orphan of Hiram Golden 5Aug1861
Golden, Nuge? Fernando	2Sept1861		Boyd, William H.	Orphan of Hiram Golden 5Aug1861
Rogers, Margaret Evaline	3Sept1861	Abt 12 yrs	Taylor, Sarah	Orphan
Rogers, Washington	3Sept1861	Abt 6 yrs	Duncan, James C.	Orphan
Province, Taylor	7Apr1862	15 yrs	Denton, James R.	
Golden, John S.	7July1862	10 yrs on 12Feb1857	Knowles, Sarah	Orphan. Canc 4Dec1865. Golden a runaway
Golden, James	7July1862	11 yrs	Crain, J. D.	Orphan
Jenkins, Altimira	6Oct1862	10 yrs on 1Mar1857	Snodgrass, Joseph	Orphan. Of color
Burden, William	3Oct1863	10 yrs on 20Mar1863	Wallace, Elizabeth	Orphan
Walker, William	3Oct1865	11 yrs	Williams, Josiah	Orphan
England, Ammon	6Nov1865	11 yrs last May	Anderson, William M.	Orphan. Of color
Carrick, John	2Jan1866	Abt 10 yrs	Carrick, John M.	Orphan. Of color
Carrick, Wash	2Jan1866	Abt 10 yrs	Carrick, John M.	Orphan. Of color
Carrick, Julia	2Jan1866	Abt 10 yrs	Carrick, John M.	Orphan. Of color
Carrick, Anderson	2Jan1866	Abt 8 yrs	Carrick, John M.	Orphan. Of color
Carrick, Patterson	2Jan1866	Abt 7 yrs	Carrick, John M.	Orphan. Of color
Hickey, Trapp	2Jan1866	13 yrs	Hickey, Carnelius	Orphan. Of color
Hickey, Sam	2Jan1866	8 yrs	Hickey, Carnelius	Orphan. Of color
Hickey, Matilda	2Jan1866	Abt 12 yrs	Hickey, Carnelius	Orphan. Of color

Name	Date	Age	Master/Guardian	Notes
Hickey, Caroline	2Jan1866	Abt 8 yrs	Hickey, Carnelius	Orphan. Of color
Lowery, Benjamin	2Jan1866	12 yrs	Lowery, Charles	Orphan. Of color
Lowery, Hattie	2Jan1866	13 yrs	Lowery, Charles	Orphan. Of color
Lowery, Mollie	2Jan1866	Abt 13 yrs	Lowery, Charles	Orphan. Of color
Lowery, Harriet	2Jan1866	Abt 10 yrs	Lowery, Charles	Orphan. Of color
Simpson, Jack	2Jan1866	Abt 9 yrs	Simpson, William M.	Orphan. Of color
Dibrell, Andy	2Jan1866	Abt 13 yrs	Dibrell, George G.	Orphan. Of color. Son of Vina Dibrell, blind & a pauper, who consents. Canc 5Mar1867
Dibrell, Joseph Watkins	2Jan1866	Abt 11 yrs	Dibrell, George G.	Orphan. Of color. Son of Vina Dibrell, blind & a pauper, who consents. Canc 5Mar1867
Dibrell, Caroline	2Jan1866	Abt 9 yrs	Dibrell, George G.	Orphan. Of color.Dau of Vina Dibrell, blind & a pauper, who consents
Dibrell, Ellen	2Jan1866	Abt 7 yrs	Dibrell, George G.	Orphan. Of color.Dau of Vina Dibrell, blind & a pauper, who consents
Dibrell, Allace	2Jan1866	Abt 5 yrs	Dibrell, George G.	Orphan. Of color.Dau of Vina Dibrell, blind & a pauper, who consents
Holder, Sidney	5Feb1866	12 yrs	Holder, Spencer	Of color. Consent of Freedmen's Bureau.
Holder, Alfred	5Feb1866	8 yrs	Holder, Spencer	Of color. Consent of Freedmen's Bureau.
Holder, Woodson	5Feb1866	6 yrs	Holder, Spencer	Of color. Consent of Freedmen's Bureau.
Rilda	5Feb1866	Abt 15 yrs	Young, Nancy	
Pistol, Charlott	5Feb1866	Abt 13 yrs	Pistol, S. C.	Orphan. Of color. Consent of Freedmen's Bureau.
Ned	5Feb1866	Abt 12 yrs	Pistol, S. C.	Orphan. Of color. Consent of Freedmen's Bureau.
Titus	5Feb1866	8 yrs	Downey, John	Orphan. Of color. Consent of Freedmen's Bureau.
Sally	5Feb1866	Abt 13 yrs	Broyles, George G.	Orphan. Of color. Cancelled 1May1876. Gone
Isaac	5Feb1866	Abt 11 yrs	Broyles, George G.	Orphan. Of color. Cancelled 1May1876. Gone
Daniel	5Feb1866	Abt 9 yrs	Broyles, George G.	Orphan. Of color. Cancelled 1May1876. Gone
Lafayett	5Feb1866	Abt 10 yrs	Young, Austin C.	Canc 6June1870, child having left Young
Frank	5Feb1866	8 yrs	Lowry, Mark	Of color. Consent of his mother and the Freedmen's Bureau
Violen (fe)	5Feb1866	10 yrs	Pall, Edley	Orphan. Of color. Consent of Freedmen's Bureau.
William	5Feb1866	14 yrs	Pall, Edley	Orphan. Of color. Consent of Freedmen's Bureau.
Henry	5Feb1866	13 yrs	Pall, Edley	Orphan. Of color. Consent of Freedmen's Bureau.

Name	Date	Age	Master	Notes
Lena	6Feb1866	Abt 9 ys	Maulden, Tucker	Orphan. Of color. Canc 1Oct1866, Lena having left Maulden
Bill	6Feb1866	Abt 7 yrs	Officer, James C.	Orphan. Of color
Elizabeth	6Feb1866	Abt 9 yrs	Officer, James C.	Orphan. Of color
Brazzile, Sarah Ann	5Mar1866	11 yrs next June	Whitaker, W. H.	Orphan
Badger, Lucreta	2Apr1866	5 yrs (March1866)	Hunter, Catherine	Orphan
Clark, Lucy	4June1866	12 yrs	Rogers, Isaac	Orphan
Leftwich, Edward	3Dec1866	Abt 9 yrs	Leftwich, Jefferson	Orphan. Of color. Consent of the Freedmen's Bureau. Child of Eliza Leftwich. Cancelled 8Jan1867, having returned to mother
Leftwich, Henry	3Dec1866	Abt 6 yrs	Leftwich, Jefferson	Orphan. Of color. Consent of the Freedmen's Bureau. Child of Eliza Leftwich. Cancelled 8Jan1867, having returned to mother
Leftwich, Joseph	3Dec1866	Abt 3 yrs	Leftwich, Jefferson	Orphan. Of color. Consent of the Freedmen's Bureau. Child of Eliza Leftwich. Cancelled 8Jan1867, having returned to mother
Payne, Sally	4Feb1867		Mitchell, Allen S.	Orphan. Abandoned by mother, Jane Payne
Annis, Samuel	4Feb1867		Lance, Henry	Orphan of Robert Annis, Dcd
Cordell, America Rome	5Aug1867	8 yrs	Fancher, Thomas H.	Orphan
England, Sarah	5Aug1867	7 yrs	Fancher, Thomas H.	Orphan of Matthew England, Dcd. 2July1866
Duncan, Nancy Elvira	5Aug1867	Abt 9 yrs	Neill, B. C.	Orphan
Duncan, James Lafayett	5Aug1867	Abt 7 yrs	Neill, B. C.	Orphan
Duncan, George Ann	5Aug1867	Abt 5 yrs	Neill, B. C.	Orphan
Clark, Lucy	6Aug1867		Smith, James W.	Orphan. Of color
Keathley, James Andrew	2Sept1867	12 yrs	Keathley, Samuel H.	Bond executed 3Feb1868
Durham, Wesley G.	7Jan1868	11 yrs	Huddleston, Wiley B.	Orphan*
Durham, Wiley B. H.	7Jan1868	10 yrs	Huddleston, Wiley B.	Orphan*
Officer, Riley	3Mar1868	5 yrs	Officer, James C.	Of color
Officer, Lewis	3Mar1868	3 yrs	Officer, James C.	Of color
Meddows, James R.	6Apr1868	3 yrs	Wiggins, Adolphus	Cancelled 2Oct1871
Rogers, Washington	6Apr1868	12 yrs	Duncan, Susan	Orphan. Cancelled 3June1872+E328

Name	Date	Age	Master	Notes
Mitchell, Milly	6Apr1868	10 yrs	Mitchell, William S.	Orphan. Of color
Mitchell, Pheby	6Apr1868	7 yrs	Mitchell, William S.	Orphan. Of color
Grasty, John	1June1868	8 yrs	Lowrey, Charles	Orphan. Son of Margaret Grasty 3Feb1868. Cancelled 4Jan1869
Grasty, John	4Jan1869	8 yrs	Lowry, William	Orphan. Son of Margaret Grasty 3Feb1868
Corder, John	1Feb1869	5 ys	Smith, Benjamin	Orphan. Cancelled 8Oct1872
Brazill, Sarah Adeline	1Mar1869	14 yrs	Worley, M. R.	Orphan
Cordell, America Rome	5Apr1869	10 yrs	Oliver, Milton B.	Orphan
Bohannan, William W.	4Oct1869	11 yrs	Holland, Seaborn	Cancelled 6Nov1871
Bohannan, John T.	4Oct1869	13 yrs	Holland, Seaborn	Cancelled 6Nov1871
Green, Piney	6Dec1869	Abt 6 yrs	Taylor, John	Orphan
Short, William	7Feb1870	Abt 7 yrs	Parker, Anthony	Orphan.Cancelled 6July1874, Short having left
Duncan, Stephen A.	2May1870	12 yrs last October	Erwin, William L.	Orphan
Leftwich, Ed	6June1870	10 yrs	Carrick, James M.	Orphan
Leftwich, Henry	6June1870	12 yrs	Carrick, James M.	Orphan
Cook, Isaac	2Aug1870	9 yrs	Cook, James	Orphan. Cancelled 7Apr1873. Isaac left Cook
Dibrell, Alice	5Sept1870	7 yrs	Dyer, Amy G.	Orphan
Cope, Eveline	7Nov1870		Rutherford, Nehemiah	Orphan. Cancelled 6Oct1879
Officer, Huston	6Feb1871		Lowery, Charles	Of color
Broyles, Albert	6Feb1871		Lowery, Charles	Of color
Miller, Martha	6Mar1871	3 yrs	Taylor, M. K.	Orphan. Cancelled 6Sept1875
Alls, Jack	6Nov1871		Crowder, Thomas P.	
Oxendine, Sally	?		Mitchell, A. S.	Indenture cancelled 6Nov1871
Sims, Rachel	5Feb1872	12 yrs	Hutson, J. L.	Orphan. Of color. Cancelled 2July1877. Runaway
Robison, Daniel	2Apr1872	9 yrs	Lee, Thomas J.	Orphan. 4June1872* Cancelled 6Jan1880
Williams, Waman	2July1872	6 yrs	Saylors, Abram	Orphan. Cancelled 6Jan1873
Corder, John	8Oct1872	8 yrs	Taylor, Obediah	Orphan. Cancelled 7Oct1878
Webster, Daniel	4Nov1872	6 yrs	Jett, John W.	Orphan. Cancelled 2Jan1877. Jett dead
Williams, Waman	6Jan1873		McBride, F. J.	
Dibrell, Alice	8Apr1873	10 yrs	Young, Daniel W.	Orphan
Mainer, William	?		Frazier, James	Indenture cancelled 2June1873

Name	Date	Age	Master	Notes
Bohannon, James	1Feb1875	9 yrs	Pitman, S. A.	At request of mother, Charity Paul. Of color
Scott, Tobe	1Mar1875	3 yrs	Cope, John W.	Orphan. Of color. Cancelled 7Jan1879
Brock, Francis U.	5Apr1875	16 mo	Chisum, James W.	Female orphan. Consent of mother, perhaps Rebecca Brock 1Dec1873*
Manard, James	7June1875	4 yrs last February	Garvison, G. T	Orphan. Shoe & boot maker
Manard, John C.	7June1875	Abt 7 yrs	Moore, David	Orphan
Miller, Martha	6Sept1875	8 yrs	Little, Thomas G.	Orphan
Lisk, Henry	1Nov1875	5 yrs	Findlay, W. S.	Orphan. Cancelled 7Aug1876
Grasty, Jeff	1Nov1875	7 yrs	Snodgrass, H. C.	Orphan. Cancelled 2July1877
Knowles, Hubbard	6Dec1875	3 yrs	Knowles, Jasper A.	Orphan
Burgess, William	?		White, J. R.	Indenture cancelled 3Apr1876. Alias William King
Lisk, Henry	7Aug1876	6 yrs	Smith, Riley	Orphan
Webster, Daniel	2Jan1877	8 or 9 yrs	Dibrell, James	Orphan
Keathley, Samuel H.	5Jan1877	18 yrs	Keathley, H. H.	Consent of father. To receive 9 Ac plus the usual remuneration at completion
Fowler, Marion	7May1877	8 yrs	Winstead, Ephraim	Orphan
Grasty, Jefferson	2July1877	Abt 9 yrs	Merideth, Elisha	Orphan
McCully, James	3Sept1877	5 yrs	Broyles, George W.	Orphan
Hutson, James	3Sept1877	13 yrs	Hutson, Lucinda	Orphan. Mother unable to provide
Hutson, George	3Sept1877	10 yrs	Hutson, Lucinda	Orphan. Mother unable to provide. Cancelled 5Jan1880. To G. W. Fisher
Clark, Henry	1Oct1877	8 yrs	Webb, Washington	Orphan. Cancelled 4Apr1887
Goolden, Lemon	2Sept1878	11 yrs	Wilson, Robert	Orphan
Howard, George	3Nov1879	4 yrs last February	Miller, Luin?	Orphan
Hutson, George	5Jan1880		Fisher, G. W.	
Hutson, Woodward	4Apr1881	12 yrs	Fisher, Alfred	Orphan. Cancelled 4Apr1887, as Isaac Woodrow Hutson
Hutson, William	4Apr1881	10 yrs	Fisher, Alfred	Orphan
Gasty, Harriet Jane	4Apr1881	6 yrs	Potts, Flem	Orphan
Young, William	4July1881	3 yrs	Lowrey, D. C.	Orphan. Of color

Name	Date	Age	Master	Notes
Crook, Wallace	6Sept1881	12 yrs	Glenn, Joseph W.	Orphan. Cancelled 4July1887, Crook having left. At latter entry called "Cook" & of color
Kerley, Albert	7Aug1882	11 yrs on 10June last	Parker, Samuel	Orphan
Jett, Frank	6Feb1883		Burgess, W. S.	Of color
Jett, Etter	6Feb1883		Burgess, W. S.	Of color
Crook, William	5Mar1883		Meredith, James	Of color
Potts, Bob	3Jan1887	8 yrs	Hyde, L. M.	Of color. Farming
Davis, William Henry	?		Snodgrass, H. C.	Indenture cancelled 4Apr1887
Master, John	?		Brogden, J. A.	Indenture cancelled 4July1887
Randall, Henry	?		Smith, Riley	Apprenticeship completed 5Dec1892. Receipt from Randall
Stacy, Bob	2Jan1893		Frazier, S. S.	
Denton, Joe Smith	2Oct1893	7 yrs	McCormack, S. H.	Son of George Denton
Denton, John Morgan	2Oct1893	5 yrs on 6Mar1893	Fisher, F. P.	Son of George Denton

Williamson County

Name	Date	Age	Master	Notes
Wadsen, John	5Aug1800	17 yrs	Smith, Alexander	Orphan
Barker, James	3Nov1802	Abt 15 yrs	Robinson, Thomas L.	Taylor
Tinney, Hardy	9Feb1803	Abt 18 yrs	Thompson, James B.	Taylor
Adams, David	10Apr1804	Abt 6 yrs	Pryor, Luke	
Robinson, Elizabeth	10July1804	11 yrs	Vaught, John	
Osteen, Prather	14Oct1805	9 yrs	Phillips, Isaac	Female
Osteen, Edward	14Oct1805	4 yrs	Phillips, Isaac	
Cochran, Aaron	14Apr1806	16 yrs	Lock, Richard S.	Orphan. Wheel wright & turner
Gamble, Kinchan	18Apr1806	Abt 12 yrs	McCollum, John	Orphan
Brown, William	13Oct1806	15 yrs	Parson, Jeremiah	Orphan
Good, Betsy Manah	14Oct1806	4 yrs	Hail, William	Orphan
Goodman, John	17Apr1807	Abt 12 yrs	Thompson, James B.	Orphan of William Goodman. Taylor
Patterson, Samuel	13July1807	15 yrs	Russel, Albert	Farming. Of color

Name	Date	Age	Master	Notes
Patterson, Moses	13July1807	11 yrs	Russel, Albert	Farming. Of color
Patterson, Daniel	13July1807	8 yrs	Russel, Albert	Farming. Of color
Patterson, William	13July1807	2 yrs	Russel, Albert	Farming. Of color
Patterson, Hannah	13July1807	Abt 4 yrs	Russel, Albert	Knitting, spinning, sewing, cooking. Of color
Patterson, Jenny	13July1807	Abt 6 yrs	Cranford, Alex	Knitting, spinning, sewing, cooking. Of color
Patterson, Fanny	13July1807	Abt 1 yrs	Cranford, Alex	Knitting, spinning, sewing, cooking. Of color
Blackshear, James	17July1807	Near 17 yrs	McBride, Joseph	Orphan. House carpenter & cabinet maker
Anderson, Jane	12 Oct1807	14 yrs	Bateman, Simon	Spinning, knitting, cooking
Blackshire, Ezekiel	12Jan1808	15 1/2 ys	McBride, Joseph	Cabinet making
Armstrong, Samuel	11July1808	15 yrs	Turner, Moses	Blacksmith
Bellenfort, John	12July1808	13 ys	Sion, John	Shop trade
Gibson, John	15Oct1808		Garrett, Thomas	For 4 yrs. Orphan. House joiner
Smith, Samuel	15Oct1808		Crockett, Samuel	For 3 yrs. Orphan. Blacksmith & gunsmith
Blackshire, Elijah	10Apr1809		McEwen, David	Shoe maker. McEwen also appt'd Elijah's guardian. Orphan of Jesse Blackshear, Dcd
Dunnavent, Claiborn	11July1809		Smith, Stephen	Taylor
Carlisle, Campbell	13July1809	13 yrs	Cummins, David	Carpenter
Carlisle, James	12Oct1809	14 yrs 5 mo	Lentz, William	Orphan. Shoes & bootmaker
Smith, Benjamin	10Apr1810		McLellan, John	House joiner
Fry, Joseph	11Oct1810		Wilson, John	Farmer
Gordon, Samuel	15Jan1811		McGann, E.	Saddler
Wilson, John	13Jan1813		Frances, Moses B.	Tanner
Anderson, John T.	14Jan1813	15 yrs on 3Sept1812	Mallory, John	Orphan. House giver
Lambert, Abram	12Apr1813		Ogilvie, John	Farmer
Fives, William	4Apr1814		Allen, George H.	Cabinet maker
Hill, Rebecca	8Apr1814		Dudley, Francis B.	Until age 21. Orphan. Needlework
Stricklin, Joseph	7July1814	16 yrs	Mallory, John	House carpenter & joiner
McCutcheon, David C.	7July1814	11 yrs	Mallory, John	House carpenter & joiner

Name	Date	Age	Name	Notes
Smith, Morgan	3Oct1814	1 yr	Mason, Martin	Orphan. Farmer
Blackshire, Elijah	4Oct1814	14 yrs last June	White, Benjamin	Blacksmith
Wilkins, John	3Jan1815	13 yrs	Hale, John H.	Orphan. Farmer
Blackshare, Jacob	6Jan1815	Bet 12 & 14 yrs	Allen, Henry	Orphan. Wagon wright
Lewis, Elizabeth	3Apr1815	Bet 2 & 3 yrs	Adams, Nathan	Until 21 yrs. House wife
Lewis, William	3Apr1815	Abt 14 yrs	Adams, Jacob	Cabnet maker
Lewis, Benjamin	4Apr1815	12 yrs	Ralston, Alex	Orphan. Cabinet maker
Lewis, Nancy	3July1815	Abt 9 yrs	Jackson, Thomas	Housekeeper
Carlisle, Robert Walker	4July1815	8 yrs	Faircloth, Cordil	Until 20 1/2 yrs. House carpenter & joiner
Lewis, David	3Oct1815	6 yrs	Carson, William	Stone & brick mason
Kennedy, Alfred	2Jan1816	Abt 12 or 13 yrs	McMillin, William	Wheel wright
Hall, Joseph	1Apr1816	18 yrs	Irion, George A.	Black smith
Blackshare, Jesse	1Apr1816	12 yrs	Geery, John	Tanner & dressing of leather
Dannell, James	1Apr1816	14 yrs	Carsey, Thomas P.	Orphan. Boot & shoe maker
Smith, Rober	1July1816	13 yrs	Pollar, Joseph	House carpenter
Roach, Bryan	8Oct1816	9 yrs	Sawyers, Demsey	Sadler
Lewis, William	8Oct1816	15 yrs	Webb, William S.	
Patton, John	10Oct1816	16 yrs	Henry, Isaac N.	Printing
Atkerson, John	6Jan1817	15 yrs	Gholston, Benjamin	House carpenter
Holt, David	6Jan1817	8 yrs	Houston, James	Hatter. Orphan
Arnold, Lucinda	7Jan1817		Hay, Balam	
Arnold, Julianna	7Jan1817		Hay, Balam	
White, Benjamin	7Apr1817	18 yrs	Dunavant, Leonard	Until March1820. House carpenter
Hay, Susan	11Apr1817	5 yrs	Nichols, John	
Laremore, James	12Apr1817	11 yrs 7 mo	Francis, Moses B.	Tanning business
Laremore, John Hamilton	12Apr1817	13 yrs 4 mo	McGilvry, William	Taylors business
Harris, Archelus	12Apr1817	16 yrs 9 mo	Gholson, Benjamin	Cabinet maker
Hobbs, Nancy	9July1817		Tomlin, Nicholas	Illegitimate child. Entry crossed out & marked rescinded
Snoden, Joseph	12July1817	12 yrs 12 days	Gholson, Benjamin	Orphan. House carpenter
Wooldridge, Loving	12July1817		Bass, Thomas	For 3 yrs 6 mo. Sadler
Lovet, John	7Oct1817	18 yrs 7 mo	Gholson, Benjamin	Until 20 yrs. House carpenter

Name	Date	Age	Master	Notes
Hopkins, William Dickson	7Oct1817	15 yrs	Sutton, Stephen	Blacksmith
Jackson, Temple	7Oct1817	7 yrs	McClaran, Franklin	Saddler
White, Joseph	9Oct1817	15 yrs	Knight, John	Until 19 yrs. Gun smith
Westbrook, Betsey	10Oct1817	7 yrs	Layne, William	House wife
Roy, Collin	13July1818		Gray, Jacob	Cancelled 15July1820 for ill treatment. Data from cancellation entry
Roy, Thomas	13July1818		Gray, Jacob	Cancelled 15July1820 for ill treatment. Data from cancellation entry. Wiliiy Roy complainant
Gholsten, Thomas	4Jan1819	14 yrs	Thrweatt, Isham	Shoe & boot maker
Gholsten, John	4Jan1819	13 yrs	Thrweatt, Isham	Shoe & boot maker
White, George	4Jan1819	16 yrs in Sept last	Meek, George B.	Taylor
White, John	4Jan1819	12yrs in June last	Meek, George B.	Taylor
Strickland, Thomas	11Jan1819	16 yrs in Oct last	Crockett, Samuel & Andrew	Gunsmith
Parks, Cullin G.	11Jan1819	11 yrs	Brooks, Samuel C.	Farmer
White, Thomas	11Jan1819	14 yrs on 7Oct next	Glass, Samuel F.	Hatter
Carlisle, Robert	5Apr1819	12 yrs	Bass, Thomas S.	Saddler. Cancelled 12Apr1819
Peebles, John	12Apr1819	8 yrs	Dugger, Joseph	Waggon maker
Threatt, Elizebeth Anne	5July1819	11 yrs	Jackson, Abner	Orphan
Thrweatt, William H.	12July1819	8 yrs	Reaves, John	Carpenter
Norman, Bethel	10Jan1820	16 yrs	Brittain, James	Cabinet maker
Fuqua, John	11Apr1820	18 yrs	White, Holland L.	Blacksmith
Roy, Collin	15July1820	17yrs on 15Sept next	Carsey, Thomas P.	Shoe & boot maker
Wooldridge, Thomas	2Apr1821	18 yrs on 7May next	Cassey, Thomas	Boot & shoe maker
McPherson, George	2July1821	14 yrs on 10June last	Cayce, Fleming	Until 19 yrs. Orphan. Blacksmith. Perhaps son of Jonathan McPherson, killed in War of 1812 Apr1819. Cancelled 2Apr1827
Ballard, Washington	2July1821	3 yrs on 7May last	Coore, Jonathan	Farming. Of color
Webb, Caleb	8Jan1822	16 yrs	Moran, Charles	Orphan. Cabinet maker

Name	Date	Age	Master	Notes
Smith, William P.	8Jan1822	13 yrs on 11Dec last	Huntsberry, Abraham	Orphan. Hater
Wright, Madison	8Jan1822	13 yrs	Nunn, Thomas	Orphan. Hatter
Webb, Thomas A.	14Jan1822	14 yrs	Moran, Charles	Orphan. Cabinet maker
Ezell, David	1Apr1822	12 yrs	Tignor, Edward W.	Orphan. Brick layer
Woodruff, Howel	10Apr1822	16 yrs on 23Oct next	Glass, Samuel F. & Park, James	Orphan. Hatter
Jackson, Barrett	14Oct1822	17 yrs on 16Sept last	Little, Joseph H.	Orphan. Waggon maker
Emma	14Oct1822	6 yrs	Adams, Nathan	Housewife. Of color
Orton, Sidney M.	6Jan1823	15 yrs	Edwards, Peter	Orphan. Blacksmith
Jackson, Hosea	6Jan1823	12 yrs	Ralston, Alexander	Orphan. Cabinet maker
Charity	14Jan1823	Abt 8 yrs	Sawyers, Virginia	House wife. Of color
Berry, James	14Apr1823	12 or 13 yrs	Ralston, Alexander	Orphan. Cabinet maker
Wright, Ann	7July1823	8 or 9 yrs	Ewing, Andrew B.	Orphan. Neat seamstress
Woodall, Washington	7July1823	11 yrs on 15Feb last	Stagg, Pleasant & Boyd, George G.	Orphan. Shoe & boot maker
Harrell, William	16July1823	14 yrs on 12Jan last	Glass, Samuel	Orphan. Hatter
Harris, James Henry	11Oct1823	13 yrs on 9July1823	Garey, James	Orphan. House carpenter
Pewitt, James	14Oct1823	14 yrs on 2Sept1823	Adams, James	Orphan. Saddle tree maker
Whitby, Richard	5Jan1824	14 yrs on 18Apr next	Currey, James W.	Orphan. Blacksmith. John Cartwright apptd adm of estate of Polly Whitby
Moore, John	5Apr1824	15 yrs on 15Sept last	Tennison, Joseph & McGan, Eli	Orphan. Shoe & boot maker
Franklin, Sally	12July1824	15 yrs	Smith, William	Sewing, spinning & housekeeping. Mulatto
Jackson, Richard	11Oct1824	4 yrs	Cayce, Fleming	Orphan. Blacksmith. On 13July & 4Oct1825 Nancy Jackson asks that indentures be cancelled. On 8Oct1825 court refused
Jackson, Polly	10Jan1825	9 yrs	Cayce, Fleming	Spinster. Of color. See above
Bailey, Richard	13Jan1825	5 yrs	Reams, Joshua	Orphan. House carpenter. Canc 4Apr1825
Ansley, Charles	14Apr1825	15 yrs in Feb last	Davis, Chesley	Orphan. Taylor

Name	Date	Age	Master	Notes
Lock, Vinacy	15Apr1825	13 yrs	Andrews, Mark L.	Orphan. Tanner & courier
Lock, Richard H.	15Apr1825	15 yrs in Dec next	Andrews, Andrew J.	Orphan. Saddler
Lock, Henry C.	15Apr1825	11 yrs in Sept next	Bond, William M.	Orphan. Shoe maker
Kennedy, William L.	16Apr1825	18 yrs	Curry, James W.	Orphan. Black smith
Askew, Hardy	3Oct1825	15 mo	Chadwell, Valentine	Orphan. Farmer. Of color
Booker, James	5Oct1825	16 yrs	Taylor, William D.	Orphan. Chair maker & painter
McCutchan, James	9Jan1826	15 yrs	Davis, Chesley	Orphan. Taylor
White, Hiram James	11Jan1826	15 yrs on 3July last	Park, James	Orphan. Hatter
Booker, Willis	11Jan1826	17 yrs	White, Benjamin	Orphan. House carpenter. Cancelled 10Oct1826 for maltreatment 2Oct1826*
Crenshaw, Jacob	3Apr1826	15 or 16 yrs	Hadley, Denny P.	Orphan. Farmer. Of color
Peebles, John	8Apr1826	15 yrs	Davis, Chesley	Until 25Dec1831. Orphan. Taylor
Anderson, Claibourne	11Apr1826	17 yrs on 1Nov1826	McGan, Eli	Orphan. Sadler
Chapman, Abram	7July1826	18 yrs on 22Feb last	Andrews, Brockenbrough	Orphan. Black smith
Anderson, Ruth	2Oct1826		Shelburne, Pettus	Orphan. Seamstress
Dunn, Machie	2Oct1826	Abt 13 yrs	McLaran, Franklin	Orphan. Saddler
Whitley, John	13Oct1826	9 yrs	Tennison, Joseph	Orphan. Boot & shoe maker
Dean, Nathan	1Jan1827	13 yrs on 6Jan inst	Thomas, Nathaniel H.	Orphan. Brick layer, maker & burner
Dean, Daniel	1Jan1827	10 yrs on 18Feb next	Thomas, Nathaniel H.	Orphan. Brick layer, maker & burner
Dean, Elijah	1Jan1827	16 yrs on 29Feb next	Thomas, Nathaniel H.	Orphan. Brick layer, maker & burner
Brown, Arthur	2Jan1827	16 yrs on 16Feb next	Montgomery, Thomas	Orphan. Taylor
Harrison, Wiley	8Jan1827	15 yrs in 1Jan inst	Thomas, Nathaniel H.	Orphan. Brick layer, maker & burner
Henry	2July1827	11 yrs	Chadwell, John	Farmer. Of color
John	2July1827	3 yrs	Chadwell, John	Farmer. Of color
America	2July1827	12 yrs	Chadwell, John	Seamstress & housewife. Of color
Nancy	2July1827	5 yrs	Chadwell, John	Seamstress & housewife. Of color

Name	Date	Term	Master	Trade / Notes
Castleman, Ahab	2July1827	16 yrs on 17Oct last	Campbell, Henry E.	Blacksmith
McCabe, Charles	2Oct1827	18 yrs	Thomas, Nathaniel H.	Orphan. Brick layer, maker & burner
Noah, Zepheniah N.	3Oct1827	18 yrs on 1Sept last	Thomas, Nathaniel H.	Orphan. Brick layer, maker & burner
Booker, Willis	8Oct1827	18 yrs	Thomas, Nathaniel H.	Orphan. Brick layer, maker & burner
Franklin, Rachel	8Oct1827	9 yrs	Core, Jonathan	Orphan. Spinning, weaving, house wifery, & seamstress. Of color. Canc 12Apr1828
Franklin, Betsey	8Oct1827	6 yrs	Core, Jonathan	Orphan. Spinning, weaving, house wifery, & seamstress. Of color. Canc 12Apr1828
Hardiston, Samuel	8Oct1827	14 yrs on 1June last	Wooldridge, Thomas E.	Orphan. Shoe & boot maker
Baker, Sterling	15Jan1828	7 yrs on 1Oct1827	Gee, David W.	Until 20 yrs. Orphan. Brick laying & stone cutting
Webb, Anonio? C.	18Jan1828	15 yrs on 2Mar next	Wooldridge, Loving H.	Orphan. Saddler
Webb, John P.	18Jan1828	17 yrs on 30Oct last	White, George	Orphan. Taylor
Edney, Milton Y.	11Apr1828	13 yrs in Oct last	West, Stephen & Fry, Joseph H.	Orphan. Cabinet maker
Franklin, Betsey	12Apr1828	8 yrs on 11May next	Smith, William	Sewing, spinning & housekeeping
Franklin, Rachel	12Apr1828	10 yrs 22Aug next	Smith, William	Sewing, spinning & housekeeping
Potts, Joseph	15July1828	15 yrs	White, George	Orphan. Taylor
Jordan, Reeves	16Jan1829	16 yrs on 10Nov last	Thomas, Nathaniel H.	Orphan. Brick maker, layer & burner
Mangrum, William D.	8Apr1829	2 yrs on 5May1829	Mangrum, William	Orphan. Farmer
Bigley, Thomas	9Apr1829	16 yrs on 7Oct1828	Eubanks, Stephen G.	Orphan. Cabinet maker. Cancelled 16Oct1830. Ill used & not taught trade
Harrel, Andrew Green	15Apr1829	12 yrs on 15Dec last	Davis, Chesley	Orphan. Taylor
Harrison, Holland	9July1829	17 yrs	Wyatt, Isaac	Orphan. Cabinet maker
Taylor, James	3Oct1829	15 yrs	Robinson, David J.	Orphan. Cabinet maker
Trantham, William M.	12Oct1829	8 yrs	Adams, James	Orphan. Farmer
Harrell, Thomas	13Jan1830	19 yrs on 14Apr1830	White, Thomas J.	Orphan. Hatter. With William Harrel, an heir of James Harrel, late a soldier in the 24th Reg of US Infantry in the late war 9July1830
McCarrol, Lemiza	5Apr1830	11 yrs	Floyd, Jones	Orphan. Housewife
Knighton, George	12Apr1830	16yrs on 16June1830	Eubanks, Stephen G.	Orphan. Cabinet maker

Name	Date	Age	Master	Notes
Powell, Martha Amanda Maury	17July1830	9 yrs on 19Feb last	Smith, Peter N.	Orphan. Seamstress. Dau of Jane Powell. Has a brother 14July1830
Ballard, Benjamin	11Jan1831	14 yrs on 25Dec next	Yancey, Philip A.	Orphan. House carpenter & joiner
Knighton, Henry A.	8July1831	14 yrs on 16June last	Fry, Joseph H.	Orphan. Cabinet maker
Caswell	4Oct1831	8 yrs	Bingham, James A.	Wheel right. Of color. Cancelled 3Jan1843
Franklin	4Oct1831	7 yrs	Bingham, William	Wheel right. Of color
Haynes, Richard	10Oct1831	12 yrs	McGan, Eli	Orphan. Sadler
Knight, Richard	10Oct1831	12yrs on 15Sept1831	McGan, Eli	Orphan. Sadler
Haynes, Franklin	10Oct1831	15 yrs on 2June1831	Carter, Fountain B.	Orphan. Shoe & boot maker
Franklin, Rachael	14July1832	14 yrs on 22Aug next	McMahon, Joseph F.	Orphan. Housewife. Of color
Franklin, Betsey	14July1832	12 yrs on 11May last	Farmer, Lemuel	Orphan. Housewife. Of color
Rogers, Mark W.	11Jan1833	2 yrs on 19Oct1832	Wooldridge, Loving H.	Orphan. Sadler
Tarkington, George	22Jan1833	17 yrs on 1Jan inst	Carter, Alexander C.	Orphan. Shoe & boot maker. Cancelled 10Jan1834. Father living
Brady, General	2Apr1833	2 1/2 yrs	Rainey, Stephen W.	Orphan. Farmer. Cancelled 5May1845. On 4Nov1851* Brady registered as free man of color, born free of Hagar Sumner
Houston, Governor	2Apr1833	4 yrs 5 mo	Rainey, Stephen W.	Orphan. Farmer. Cancelled 5May1845. On 4Nov1851* Houston registered as free man of color, born free of Hagar Sumner
Haley	8Apr1834	7 yrs	Conn, George A.	Farmer. Of color
Smith, Ezekial	17Apr1834	16 yrs	Wooldridge, Loving H.	Orphan. Sadler
Rhodes, Josephus	7July1834	10 yrs on 25Mar last	Gantt, James M	Orphan. Brick maker, layer & burner
Lewis	17Jan1835	4 yrs 6 mo	Carter, Alexander C.	Shoe & boot maker. Orphan. Of color. Cancelled 6Mar1843
Barnett, William B.	5Oct1835	14 yrs on 21Mar last	Carter, Fountain B.	Orphan. Shoe & boot maker

Name	Date	Age	Master	Trade / Notes
Edlin, James H. B. T.	5Oct1835	14 yrs	Carter, Fountain B.	Shoe & boot maker. Son of Oswald Edlin, who has abandoned his wife & children. Cancelled 20Jan1836
Jones, James	4Jan1836	5 yrs on 4Oct last	Hicks, Benjamin A.	Orphan. Shoe & boot maker
Johnson, Andrew Jackson	4Jan1836	6 yrs on 6May last	Jones, Richard C.	Orphan. Farmer
Owens, Catherine	11Jan1836	8 yrs in June last	Chrisman, Jacob	Orphan. Housewife. Cancelled 5June1837
Edlin, James H. B. T.	20Jan1836		Wright, John N.	Shoe & boot maker
Lannear, Christopher A.	20Jan1836	17 yrs last May	McGan, Alfred	Orphan. Sadler
Holland, John	4Apr1836	8 yrs	McKay, Milton R.	Orphan. Farmer
Trentham, Henry	6Sept1836		Woldridge, Loving H.	Sadler
Lester, Benjamin L.	3Oct1836	17 yrs	Thomas, Nathaniel H.	Orphan. Stone cutter
Lester, George F.	3Oct1836	12 yrs	Thomas, Nathaniel H.	Brickmaker & bricklayer
Lester, William R.	3Oct1836	10 yrs	Thomas, Nathaniel H.	Brickmaker & bricklayer
Sudbury, Patrick	8Nov1836	12 yrs	Herbert, John B.	Orphan. Saddler
Haynes, John	5Dec1836	15 yrs	Wright, John N.	Orphan. Shoemaker
Thompson, Martha Jane	1May1837	7 yrs	Stevens, Silas	Orphan. Housewifery
Haley	5June1837	9 yrs	Conn, George A.	Farmer. Of color
Thompson, Page	5June1837	10 yrs on 20Apr last	McAlpin, Daniel	Orphan. Stone mason
Thompson, Samuel	5June1837	12 yrs on 7May last	Macham, James	Orphan. Farmer
Brown, Jack	3July1837	12 yrs last January	Bullock, John H.	Common labourer. Of color
Barnett, John Willis	2Oct1837	14 yrs on 13Apr next	Woldridge, Thomas E.	Orphan. Boot & shoe maker. Consent of John Willis & of Sarah Barnett, mother
Deason, James H.	6Nov1837	3 yrs	Henderson, Samuel	Orphan. Farmer
Deason, William R.	6Nov1837	5 yrs	Henderson, Samuel	Orphan. Farmer
Deason, Henry H.	6Nov1837	8 yrs	Henderson, Samuel	Orphan. Farmer
Sam or Major	4Dec1837	11 or 12 yrs	Peay, Susan	Farmer. Of color
Melson, Henry A.	1Jan1838	12 yrs	Crichlow, Joseph E.	Orphan. Saddler
Meadow, Samuel	1Jan1838	16 yrs	White, Franklin P.	Orphan. House carpenter
Jackson, John	1Apr1839	11 yrs	Sutton, Jonas	Tanner. Sutton also apptd guardian
Askew, Hady	2Apr1839	15 yrs	Chadwell, Elizabeth	Farmer. Of color
Hodges, Albert	6Jan1840	13 yrs	Hill, John D.	Orphan. Farmer

Name	Date	Age	Master	Notes
Williams, James R.	1Mar1841	13 yrs on 20Aug next	Anderson, William	Orphan. Tailor
Williams, John Nicholas	1Mar1841	9 yrs on 2July next	Crichlow, Joseph E.	Orphan. Saddler
Williams, William James	1Mar1841	11 yrs on 22Mar inst	Brown, Willie	Orphan. Cabinet maker
Barham, John H.	2Mar1841	13 yrs on 29Apr next	Berson, Solomon W.	Orphan. Silversmith
George	3Jan1843	Abt 14 yrs	Rotterock, George	Tanner & currier. Of color
Caswell	3Jan1843		White, Franklin P.	Carpenter. Of color
Henry	6Feb1843	13 yrs on 9April next	Ratcliffe, John W.	Of color. House carpenter
Sally	6Feb1843	11 yrs on 8April next	Graham, William	Of color. Seamstress & weaver
Brown, Louis	6Mar1843		White, Franklin P.	Of color. House carpenter. 6Feb1843*
Goley, Martha	3Oct1843	9 yrs in Sept last	Chrisman, Marcus L.	Orphan. Weaver & housewifery. Cancelled 5May1845
Wells, Henry	3Oct1843	12 yrs on 23Mar last	Wells, Reuben M.	Orphan. Farmer. Cancelled 5May1845
Poteete, David	3Mar1845		Andrews, George	Blacksmith. Of color. On 1June1846 suit by Barbara Poteet to cancel indenture denied. Boy's name given as David McSevean?
Bond, Thomas	5May1845	15 yrs on 11July next	Bochens, Joseph A.	Orphan. Saddler. Cancelled 1Sept1845
Poteet, Brice	3Feb1846	14 yrs in Jan next	Short, John J.	Orphan. Stonecutter
Sturdivant, James	6Apr1846	17 yrs on 21Jan last	Sampson, Emanuel	Orphan. Farmer
Butler, Isaac H.	7Dec1846	14 yrs	Barker, George W.	Farmer
Butler, John	7Dec1846	13 yrs	McAlpin, Daniel	Bricklayer
Loftin, Albert	5Apr1847		Rogers, William A.	Tanner. Of color
Mayfield, Alfred	6Mar1848	Abt 12 yrs	Pinkston, David	Tanner
Newcomb, Nelson	7May1849	13 yrs	Bridges, Samuel B.	Orphan. Farmer
Burney, Cornelia F.	5Mar1850		Rainey, Robert	Housewife. Abandoned by father, Charles G. Burney
Robinson, Lewis	7Jan1851		Duke, Beverly	Taylor
Harrison, James	7Apr1851		Waddy, James	Wagon making
Bagley, James	1Dec1851		Anderson, Stanfield	Orphan. Farmer

Name	Date	Age	Name	Notes
Bagley, John	1Dec1851		Hartley, Laban	Orphan. Blacksmith
Bagley, Calvin	1Mar1852		Sweeney, Sillas W.	Cooper
Harris, John Wilson	2Aug1852		Barnett, Josephus	Orphan. Farmer
Owen, James M.	4Oct1852		Jamison, Jacob	Both of color
Askins, Mary A. E.	4Oct1852		Jamison, Jacob	Both of color
Askins, John Eli	4Oct1852		Jamison, Jacob	Both of color
Robinson, Lewis	3Nov1852	Abt 12 yrs	Bochens, William G. D.	Orphan. Saddler
Roberts, George Andrew Jackson	7Feb1859	9 yrs	Cody, Bailey H.	Orphan. Shoe & boot maker
Burnett, Caunsil	2Jan1866		Burnett, W. W.	Of color
Burnett, William	2Jan1866		Burnett, W. W.	Of color
Burnett, Mat	2Jan1866		Burnett, W. W.	Of color
Maybery, Lyla	2Jan1866		Rainy, Robert	Of color
Turley, Elwood	3Jan1866		Turley, T. W.	Of color
Darden, Martha	3Jan1866		Bond, Thomas B.	Of color
Darden, Balin	3Jan1866		Bond, Thomas B.	Of color
Furgerson, Andrew	9Jan1866		Furgerson, John R.	Of color
Furgerson, Mariah	9Jan1866		Furgerson, John R.	Of color
Copeland, Mary	7May1866		Copeland, Samuel	Until 21 yrs. Housekeeping & housewifery. Of color. Req of mother, Lella Copeland
Crutcher, Mary	4June1866		Crutcher, Nancy P.	Until 21 yrs. Housekeeping. Of color
Bolerjack, Taswell	9July1866		Bolerjack, John	Of color
Bolerjack, Ura	9July1866		Bolerjack, John	Of color
Bolerjack, Nelius	9July1866		Bolerjack, John	Of color
Ozbourne, Vina	9July1866		Ozbourne, Robert A.	Of color
Beasly, Dick	9July1866		Beasly, William	Of color
White, Jacob	9July1866		Kelly, A. M. W.	Of color
Bittick, Sam.	6Aug1866		Bittick, Cyrus S.	Of color
Bittick, Ed.	6Aug1866		Bittick, Cyrus S.	Of color
Bittick, Sam. Houston	6Aug1866		Bittick, Josephus	Of color
Bittick, Albert	6Aug1866		Bittick, Josephus	Of color

Name	Date	Age	Master	Notes
King, Joseph	13Aug1866		King, John	Of color
King, Jerry	13Aug1866		King, John	Of color
Crass, Martha	6Nov1866		Bond, Thomas K?	
Green, Matty	8Jan1867		Coke, Daniel F.	Of color
Green, Julious	8Jan1867		Coke, Daniel F.	Of color
Alexander, William J.	18Feb1867		Brown, Benjamin T.	
Smith, Joseph	6May1867		Stephens, John P.	Of color
Jones, Thomas	10June1867		Averett, M. D. L.	Of color
Wells, Catharine	1July1867	9 yrs	Wells, J. B.	Of color
Reid, Price	2July1867		Reid, Alexander	Of color
Reid, Lucy	2July1867		Reid, Alexander	Of color
Rice, Susan	2July1867		Robinson, Nancy	Of color
Baugh, Nicholas	12July1869	Abt 12 yrs	Baugh, Joseph W.	Of color
Baugh, Harriett	12July1869	Abt 10 yrs	Baugh, Joseph W.	Until 21 yrs. Of color
Maybery, Louisa	13Nov1871	8 yrs	Maybery, H. G. W.	Orphan. Housekeeping. Of color
Andrews, John	18Dec1871	6 yrs	Tulloss, Joseph R.	Bastard. Mother dead. Farming. Of color
Rucker, Eli	8Jan1872	14 yrs	Rucker, A. D. A.	Orphan. Farming. Of color
Logan, Richard	12Feb1872	18 yrs	Logan, Thomas P.	Orphan. Farming. Of color
McPhail, Kate M.	5Mar1872		Baltishurler, F. G.	Housekeeping. Of color
Gardner, James	21July1873		Pointer, Samuel A.	
Chapman, George	21July1873		Pointer, Samuel A.	
Chapman, James	21July1873		Pointer, Samuel A.	
Chapman, Martha	21July1873		Pointer, Samuel A.	
Jones, Francis M. Lavender	21July1873		Brown, G. W.	
Chapman, Jack	21July1873		Chapman, C. C.	Next of kin present in court
Chapman, Mary Francis	21July1873		Chapman, C. C.	Next of kin present in court
Chapman, Martha	21July1873		Chapman, C. C.	Next of kin present in court
Chapman, William	21July1873		Chapman, C. C.	Next of kin present in court
Beard, John	16Apr1874		Allen, Samuel	Written consent of parents, W. B. & Nancy Beard. Farming

Name	Master	Date	Age	Notes
McLaughlin, Lige	Kernan, James T.	30Jan1875	Abt 13 yrs	Farming. Father & mother dead. Of color
Pointer, William	Harrison, William	2Feb1875	Abt 6 yrs	Farming. Bastard. Mother unable to provide. Of color
Wade, Rachel	Wade, E. L. (Mrs)	?		Cancelled 14Sept1875. Unable to control. Of color. To custody of sister, Mollie Pigg
Lantern, Reuben A.	Lantern, Joseph	7Dec1875	Abt 7 yrs	Farming. Bastard. Mother unable to provide, consents. Surname "Lantern" given to minor at this time
Smith, Charles	Gray, G. W.	16Feb1876	Abt 8 yrs	Farming. On 4Mar1876 Gray allowed to remove Smith to Williamsport, Maury Co
Rutledge, Dora A.	Paschall, B. H.	4Sept1876	Abt 10 yrs	Housekeeping. Parents dead
Patton, Andrew	Pointer, S. J.	5Oct1877	13 yrs	Consent of mother. Of color
West, Wallace	Pollard, Elizabeth	10Sept1878		Farmer. Of color

Wilson County

Name	Master	Date	Age	Notes
Bloodworth, Jesse	Rhea, John	26Mar1805		Black smith
Jmpson, John	Youm, Patrick	24Sept1806		Orphan. Blacksmith
Searcy, Robert	Taylor, Elisha	17June1816	10 yrs	Orphan
Toliver, Zachariah	Shoville, Samuel, of Lebanon	17Sept1816		Taken from jail. Bound until 24Aug1819. Blacksmith
Akin, Aaron Johnson	Finly, Obediah G	17Dec1816		For 4 yrs. Son of Harrison.
McKinney, John R.	Moon, Isaac	17Dec1816		Orphan
McKenney, Joel	Dew, Nathaniel	17Mar1817		
Jackson, William	Horn, Jeremiah	17Mar1817		
Melton, Garrett	Cross, Elijah	17Mar1817		
Wright, John J.	McMinn, John	17Mar1817		
Robertson, Lucy	Bettis, Wyatt	18Mar1817	1 yr	Orphan
Willard, William	Williard, James	19Mar1817	3 yrs	
Mathews, Joshua	State, William N.	17Sept1817	6 yrs	Orphan. Blacksmith
Cannon, Thomas M.	Roberts, Robert B.	16Dec1817		Until 15Aug1821. Cancelled 2Aug1819
Echols, Abner	Hansbro, Smith, of Lebanon	16Dec1817	16 yrs on 7May last	Orphan

Name	Date	Age	Master	Notes
Ash, Frederick	2Feb1818		Stewart, Abner	Orphan. Wheelwright
Wallis, Samuel	3Feb1818	9 yrs	Stone, John	Deserted by father
Chaddock, Alexander	3Feb1818		Sherrell, Samuel W.	
McClendon, Jacob	?		Algood, William	Left Algood in Oct1817. Cancelled 8May1818
Williams, Elisha	3Aug1818	12 ys	McCaffy, John	
Smith, Allen	3Nov1818	7 yrs	Milligan, James	Cooper
Hodge, William	3May1819		Hartsfield, William	
Moore, Zachariah	3May1819		Moore, Warren	
Moore, Evalina	3May1819		McWhirter, George	
Wood, John	3May1819	15 yrs	Rhodes, Hezekiah	Mulatto
McCarty, Jane	?		Corner, Reuben	Orphan. Cancelled 2Aug1819, motion of John Muckleyea. To possession of Muckleyea
Dunbar, Stephen	2Aug1819		Walker, Harbert	
Jackson, Robert	1Nov1819		Chasten?, Elisha	Orphan
Blackwell, Malinda	7Feb1820		Carruth, James	
Mitchell, Jesse William	7Feb1820		Mitchell, Lamech	
Mitchell, Martha Ann Elizabeth	7Feb1820		Mitchell, Lamech	
Morgan, Alston	1May1820		Dismukes, Elisha	
Wallis, Samuel	1May1820		Phelps, Benjamin	
Jones, Ealender	1May1820		Rogers, William	Female
Duncan, Stephen	7Aug1820		Durk, Samuel	
James, Carey	6Nov1820	13 yrs	Lane, Drury	Female orphan
Snell, Riley	6Nov1820	10 yrs	Sypert, Lawrence	Orphan
Snell, James	7Nov1820	5 yrs	Cross, James	Orphan
Hall, James	6Aug1821	18 yrs	Seawell, Hardy M.	Orphan
Harrell, Asa	6Aug1821	16 yrs	Wade, William H.	Orphan
Miller, Samuel	25Mar1822	12 yrs	Aston, Alexander	Orphan
Beasley, Washington	25Mar1822		Woodward, Hezekiah	Orphan

Apprentice	Date	Term/Age	Master	Notes
Burrus, Asbury	25Mar1822	8 yrs	Walk, Wesley	
Quarles, Milton Houston?	26Mar1822		Davidson, John B.	For 4 yrs. Cabinet maker
Brown, Mason	24June1822	11 yrs (17?)	Loyd, Jarratt	Until 20 yrs
Brown, Irwin	24June1822		Loyd, Jarrat	
Gallagly, [Joseph]	?		State, William N.	Badly treated. Cancelled? 26June1822. Entry incomplete. 26Mar1822*
Dinah	23Dec1822	5 yrs	Leawell, Hardy M.	Of color
King, Dennis	22June1823	16 yrs last Christmas	Jennings, Abel	Orphan. For 5 yrs. Farming
Butler, Bretton	22Sept1823		Allen, Eli	
Mallaga, James C.	22Sept1823		Cowper, Francis	
Brown, Edward	22Sept1823		Roane, Hugh	
Millegan, Joseph	22Sept1823		Bryson, Joseph	
Mitchell, John	22Sept1823		Hartsfield, William	
Pennal, Ryal	22Dec1823		Jennings, John A.	
Somers?, George	22Dec1823		Tucker, Green	Orphan
Pennal, Willer	22Dec1823		Short, Theophalus W.	
Scott, James P.	22Mar1824	14 yrs	Carruth, Walter	
Pennel, Sally	27Sept1824		Ward, John	Until 21 yrs
Moore, Edward	25Sept1826		Sevan, Andrew	
Moore, Haywood	25Sept1826		Sevan, John	
Lewis, William	27Dec1826		Baxter, George	
Jones, Henry L.	?		Chance, Joseph B.	Blacksmith. Cancelled 5Apr1827 for ill treatment. Plaintiff was Henry's next friend, Susannah Jones. Chance appealed to Circuit Court
Aust, Thomas B.	24Dec1827	Abt 17 yrs	Aust, Frederick	
Jackson, Isaac	29Dec1827		Gibson, Jesse	Also recorded 3Jan1828
Lasater, Calvin	24Mar1828		Bettis, William	
Billingsly, Charles	22Sept1828		?	Son of John Billingsly. Probably bound. Entry incomplete
McDermet, Ann	22Sept1828		Dickins, Samuel	
Booker, Polly	22Sept1828		Cox, Jr, John	Orphan

Name	Date	Age	Master	Notes
Bell, Nancy	22Sept1828		Merett, James	Until age 21. Merrett also appointed guardian. Orphan
Osburn, James A.	22Sept1828		Moore, George	
Romine, Thomas	28Dec1828		Toliver, Zachariah	
Underwood, Johnson	23Mar1829		Scoggins, George W.	
Underwood, William	23Mar1829		Jones, Henry	
Nighbors, John	23Jun1829		Danl, James	
Jacobs, Joel	23Jun1829		Kirkpatrick, Thomas	Orphan
Bowers, Lemuel	24June1829		Irwin, James M. & Vick, Allen W.	
Jacobs, Joel	30June1829		Hancock, Nelson D.	
Crook, Polly	28Sept1829		Bradford,	
Crook, George	28Sept1829		Williams, Julias H.	
Brown, Martin	28Dec1829		Donnell, Leo	
Tucker, Nancy	28Dec1829		Clemmons, John	Cancelled 26Dec1831
Bowers, William	4Jan1830		McConnell, David	
Lindsey, John	22Mar1830		Caplinger, Soloman	Orphan
Lindsey, Wyatt	22Mar1830		Carruth, James	
Lindsey, Joseph	22Mar1830		Carruth, James	
Bell, Nancy	28June1830		Hollaway, Levi	
Booker, Polly	28June1830		Phillips, Benjamin	
Mitchell, Richard	27Sept1830	Abt 9 yrs	Carruth, Alexander	Orphan
Fullerton, William	4Oct1830	Abt 9 yrs	Johnson, Philip	
Grissom, Timothy	28June1831	Abt 15 yrs	Smith, Nicholas	Orphan
Grissom, Young	28June1831	Abt 11 yrs	Smith, Nicholas	Orphan
Tucker, Nancy	26Dec1831		Young, Gilbert	
Wetherspoon, Malinda	27Dec1831	Abt 8 yrs	Sherrell, Alanson N.	Orphan
Tomblin, John	27Dec1831	Abt 15 yrs	Holman, John	Orphan. Released August1837, as John Tumblin. Now 21 yrs.
Clymer, Noah R.	24Mar1834	Abt 8 yrs	Brown, James M.	Orphan. Cabinet maker
Partian, James	24Mar1834	Abt 14 yrs	Kirkpatrick, Thomas	Orphan. Saddler

Orphan	Date	Age	Master	Notes
Climer, James	24Mar1834	Abt 6 yrs	Swain, Caleb	Orphan. Hatter. Cancelled 1Jan1844
Lindsey, Elisha	24Mar1834	Abt 18 yrs	McKnight, William	Orphan. Waggon making
Breedlove, James	?		Tolliver, Zechariah	Blacksmith. Cancelled 28Mar1834. To Edward Travilian, Guardian
Climer, John	23June1834		Hancocke, Nelson	Orphan. Saddling
Neely, William	23June1834		Hammonds, Thomas	Sadler. Cancelled 1Aug1836, as William Neal. "Hamblin" leaving state
Garrison, George W.	22Sept1834	Abt 17 yrs	Kirkpatrick, Thomas	Sadler. Cancelled 28Mar1836
Dallis, Jr, Robert	22Sept1834	Abt 7 yrs	Dallas, Sr, Robert	Orphan. Farming
Tompkins, Washington	22Dec1834	Abt 14 yrs	McNiel, John	Orphan
Jacobs, Allen	25Dec1834	Abt 14 yrs	Stewart, Elijah R.	Orphan. Cabinet maker
Hunt, James	23Mar1835	Abt 15 yrs	Wilburn, William L.	Orphan. Cabinet maker
Wheeler, Henry	23Mar1835	Abt 10 yrs	Provine, Alexander M.	Orphan. Taning. Cancelled 6July1840* and Robert Daughty apptd guardian of Henry and Mary Wheeler, orphans of John Wheeler, Dcd. Provine leaving country 1June1840*
Hunt, James	23Mar1835	Abt 16 yrs	Holman, Robert M.	Orphan. Bricklayer
Farr, John	23June1835	Abt 14 yrs	Holman, Robert M.	Orphan. Bricklayer
Gillard, Finly S.	28Sept1835	Abt 8 yrs	Gold, Pleasant	Farmer. Cancelled Nov1836. Returned to father, Edward Dillard
Gillard, Thomas G.	28Sept1835	Abt 7 yrs	Gold, Pleasant	Farmer. Cancelled Nov1836. Returned to father, Edward Dillard
Smith, John A.	1Oct1835		Cain & Latimore.	Orphan. Tailoring
Stanly, Judah Martha Ann	28Dec1835	Abt 8 yrs	Bryson, Hiram	Until 21 yrs
Ellis, Alfred	28Dec1835	Abt 13 yrs	Bass, Solomon	Request of mother
John	?		Blaze, George	Cancelled 6Feb1837 for ill use. To mother, Dianna Valentine. Of color. 28Dec1835*
Eli	?		Blaze, George	Cancelled 6Feb1837 for ill use. To mother, Dianna Valentine. Of color. 28Dec1835*
Foster, John W.	28Mar1836	Abt 8 yrs	More?, Hiram S.	Orphan. Sadler
Cothern, William C.	28Mar1836	Abt 19 yrs	Gwyn, Ransom	Orphan. Blacksmith. Canc 6June1836. William diseased in mind and body

Name	Date	Age	Master	Notes
Latimer, Alpheus R.	5Sept1836	Abt 17 yrs	Latimer, Benjamin A.	Tailor
Grovins, William	2May1836		Parham, Samuel H.	Grovins binds himself for 2 yrs. A minor?
Fortress, John	1May1837	Abt 7 yrs	Holmes, William	Shoe & boot making
Carroll, George	5June1837	Abt 10 yrs	Goldston, John N.	Orphan. Machine & cabinet maker
Graves, William	4Sept1837	Abt 19 yrs	Underwood, Johnson	For 1 yr 11 mo. Tailor
Finny, Harris	7Nov1837	Abt 11 yrs	Gregory, Richard	Orphan. Wool carding
Sanders, Maria Ann	7Nov1837	Abt 12 yrs	Anderson, Joseph M. (Dr)	Orphan. Of color
Wheeler, John	7Nov1837	Abt 9 yrs	Doughty, Robert	Orphan. Farmer
Dickson, Thomas	1Jan1838	Abt 15 yrs	Kirkpatrick, Thomas	Orphan. Sadler
Campbell,	?		Stewart, Elijah R.	Cabinet maker. Canc 5Feb1838. Now 21 yrs
Wright, John H.	6Mar1838	Abt 14 yrs	Jennings, William B.	Orphan. Farmer
Holmes, Elizabeth	6Aug1838	Abt 9 yrs	Tarpley, Lindsey B.	Of color. Cancelled 4Aug1846, Tarpley having left the state. Dau of Mary Holmes. Ordered returned to family
Holmes, Robert	6Aug1838	Abt 7 yrs	Tarpley, Lindsey B.	Blacksmith. Of color
Dickson, Franklin H.	5Nov1838	Abt 18 yrs	Kirkpatrick, Thomas	Orphan. Sadler
Arnold, William	4Feb1839	Abt 11 yrs	Robins, William C.	Orphan. Sadler
Green, Albert	2Apr1839		Hancock, Dawson A.	Sadler. Illegitimate son of Barbary Green
Jefferson, Eneas	4Nov1839	11 yrs on 31Jan next	Holmes, William	Illegitimate son of ___ Duff, formerly ___ Green. Shoe & boot making. Name may be Eneas Jefferson Green. Record unclear
Hinson, Anthony	4Nov1839	7 yrs on 9April last	Holmes, William	Illegitimate son of ___ Duff, formerly ___ Green. Shoe & boot making. Name may be Anthony Hinson Green. Record unclear
Green, Bryant	6Jan1840	Abt 11 yrs	Lane, Thomas B.	Illegitimate son of Barbary Green.* On 6Apr1840 appropriation made for support of Barbary Green, pauper
Clopton, Benjamin A.	3Feb1840	Abt 14 yrs	Duffy, William C.	For 6 yrs. Tailor
Wade, Michael	2Mar1840	Abt 15 yrs	Fisher, Phillip	Orphan
Collins, Hiram K.	2Mar1840	Abt 16 yrs	Rickets, John S.	
Green, Briant	7Dec1840	Abt 13 or 14 yrs	McClain, William P.	Printer
Green, Samuel	1Feb1841	7 yrs on 19th this	Holmes, William	Shoe and boot making. Consent of mother

Name	Date	mo / Age	Bound to	Remarks
Dehart, William	7June1841	Abt 12 yrs	Hancock, Eli	Orphan. Manufacturing hemp rope. Cancelled same day at William's request. AKA William McDougal
Mahaffy, Noah Washington	7June1841	13 yrs on 26Nov next	Hancock, John	Farmer. Cancelled 5Feb1844
Mahaffy, Robert Henry	7June1841	Abt 6 yrs	M____, William	Until 20 yrs. Entry poorly legible
McDougal, William	7June1841	Abt 12 yrs	Johnson, ____	Entry poorly legible
Casselman, Benjamin	5July1841	18 yrs	Cartmell, Nathan	Orphan. Tanning & currying leather
Bumpass, Grief Andrew Jackson	7Feb1842		Jewell, Elihu B.	Blacksmith. Abandoned by mother
Thompson, Warfield	8Mar1842	Abt 16 yrs	Cartmell, Nathan	Orphan. Tanning & currying
McLaimer?, John G.	8Mar1842	Abt 14 yrs	Bell, Nathaniel	Cabinet maker
Reed, Thomas	4Apr1842	Abt 7 yrs	Owen, John	Farmer. Illegitimate son of Betsy McGee
Craddock, Grief Andrew Jackson	4Apr1842	Abt 8 yrs	Jewell, Elihu B.	Blacksmith. Illegitimate son of Elizabeth T. Bumpass, formerly Craddock
Parker, Hiram K.	2May1842	Abt 7 yrs	Whitlock, Thomas K.	Orphan. Farmer
Mahaffy, Lycurgus C.	6June1842	Abt 11 yrs	Johnson, Harrison A.	Farmer. Cancelled 2Nov1846, as Lycurgus Clinton Mahaffy. To H. H. Hancock
Zachary, Joshua	5Sept1842	11 yrs on 11June last	Robins, William C.	Orphan. Sadler
Mahaffy, Robert	3Oct1842	Abt 6 yrs	Reed, Robert D.	Cancelled 4Dec1843
Criswell, Kitty Ann	5Dec1842	Abt 17 yrs 6 mo	Jenkins, Selon	Illegitimate girl of color
Edmund	1May1843	17 yrs	Burton, Robert N.	Of color. Emancipated slave of Elizabeth Mansher, Dcd
Harry	1May1843	15 yrs	Burton, Robert N.	Of color. Emancipated slave of Elizabeth Mansher, Dcd
Couch, Andrew	4Sept1843	Between 6 & 7 yrs	Orrand, John	Illegitimate son of Martha Couch. Farmer. Of color
Partain, John	4Dec1843	Abt 8 yrs	Williams, Bennett	Orphan. Cancelled 1July1844
Partain, Robert	4Dec1843	Abt 6 yrs	Williams, Bennett	Orphan. Cancelled 1Oct1846. Robert gone to live with his friends
Mehaffee, Robert	4Dec1843	Abt 8 yrs	Jerrett, Hiram	Cancelled 6Oct1845
Puckett, George R.	5Feb1844		Kirkpatrick, Thomas	Sadling
Ozment, Marcus D.	5Feb1844		Kirkpatrick, Thomas	Sadling

269

Name	Date	Age	Master	Notes
Robertson, James C.	5Feb1844		Kirkpatrick, Thomas	Sadling
Mehaffy, Noah	5Feb1844		Hancock, John F.	Until 20 yrs.
Winter, Julia Ann	4Mar1844	Abt 13 or 14 yrs	Brown, William	Orphan
Partain, John	1July1844	Abt 8 yrs	Kittrell, Marion B.	Orphan
Bradberry, Cullen	5Aug1844	Abt 13 yrs	Hudson, Paschal P.	Cancelled 1May1848, as Cullen Bradly
Trusty, Josiah	3Sept1844	Abt 13 yrs	Edge, Elam	Orphan of William Trustee, Dcd. Carpenter. Mother consents. Cancelled 7Sept1846. To mother
Guill?, Vincent	7Oct1844	Abt 13 yrs	Brown, Robert	Orphan. Farmer
Trusty, William Henry	2Dec1844	Abt 9 yrs	Edge, Elam	Orphan. House carpenter. Cancelled 7Sept1846. To mother
Hunt, Andrew	3Mar1845	Abt 11 yrs	Hunt, John	Orphan. Farmer
Wooly, Nancy	2Jun1845	Abt 18 yrs	Dowell?, Jesse J.	Of color. A prior indenture with Thomas J. Smith cancelled
Mehaffee, Robert	6Oct1845		Holt, Jesse W.	Orphan. Farmer. Cancelled 5July1847. Holt leaving the state
Marly, John	6Jan1846	Abt 18 yrs	Summerhill, William	Of color. Cancelled 3Mar1846 at request of mother, Nancy Marly, & of Eliza Marly. Mom to select new master & return to court
Marly, Lucy	6Jan1846	Abt 14 yrs	Summerhill, William	Of color. See above
Marly, Chancy	6Jan1846	Abt 7 yrs	Summerhill, William	Of color. See above
Marly, Joe	6Jan1846	Abt 4 yrs	Summerhill, William	Of color. See above
Marly, Amanda	6Jan1846	Abt 4 yrs	Summerhill, William	Of color. See above
Sullivan, William R.	4Jan1847	9 yrs on 26Sept last	Sullivan, Benjamin L.	Orphan. Wagon maker
Mehaffee, Robert	5July1847	Abt 10 yrs	Dill, Hiram M.	Orphan.
Moran, Emily	6Sept1847	Abt 15 yrs	Dunn, Thomas B.	Consent of mother. On 4Oct1847 Evaline Moran, orphan, ordered taken from ___ Alexander & delivered to Dunn
Wright, Thomas	6Dec1847	Abt 17 yrs	Haynes, John A.	Orphan. Boot & shoe making
Chambless, David	6Dec1847	Abt 19 yrs	Haynes, John A.	Orphan. Boot & shoe making
Marly, Lucy	4Jan1848	Abt 16 yrs	Brien?, John P.	Child of Nancy Marly, who consents
Marly, Candy	4Jan1848	Abt 8 yrs	Brien?, John P.	Child of Nancy Marly, who consents
Marly, Amanda	4Jan1848	Abt 3 yrs	Brien?, John P.	Child of Nancy Marly, who consents
Marly, Jo	4Jan1848	Abt 5 yrs	Brien?, John P.	Child of Nancy Marly, who consents

Name	Date	Age	Guardian	Notes
Marly, Ann	4Jan1848	Abt 2 yrs	Brien?, John P.	Child of Nancy Marly, who consents
Bradly, Cullen	1May1848	Abt 17 yrs	Tolliver, Zachariah	Orphan. See Cullen Bradberry
Chambless, Berry Lafayette	7Aug1848	b. 15Mar1835	Price, M. A.	Orphan of Henry Chambless, Dcd
Bruius?, Grief Andrew Jackson	2Jan1849	16 yrs	Wroe, Hiram S.	Orphan. Sadler
Parsons, James	5Feb1849	Abt 10 yrs	Alexander, William P.	Orphan. See Bumpass
Parson, William L.	5Feb1849	Abt 15 yrs	Marshall, John W.	Orphan. Farmer
Pugh, George B.	5Feb1849	16 yrs on 15Nov last	Pugh, Elijah A.	Orphan. Farmer
Sweatman, John	5Mar1849	16 yrs	Posey, Alexander	Orphan. Farmer. Mother dead. Abandoned by father 6Feb1849*
Blankenship, John	2Apr1849	Abt 2 yrs	Williamson, Zachariah	Illegitimate child of Rebecca Blankenship. Farmer
Allen, David Lawson	7May1849	Abt 8 yrs	George, William H.	Orphan. Stone mason
Byter, Josephus	4June1849	Abt 8 yrs	Myres, Peter	Consent of mother. Abandoned by father. Farmer
Moore, Eliza	6May1850	Abt 12 yrs	Drinnan, Hiram A.	Of color
Moore, Amanda	6May1850	Abt 10 yrs	Drinnan, Hiram A.	Of color
Moore, Sarah	6May1850	Abt 8 yrs	Drinnan, Hiram A.	Of color
Moore, James	6May1850	Abt 4 yrs	Drinnan, Hiram A.	Of color
Moore, William	6May1850	Abt 2 yrs	Drinnan, Hiram A.	Of color
Moore, John	6May1850	Abt 2 mo	Drinnan, Hiram A.	Of color
Bull, Jasper	4Nov1850	Between 8 & 9 yrs	England, John	Orphan. Farmer
Sadler, Samuel	7Jan1851	Abt 7 yrs	McIntire, William	Illegitimate son of Rena Sadler
Biter, Peter Franklin	7Apr1851	6 yrs on 5Dec last	Rice, William Carroll	Farmer. Illegitimate child of Nancy Biter
Haley, James Y.	5May1851	5 yrs on 13Mar last	Green, Isham S.	Orphan. Farmer
Haley, Richard Thomas	5May1851	14 yrs on 21Nov	Goldstone, John M.	Orphan. Farmer
Bett, George Washington	2Jun1851	Abt 10 yrs	Bond, John	Abandoned by father, Houston Bett. Mother afflicted, consents. Canc 6Oct1851. Father returned & removed family from county
Bett, Anderson	2Jun1851	Abt 8 yrs	Bond, John	Abandoned by father, Houston Bett. Mother afflicted, consents. Canc 6Oct1851. Father returned & removed family from county

Name	Date	Age	Master	Notes
Bett, Pinkney	2Jun1851	Abt 5 yrs	Bond, John	Abandoned by father, Houston Bett. Mother afflicted, consents. Canc 6Oct1851. Father returned & removed family from county
Cox, John	8July1851	Abt 12 yrs	Burgess, Charles L.	Tailor. Son of William Cox, Dcd
Wilkerson, Benjamin F.	5Aug1851	4 yrs on 24Jan last	Climer, William	Illegitimate child. Farmer
Ricketts, William	3Feb1852	In 16th year	Simpson, John L.	Orphan
Daniel, Carroll	3Feb1852	Abt 16 yrs	Simpson, Charles W.	Orphan
Bryant, Lorenzo Dow	1Mar1852	10 yrs on 2Sept next	Rhea, Archibald	Farmer
Canns?, Berry	6July1852	Abt 14 or 15 yrs	McMinn, Samuel N. (Dr)	Mother dead. Father too old to care for him
Bailey, William	4Jan1853	16? yrs on 13Nov last	Powell, Benajmin D.	Orphan of Washington Bailey, Dcd
Griggs, Mack	7Feb1853	8 yrs mid Nov last	Thomas, H. N.	Orphan. Farmer
Griggs, John	4Apr1853	Abt 11 yrs	Kennedy, E. A.	Orphan. Farmer
Edwards, Samuel	5Sept1853	8 yrs on 15Oct next	Thomas, Albert C.	Orphan. Farmer
Coleman, Mary Ann	5Dec1853	Abt 12 yrs	Coleman, William J.	Until 20 yrs. Orphan. Same date Sampson Knight apptd administrator of estate of Elizabeth Coleman. Cancelled 2Apr1855, as Coleman leaving country. To her sisters care
Coleman, George	5Dec1853	Abt 14 yrs	Coleman, Robert H.	Orphan. Same date Sampson Knight apptd administrator of estate of Elizabeth Coleman
Coleman, John	5Dec1853	Abt 9 yrs	Coleman, Robert H.	Orphan. Same date Sampson Knight apptd administrator of estate of Elizabeth Coleman
Nowlen, Robert	3Apr1854	Abt 15 yrs	Forbes, F. C.	Orphan. Farmer
Loyd, Joseph	2Oct1854	12 yrs in June last	Brassell, Reuben	Orphan. Farmer. Cancelled 2Jan1855
Sims, John	6Nov1854	Abt 4 yrs	Kirkpatrick, John B.	Father dead. Mother very poor. Of color. Cancelled 1Oct1855. Kirkpatrick leaving the county
Sims, William	6Nov1854	Abt 6 yrs	Kirkpatrick, Thomas	Father dead. Mother, very poor, to receive $20 per annum. Of color. Canc 4June1867

Name	Date	Master	Age	Notes
Sims, George W.	6Nov1854	Kirkpatrick, Thomas	Abt 11 yrs	Father dead. Mother, very poor, to receive $20 per annum. Of color
Loyd, Joseph	2Jan1855	Ingram, James	13 yrs next summer	Orphan. Farmer. Ingram is brother-in-law of Loyd (or of Brassell/Brazel, former master). Wording unclear
Crouse, John	5Feb1855	Kelly, Calvin	Abt 12 yrs	Orphan. Farmer
Tate, Moses	5Feb1855	Finney, Horace C.	Near 5 yrs	Orphan. Farmer
Buckner, Thomas	2July1855	Jennings, Uriah	9 or 10 yrs	Orphan
Sims, John	1Oct1855	Kirkpatrick, Thomas	Abt 6 yrs	Of color. Cancelled 4June1867
Ball, John Jasper	1Oct1855	Rutherford, Chesseldon	Abt 13 yrs	Orphan
Day, Thomas	3Dec1855	Day, Mary		Orphan. Mary is grandmother. Of color
Day, Jacob	3Dec1855	Day, Mary		Orphan. Mary is grandmother. Of color
Day, Margaret	3Dec1855	Day, Mary		Orphan. Mary is grandmother. Of color
Day, Abram	3Dec1855	Day, Mary		Orphan. Mary is grandmother. Of color
Vivrett, Cage Thomas	3Mar1856	Jolly, Isham	13 yrs	Orphan. Farmer. On 2June1856 John Perkins, next friend of Vivrett, asks for cancellation of indenture. Action deferred
Winter, Joseph	?	Robertson, William A.		Brickmason. Cancelled 5Aug1856 at request of mother, a widow
Bryant, James Washington	1Sept1856	Clopton, John A.	12 yrs on 25th inst	Orphan. Farmer
Baw, James	2Feb1857	Smith, John	Abt 10 yrs	Orphan. Farmer. 2Aug1858*
Goldstone, Charles R.	7Sept1857	Goldstone, William B.	Abt 10yrs in Oct next	Orphan. Farmer
Patton, James Gideon	2Nov1857	Davis, Anderson	9 yrs on 25Nov1857	Orphan. Farmer. Cancelled 2May1859, as Patterson. To mother
Gray, Smith	1Mar1858	Coppage, James M.	Abt 16 yrs	Orphan. Blacksmith
Goldson, Mary	2May1859	Williams, A. R.	8 yrs 6 mo	Orphan. Cancelled 7May1860. Name taken from cancellation entry. To grandfather, David C. Jackson, per wishes of her friends
Sullivan, James N.	6Feb1860	Robbins, Thomas R.	13 yrs on 3Nov last	Son of Eleazer Sullivan. Making saddles
Sims, Jemima	1May1865	Kirkpatrick, Thomas (Maj)	Abt 12 yrs	Of color. Cancelled 4June1867
Julia	5June1865	McCorkle, M. (Dr)	Abt 11 yrs	Housekeeping. Mother dead. Of color

Name	Date	Age	Master	Notes
Smith, Mary D.	8Jan1867	9 yrs	Smith, E. J. (Mrs)	Base born mulatto
Clark, Alex	8Jan1867	Abt 10 yrs	Tarver, Burrell	Orphan. Farmer
Johnson, Andrew	2Apr1867		McFarland, James P.	Orphan. Of color. Previously bound by FB, now filed with County Clerk
Brown, Eliza Jane	2Apr1867		Brown, William	Orphan. Of color. Previously bound by FB, now filed with County Clerk
Swain, Ann	2Apr1867		Winter, E. D.	Orphan. Of color. Previously bound by FB, now filed with County Clerk
Hill, Ben	2Apr1867	Abt 13 yrs	Foust, William E.	Orphan. Of color. Previously bound by FB, now filed with County Clerk. Cancelled 3Feb1868. Ben gone to parts unknown
Hill, Adeline	2Apr1867		Gaskell, D. W.	Orphan. Of color. Previously bound by FB, now filed with County Clerk
McMurry, Frank	2Apr1867		McMurry, M.	Orphan. Of color. Previously bound by FB, now filed with County Clerk
Norris, Berry	2Apr1867		McFarland, James	Orphan. Of color. Previously bound by FB, now filed with County Clerk
Sherrell, Ruthy	2Apr1867		Sherrell, S. W.	Orphan. Of color. Previously bound by FB, now filed with County Clerk
Sherrell, Lucy	2Apr1867		Sherrell, S. W.	Orphan. Of color. Previously bound by FB, now filed with County Clerk
Milton, William	2Apr1867		Easterly, T. B.	Orphan. Of color. Previously bound by FB, now filed with County Clerk
Hatton, Amy	2Apr1867		Patton, J. H.	Orphan. Of color. Previously bound by FB, now filed with County Clerk
McFarlan, Isabella	2Apr1867		McFarland, J. M.	Orphan. Of color. Previously bound by FB, now filed with County Clerk
Whitmore, Joseph	6May1867	14 yrs	Wollard, J. M.	Father ___ Whitmore, Dcd
Thompson, Jacob	6May1867	14 yrs	Robinson, William A.	Orphan. Of color. Cancelled 4May1868

Name	Date	Age	Bound to	Notes
Owens, Frank	6May1867	12 yrs	Lester, Henry D.	Orphan. Of color. Previously bound by FB, now filed with County Clerk. Cancelled 3Feb1868. Frank gone to parts unknown
Carver, Caroline	6May1867	9 yrs	Swingly, Martha (Patsy)	Orphan. Of color. Previously bound by FB, now filed with County Clerk. Cancelled 6Aug1867. Swingley too old to manage her
Latimer, Sally	6May1867	14 yrs	Word, John	Orphan. Of color. Previously bound by FB, now filed with County Clerk
Carver, Nancy	6May1867	11 yrs	Swingly, Martha (Patsy)	Orphan. Of color. Previously bound by FB, now filed with County Clerk. Cancelled 6Aug1867. Swingley too old to manage her
Gwynn, Albert	6May1867	6 yrs	Walker, John	Orphan. Of color. Previously bound by FB, now filed with County Clerk
Alexander, Harrison Green	6May1867	11 yrs	Skeen, Mathew	Orphan. Of color. Previously bound by FB, now filed with County Clerk. Canc 1Feb1876 as Hiram Green Alexander. Unmanagable
Alexander, Margaret	6May1867	9 yrs	Skeen, Mathew	Orphan. Of color. Previously bound by FB, now filed with County Clerk
Baird, Samuel	6May1867	11 yrs	Word, John	Orphan. Of color. Previously bound by FB, now filed with County Clerk
Palmer, Henry	6May1867	6 yrs	Rogers, W. R.	Orphan. Of color. Previously bound by FB, now filed with County Clerk
Joseph	3June1867	13 yrs	Tiller, Mason	Farming. Of color
Baird, John	3June1867	Abt 7 yrs	Rogers, B. D.	Father & mother dead. Of color
Jackson, Foster	4June1867	11 yrs	Jackson, William H.	Of color
Jackson, Isham	4June1867	13 yrs	Jackson, Thomas R.	Of color
Williams, William	4June1867	16 yrs	Jackson, Thomas R.	Of color
Cartwright, Francis	4June1867	13 yrs	Jackson, Thomas R.	Of color
Edwards, Finis	2July1867	12 yrs	Harlin, Lewis	Orphan

Name	Date	Age	Master	Notes
Hamilton, Alex	6Aug1867	9 yrs	Fite, J. L. (Dr)	Orphan. Of color. Cancelled 18July1876. Alex unmanageable, fights with others
Hamilton, Betsy	6Aug1867	11 yrs	Everston, Walter D.	Orphan. Of color
Clemmons, J. Turner	6Aug1867	16 yrs	Kelly, D. C.	Orphan. Of color
Clemmons, Andrew Jackson	6Aug1867	14 yrs	Kelly, D. C.	Orphan. Of color
Hamilton, William	6Aug1867		Hudson, Charles F.	Orphan. Of color
McCorkle, Jenny	6Aug1867	Abt 13 yrs	Woolard, James M.	Orphan. Of color
McFarland, Bill	8Oct1867	7 or 8 yrs	Vance, E. R.	Orphan. Of color. Consent of Matilda McFarland, destitute June1874*
Ellen	8Oct1867	Abt 4 yrs	Tribble, Peter	Orphan. Of color
Smith, Lafayette	4Nov1867	Abt 9 yrs	Smith, Josiah	Orphan. Of color
Thompson, Albert	2Dec1867	Abt 14 yrs	Thompson, Peter	Orphan. Of color
Dobson, Isaac	7Jan1868		Dykes, James H.	Until 1Jan1876. Orphan. Of color. Farming
Campbell, Dewitt	7Jan1868	5 yrs	Hancock, J. H.	Orphan. Of color
Smith, Levy	4Feb1868	8 yrs	Smith, E. J. (Mrs)	Orphan. Of color
Smith, Lethe	4Feb1868	Abt 5 yrs	Jackson, Thomas R.	Orphan. Of color
Bond, Charley	2Mar1868	8 yrs	Bond, Jack	Orphan. Of color
Bryant, John Thomas	8Apr1868	16 yrs	Bryant, Joseph E.	Orphan. Of color
Martin, John A.	4May1868	Abt 11 yrs	Martin, W. D.	Orphan. Of color
Baird, Charley	5May1868	Abt 17 yrs	Baird, Dan W.	Orphan. Of color
Hill, Adaline	?		Gaskill, D. W.	Alias Adaline McFarland. Was bound by FB but never completed. Voided 9May1868. To be delivered to "her natural guardians"
Coe, Ned	8Sept1868	11 yrs	Coe, Jesse F.	Orphan. Farming. Of color. Cancelled 7Feb1870. Ned a runaway
Edwards, Frank	4Nov1868	Abt 11 yrs	Bond, G. W. C.	Orphan. Of color
Hill, Caroline	9Dec1868	13 yrs	Goldston, John M.	Housework. Of color. Rescinded 7Mar1870. Taken to Illinois by an uncle, whom the mother had wished have him
Hill, Young B.	9Dec1868	11 yrs	Goldston, John M.	Farming. Of color. Brother of Caroline

Name	Date	Term	Master	Remarks
Hamilton, Eliza	7Jan1869		O'Brien, Pat	Recorded as Pat-O-Brien. Until age 21 yrs (1Jan1882). Orphan. Of color
Edwards, Elizabeth Alice	3May1869	Abt 4 yrs	Edwards, T. M.	Until 1Jan1886 (age 21 yrs). Orphan. Of color
Thompson, Margaret	7Feb1870	11 yrs	Byres, M. A.	Orphan. Of color. Cancelled 3Jan1876. Margaret unmanagable & has left Byers
Green, Thomas	7Mar1870	13 yrs	Jones, B. W.	Orphan. Farming
Sanders, L. A. O.	2May1870	10 yrs on 11Feb1870	Grissom, A. H.	Until 11Feb1881. Orphan. Farming
Preston, Susan	2May1870		Huddleston, G. A.	Until 1Jan1878 (age 18 yrs). Orphan. Housework. Of color
Lasater, Sarah A.	6June1870	12 yrs	Estes, Matthew	Until 4July1876 (age 18) Orphan. Housework
Thompson, Sandy	5Dec1870	9 yrs on 1Mar1871	Hancock, Abraham J.	Farming. Orphan. Of color
Cooper, Samuel H.	6Mar1871	9 yrs	Wheeler, Y. C.	Until 9Feb1883. Farming. Cancelled 4Mar1872, Cooper having left Wheeler
Glenn, Anderson	6May1872	14 yrs on 7June1872	Arnold, John B.	Orphan. Farming. Of color
Glenn, Nelson	6May1872	10 yrs on 6May1872	Arnold, John B.	Orphan. Farming. Of color
Tilghman, Pink	5Aug1872	13 yrs	Tilghman, T. O.	Until 21 yrs. Housework. Of color
Scobey, Nathan	20Oct1873	13 yrs	Bryant, F. F.	Until 18Oct1881. Orphan. Of color*
Lane, Edmund	3Nov1873	Abt 15 yrs	Estes, James S.	Orphan. Of color
Johnson, Andrew	4May1874	15 yrs on 4May1874	Camper, Joseph	Orphan. Of color
Denton, Martha Elizabeth	4May1874	8 yrs in Oct1874	Baird, D. W.	Of color
Denton, Edmund Hutran	4May1874	6 yrs on 1July1874	Baird, D. W.	Of color
Denton, Osman Horatio	4May1874	10 yrs on 4Dec1874	Baird, D. W.	Of color
Thomas, Samuel	June1874	14yrs on 14Jan1875	Barrett, John A.	Farm work. Mother in poor house. No recognized father
Bolin, Doss	5Jan1875		Byrne, William M.	Orphan. Farming
Bolin, G. W.	7Jan1876		Jennings, J. R.	Orphan. Farming
Helton, Robert Lee	4Mar1878	12 yrs	Ferrill, B. B.	Orphan. Farming
Graves, Maggie	2Apr1878	10 yrs	Mitchell, Martha	Orphan. Of color
Graves, Ophelia	2Apr1878	2 yrs	Steel, Clancy	Housekeeping & domestic economy. Abandoned by father. Mother dead

INDEX

Note: Names may appear more than once on a page

R. B., 190
R. E., 190
Richard, 39
Robert, 29, 30
Samuel, 108
Stanley H., 62
Wiley, 71
William, 214
Bell [Ball],
David G., 51
Bellenfort
John, 252
Ben, 29, 142,
221, 223
Benedict
Joseph, 104
Benford
J. W., 3
Benner
Henry E., 140
Bennet
Risden, 201
Samuel, 201
Bennett
Henry, 55
James, 21
John, 23, 25
R. A., 223
Thomas, 55
William, 101
William J., 235
Benning
James, 22, 25,
28
Bennington
Ann, 238
Henry, 238
Benson
George, 163
Phils, 173
William, 174
Benston
Mathias, 109
Benthall
Daniel, 212
Enos, 210
Laban, 212
Bentley
Andrew, 189
W. R., 103
Bently
Bently, 66
D. A., 103
Leonidas M.,
100
Sam, 66
William R.,
103
Benton
Clarisa Jane,
241
Franklin, 167
James W., 234
Jesse Lewis,
241

John, 241
Lewis, 157
R., 175
William, 175
Bernard
Elisha, 215
John, 222
Walter, 186
Berron
Bxter, 2
Berry
A. D., 54
Charles M., 20
David W., 47
Elizabeth, 179
Henry S., 214
James, 255
John, 25
John G., 19
Leynard, 156
Simeon, 200
William L.,
108
William
Lawson, 19
Berryhill
William M., 29
Berryman
Allen, 133
H. T., 91
Samuel, 128
Berson
Solomon W.,
260
Bertrand
Joseph N., 218,
219
Bess
Bazel, 228
Beterworst
Adira, 197
Bethel
Price, 8
Bethune
Elizathun, 120
Betsey, 49
Bett
Anderson, 271
George
Washington,
271
Houston, 271,
272
Pinkney, 272
Bettie, 222
Bettis
William, 265
Wyatt, 263
Betts
Zachariah, 207
Bevans
James, 181
Beverly
Thomas B., 86
Bevers

Kesiah, 68
Bias
James Abner,
110
Bibb
Minor, 69
Bibee
Johnnie, 63
Bickam
John, 232
Biffle
Adam, 148
William, 148
Bigbee
John J., 172
Bigger
James, 118
Biggs
Elijah, 171
Jason, 181
John, 52
Bigley
Thomas, 43,
133, 257
Bilbrey
Isaac, 168
Bilbry
Dawson, 169
Biles
Jonathan, 228
Bill, 29, 248
Billiff
Valentine, 193
Billings
James, 192
William, 49
Billingsly
Charles, 265
John, 265
John M., 226
Billington
J. M., 151
Bills
Jonathan D.,
130
Billy, 132
Bingham
J. J., 152
James, 138
James A., 258
John, 201
Martin, 200
Samuel H.,
147
William, 258
Binion
John, 193
Binkley
Charles, 42, 72
Elenora, 72
Ellen, 73
F. M., 71, 73
Henry, 72
Hiram B., 174
Jacob, 172

Jerry, 72
Samuel, 72
Sarah Ann, 9
William, 9
Binkly
A. J., 176
Binum
Mose
Patterson,
131
Binyard
Rosetta A., 38
Bird
James, 13
John, 102, 103
Bishop
Alfred, 100
Betsey, 19
Eliza J., 101
Epson, 20
Gabriel A.,
100
John W., 100
Joseph, 203
L. B., 102
Lindsey B.,
100, 101
Sally, 19
W. J., 100
Wiley, 100
Wilie, 102
William, 68
William J.,
100, 101
William
James, 100
Biter
Nancy, 271
Peter, 271
Bitter
Bernard, 103
Bittick
Alberta, 261
Cyrus S., 261
Ed, 261
Josephus, 62,
261
Sam, 261
Sam. Houston,
261
Bivins
James, 183
Black
Alexander, 201
Almira, 162
Alphonzo, 152
Amanda, 203
Amanda
Catherine,
203
Amzi, 135
Catherine, 203
David, 197
Elizabeth, 202
G. W., 162

285

John Thomas, 276
Joseph E., 276
Lorenzo Dow, 272
Louisa, 111
M. R., 127
Myra, 149
Reps, 9
Robert, 125
Robertson, 149
Samanthy, 9
Sterling, 112
Susan, 125
William R., 108
Brymer
Henry, 226, 227
Brysen
J. H., 115
Bryson
Hiram, 267
Joseph, 265
William, 4
Buchanan
Bud, 124
Hattie, 124
James B., 54
John W., 115
Laban, 53
Moses, 106
W. J. (Mrs), 104
Buchannan
Charley, 124
John, 124
Ruth, 124
William, 124
Buchinsan?
William, 195
Buck
E. B., 224
Elijah, 132
James, 30
Samuel, 196, 197
Thomas M., 46
Buckham
Dolly, 127
Buckner
Thomas, 273
William L, 12
Bucks
Elias, 132
Bugg
Bob, 218
Jacob, 133
James C., 120
John B., 120
Joseph D., 120
Louisa, 120
Robert M., 83
William, 120
Buie

Daniel, 30
Buler
Mary F., 101
Bull
Jasper, 271
Richard, 211
Bullard
Elizabeth, 7
James W., 7
Bullin
W. S., 230
Bullock
Asbury, 192
David P., 221
George, 205
John E., 192
John H., 259
Julia, 221
Rufus, 151
William, 192
Bumpass
Catharine, 161
Elizabeth T., 269
Gebidee, 161
Grief Andrew
Jackson, 269
Mary, 100
William, 161
Bunckley
Jonathan, 208
Bunten
John, 158
John D., 158
Bunton
Henry, 67
James, 158
William R., 173
Burch
Bernard, 82
Bernard M., 83
Irvin, 85
Stephen C., 99
Burchett
Elias, 153
John, 153
Burden
William, 238, 241, 246
Burdin
John B., 198
Burgess
Charles L., 272
W. S., 251
William, 250
Willis, 119
Burk
Arter, 96
Arter?, 96
Ruthy, 96
Burke
E. K., 55
Franklin A., 142

Henry Alonzo, 86
Malissa Ann, 86
Matilda Ann, 86
Melissa Ann, 86
Burket
Arthur H., 4
George E., 4
Burkett
Burgess, 82
Burnet
Fanney, 21
Thomas B., 110
Burnett
Ally, 19
Caunsit, 261
Cora Aldridge, 62
John P., 40
Kinchen, 53
Mat, 261
Parnell, 41
Peter, 19
Rachael, 20
Thomas, 57
Venis, 20
W. W., 261
William, 179, 261
Burney
Charles G., 260
Cornelia F., 260
William L., 178
Burns
Alexander, 232
Celia, 232
Milton, 135
W. C., 232
Burnsides
Nancy, 60
Burress
Charles, 163
David, 163
Henry, 163
Hester, 163
Burris
John M., 95
Nancy, 204
Timothy, 10
Burrow
William, 3
Burrows
Russel, 89
Thomas, 11
Victory, 89
Burrus
Asbury, 264
Burt

Fredrick, 78
Tenham, 42
Burthoon
Betsy, 120
Burton
D. L., 95
Edith, 95
George H., 50
Goerge H., 47
Henry S., 186
Jack, 95
John P., 95
Lewis, 214
Mattie, 95
Morris G., 183
Moses, 35
Robert N., 269
Thomas, 48
Burtrand
Joseph N., 217
Busby
George
Stanton, 168
James H., 218
Martha E., 204
Bush
Andrew I., 163
Asa Martin, 194
Barberry E., 7
Bery
Zachariah, 7
Carter?, 175
Delila, 175, 176
Elizabeth, 176, 177
F. R., 7
George, 208
Granderson, 174
Grandison, 195
Harvey, 8
Irena, 195
Irrena, 174
Jane, 58, 176
John Calvin, 176
Louisa, 58, 176
Moltan, 193
Shelton, 223
William, 176
Bushnel
Ezra, 16
Bushnell
Eusebius, 16
Bushrod, 50
Busick
L. J. M., 84
Bussel
Albert, 206
Bussell
George, 207
John E., 241

Solomon, 30,
34, 39, 40
Theoderick, 49
Thomas, 104
Thomas D.,
130
William E. W.,
217
William M.,
100
Clarke
J. P., 228
Clary
Vachel, 212
Clay
Green, 11
Mark, 22
Sidney, 11
Clayton
Thomas, 103
William, 240
Cleavland
Mary S. J., 116
Cleek
James, 117
Clem
George M.,
117
Jasper N., 117
Clements
Alfred Haynes,
82
Andrew J., 10
Louis F., 185
Read, 207
William W.,
66
Clemmons
Andrew E., 51
Andrew
Jackson, 276
J. Turner, 276
John, 266
Jonas, 66
Clendenon
Jackson, 228
Clenny
James T., 239
Samuel, 244
Clevenger
George, 127
Clift
James, 229
Clifton
J. K., 73
Climer
James, 266
John, 266
William, 272
Clingan
J. M., 74
Clinker
Humphrey, 54
Cloar
Absolam, 210

Hubert, 219
William, 214
Clopton
Benjamin A.,
268
John A., 273
Clounch
Allice, 115
George W.,
115
James, 115
Jennie, 115
Clounch, Sr
James, 115
Cluck
Martha, 218
Clymer
Noah R., 266
Coan
John E., 234
Coates
William A., 87
Coats
Paton H., 1
Thomas, 105
William, 86
Cobal
Terry H., 138
Cobb
James H., 109
Robert S., 39
Cobbs
Paulina, 82
Cobler
Davis, 44
Cochran
Aaron, 251
John, 193
Simeon, 195
Cock
Jurrett, 123
Cocke
Stephen, 157
Cockrill
George, 59
Mark R., 42
Robert, 43
Cody
Bailey H., 261
Burnett, 236
Pierce, 81, 236
Sally, 81, 236
Coe
Jesse F., 276
Ned, 276
Coffee
Humphrey, 59
Joseph, 33
Mary, 144
Coffer
Allen, 119
Coffman
Isaac, 31
Coggins

Jeremiah C.,
198
Cohron
James, 105
Coke
Daniel F., 262
Coker
Job, 99
John M., 84
Mary, 99
Cokley
Charles, 220
John, 220
Coldwell
John, 29, 119
Coldwell, Jr
William, 32
Cole
Alfred B., 232
Bennet, 232
Edward, 19
Eli, 106
Elizabeth, 108
F. M., 111
Hartwell, 232
John, 108, 110
John H., 232
L. L., 115
M. S. (Dr), 177
Robert A., 51
William, 20,
135
William F.,
112
Coleman
Alfred, 217
Bridget, 146
Daniel, 135
Elizabeth, 272
George, 272
George W.,
160
James, 188
Jesse, 192
John, 272
Joseph S., 187
Martin, 146
Mary Ann, 82,
272
Robert H., 272
Royal, 207
Thomas A., 76
Thomas F., 5
William, 134
William
Henry, 77
William J., 272
Colier
Brown L., 99
John E., 111
Colley
Richard R., 52
Collier
Elen, 192
John A., 55

William, 144,
199
Collin
Riley, 71
Collins
Ben, 121
Charles, 121
Disa, 121
Ebsworth, 32
Edmund, 6
Elisha, 124
Elizabeth, 121
Feraly, 242
Francis, 138
George H.,
156, 157
Hanah, 201
Harriet, 6
Hiram K., 268
James, 32
James W., 12,
124
John, 12, 119
John G., 216
John W., 231
Joseph, 194
Joseph A., 84
Lafayette K.,
137
Lewis, 12
Manerva, 242
Mary Jane, 242
Nancy, 118
Overton, 167
Robert, 156,
157
Robert M., 12
Samuel F., 87
Seth, 15, 231
Sylvia, 121
Thomas, 15,
44
Wade, 65
William, 12,
32, 109, 138
William F.,
126
William W.,
201
Wshington,
121
Colman
W. D., 74
Colter
Alexander, 113
H. H., 113
Coltharp
John, 38
William, 39
Colthorp
John, 37, 39
Norvell, 37
Norvelle, 39
William, 37
Combs

Cowper
Francis, 265
Cox
A. D., 60
John, 32, 33,
272
Lewis, 172
Lizzie, 87
Mary Jane, 60
Mickey, 85
Peter G., 93
W. G., 93
William, 85,
180, 272
William B., 35
Cox, Jr
John, 265
Cozeans
John Bartley,
171
Crabb
Henry, 28
Crabtree
Samuel, 237
Craddick
Elizabeth, 65
Craddock
Elizabeth T.,
269
Grief Joseph,
269
Craften
George W., 84
John B., 84
Crafton
John B., 131
Cragg
James T., 43
Craggot
Peter, 193
Robert, 193
Craig
Alexander, 21
Frank B., 149
John F., 144
Craighead
Alexander, 59
James, 59
W. H., 93
Crain
Axes?, 225
Axies? (fe),
225
Emily, 225
J. D., 246
Jesse, 225
Mason, 225
Moses, 225
Sarah L., 225
Cramer
Henry, 24
Cranfield
Isom, 106
Cranford
Alex, 252

Cranford Sr
William, 132
Cranford, Jr
William, 132
Cranister
Adam, 96
Crass
Martha, 262
Craven
Solomon, 231
Crawell
M. M., 199
Crawford
Abraham L.,
103
Alexander, 131
Jack, 8
James A., 106
Robert N., 242
Thomas, 165
William H.,
166
Crawley
James
Madison,
235
Thomas
Jasper, 13
Crawly
Martha
Narissa, 13
Crealy
Lavisa, 225
Marion, 225
William, 225
Creasey
Thomas, 223
Creasy
Josephus, 198
Thomas, 223
Creeley
Angaline, 225
Emeline, 225
Isaac T., 225
Creely
Emeline, 225
Creighton
Joseph, 59
Creley
William, 225
Crenshaw
Jacob, 256
Richard, 33
William T., 37
Crews
Lilly, 104
Crichlow
Joseph E., 259,
260
Crick
John, 204
Criddle
John, 22
Crighton
Joseph, 45

Crisp
Mansil, 96
Criswell
Kitty Ann, 269
Crockarell
Barnet, 204
Crocket
Jane, 170
William, 170,
172, 212,
214, 216
Crockett, 229
Andrew, 254
Matilda, 191
Samuel, 252,
254
W. W. T., 64
Crofford
Alexander C.,
138
Crook
Bignal, 22
Eiben, 209,
210
George, 266
Polly, 266
T. J., 207
Wallace, 251
William, 251
Crooks
Robert, 42
Crosby
Horace, 146
Medora, 146
Thomas J., 146
Crosley
Josiah, 98
Cross
Charles, 148
David, 150
Elijah, 263
James, 264
Jane, 148
Robert, 142
Sarah, 148
Thomas, 58
Crosslen
Harvey, 15
Polly Ann, 15
William
Harvey, 15
Crossway
Nicholas, 19
Crosswell
Nimrod, 202
Crosswey
Elias, 41
Crosswhite
Elijah, 84
Crosthwait
James, 188
William, 188
Crotzer
Jane, 164
Crouch

Thomas J., 55
Crouse
Elizabeth, 186
John, 273
Spencer, 186
Crow
James, 170
Lucinda, 89
Mary, 170
Nelly, 90
Crowder
Isaac, 81
M. N., 95
Nathaniel, 133
Thomas P.,
249
Crowell
David, 152
John, 169
Crownover
James, 182
Crozier
C. W. (Dr),
163
Cruch
Edwin, 189
Crunk
J. B., 224
Crutcher
Annie, 127
Eliza, 227
Fanny, 148
Henry, 227
James P., 127
John, 127
John H., 34
Mack, 125
Mary, 261
Mat., 127
Nancy P., 261
Oliver, 127
R. P., 127
William, 127
Crutchfield
Jesse, 138
Richard, 156
Cryer
James, 208
John, 208
Culbertson, 154
John, 154
Culbreath
Polly, 195
Cull
Reece, 144,
145, 146
Cullam
D. W., 10
Cumings
Thomas, 169
Cumming
Eunen, 118
Cummings
JoDeny, 227
Joseph J., 239

John W., 231
Joseph, 118
Laura, 87
Loyd, 39, 42
Luckett, 190
M. W., 168
Maris?, 159
Micajah C.,
127
N. S., 121
Nathan, 211
Nathan C., 237
Ritta, 151
Robert, 7, 28
Robert G., 11
Sam, 126
Samuel, 119,
217, 224
Solomon, 68
Thomas, 7
Thomas B.,
168
William, 7,
118, 167,
186
William
Henry, 251
Zachariah, 44,
47
Dawes
Isaac, 57
James, 57
Lafayette, 57
Mary V., 57
Robert, 57
Sarah Francis,
57
Susannah, 57
Dawson
Elisha, 202
Ephraim, 238
Day
Abraham, 58
Abram, 273
Jacob, 58, 273
Jane, 58
John, 58
Madison, 58
Margaret, 273
Margaret Ann,
58
Mary, 273
Thomas, 58,
273
Days
L., 56
Deaderick
Fielding, 56
Deadrick
George M., 19
Deadridge
Thomas, 18
Dean
Alick, 86
Anderson, 152

Clementine,
152
Daniel, 256
Elijah, 256
Houston, 152
Julia, 86
Mollie, 152
Nathan, 256
Thomas, 212
Deason
Henry H., 259
James H., 259
William R.,
259
Deatherage
Bird C., 239
Deathrige
John, 20
Thomas, 20
Deavenport
Nathan, 83
Debrell
Edwin, 41
Deel
Bluford, 134
Wesley, 133
Wilford, 134
Defoe
John W., 91
Polly, 81
Dehart
William, 268
Deloach
Ann, 75
Gid, 75
Sallie, 7
Simon, 69
W. T., 75
Delzell
William, 79
Dempsey, 221
Margarett, 239
Sarah, 239
Dempsy
Butch, 245
Tennessee, 245
Demumbra
William, 9
Wilson, 10
Demumbram
Richard, 177
Denham, 198
Elizabeth, 198
Denison
William, 116
Denney
Francis, 188
Denning
William, 55
Dennis, 227
Briant, 84
Lemuel P. M.,
111
Samuel, 106
Susan Ann, 95

Will Henry, 95
Denny?
L. D., 197
Denson
Reuben, 203
Denton
Corda, 143,
144
Edmund
Hutrand,
277
James R., 246
James W., 195
Joe Smith, 251
John, 251
Lemuel B., 98
Martha
Elizabeth,
277
Osman
Horatio, 277
Samuel, 237
Derham
Silas Herndon,
174
Zechariah, 173
Derr
Daniel, 82
Derrons
Hiram, 136
Deshan
Leach, 21
Devenport
Thomas, 83
Dew
Jose C., 242
Nathaniel, 263
DeWyer
Lucy A., 163
Dial
Mary Jane, 14
Mary M., 133
Wyatt
Hawkins,
133
Dibrell
Alice, 249
Allace, 247
Andy, 247
Caroline, 247
Ellen, 247
George G., 247
James, 250
Joseph
Watkins,
247
Vina, 247
Dick, 130
Dickerson
Francis, 63
George, 63
James, 63
Jefferson, 63
Thomas A.,
168

W. J., 233
William, 218
Dickey
Alfred, 132
Benjamin, 84
Ebenezer, 62
George, 130
George M.,
127
Sims, 62
William
Henry, 85
Dickins
Samuel, 265
Dickson
Enos H., 185
Franklin H.,
268
J. C., 92
John, 181
John M., 33
Marena M., 73
Robert, 105,
106
Thomas, 268
Dicky
James, 213
Dill
Hiram M., 270
Dillard
Edward, 267
Newton, 206
Dillen
John, 162
Dilliard
Gabrial, 217
Dilling
W. H., 162
Dillion
Daniel, 215
Dillon
Charles R.,
130, 135
Daniel, 194
George W.,
196
William B.,
196, 197
William T.,
166
DiMills
Benjamin, 18
Dinah, 265
Dinkins
Robert, 206
Dismukes
Elisha, 264
Dixon
William W.,
172
Dixson
Ephraim, 204
Doak
Nelson, 186
Dobbins

Dunlap
  Alexander, 29
  E. S., 230
  Robert R., 92
Dunlop
  Mattie, 163
Dunly
  John W., 114
Dunn
  Benjamin, 155
  John, 155
  Machie, 256
  Thomas B.,
    270
  William H., 51
Dunnavent
  Claiborn, 252
Dunnaway
  Cumbey, 191
Dunnegan
  Norman, 70
Dunnegin
  Andrew, 70
  Benton, 70
  James, 70
  John, 70
Dunnigin
  Thomas, 241
Durant
  Thomas, 194
Durard
  Joseph, 9
  Ruth, 9
  Timothy, 9
Durell
  John, 69
Duren
  Emeline, 53
Durham
  A. M., 222
  Charlie, 224
  Henry, 223
  Ila, 138
  J. G., 223
  James, 219,
    220
  John, 101
  John Wesley,
    223
  Jonathan, 221,
    223
  Mary Caroline,
    223
  Nancy, 111
  Napoleon B.,
    101
  Presly, 138
  Thomas, 67
  Wesley G.,
    248
  Wiley B. H.,
    248
Durk
  Samuel, 264
Dusenberry

John, 105
Duty
  George, 209,
    211
  Henry, 81, 211
  Malinda, 81
  Philip, 211
Duvall
  Alexander, 104
Dyar
  James, 27
  Wiley, 27
Dye
  D. B. F., 224
  Jimmie, 15
  Malinda, 15
Dyer
  Amy G., 249
  Appollus, 240
  C. C., 169
  Caroline, 70
  David, 26, 37
  Filmont, 71
  Francis
    Marion, 238,
      240
  James Robert,
    2
  Joel, 193
  John Filmore,
    2
  John W., 71
  Lydia, 240
  Robert, 2
  S. G., 2
  Simpson, 37
  William, 26
Dykes
  James H., 276
Dysart
  G. B., 126
  Mary, 126
Eagleman
  Joseph, 18
Eakin
  Lucretia, 2
  Moses, 21
Earheart
  Abraham, 171
Earle
  William H.,
    173
Earles
  Nathan, 225
Earthman
  Lewis, 33
Easley
  Cora, 75
  Francis P., 175
  Ida, 75
  J. B., 91
  William, 151
Easly
  W. T., 91
Eason

E. J. (Mrs), 61
J. R., 91
East
  Benjamin J.,
    61
  Edward H., 28
Easterly
  B. H., 10
  T. B., 274
Eastin
  Thomas, 19,
    20
Eastland, 237
  Thomas, 237
Eastman
  John W., 15
  Sarah Jane, 15
Eaton
  George W.,
    103, 233
  M. E., 233
  T. T., 191
Eavins
  W. H., 74
Echols
  Abner, 263
  Augustus T.,
    113
  Martha Ann,
    112
  Silas, 22
  William, 113
Edde
  Moses P., 110
Eddington
  Edward J., 109
Elizabeth
  Eleanor, 109
  John E., 110
  Mary Jane, 109
  Miles Newton,
    109
  Rebecca
    Frances, 109
Eddins
  Nabo, 114
  William, 114
Edens
  Elmira J., 164
  Samuel, 164
Edge
  Elam, 270
Edington
  Joseph, 228
Edlin
  James, 162
  James H. B. T.,
    258, 259
  Oswald, 258
Edmiston
  William A., 98
Edmond, 143,
  196, 221
Edmondson
  James, 96

Maggie, 117
Polley Ann,
  117
Samuel, 36
Edmund, 60, 269
Edney
  Milton Y., 257
William
  Britan, 27
Edson
  J. B., 177
Edward
  Elizabeth, 172
  James A., 78
Edwards
  Andrew J., 121
  Arthur, 126
Elizabeth
  Alice, 277
  Finis, 275
  Frank, 276
  James, 226
  John, 209
  Joseph, 182
  Josephine, 63
  Peter, 255
  Samuel, 6, 272
  T. M., 277
  Viney, 174
  William W.,
    110
Edy, 47
Elam
  Edward, 181
  John, 184
Elder
  Manira Jane,
    165
  Reuben, 163
  William, 165
Eldridge
  Charley, 168
  James, 168
  Jesse, 167
  Polly, 235
  Sally, 235
  Samuel, 31
  William D.,
    168
Eleazer?
  Mike, 75
Eli, 267
  Jacob, 82
Eliza, 143
Eliza Ann, 145
Elizabeth, 2, 160,
  187, 248
Elkins
  Allen, 80
  J. D., 8
  Thomas, 4
Ellanora, 222
Ellen, 80, 154,
  276
Elleston

Joshua, 28
William, 185
Furgason
Rittenhouse,
185
Furgerson
Anderson J.,
187
Andrew, 261
John, 107
John R., 261
Mariah, 261
Nelson, 107
William, 187
Furgurson
Nancy, 159
Furguson
Samuel, 159
Furn
Richard, 229
Furr
Nancy, 136
Fussell
J. W., 71
Fuston
J. S., 231
Fyke
John P., 175
Mathew V.,
175
Gabel
Barnabas, 98
Gafford
James M., 160
Gage
Maryann, 75
Gainer
Jesse, 68
Gaines
Andrew, 88
James H., 236
Gains
Adaline, 196
Fletcher, 196
Polly, 196
Thomas, 229
Washington,
196
Gainwell
J. C., 167
Gaither
Philip D., 78
Galagher
Charles, 41
Gallagher
John, 41
Gallagly
Joseph, 264
Gallaspy
William, 16
Gallion
George, 69
Gamble
Andrew, 239
Edmond, 17

Edmund, 26
Kinchan, 251
Gambling
James, 210
Gamer
William, 54
Ganaway
Burwell, 180
Gann
Patsy, 4
Willis, 4
Gant
Jackson, 120
William M.,
84, 120
Gantt
James M., 258
Gardiner
John S., 180
Samuel G., 82
Gardner
Britain, 140
Harriet, 128
Henry, 173
Hughey, 99
James, 262
John, 173
Samuel G.,
182
William, 210
Garey
James, 255
Garner, 25, 45
James Monroe,
174
John, 25
William, 39,
40, 51
Garner, Renfro,
91
Garnett
J. L., 230
J. S., 230
Garrard
Thomas, 128
Garratt
George, 167
Green, 191
Henry, 191
L. M., 191
Polley, 167
Simon, 191
Garret
Richard, 32
Garrett
Elisha, 120
Elizabeth, 168
George, 167
Jacob, 168
Richard, 24
Robert E., 13
Stephen J., 141
Thomas, 23,
252
William, 208

Willis, 164
Garrison
Agnes, 195
George W.,
267
Lucretia, 195
Patsey, 195
Garth
Florence, 177
Jessee T., 228
W. C., 177
Garvison
G. T., 250
Gasaway
John, 182
Gaskell
D. W., 274
Gaskill
D. W., 276
Gass
Fountain E. P.,
199
Joseph, 199
Gaston
Maury, 75
Richard, 70
Gasty
Harriet Jane,
250
Gately
Thomas W.,
204
Gatewood
William, 83
Gatlin
James, 199
Gatny
Westly, 76
Gault
Carrie D., 207
Gavin
Andrew, 52
Gayle
Matthew W.,
137
Gee
David W., 257
John M., 197
Geery
John, 253
Genir
Wade, 2
Gentry
Jefferson, 203
John R., 53, 54
Nicholas, 17
George, 28, 107,
109, 145, 222,
223, 260
Caswell, 238
David W., 107
Henry, 238
James N., 173
James W., 174
Mack, 238

Patsy, 238
William, 36,
107
William H.,
198, 271
George A., 102,
182
Georgia, 88
Gess
Richard, 55
Ghaskey
Nancy Ann,
244
Gholson
Benjamin, 253
Gholsten
John, 254
Thomas, 254
Gholston
Benjamin, 253
John, 42
Gibbs
James F., 90
John, 90
Mary, 90
Sarah F., 90
William, 111
Gibson
Albert G., 108
Jesse, 265
John, 252
Joseph N., 118
Levander, 181
Lewis, 106
Gideon
Daniel, 118
Gidon T., 135
Gifford
William, 134
Gilbert
Eliza, 84
James, 85
Giles
Care J., 90
Gilespie
John, 208
Gilham
Samuel, 82
Gill
Alanson G.,
111
Francis P., 198
Jo J. S., 126
John, 130
W. W., 2
Gillam
Samuel, 89
Gillard
Finly S., 267
Thomas G.,
267
Gillaspie
Arguile C., 77
Tipton L., 78
William, 202

301

George
  Washington,
  130
Green T., 187
Sallie, 152
Samuel, 259
William P.,
  191
William T.,
  192
Hendley
  Hugh, 153
Hendrick
  T. W. (Mrs),
  74
  Thornton W.,
  71
Hendrix
  Laban, 92
  Peyton, 191
Henley
  William, 220
Henly
  Charles R.,
  173
  Patrick L., 219
Hennessee
  P. S., 228
Henry, 31, 34,
  36, 38, 49, 79,
  132, 143, 203,
  204, 221, 247,
  256, 260
  F. A., 46
  G. A., 164
  Isaac N., 253
  John M., 176
  Lemuel B., 43
  Rebecca, 54
  Samuel T., 10
  Sarah Francis,
  10
Henry Buchanan,
  222
Henseley
  James, 157
Henson
  Cathom W., 92
Herbert
  James, 103
  John B., 259
  Richard, 22
  S. B., 103, 104
Herd
  James R., 240
  Joseph, 238
  Joseph W.,
  242, 243
Herndan
  Joseph, 134
Herndon
  Cornelius, 210
  George, 42
  R. M., 207
Herod

Jane, 188
  Margaret A.,
  95
  William, 197
Herrald
  James W., 119
Herriman
  John, 5
Herrin
  C. J., 102
  Charles J., 98
  Thomas, 61
Herring
  Stephen, 178
Hesselbein
  Charles D., 61
Hester
  Alexander, 205
  Leander, 206
Hettan
  William, 96
Heuser
  John J., 61
Hewitt
  Henry W., 188
Hewlett
  Edmond, 28,
  29
  Edmund, 24
  George, 28, 29,
  32
  William, 33,
  40, 42
Hewlett &
  Peterson, 41
Heynie
  William, 198
Hibit
  Laura B., 10
Hibits
  James, 193
Hickerson
  Ezekiel, 70
  Henry M., 75
  Wiley, 15
  William A., 12
Hickey
  Carnelius, 246
  Caroline, 246
  Cornelius, 243,
  245
  Matilda, 246
  Obidiah, 166
  Sam, 246
  Trapp, 246
Hickman
  A., 152
  Amalia S. A.,
  197
  Edwin, 19
  James C., 152
  John _oyer, 19
  Lille D., 12
  Simon W., 197
  Stephen, 197

Willis, 59
Hicks
  Alfred, 82
  Benjamin A.,
  259
  Charles, 98
  Charlotte, 81
  Elijah, 31
  Florence, 164
  George W., 70
  Henry, 160
  James G., 25
  James R., 198
  James S., 192
  Jefferson, 180
  Jesse, 206
  John, 66, 106
  John C., 29, 33
  Thomas, 31,
  81, 219
  W. D., 191
  William, 180
Hiett
  Isaac, 174
  Lewis, 218
Higden
  Edney, 9
  Eliza, 9
  James, 9
Higdon
  Coley, 87
  D. K., 85
  James J., 74
  Mrs, 74
  Thomas, 87
Higgins
  Bernard, 212
  Michael, 138
  William, 3
Hightower
  Harriet, 154
Higlin
  James, 134
Hill
  Adaline, 276
  Adeline, 274
  B. J., 229
  Ben, 274
  Benjamin, 12,
  77
  Caroline, 276
  Dan, 17
  E. L., 227
  Elizabeth Jane,
  218
  Female, 122
  H. B., 60
  Henry, 58
  Houston C.,
  109, 110
  Isaac, 184
  Isaac H., 134
  Issabella, 218
  J., 133
  J. H., 125

J. W., 73
James, 120
Jesse, 109
Joab, 239
John, 79, 119
John D., 259
John G., 54
John R., 122
Mary
  Elizabeth,
  77
Mary Jane, 12
Nancy, 79, 218
Rebecca, 252
Reuben, 76
Rhoda
  Adaline, 218
Richard J., 50
Robert S., 47
Samuel, 110
Susan, 230
Tennessee, 86
Thomas, 11
Thomas
  Hickman, 15
Thomas J., 43
William, 46,
  79
William B.,
  119
Willis, 66
Young B., 276
Hill, Jr
  William, 46
Hillis
  H. L., 226
  L. H., 226
  Murph, 227
Hindman
  Eli, 109, 110
Hines, 78
Hinkle
  Samuel, 107
Hinson
  Anthony, 268
  E. L., 170
  Thomas H.,
  162
  Warren, 126
Hinton
  Jeremiah, 20
  William N. (or
  M.), 40
Hitchcock
  Ann, 55
Hix
  Thomas, 102
Hobbs
  Colin S., 46
  Edwin, 45
  James, 230
  John, 51
  John A., 115
  John M., 160

313

Peter, 154
Lytle
Frank, 189
William, 133, 135, 136
Lyttle
Betsey, 213
Nancy, 213
Polley, 213
Maberry
Thomas, 136
William, 178
Willis, 138
Mabrey
Francis H., 81
Macham
James, 259
Mack
John, 129, 133, 134
London, 153
Robert, 134
Mackanaw, 108
Mackey
George, 151
John B., 3
Marian, 3
Macklin
Resdin?, 160
Macon
J. E. J., 229
John, 230
John Ess, 229
Madden
William, 52
Maddox
Ellis, 23
Maddrn
John M., 1
William A., 1
Maddux
William D, 57
Maden
Thomas, 193
Walter D., 162
Madison
Murphy, 61
William, 14
Mahaffy
Lycurgus C., 269
Lycurgus Clinton, 269
Noah Washington, 268
Robert, 269
Robert Henry, 268
Mahan
Thomas E., 139
Mahon
Thomas, 139
Thomas E., 142
Mahoney
Timothy T., 61
Mainer
William, 249
Mainyard
Levi, 241
Major, 186, 259
Majors
Robert W., 160
Malissa, 168
Mallaga
James C., 265
Mallard
Cyrus, 80
John, 211
Joseph, 211
Mary, 80
Mallory
James H., 164
John, 252
Malone
Ervin B. J., 2
H. R., 103
Meredith Erskine, 71
R. R., 162
Maloney
Nathaniel, 111
Malory
Thomas Eaton, 47
Malugian
Jonathan, 69
Malugin
William, 69
Malvina, 88
Man
Timothy W., 198
Manard
James, 250
John C., 250
Mandlebeum
Henry, 68
Maney
W. B., 63
Mangrum
William, 257
William D., 257
Manley
Pinkney Fillmore, 62
Mann
Eudora M., 55
George, 55
George W. M., 57
Josiah, 55
Robert, 155
Samuel, 155
Sarah V., 55
Manner
Levi, 241
Manning
John, 229
Matthew, 204
Tapley M., 203
William, 27
Willis, 201
Manon
John, 54
Manscoe
Archibald E., 44
Mansher
Elizabeth, 269
Mansmill?
John, 57
Manson
J. E., 189
Mantlow
James W., 120
Manuel, 186
Manus
Tillman C., 229, 230
Maples
Levi, 167
Susan, 167
Mappin
Charles, 191
Marable
Benjamin, 163
Catharine, 163
Kitty, 163
March
Jesse D., 42, 44, 45, 49, 52
Lewis, 62
Moses, 189
Marcham
S. T., 8
Marchant
Margaret, 8
Marchbanks
Walter, 93
Margaret, 49, 137, 221, 224
Mariah, 74, 196
Marion
Francis, 157
Maris
Lucy, 10
Marthy, 10
Mark
D. S., 115
Markham
Sabrina, 216
Markum
Charles, 7
Marlin
Augustin, 172
James, 179
Thomas, 179
Marly
Amanda, 270
Ann, 270
Candy, 270
Chancy, 270
Eliza, 270
Jo, 270
Joe, 270
John, 270
Lucy, 270
Nancy, 270
Marrable
J. H., 163
Marsh
A., 72
Marshall
Balis L., 112
Benjamin, 112
Elihu, 25, 29
Ezekial, 219
Honea, 159
Horace, 159
John W., 270
W. R., 207
William H., 219
Martan?
Washington, 197
Martha, 44, 47, 49, 50, 51, 108
Martin
Amzi, 187
Ben, 231
Blackman, 44
Campbell, 19
Caroline, 231
D. A., 178
Henry, 36
James, 82
James L., 216
Jeremain G., 202
Jeremiah, 34
Jeremiah G., 202
John, 82, 231
John A., 276
John B., 100, 101
Joseph, 16
M. T., 68
Margaret, 160
Mart, 8
Martha A. A., 112
Mary, 231
Mary C., 107
Matt, 13
Morgan L., 156
Nancy, 58
Peter, 29
Peter H., 30, 31, 214
Polly, 234
Robert, 63

Milly, 248
Peter, 128, 133
Pheby, 249
Richard, 266
Robbert S.,
 225
Sally, 143
Saluda Ann,
 228
Samuel, 138,
 139
Sarah, 142,
 145
Stephen, 209
Susan, 142,
 144
Thaddeus, 142
Thadeus, 145
Thomas, 11
William, 143
William S.,
 248, 249
Willie, 50
Mixon
 Mrs, 74
 Nuton, 74
Mobias
 Charles F., 195
 Elizabeth, 194
Modgelin
 Elijah, 129
Moffets
 Aaron, 228
 G. P., 228
Moffett
 James S., 112
Mohon
 Thomas E.,
 139
Molton
 Amos, 22
 Michael, 68
Monk
 Elizabeth, 101
 William J., 101
Monroe
 Ed, 91
 J., 175
 Marshall, 91
 Vandever, 167
Monsor?, 176
Montague
 John, 180
 Thomas, 180
Montgomery
 Cynthia Ann,
 98
 John J., 82
 Sandy, 14
 Stephen, 215
 Thomas, 256
 W. M., 115
 William, 17
Moody
 Bennet, 220

David, 187
Robert, 52
Moon
 Eliza, 191
 Elvira, 7
 Isaac, 263
 Jim, 125
 William, 191,
 211
Mooningham
 John E., 9
Moony
 Loucinda, 89
Moor
 Elizabeth, 80
 James, 74
Moore
 A. S., 108
 Alford, 29
 Amanda, 271
 Amos, 18
 Anna, 191
 Benjamin, 194
 Charles, 151
 D. D. (Dr), 191
 David, 18, 152,
 225, 250
 Della, 80
 Edward, 265
 Eleanor, 237
 Eliza, 271
 Elleck, 124
 Emeline, 151
 Evalina, 264
 G. B., 49
 George, 61,
 265
 Haywood, 265
 Isaac, 133
 J., 43
 James, 237,
 271
 James B., 126
 James D., 28,
 44, 45, 46
 James T., 142,
 149
 James W., 135,
 138
 Jefferson, 181
 John, 22, 31,
 32, 206,
 255, 271
 John D., 206
 John T., 86,
 191
 Joseph, 34
 Lewis, 178
 Mark H., 46
 Matilda, 149
 Milly, 183
 Nathan, 126
 Richard B., 76
 Samuel, 19,
 136, 208

Samuel W.,
 219
Sarah, 271
Sarah Jane,
 149
Satty, 205
Talitha, 185
Thomas D.,
 120
Thum, 205
Tomothy, 210
W. E., 113
Warren, 264
William, 28,
 43, 44, 81,
 106, 178,
 193, 237,
 271
William G.,
 120
William H.,
 45, 46, 49,
 54
William T., 55
William W.,
 243
Zachariah, 264
Moore &
 McClain, 110
Moore, Jr
 Samuel, 225
Moran
 Charles, 25,
 254, 255
 Emily, 270
 Evaline, 270
More
 William, 225
More?
 Hiram S., 267
Morehead
 William, 204
Morgan
 Alston, 264
 Cabal, 61
 Elizabeth, 169
 Ida, 61
 J. L., 170
 J. W., 95
 John S., 107
 John T., 107,
 109, 110
 Salley, 74
 Thomas, 17
 W. L., 169
Morgan & Jones,
 106
Moris
 George W.,
 104
Morlam
 John R., 140
Morrias?
 William, 241
Morris

Ann, 211
Daniel, 26,
 180, 193
Even, 173
Evin, 174
George, 175
George C.,
 138, 155,
 175
Isaac, 27
James, 180
James L., 120
Jane, 177
Jesse, 201
John, 175
John G., 233
Joseph, 120
Margaret, 167
Margaret J., 87
Mary, 175, 182
Simantha, 167
Thomas, 26,
 212
Washington,
 172
William B.,
 167
William P.,
 138
Morrisett
 Zachariah, 93
Morrish
 Catey, 209
 Caty, 209
 Moses, 209
 Nelley, 209
 Neuben, 210
 Newburn, 209
Morrison
 Andrew, 51
 John, 213, 218
 Samuel, 213
 William, 181
Morrow
 Benjamin, 97
 John, 51
Morrrow
 James, 140
Morton
 Hamman, 89
 John B., 55
 John J., 89
 Lewis, 234
 Mary E., 232
 Moses, 228
 Sarah, 234
 Solomon, 55
 William, 89,
 234
 Wright H., 52
Mosby
 Fountain C.,
 186
Mosely
 Henry, 13

James A., 165
Nancy, 165
Washington
V., 165
William C.,
220
Odom
C. B., 8
O'Donnell
Connell, 59
Officer
Alexander, 242
Huston, 249
James C., 248
John, 165
Lewis, 248
Riley, 248
Ogalsby
Daniel, 155
Ogden
Albert, 163
Betsey, 163
Ogelvie
Richard H.,
149
Ogilvie
Dnira, 124
John, 252
Ogwin
James, 170
John R., 170
Olds
James, 144
Oliphant
James, 17, 179
Olium?
Robert H., 76
Oliver
Asa, 116
Edmund, 183
Enoch, 17
George, 30
George W., 78,
183
J. R., 7
John, 78
Lem, 86
Levi, 236
Milton B., 249
Pleasant, 183
Polly, 36, 37
Roderick, 22,
29
Sally, 36
Sarah, 38
Oneal
John M., 125
M. T., 125
Orear
William, 77
Orgain
William D.,
158
Orman
Lucy, 123

Sarah F., 123
Ornstreet
William, 214
Orr
John, 118, 126
Joshua, 127
Thomas, 135
Orran
Ann, 8
Samuel, 8
Orrand
John, 269
Orren
William, 197
Orth
Peter, 104
Orthelia, 229
Orton
Ray S., 52
Sidney M., 255
Osbin
John Wesley,
175
Osborn
Alfred M., 32
Osborne
Alfred M., 39
Joe, 14
William, 39
Osburn
James A., 265
John, 135
Osteen
Edward, 251
Prather, 251
Othello, 30
Ouinding
John, 243
John P., 242
Ousburn
Joseph, 175
Ousler
Orlander, 172
Outland
Briant, 201
Outlaw
John C., 212,
214
Tabitha, 231
Overall
Aaron, 190
Abraham, 183
Overdeer
Jacob, 185
Overton
E., 74
Thomas, 74
Owen
Dempsey, 186
Edward L.
Edward, 167
Hannibal, 52
J. W., 178
James, 187
James M., 261

John, 269
John Smith,
180
Joseph, 111
Logan, 78
M. P., 77
Rebecca E., 5
William, 48,
51, 132
Zadac, 174
Owens
Adrian, 238
Amanda, 47
Andrew, 47,
52
Carroll, 49
Catherine, 259
David, 180
David T. M.,
198
Frank, 275
James, 45, 235
Robert, 201
Samuel, 133
Oxandine
John P., 243
Oxendine
Sally, 249
Ozbourne
Robert A., 261
Vina, 261
Ozburn
Budd, 16
Samuel, 16
Ozment
Marcus D.,
269
P. W. Maxey &
Co., 59
Paccand
Ferdinan, 162
Pace
Barnet, 21, 25
Harriet, 21
Lucinda, 25
Richard, 25
Pack
Bartemus, 67
John, 68
Mary, 68
Matilda, 68
Monroe, 67
Nancy, 67
Page
Absalom, 39
George, 172
George, 22
Henny, 203
Jefferson, 41
Jesse, 41
Jesse W., 44,
47
Patsey, 39
Thomas B., 56
Warren, 39

Paine
Hardin, 97
James, 97
Martha Jane,
97
Mary L., 229
Maryan, 97
Robert, 97
Susan J., 103
Thomas, 171
Winsted, 97
Paisley
James, 83
John M., 87
Samuel, 172
Pall
Edley, 247
Palmer
Henry, 275
William, 197
Pamplin
James, 116
Niel, 116
Sharper, 116
Pankey
Uzzi, 195
Pantel
Ankey Y., 139
Papous
William, 244
Parchiner
J. T., 205
Parchman
Bell, 205
Dennis, 205
Dora, 205
Ella, 205
Jacob H., 205
Jesse, 205
Lizza, 205
Mary, 205
Neely, 205
Parchmen
James W., 204
M. J., 205
Parchment
John, 202
Pardue
G. M., 72
Martha A., 10
Parham
Samuel H.,
267
Parish
David, 76
James, 23
Richard, 76
Park
James, 255,
256
James A., 118
James P., 118
William M.,
118
Parke

George, 99
Joseph, 44
Parker
  Anthony, 249
  Daniel, 2, 210
  David H., 175
  Frank, 2
  Harvey, 13
  Hiram K., 269
  James M., 92
  John, 68, 92,
    214
  John C., 176
  John W., 224
  Katherine E.,
    92
  Laban, 204
  Noah, 99
  Paradise, 30
  Pityl M., 92
  Sam, 2
  Samuel, 251
  William, 99,
    211, 214
Parker, Jr
  Felix, 175
Parkerson
  James B., 50
Parkes
  Thomas, 61
Parks
  Cullin G., 254
  Florence, 164
  George, 58
  J. C., 152
  Jim, 114
  John L., 84
  L. P., 164
  Nancy, 114
  Thomas, 126
  William, 101,
    107
  Willie S., 98
Parmelton
  Maria, 211
Parmer
  Daniel, 208
  Philip, 194
  Wilson Lee,
    208
Parnell
  Archibald, 120
Parrett
  Thomas J., 83
Parris
  Jonathan, 231
  Obadiah, 195
Parrish
  Benjamin, 213
  Eaton, 118
  Frank, 59
  Garland, 118
  George W., 41
  Henry, 63
  Hue, 71

Huel, 70
Joseph, 139
Mary Ann, 106
Mary K., 118
Samuel L., 186
Thomas L.,
  188
William G.,
  183
Parrott
  Thorpe, 194
Parsly
  Nicholas, 66
Parson
  David N., 87
  Henry, 151
  Jeremiah, 251
  William L.,
    270
Parsons
  Elin, 239
  Francis
    Marion, 239
  James, 270
  John, 209
  Major, 239
  Samuel A., 85
  Sarah Ann,
    239
Partain
  John, 269
  Robert, 269
Partee
  Benjamin, 153
  Jacob, 153
  Phill, 151
  William, 151
Parten
  John H., 139
Parter
  Alexander B.,
    172
Partian
  James, 266
Partin
  Peter, 77
Parton
  Forest, 87
  Isaac, 9
  J. L., 8
  Lewis, 229
  Marnetta, 9
  William P., 8
Paschal
  Jackson, 197
Paschall
  B. H., 263
Pass
  Dicy, 204
  Frances, 204
  John A., 242
  Robert N., 204
Passons

Major
  Washington,
    239
Pate
  Lucinda, 40,
    41
  S. H., 199
  Stephen, 195
  William, 181
Patengell
  Samuel, 70
Patrick
  James A., 5
  Jesse, 3
  Katherine, 3
  Levi, 3
  Moses, 89
  Polly Ann, 5
  Polly Anne, 4
  Robert, 5
  Timothy, 52
  William, 227
  William F., 5
Patry
  A., 170
Patterson
  Adeline, 139
  Andrew, 92
  Betsy
    Caroline,
      131
  Catharine, 137,
    140
  Daniel, 252
  Elizabeth R.,
    113
  Fanny, 252
  Hannah, 252
  J. L., 68
  James Gideon,
    273
  Jenny, 252
  John, 42, 83,
    137, 221,
    222, 224
  Julia, 137
  Lee, 68
  Luke, 129
  Margaret, 137
  Mary, 83, 137
  Matilda, 161,
    162
  Matthew, 40
  Moses, 252
  Narcissa, 137,
    140
  Narcissa A.,
    140, 143,
    144
  Nelson, 81
  Ready, 3
  Robert, 40
  Samuel, 251
  Tom, 113

William, 131,
  252
Patteson
  Moses, 82
  Thomas, 40
Patton
  Andrew, 263
  David, 210
  Eliza, 189
  Francis M., 57
  J. H., 274
  James, 23, 25,
    181
  James Gideon,
    273
  John, 24, 154,
    156, 253
  John A., 189
  Robert J., 5
  Samuel, 181
  Soleman, 57
  Thomas J., 5
  William, 30,
    217
Pattrick
  Levi, 3
  William, 3
Paul
  Charity, 250
  Isaac, 58
  James A., 60
Paulk
  James L., 104
Paull?
  Wiley B., 59
Pauly
  William, 171
Payne
  Benjamin, 193
  Elana?, 191
  G. W. G., 54
  George, 194
  J. A., 64
  Jane, 248
  Sally, 248
  W. W., 2
Payzer
  George, 23
Pea
  David W., 11
Peabody
  John, 49
Peachey
  P., 157
Peacock
  Sarah, 124
  William, 68
Peacock &
  Williams, 41
Peak
  Gilliam A., 85
Pearce
  Anna, 97
  John, 136
  John D., 120

Samuel, 98
Spencer, 98
Pearcell
James, 128
Pearsell
James, 128
Pearson
Calvin W., 219
Meredith, 78
Samuel, 80,
184, 185
Simon, 82
Solamon, 228
Thomas, 184
William, 184
William J., 88
William M.,
184
Peay
Susan, 259
Peck
Thomas R.,
183
Peebles
John, 254, 256
Peek
William M.,
165
Peggy, 35
Pegram
John P., 53, 54
Roger, 52
William, 45
Pelham
Isham, 5, 6
Pellam
C. H., 155
Pendarris
William, 193
Pendergrass
John, 209
Penell
Washington,
197
Pennal
Ryal, 265
Willer, 265
Pennel
Sally, 265
Pennington
Isaac D., 99
Jacob M., 101,
102
Jacob W., 99
James J., 99,
102
Philip M., 99
Pepper
Calvin, 150
Leander, 175
Richard, 198
Perdue
T. B., 10
Peregin
Mathew, 85

William, 85
Perkins
Edmund B., 35
James W., 67
John, 273
Sophia, 35
Permenter
Malachi, 174
Perrin
Jerry, 62
Perry
James H., 180
Jesse, 179
Josiah, 173
Keeble, 119
Macinas G., 90
Powell, 140
Richard B.,
120, 149
Robert R., 113
Rolls, 209
Ruffin, 69
William S.,
174
William W.,
113
Persell
James, 129
Persise
John B., 155,
156
Peter, 79, 133,
134
Peterson
Basil, 157
Isaac, 156
Morton, 46,
47, 49
Petty
David, 100
Dennis, 192
G. H., 74
James D., 74
Joseph, 189
Newton, 8
Thomas, 189
Petzer
George, 75
Pewatt
John, 209
Pewitt
James, 255
Peyton
Balie, 222, 223
Benjamin A.,
183
Emily F., 222
Joshua, 7
Minerva, 222
Mry Jane, 7
William H.,
183
Pharo, 143
Pheiffer
Fanny, 63

Phelps
Benjamin, 264
Charles, 1, 17
Daniel, 179
Elisha, 16, 17
Jackson, 179,
180
John, 16
Josiah, 27
Mary, 16
Micajah, 16,
17
Solomon, 16
Zadoch, 179
Phenix
Henry, 81
Philips
Absolom L.,
231
Britain, 105
Cynthia Ellen,
108
David L., 231
Elizabeth, 105
Fanny, 108
Frances, 110
Francis, 108
George, 178
Israel, 105
James, 108
Joseph, 170
Lewis, 109
Mark, 24
Preston D.,
174
Rebecah, 105
Richard B.,
156
Sarah Luvinia,
230
William, 69,
178
Phillips
Alice, 125
Allice, 121
Benjamin, 266
Charles, 119
Giles, 121, 125
Hannah, 121,
125
Hariet, 125
Harriett, 121
Horatia M.,
120, 121
Isaac, 251
Jo, 125
John, 105
John H., 107,
109
Joseph, 120,
125
Lemuel, 138
Louisa, 179
Monroe, 120
Robert L., 125

S. B., 3
Samuel, 121,
125
Simon, 225,
226
Thadeus, 217
Thomas, 120
W. R., 125
W. W., 176
William, 7, 64,
69
Philpot
Franklin, 112
Phippen
Charles, 207
Phipps
Charles, 210
Phulfar
Joseph, 45
Lucinda, 46
Phulphar
Lucinda, 46
Pick
Nathaniel, 30
Pickard
John, 103
Mary
Elizabeth,
92
Spencer, 92
Pickens
Ann J., 118
Louise, 95
Margaret E.,
118
Mary E., 118
Matthew G.,
129
Picket
John, 229
Pickett
Alford, 74
J. J., 74
Pickins
David B., 124
James H., 80
Nannie, 124
Pierce
John, 16
Pigg
Mollie, 262
William, 116
Pilant
Pinkney, 105
Pillow
Albert, 151
Pincham
Peter, 217
Piner
Thomas, 69
Pinkerton
James H., 91
Pinkley
Asa, 193
Daniel, 171

Rigsby
Frances
Malvin, 66
Lawson, 197
Layfayette, 66
R. J., 221
William T., 66
Rilda, 247
Riley
James, 157
Samuel G.,
110
Samuel J., 111
Rily
Henry Brown,
190
John, 130
Louisa F., 190
Rineheart
Andrew, 161
Riner, 126
William N.,
126
Ring
B. S., 9
William, 7, 9
Rippy
Amanda J.,
221
Eli, 221
Josiah, 220
Sally, 220
Risen
James Emery,
234
Rison
Rison, 196
Riter
Charles, 162
John, 162
Malinda, 162
Polk, 162
William, 162
Riveer
William, 144
Rivers
John H., 81
Rives
Robert, 124
Roach
Bryan, 253
James, 107
James P., 113
John, 28, 107,
155
John Griffin,
23
Martha, 108
Stephen, 181
Susan S., 109
William D.,
107
Roads
James, 28
Roand

Henry, 119
Roane
Hugh, 265
Roark
Asa, 194
Robb
W. D., 219
Robbins
Almira, 185
Atalanta Ann,
185
Atkinson, 184
Elmira Ann,
185
Hull, 185
James H., 184
Thomas, 185
Thomas R.,
273
Roberson
Lucinda, 98
Rufus Scott,
150
Robert, 173, 188
Roberts
Alsira, 246
Collins H., 159
Cyrus L., 186
Dilla, 72
George, 179
George
Andrew
Jackson, 261
Hellen, 72
James, 198
James A., 112
James M. F.,
94
John, 238
John G., 65
Julia, 94
Lewis E., 94
Lucinda, 238,
246
M. T., 56, 58
Melvina, 148
Phillip, 76
Philop, 12
R. W., 159
Richard G.,
239
Robert, 72
Robert B., 263
Sally, 238
Squire L. E.,
94
W. R., 15
William, 75,
88
Zepheniah, 14
Robertson
Betsy P., 62
Charles, 62
David W., 77
Elijah, 215

Henry, 201,
203
James C., 42,
269
John, 160
Joseph, 173
Lucy, 263
Mernari, 203
Nicholas, 160
Norvell H., 38,
39
R. S., 9
Thomas, 160
William, 172,
173
William A.,
273
Robins
Atkinson D.,
185
Betsy, 171
John, 171
Polly, 171
Samuel, 171
William C.,
268, 269
Robinson
Benjamin, 127
Bennett, 133
David I., 180
David J., 257
Edward, 67
Elizabeth, 251
Hugh, 180
Jimmie, 191
John, 131
Lewis, 260,
261
M. W., 77
Nancy, 262
Thomas L.,
251
William A.,
274
William B.,
109
William
Francis
Asbury, 158
William H.,
243
Robison
Alexander C.,
243
Daniel, 249
John, 131
Robison?,
Frederick, 3
male
children of,
190
Rod
Anderson, 136
Rodes
Iverson T., 13

Rodgers
D. C., 226
Enos, 217
Jacob, 133
John H., 52
Joseph, 40
Roe
Allen, 8
Rogers
Alexander M.,
155
Anderson S.,
244
B. D., 275
David, 202,
217
Edward H., 49
Elizabeth, 6
Isaac, 248
Isam, 178
Isham, 170
Jacob, 138
James, 5, 6
James Edward,
66
John, 6, 136,
170
John M., 242
John W., 65
Margaret
Evaline, 246
Mark W., 258
S. M., 151
Samuel P., 134
W. R., 275
Washington,
246, 248
William, 160,
264
William A.,
260
William W.,
243
Roland
Delilah, 35
Elizabeth, 41
James, 46
Joel, 40
John, 35
Jordan, 35
Jordon, 38
Rebecca, 35
Richard W.,
108
William, 46
Roller
John, 57
Rollicoffer
Elizabeth, 153
Rollicoffer, Jr
Elizabeth, 153
Rollins
A. M., 74
Mary Ann, 74

Timmins
  Ambrose, 110
  Solemn, 74
Timmons
  Squire H., 142,
    145
  William, 110
Timms
  James, 111
  Rosanna, 111
Timothy, 221
Tin, 221
Tindal
  Henry, 40
Tines
  West, 196
Tinnen
  James, 80
Tinney
  Hardy, 251
Tinsley
  Tipton, 211
Titus, 247
Todd
  C. W., 192
  J. A., 7
  J. P., 9
Toliver
  James T. A.,
    13
  Zachariah,
    263, 265
Tolliver
  Zachariah, 270
  Zechariah, 266
Tom, 136
Tomblin
  John, 266
Tomlin
  James S., 101
  Nicholas, 253
Tompkins
  James S., 223
  Joel M., 223
  Washington,
    267
Tompson
  George M.,
    165
Tonage
  Margaret
    Grimes, 154
  Polly, 154
Toney
  Thomas, 65,
    66
Tool
  James, 111
Tooly
  Joseph H., 52
Toomy
  James, 218
Tosh
  Andrew J., 12
  Frances, 13

Martin V. V,
  228
  William, 227
Tovnor
  Joseph, 217
Towery
  William, 109
Towler
  Angeline, 123
  John W., 231
Towns
  Herbert, 38
Towrey
  James, 107
  Josiah, 108
  Thomas
    Jefferson,
    107
Trabue
  Henry, 63
Tramble
  Hollingsworth,
    105
Tramell
  James, 70
Trantham
  William M.,
    257
Trapenanfearey
  Philip, 211
Traughbor
  Henry, 172
Travilian
  Edward, 266
Travis
  Sam, 206
Traylor
  H. F., 66
Tremble
  John, 172
Trentham
  Henry, 259
Tribble
  Peter, 276
Trible
  Elvis Huston,
    223
Trice
  James Simon,
    163
  Mary Ann, 163
  Washington,
    33
  Wiley, 163
Trigg
  James, 40
Trimble
  Porter, 223
Trinkle
  Henry, 204
Trip
  Jonathan, 110
Tripp
  G. W., 101
Troop

James M., 106
Trott
  George, 183
  Henry, 180
Trotter
  J. K., 164
Trousdale
  James, 155
  James W., 142
Truett
  John B., 209
Trumbo
  Ambrose, 210
Trustee
  William, 270
Trusty
  Josiah, 270
  William
    Henry, 270
Tucker
  Abram, 140
  Alexander, 159
  Caswell, 182
  Elisabeth, 171
  Franklin, 120
  George M., 56
  George W.,
    104
  Green, 265
  Henry, 171
  Jackson, 83
  James, 159,
    179
  John, 83, 170,
    171, 183
  Kenton, 77
  Marion, 104
  Nancy, 170,
    266
  Peggy, 170
  Phebe, 171
  Riggs, 170,
    171
  Robert, 159
  Samuel, 171
  Samuel G., 56
  Samuel L., 110
  Sarah, 170
  Silas, 170, 171
  Thomas, 182,
    183
  William, 184,
    192
  William R.,
    239
Tuckness
  Felix F., 137
  Gilbert, 137
Tulloss
  Joseph R., 262
Tumblin
  John, 266
Tunes
  Demarous M.,
    78

Turley
  Charles A., 53
  Elwood, 261
  T. W., 261
Turnage
  Shelby, 215
Turnbull
  William, 17
Turner
  Abner, 59
  Betsey, 209
  Buford, 129
  Creacy, 40
  Eli, 7
  George, 6
  Henry, 229
  J. E., 10
  James, 173
  James N., 221
  John, 176, 212
  John B., 78
  John E., 236
  M. G., 160
  Martin, 210
  Moses, 252
  Philip, 149,
    213
  Randolph, 235
  Roberson J.,
    77
  Robert, 195
  Samuel, 208
  Sarah A., 129
  Thomas, 46,
    54, 235
  Thomas A., 65
  William, 165,
    192, 211,
    217
  William W.,
    47
  Wilson, 198
Turney
  H. L. (Mrs), 80
  Hopkins Lacy,
    193
  J. B., 116
  Jacob B., 107
  Peter, 193
Turpin
  T. W., 141
Tuttle
  John A., 224
Twidwell
  Polly, 180
Twitty
  P. L., 114
Tycer
  Ellis, 69
Tye
  W. M., 152
Tyler
  Amanda
    Elizabeth,
    189

Stephen, 214
Tyre
Connsil, 153
Elizabeth, 153
Parilee, 30
Richardson, 22
Thomas J., 196
Tyree
Abner C., 196
Henry P., 56
Samuel S., 67
Susan, 119
Ubanks
George, 33
Stephen, 33
Thomas, 40
Uhles
Frederick J., 194
Uhles, Sr
Frederick J., 194
Uhls
Richard, 195
Underwood
Benjamin, 236
Brice, 236
Edward, 141
Johnson, 265, 267
Noah, 66
Sally, 141
Seth, 236
Thomas, 236
William, 266
Uptain
Amanda M. A., 112
Upton
Lewis, 168
Lewis C., 167
Louis, 165
Malisa J., 167
Nancy, 196
William, 165
Ursery
William, 236
Ursey, 30
Ury
Robert, 173
Usery
William, 53, 82, 237
Utley
Gloster, 175
Lemuel, 175
Piety?, 175
Uzzell
Elisha, 128
Jzzell, 138
Uzzell & Kirkpatrick, 131
Uzzle
Jourdan, 212

Vale
Caty, 156
Valentine
Dianne, 267
Emiline, 191
Valines
Amanda, 223
Van Hooser
P. F., 95
Van Pelt
Henry, 37
Vance
E. R., 276
Vancleve
James B., 99
Vanderver
Emma, 151
Vanderville
John, 41
Vanhook
Hiram, 218
William, 73
Vanhooser
Eulysses, 229
Vanleer
Bernard, 37
Vanlier
Daniel, 73
Tennessee, 74
Vardell
John, 180
Moore J., 180
Moore
Johnson, 180
Thomas, 179
Varen
Friet?, 104
Varnon
Nehemiah, 171
Vaughan
Archibald, 46
Edward, 20
Joel, 215
John, 20
Lemuel, 183
Nancy, 155
Richard, 65
William, 244
Vaughn
Archibald, 34
John, 45
Thomas, 126
William, 243
Vaught
John, 251
Malinda, 179
Matilda, 179
Nathan, 138, 139
Thornton, 130
Vernon
William, 106, 107
Vernor

James, 16
Samuel, 16
Vest
Berry, 36
Vick
Allen W., 266
Nathan, 157
Vickers
Thomas M., 206
Villines
Henry, 177
Rebecca, 177
William, 174, 177
Vincent
John, 19, 23
Vincents
John, 238
Vines
Benjamin, 107, 109
Betsey, 108
Elizabeth, 108
Milly, 107
Viney, 140
Vineyard
John, 70
Orren, 70
Vinson
E. L., 87
J. C., 206
Rebecca, 20
Richard, 20
William, 181
Violen, 247
Violet, 222, 223
Virgil
Samuel, 49
Virgin
Samuel J., 44
Vivrett
Cage Thomas, 273
Volisa
James, 241
Voorheiz
Peter, 127
William, 127
Voorhies
Peter J., 130
William, 129, 130
Voorvaart
Henry, 59
Vorhees
William, 135
Vorhies
P. J., 129
Voss
Alexander, 245
Vought
Nathan, 127
Stephen, 127
Vowel

Thomas, 65
Waddle
Allan, 23
Allen, 26
James, 30
Samuel, 180
Waddy
James, 260
Wade
E. L. (Mrs), 262
Jeremiah, 182
Michael, 268
Rachel, 262
T. B., 86
William H., 264
Wadsen
John, 251
Wafford
John, 101
Waganer
J. W., 15
Wages
James, 155
Waggoner
Catherine, 109
Henry, 65
J. W., 14
William, 51
Wagner
George F., 231
Sarah, 231
Wain
Mary, 163
Mrs, 163
Wainwright
Hadly, 149
Wair
George L., 39
Waitten?
Thomas W., 198
Walbridge
Porter, 128
Walden
John, 14
Thomas, 190
Walder
Pricilla, 50
Waldrup
Julia, 87
Wale
James H., 7
Walk
Isaiah, 156
Wesley, 264
Walker
Albert, 150
Andrew W., 110
Benjamin, 39, 40, 98
Brooks, 119
Charles, 83

www.ingramcontent.com/pod-product-compliance
Lightning Source LLC
Chambersburg PA
CBHW070547270326
41926CB00013B/2233